AF838121

Please send any correspondence regarding permissions to:
UniversityOfHealthCare
PO Box 48891A
Los Angeles, CA 90048

ISBN: 1594910995

Library of Congress Catalog Number: 2004096191

UniversityOfHealthCare website: www.uohc.com

Contents

Introduction	1
The Author	1
45 CFR 160, 162, and 164	2
Guidance Published 12/02	44
45 CFR 142	87

Introduction

This product consists of a combination of this manual and a CD. The manual is a summary of the more important documents presented on the CD.

When you place the CD in your computer, it should load automatically and install with some simple steps. If it does not start automatically, open up Windows Explorer (from Start, Programs, Accessories) and navigate to the setup file with the abstract arrow icon on your CD drive. Then double click it. It will then install on your computer. After that, you may open the program by clicking on Start, Programs, and then the name of the program. This will open the program file. After you run it the first time, an icon will automatically be added to your desktop.

This CD program is protected with anti-piracy software. The library edition is licensed to one user on one computer for one time for borrowers from a library. As a result, if you decide to purchase the product, you will need to follow the instructions after you install the CD. One complimentary activation is allowed per library for a computer at the library. The request must come from an email with the library URL in the return address.

You must have Internet Explorer 4.0 or higher running on your computer. Supported operating systems are Windows 95, 98, 98 SE, ME, 2000, or XP.

For any questions about your license or the program, contact us at license@uohc.com.

About the Author

M. Daniel Farb, CEO of UniversityOfHealthCare and UniversityOfBusiness, is a leader in the field of interactive management and healthcare e-learning. He received a BA in English Literature from Yale (where he set an academic record and studied with writers like Robert Penn Warren), an M.D. from Boston University, a degree in Executive Management from the Anderson School of Business at UCLA, and is currently working on a degree at UCLA in International Trade. He is a practicing ophthalmologist. He also has received two patents in ophthalmology and is working on others, has worked with the World Health Organization in Geneva and the National Institutes of Health in Washington, D.C. He has written scientific and popular articles, and has worked as a newspaper reporter. He helped Dr. Robbins edit one of the editions of Robbins' "Pathology" textbook for readability. He wrote an article on humor for the Massachusetts Review. He has experience in theater and television, including acting, directing, and stage-managing. He has programmed his own patient records database. He has written and edited hundreds of e-learning courses.

Dr. Farb is a member of the American Academy of Ophthalmology, the Union of American Physicians and Dentists, the AOJS, the American Association of Physicians and Surgeons, the ASTD (American Society for Training and Development), the E-Learning Forum, the Southern California Biomedical Council, the PDA (Parenteral Drug Association), and the Medical Marketing Association.

He has taken the same training as the FDA on electronic records enforcement.

HIPAA Documents

The first set of documents are 45 CFR 160, 162, and 164.

[Federal Register: February 20, 2003 (Volume 68, Number 34)]
[Rules and <strong>Regulations</strong>]
[Page 8333-8381]
From the Federal Register Online via GPO Access [wais.access.gpo.gov]
[DOCID:fr20fe03-4]

[[Page 8333]]

Part II

Department of Health and Human Services

Office of the Secretary

----

45 CFR Parts 160, 162, and 164

Health Insurance Reform: Security Standards; Final Rule

[[Page <strong>8334</strong>]]

DEPARTMENT OF HEALTH AND HUMAN SERVICES

Office of the Secretary

45 CFR Parts 160, 162, and 164

[CMS-0049-F]
RIN 0938-AI57

Health Insurance Reform: Security Standards

AGENCY: Centers for Medicare & Medicaid Services (CMS), HHS.

ACTION: Final rule.

SUMMARY: This final rule adopts standards for the security of electronic protected health information to be implemented by health plans, health care clearinghouses, and certain health care providers. The use of the security standards will improve the Medicare and Medicaid programs, and otherFederal health programs and private health programs, and the effectiveness and efficiency of the health care industry in general by establishing a level of protection for certain electronic health information. This final rule implements some of the requirements of the Administrative Simplification subtitle of the Health Insurance Portability andAccountability Act of 1996 (HIPAA).

DATES: Effective Date: These <strong>regulations</strong> are effective on April 21,
2003.

Compliance Date: Covered entities, with the exception of small health plans, must comply with the requirements of this final rule by April 21, 2005. Small health plans must comply with the requirements of this final rule by April 21, 2006.

FOR FURTHER INFORMATION CONTACT: William Schooler, (410) 786-0089.

SUPPLEMENTARY INFORMATION:

Availability of Copies and Electronic Access

To order copies of the Federal Register containing this document, send your request to: New Orders, Superintendent of Documents, P.O. Box
371954, Pittsburgh, PA 15250-7954. Specify the date of the issue requested and enclose a check or money order payable to the Superintendent of Documents, or enclose your Visa or Master Card number
and expiration date. Credit card orders can also be placed by calling the order desk at (202) 512-1800 or by faxing to (202) 512-2250. The cost for each copy is $10. As an alternative, you can view and photocopy the Federal Register document at most libraries designated as Federal Depository Libraries and at many other public and academic libraries throughout the country that receive the Federal Register.

This Federal Register document is also available from the Federal Register online database through GPO access, a service of the U.S.

Government Printing Office. The Web site address is
<A HREF="http://www.access.gpo.gov/nara/index.html">.

I. Background

The Department of Health and Human Services (HHS) Medicare Program, other Federal agencies operating health plans or providing health care, State Medicaid agencies, private health plans, health care providers, and health care clearinghouses must assure their customers (for example, patients, insured individuals, providers, and health plans) that the integrity, confidentiality, and availability of electronic protected health information they collect, maintain, use, or transmit is protected. The confidentiality of health information is threatened not only by the risk of improper access to stored information, but also by the risk of interception during electronic transmission of the information. The purpose of this final rule is to adopt national standards for safeguards to protect the confidentiality, integrity, and availability of electronic protected health information. Currently, no standard measures exist in the health care industry that address all aspects of the security of electronic health information while it is being stored or during the exchange of that information between entities.

This final rule adopts standards as required under title II, subtitle F, sections 261 through 264 of the Health Insurance Portability and Accountability Act of 1996 (HIPAA), Pub. L. 104-191. These standards require measures to be taken to secure this information while in the custody of entities covered by HIPAA (covered entities) as well as in transit between covered entities and from covered entities to others.

The Congress included provisions to address the need for safeguarding electronic health information and other administrative simplification issues in HIPAA. In subtitle F of title II of that law, the Congress added to title XI of the Social Security Act a new part C, entitled ``Administrative Simplification" (hereafter, we refer to the Social Security Act as ``the Act"; we refer to the other laws cited in this document by their names). The purpose of subtitle F is to improve the Medicare program under title XVIII of the Act, the Medicaid program under title XIX of the Act, and the efficiency and effectiveness of the health care system, by encouraging the development of a health information system through the establishment of standards and requirements to enable the electronic exchange of certain health information.

Part C of title XI consists of sections 1171 through 1179 of the Act. These sections define various terms and impose requirements on HHS, health plans, health care clearinghouses, and certain health care providers. These statutory sections are discussed in the Transactions Rule, at 65 FR 50312, on pages 50312 through 50313, and in the final rules adopting Standards for Privacy of Individually Identifiable Health Information, published on December 28, 2000 at 65 FR 82462 (Privacy Rules), on pages 82470 through 82471, and on August 14, 2002 at 67 FR 53182. The reader is referred to those discussions.

Section 1173(d) of the Act requires the Secretary of HHS to adopt security standards that take into account the technical capabilities of record systems used to maintain health information, the costs of security measures, the need to train persons who have access to health information, the value of audit trails in computerized record systems, and the needs and capabilities of small health care providers and rural health care providers. Section 1173(d) of the Act also requires that the standards ensure that a health care clearinghouse, if part of a larger organization, has policies and security procedures that isolate the activities of the clearinghouse with respect to processing information so as to prevent unauthorized access to health information by the larger organization. Section 1173(d) of the Act provides that covered entities that maintain or transmit health information are required to maintain reasonable and appropriate administrative, physical, and technical safeguards to ensure the integrity and confidentiality of the information and to protect against any reasonably anticipated threats or hazards to the security or integrity of the information and unauthorized use or disclosure of the information. These safeguards must also otherwise ensure compliance with the statute by the officers and employees of the covered entities.

II. General Overview of the Provisions of the Proposed Rule

On August 12, 1998, we published a proposed rule (63 FR 43242) to establish a minimum standard for security of electronic health information. We proposed that the standard would require the safeguarding of all electronic health information by covered entities. The proposed rule also proposed a

[[Page 8335]]

standard for electronic signatures. This final rule adopts only security standards. All comments concerning the proposed electronic signature standard, responses to these comments, and a final rule for electronic signatures will be published at a later date. A detailed discussion of the provisions of the August 12, 1998 proposed rule can be found at 63 FR 43245 through 43259.

We originally proposed to add part 142, entitled ``Administrative Requirements," to title 45 of the Code of Federal <strong>Regulations</strong> (CFR).
It has now been determined that this material will reside in subchapter C of title 45, consisting of parts 160, 162, and 164. Subpart A of part 160 contains the general provisions applicable to all the Administrative Simplification rules; other subparts of part 160 will contain other requirements applicable to all standards. Part 162 contains the standards for transactions and code sets and will contain the identifier standards. Part 164 contains the standards relating to privacy and security. Subpart A of part 164 contains general provisions applicable to part 164; subpart E contains the privacy standards. Subpart C of part 164, which is adopted in this final rule, adopts standards for the security of electronic protected health information.

III. Analysis of, and Responses to, Public Comments on the Proposed Rule

We received approximately 2,350 timely public comments on the August 12, 1998 proposed rule. The comments came from professional associations and societies, health care workers, law firms, health insurers, hospitals, and private individuals. We reviewed each commenter's letter and grouped related comments. Some comments were
identical. After associating like comments, we placed them in categories based on subject matter or based on the section(s) of the <strong>regulations</strong> affected and then reviewed the comments.

In this section of the preamble, we summarize the provisions of the proposed <strong>regulations</strong>, summarize the related provisions in this final
rule, and respond to comments received concerning each area.

It should be noted that the proposed Security Rule contained multiple proposed ``requirements" and ``implementation features." In this final rule, we replace the term ``requirement" with ``standard." We also replace the phrase ``implementation feature" with ``implementation specification." We do this to maintain consistency with the use of those terms as they appear in the statute, the Transactions Rule, and the Privacy Rule. Within the comment and response portion of this final rule, for purposes of continuity, however, we use ``requirement" and ``implementation feature" when we are referring specifically to matters from the proposed rule. In all other instances, we use ``standard" and ``implementation specification."

The proposed rule would require that each covered entity (as now described in Sec. 160.102) engaged in the electronic maintenance or transmission of health information pertaining to individuals assess potential risks and vulnerabilities to such information in its possession in electronic form, and develop, implement, and maintain appropriate security measures to protect that information. Importantly, these measures would be required to be documented and kept current.

The proposed security standard was based on three basic concepts that were derived from the Administrative Simplification provisions of HIPAA. First, the standard should be comprehensive and coordinated to address all aspects of security. Second, it should be scalable, so that it can be effectively implemented by covered entities of all types and sizes. Third, it should not be linked to specific technologies, allowing covered entities to make use of future technology advancements.

The proposed standard consisted of four categories of requirements that a covered entity would have to address in order to safeguard the integrity, confidentiality, and availability of its electronic health information pertaining to individuals: administrative procedures, physical safeguards, technical security services, and technical mechanisms. The implementation features described the requirements in greater detail when that detail was needed. Within the four categories, the requirements and implementation features were presented in alphabetical order to convey that no one item was considered to be more important than another.

The four proposed categories of requirements and implementation features were depicted in tabular form along with the electronic signature standard in a combined matrix located at Addendum 1. We also provided a glossary of terms, at Addendum 2, to facilitate a common understanding of the matrix entries, and at Addendum 3, we mapped available existing industry standards and guidelines to the proposed security requirements.

A. General Issues

The comment process overwhelmingly validated our basic assumptions that the entities affected by this regulation are so varied in terms of installed technology, size, resources, and relative risk, that it would be impossible to dictate a specific solution or set of solutions that would be useable by all covered entities. Many commenters also supported the concept of technological neutrality, which would afford them the flexibility to select appropriate technology solutions and to adopt new technology over time.

1. Security Rule and Privacy Rule Distinctions

As many commenters recognized, security and privacy are inextricably linked. The protection of the privacy of information depends in large part on the existence of security measures to protect that information. It is important that we note several distinct differences between the Privacy Rule and the Security Rule.

The security standards below define administrative, physical, and technical safeguards to protect the confidentiality, integrity, and availability of electronic protected health information. The standards require covered entities to implement basic safeguards to protect electronic protected health information from unauthorized access, alteration, deletion, and transmission. The Privacy Rule, by contrast, sets standards for how protected health information should be controlled by setting forth what uses and disclosures are authorized or required and what rights patients have with respect to their health information.

As is discussed more fully below, this rule narrows the scope of the information to which the safeguards must be applied from that proposed in the proposed rule, electronic health information pertaining to individuals, to protected health information in electronic form. Thus, the scope of information covered in this rule is consistent with the Privacy Rule, which addresses privacy protections for ``protected health information." However, the scope of the Security Rule is more limited than that of the Privacy Rule. The Privacy Rule applies to protected health information in any form, whereas this rule applies only to protected health information in electronic form. It is true that, under section 1173(d) of the Act, the Secretary has authority to cover ``health information," which, by statute, includes information in other than electronic form. However, because the proposed rule proposed to cover only health information in electronic form, we do not include security standards for health information in non-electronic form in this final rule.

[[Page 8336]]

We received a number of comments that pertained to privacy issues. These issues were considered in the development of the Privacy Rule and many of these comments were addressed in the preamble of the Privacy Rule. Therefore, we are referring the reader to that document for a discussion of those issues.

2. Level of Detail

We solicited comments as to the level of detail expressed in the required implementation features; that is, we specifically wanted to know whether commenters believe the level of detail of any proposed requirement went beyond what is necessary or appropriate. We received numerous comments expressing the view that the security standards should not be overly prescriptive because the speed with which technology is evolving could make specific requirements obsolete and might in fact deter technological progress. We have accordingly written the final rule to frame the standards in terms that are as generic as possible and which, generally speaking, may be met through various approaches or technologies.

3. Implementation Specifications

In addition to adopting standards, this rule adopts implementation specifications that provide instructions for implementing those standards.

However, in some cases, the standard itself includes all the necessary instructions for implementation. In these instances, there may be no corresponding implementation specification for the standard specifically set forth in the <strong>regulations</strong> text. In those instances, the standards themselves also serve as the implementation specification. In other words, in those instances, we are adopting one set of instructions as both the standard and the implementation specification. The implementation specification would, accordingly, in those instances be required.

In this final rule, we adopt both ``required" and ``addressable" implementation specifications. We introduce the concept of ``addressable implementation specifications" to provide covered entities additional flexibility with respect to compliance with the security standards.

In meeting standards that contain addressable implementation specifications, a covered entity will ultimately do one of the following: (a) Implement one or more of the addressable implementation specifications; (b) implement one or more alternative security measures; (c) implement a combination of both; or (d) not implement either an addressable implementation specification or an alternative security measure. In all cases, the covered entity must meet the standards, as explained below.

The entity must decide whether a given addressable implementation specification is a reasonable and appropriate security measure to apply within its particular security framework. This decision will depend on a variety of factors, such as, among others, the entity's risk analysis, risk mitigation strategy, what security measures are already in place, and the cost of implementation. Based upon this decision the following applies:

(a) If a given addressable implementation specification is determined to be reasonable and appropriate, the covered entity must implement it.

(b) If a given addressable implementation specification is determined to be an inappropriate and/or unreasonable security measure for the covered entity, but the standard cannot be met without implementation of an additional security safeguard, the covered entity may implement an alternate measure that accomplishes the same end as the addressable implementation specification. An entity that meets a given standard through alternative measures must document the decision not to implement the addressable implementation specification, the rationale behind that decision, and the alternative safeguard implemented to meet the standard. For example, the addressable implementation specification for the integrity standard calls for electronic mechanisms to corroborate that data have not been altered or destroyed in an unauthorized manner (see 45 CFR 164.312(c)(2)). In a small provider's office environment, it might well be unreasonable and inappropriate to make electronic copies of the data in question. Rather, it might well be more practical and afford a sufficient safeguard to make paper copies of the data.

(c) A covered entity may also decide that a given implementation specification is simply not applicable (that is, neither reasonable nor appropriate) to its situation and that the standard can be met without implementation of an alternative measure in place of the addressable implementation specification. In this scenario, the covered entity must document the decision not to implement the addressable specification, the rationale behind that decision, and how the standard is being met. For example, under the information access management standard, an access establishment and modification implementation specification reads: ``implement policies and procedures that, based upon the entity's access authorization policies, establish, document, review, and modify a user's right of access to a workstation, transaction, program, or process" (45 CFR 164.308(a)(4)(ii)(c)). It is possible that a small practice, with one or more individuals equally responsible for establishing and maintaining all automated patient records, will not need to establish policies and procedures for granting access to that electronic protected health information because the access rights are equal for all of the individuals.

a. Comment: A large number of commenters indicated that mandating 69 implementation features would result in a regulation that is too burdensome, intrusive, and difficult to implement. These commenters requested that the implementation features be made optional to meet the requirements. A number of other commenters requested that all implementation features be removed from the regulation.

Response: Deleting the implementation specifications would result in the standards being too general to understand, apply effectively, and enforce consistently. Moreover, a number of implementation specifications are so basic that no covered entity could effectively protect electronic protected health information without implementing them. We selected 13 of these mandatory implementation specifications based on (1) the expertise of Federal security experts and generally accepted industry practices and, (2) the recommendation for immediate implementation of certain technical and organizational practices and procedures described in Chapter 6 of For The Record: Protecting Electronic Health Information, a 1997 report by the National Research Council (NRC). These mandatory implementation specifications are referred to as required implementation specifications and are reflected in the NRC report's recommendations. Risk Analysis and Risk management are found in the NRC recommendation title System Assessment; Sanction Policy is required in the Sanctions recommendation; Information system Activity Review is discussed in Audit Trails; Response and Reporting circumstances.

In addition, a number of voluntary national and regional organizations have been formed to address HIPAA implementation issues and to facilitate

[[Page 8337]]

communication among trading partners. These include the Strategic National Implementation Process (SNIP) developed under the auspices of the Workgroup for Electronic Data Interchange (WEDI), an organization named in the HIPAA statute to consult with the Secretary of HHS on HIPAA issues. Some of these organizations have developed white papers, tools, and recommended best practices addressing a number of HIPAA issues, including security. Covered entities may wish to examine these products to determine if they are relevant and useful in their own implementation efforts. A partial list of these organizations can be found at <A HREF="http://frwebgate.access.gpo.gov/cgi-bin/leaving.cgi?from=leavingFR.html&log=linklog&to=http://www.wedi/snip./org">http://www.wedi/snip./org</A>. We believe that these and other future industry-developed guidelines and/or models may provide valuable assistance to covered entities implementing these standards but must caution that HHS does not rate or endorse any such guidelines and/or models and the value of its content must be determine by the user.

b. Comment: Many commenters asked us to develop guidelines and models to aid in complying with the Security Rule. Several commenters either offered to participate in the development of guidelines and models or suggested entities that should be invited to participate.

Response: We agree that creation of compliance tools and guidelines for different business environments could assist covered entities to implement the HIPAA Security Rule. We plan to issue guidance documents after the publication of this final rule. However, it is critical for each covered entity to establish policies and procedures that address its own unique risks and circumstances.

In addition, a number of voluntary national and regional organizations have been formed to address HIPAA implementation issues and to facilitate communication among trading partners. These include the Strategic National Implementation Process (SNIP) developed under the auspices of the Workgroup for Electronic Data Interchange (WEDI), an organization named in the HIPAA statute to consult with the Secretary of HHS on HIPAA issues. Some of these organizations have developed white papers, tools, and recommended best practices addressing a number of HIPAA issues, including security.

Covered entities may wish to examine these products to determine if they are relevant and useful in their own implementation efforts. A partial list of these organizations can be found at <A HREF="http://frwebgate.access.gpo.gov/cgi-bin/leaving.cgi?from=leavingFR.html&log=linklog&to=http://www.snip.wedi.org">http://www.snip.wedi.org</A>.

We believe that these and other future industry-developed guidelines and/or models may provide valuable assistance to covered entities implementing these standards but must caution that HHS

does not rate or endorse any such guidelines and/or models and the value of its content must be determined by the user.

4. Examples

Comment: We received a number of comments that demonstrated confusion regarding the purpose of the examples of security solutions that were included throughout the proposed rule. Commenters stated that they could not, or did not wish to, adopt various security measures suggested in examples. Other commenters asked that we include additional options within the examples. Some commenters referred specifically to the example provided in the proposed rule demonstrating how a small or rural provider might comply with the standards. One commenter asked for clarification that the examples are not mandatory measures that are required to demonstrate compliance, but are merely meant as a guide when implementing the security standards. Another commenter expressed support for the use of examples to clarify the intent of text descriptions.

Response: We wish to clarify that examples are used only as illustrations of possible approaches, and are included to serve as a springboard for ideas. The steps that a covered entity will actually need to take to comply with these <strong>regulations</strong> will be dependent upon

its own particular environment and circumstances and risk assessment. The examples do not describe mandatory measures, nor do they represent

the only, or even the best, way of achieving compliance. The most appropriate means of compliance for any covered entity can only be determined by that entity assessing its own risks and deciding upon the measures that would best mitigate those risks.

B. Applicability (Sec. 164.302)

We proposed that the security standards would apply to health plans, health care clearinghouses, and to health care providers that maintain or transmit health information electronically. The proposed security standards would apply to all electronic health information maintained or transmitted, regardless of format (standard transaction or a proprietary format). No distinction would be made between internal corporate entity communication or communication external to the corporate entity. Electronic transmissions would include transactions using all media, even when the information is physically moved from one

location to another using magnetic tape, disk, or other machine readable media. Transmissions over the Internet (wide-open), extranet (using Internet technology to link a business with information only accessible to collaborating parties), leased lines, dial-up lines, and private networks would be included. We proposed that telephone voice response and ``faxback" systems (a request for information made via voice using a fax machine and requested information returned via that same machine as a fax) would not be included but we solicited comments

on this proposed exclusion.

This final rule simplifies the applicability statement greatly. Section 164.302 provides that the security standards apply to covered entities; the scope of the information covered is specified in Sec. 164.306 (see the discussion under that section below regarding the changes and revisions to the scope of information covered).

1. Comment: A number of commenters requested clarification of who must comply with the standards. The preamble and proposed Sec. 142.102

and Sec. 142.302 stated: ``Each person described in section 1172(a) of the Act who maintains or transmits health information shall maintain reasonable and appropriate administrative, technical, and physical safeguards." Commenters suggested that this statement is in conflict with the law, which defines a covered entity as a health plan, a clearinghouse, or a health care provider that conducts certain transactions electronically. The commentors apparently did not realize that section 1172(a) of the Act contains the definition of covered entities.

Response: Section 164.302 below makes the security standards applicable to ``covered entities." The term ``covered entity" is defined at Sec. 160.103 as one of the following: (1) A health plan; (2) a health care clearinghouse; (3) a health care provider who transmits any health information in electronic form in connection with a transaction covered by part 162 of title 45 of the Code of Federal <strong>Regulations</strong> (CFR). The rationale for the use and the meaning of the term ``covered entity" is discussed in the preamble to the Privacy Rule (65 FR 82476 through 82477).

As that discussion makes clear, the standards only apply to health care providers who engage electronically in the transactions for which standards have been adopted.

[[Page 8338]]

2. Comment: Several commenters recommended expansion of applicability, either to other specific entities, or to all entities involved in health care. Others wanted to know whether the standards apply to entities such as employers, public health organizations, medical schools, universities, research organizations, plan brokers, or non-EDI providers. One commenter asked whether the standards apply to State data organizations operating in capacities other than as plans, clearinghouses, or providers. Still other commenters stated that it was inappropriate to include physicians and other health care professionals in the same category as plans and clearinghouses, arguing that providers should be subject to different, less burdensome requirements because they already protect health information.

Response: The statute does not cover all health care entities that transmit or maintain individually identifiable health information. Section 1172(a) of the Act provides that only health plans, health care clearinghouses, and certain health care providers (as discussed above) are covered. With respect to the comments regarding the difference between providers and plans/clearinghouses, we have structured the Security Rule to be scalable and flexible enough to allow different entities to implement the standards in a manner that is appropriate for their circumstances. Regarding the coverage of entities not within the jurisdiction of HIPAA, see the Privacy Rule at 82567 through 82571.

3. Comment: One commenter asked whether the standards would apply to research organizations, both to those affiliated with health care providers and those that are not.

Response: Only health plans, health care clearinghouses, and certain health care providers are required to comply with the security standards. Researchers who are members of a covered entity's work force may be covered by the security standards as part of the covered entity. See the definition of ``workforce" at 45 CFR 160.103. Note, however, that a covered entity could, under appropriate circumstances, exclude a researcher or research division from its health care component or components (see Sec. 164.105(a)). Researchers who are not part of the covered entity's workforce and are not themselves covered entities are not subject to the standards.

4. Comment: Several commenters stated that internal networks and external networks should be treated differently. One commenter asked for further clarification of the difference between what needs to be secured external to a corporation versus the security of data movement within an organization. Another stated that complying with the security standards for internal communications may prove difficult and costly to monitor and control. In contrast, one commenter stated that the existence of requirements should not depend on whether use of information is for internal or external purposes.

Another commenter argued that the regulation goes beyond the intent of the law, and while communication of electronic information between entities should be covered, the law was never intended to mandate changes to an entity's internal automated systems. One commenter requested that raw data that are only for the internal use of a facility be excluded, provided that reasonable safeguards are in place to keep the raw data under the control of the facility.

Response: Section 1173(d)(2) of the Act states: Each person described in section 1172(a) who maintains or transmits health information shall maintain reasonable and appropriate administrative, technical, and physical safeguards--(A) to ensure the integrity and confidentiality of the information; (B) to protect against any reasonably anticipated--(i) threats or hazards to the security or integrity of the information; and (ii) unauthorized uses or disclosures of the information; and (C) otherwise to ensure compliance with this part by the officers and employees of such person.

This language draws no distinction between internal and external data movement. Therefore, this final rule covers electronic protected health information at rest (that is, in storage) as well as during transmission. Appropriate protections must be applied, regardless of whether the data are at rest or being transmitted. However, because each entity's security needs are unique, the specific protections determined appropriate to adequately protect information will vary and will be determined by each entity in complying with the standards (see the discussion below).

5. Comment: Several commenters found the following statement in the proposed rule (63 FR 43245) at section II.A. confusing and asked for clarification: ``With the exception of the security standard, transmission within a corporate entity would not be required to comply with the standards."

Response: In the final Transactions Rule, we revised our approach concerning the transaction and code set exemptions, replacing this concept with other tests that determine whether a particular transaction is subject to those standards (see the discussion in the Transactions Rule at 65 FR 50316 through 50318). We also note that the Privacy Rule regulates a covered entity's use, as well as disclosure, of protected health information.

6. Comment: One commenter stated that research would be hampered if proposed Sec. 142.306(a) applied. The commenter believes that research uses of health information should be excluded or the standard should be revised to allow appropriate flexibility for research depending on the risk to patients or subjects (for example, if the information is anonymous, there is no risk, and it would not be necessary to meet the security standards).

Response: If electronic protected health information is de-identified (as truly anonymous information would be), it is not covered by this rule because it is no longer electronic protected health information (see 45 CFR 164.502(d) and 164.514(a)). Electronic protected health information received, created, or maintained by a covered entity, or that is transmitted by covered entities, is covered by the security standards and must be protected. To the extent a researcher is a covered entity, the researcher must comply with these standards with respect to electronic protected health information. Otherwise, the conditions for release of such information to researchers is governed by the Privacy Rule. See, for example, 45 CFR 164.512(i), 164.514(e) and 164.502(d). These standards would not apply to the researchers as such in the latter circumstances.

7. Comment: One commenter asked to what extent individual patients are subject to the standards. For example, some telemedicine practices support the use of diagnostic systems in the patient's home, which can be used to conduct tests and send results to a remote physician. In other cases, patients may be responsible for the filing of insurance claims directly and will need the ability to verify facts, confirm receipt of claims, and so on. The commenter asked if it is the intent of the rule to include electronic transmission to or from the patient.

Response: Patients are not covered entities and, thus, are not subject to these standards. With respect to transmissions from covered entities, covered entities must protect electronic protected health information when they transmit that information. See also the discussion of encryption in section III.G.

[[Page 8339]]

C. Transition to the Final Rule

The proposed rule included definitions for a number of terms that have now already been promulgated as part of the Transactions Rule or the Privacy Rule. Comments related to the definitions of ``code set,'' ``health care'' clearinghouse,'' ``health plan,'' ``health care provider,'' ``small health plan,'' ``standard'' and ``transaction,'' are addressed in the Transactions Rule at 65 FR 50319 through 50320. Comments concerning the definition of ``individually identifiable health information'' are discussed below, but are also addressed in the Privacy Rule at 65 FR 82611 through 82613. In addition, a few terms were redefined in the final Standards for Privacy of Individually Identifiable Health Information (67 FR 53182), issued on August 14, 2002 (Privacy Modifications). Certain terms that were defined in the proposed rule are not used in the final rule because they are no longer necessary. Other terms defined in the proposed rule are defined within the explanation of the standards in the final rule and are discussed in the preamble discussions in Sec. 164.308 through Sec. 164.312.

Definitions of terms relevant to the security standards now appear in the <strong>regulations</strong> text provisions as indicated below:

Sec. 160.103: Definitions of the following terms relevant to this rule appear in Sec. 160.103: ``business associate,'' ``covered entity,'' ``disclosure,'' ``electronic media,'' ``electronic protected health information,'' ``health care,'' ``health care clearinghouse,'' ``health care provider,'' ``health information,'' ``health plan,'' ``individual,'' ``individually identifiable health information,'' ``implementation specification,'' ``organized health care arrangement,'' ``protected health information,'' ``standard,'' ``use,'' and ``workforce.'' These terms were discussed in connection with the Transaction and Privacy Rules and with the exception of the terms ``covered entity'' ``disclosure'' ``electronic protected health information,'' ``health information,'' ``individual,'' ``organized health care arrangement,'' ``protected health information,'' and ``use,'' we will not discuss them in this document. We note that the definition of those terms are not changed in the final rule.

Sec. 162.103: We have moved the definition of ``electronic media'' at Sec. 162.103 to Sec. 160.103 and have modified it to clarify that the term includes storage of information. The term ``electronic media'' is used in the definition of ``protected health information.'' Both the privacy and security standards apply to information ``at rest'' as well as to information being transmitted.

We note that we have deleted the reference to Sec. 162.103 in paragraph (1)(ii) of the definition of ``protected health information,'' since both definitions, ``electronic media'' and ``protected health information,'' have been moved to this section. Also, it is unnecessary, because the definitions of Sec. 160.103 apply to all of the rule in parts 160, 162, and 164.

We have also clarified that the physical movement of electronic media from place to place is not limited to magnetic tape, disk, or compact disk. This clarification removes a restriction as to what is considered to be physical electronic media, thereby allowing for future technological innovation. We further clarified that transmission of information not in electronic form before the transmission, for example, paper or voice, is not covered by this definition.

Sec. 164.103: The following term ``plan sponsor'' now appears in the new Sec. 164.103, which consists of definitions of terms common to both subpart C and subpart E (the privacy standards). This definition was moved, without substantive change, from Sec. 164.501 and has the meaning given to it in that section, and comments relating to this definition are discussed in connection with that section in the Privacy Rule at 65 FR 82607, 82611 through 82613, 82618 through 82622, and 82629.

Sec. 164.304: Definitions specifically applicable to the Security Rule appear in Sec. 164.304, and these are discussed below. These definitions are from, or derived from, currently accepted definitions in industry publications, such as, the International Organization for Standards (ISO) 7498-2 and the American Society for Testing and Materials (ASTM) E1762-95.

The following terms in Sec. 164.304 are taken from the proposed rule text or the glossary in Addendum 2 of the proposed rule (63 FR 43271), were not commented on, and/or are unchanged or have only minor technical changes for purposes of clarification and are not discussed below: ``access,'' ``authentication,'' ``availability,'' ``confidentiality,'' ``encryption,'' ``password,'' and ``security.''

Sec. 164.314: Four terms were defined in Sec. 164.504(a) of the Privacy Rule (``common control,'' ``common ownership,'' ``health care component,'' and ``hybrid entity''). Because these terms apply to both security and privacy, their definitions have been moved to Sec. 164.103 without change. Those terms are discussed in the Privacy Rule at 65 FR 82502 through 82503 and at 67 FR 53203 through 53207.

1. Covered Entity (Sec. 160.103)

Comment: One commenter asked if transcription services were covered
entities. The question arose because transcription is often the first electronic or printed source of clinical information. Concern was expressed about the application of physical safeguard standards to the transcribers working for transcription companies or health care providers, either as employees or as independent contractors.

Another commenter expressed concern that scalability was limited to only small providers. The commenter explained that Third Party Administrators (TPAs) allow claim processors to work at home. Some TPAs
have noted that it would be impossible to comply with the security standards for home-based claims processors.

Response: A covered entity's responsibility to implement security standards extends to the members of its workforce, whether they work at home or on-site. Because a covered entity is responsible for ensuring the security of the information in its care, the covered entity must include ``at home'' functions in its security process. While an independent transcription company or a TPA may not be covered entities,
they will be a business associate of the covered entity because their activities fall under paragraph (1)(i)(a) of the definition of that term. For business associate provisions see proposed preamble section III.E.8. and Sec. 164.308(b)(1) and Sec. 164.314(c) of this final rule.

2. Health Care and Medical Care (Sec. 160.103)

Comment: One commenter asked whether ``medical care,'' which is defined in the proposed rule, and ``health care,'' which is not, are synonymous.

Response: The term ``medical care,'' as used in the proposed rule (63 FR 43242), was intended to be synonymous with ``health care.'' The term ldquo;medical care'' is not included in this final rule. It is, however, included in the definition of ``health plan,'' where its meaning is not synonymous with ``health care.'' For a full discussion of this issue and its resolution, see the Privacy Rule (65 FR 82578).

[[Page 8340]]

3. Health Information and Individually Identifiable Health Information 160.103)

We note that the definitions of ``health information'' and ``individually identifiable health information'' remain unchanged from those published in the Transactions and Privacy Rules.

a. Comment: A number of commenters asked that the definition of ``health information'' be expanded to include information collected by additional entities. Several commenters wanted the definition to include health information collected, maintained, or transmitted by any entity, and one commenter suggested the inclusion of aggregated information not identifiable to an individual. Several commenters asked that eligibility information be excluded from the definition of information. Several commenters wanted the definition broadened to include demographics.

Response: Our definition of health information is taken from the definition in section 1171(4) of the Act, which provides that health information relates to the health or condition of an individual, the provision of health care to an individual, or payment for the provision of health care to an individual. The statutory definition also specifies the entities by which health information is created or received. We note that, because ``individually identifiable health information'' is a subset of ``health information'' and by statute includes demographic information, ``health information'' necessarily includes demographic information. We think this is clear as a matter of statutory construction and does not require further regulatory change.

b. Comment: Several commenters asked that we clarify the difference between ``health information'' and ``individually identifiable'' and ``health information pertaining to an individual'' as used in the August 12, 1998 proposed rule (63 FR 43242). Additionally, commenters
asked that we be more consistent in the use of these terms and

recommended use of the term ``individually identifiable health information."

Two commenters stated that it is important to distinguish between ``health information pertaining to an individual" and ``individually identifiable health information," as in reporting statistics at various levels there will always be a need to bring forth information pertaining to an individual.

One commenter recommended that the standards apply only to individually identifiable health information. Another stated that in Sec. 142.306(b) of the proposed rule, ``health information pertaining to an individual" should be changed to ``individually identifiable health information," as nonidentifiable information can be used for utilization review and other purposes. As written, the regulation text could limit the ability to use data, for example, from a clearinghouse for compliance monitoring.

Response: In general, we agree with these commenters, and note that these comments are largely mooted by the decision, reflected in Sec. 164.306 below and discussed in section III.D.1. of this final rule, to cover only electronic protected health information in this final rule.

c. Comment: Several commenters stated that the definition of ``individually identifiable health information" is not in the <strong>regulations</strong> and should be added.

Response: We note that the definition of ``individually identifiable health information" appears at Sec. 160.103, which applies to this final rule.

4. Protected Health Information (Sec. 160.103)

This term is moved from Sec. 164.501 to Sec. 160.103 because it applies to both subparts C (security) and E (privacy). See 67 FR 53192 through 531936 regarding the definition of ``protected health information."

Also, the term ``electronic media" is included in paragraphs (1)(i) and (ii) of the definition of ``protected health information," as specified in this section.

In addition, we added the definitions of ``covered functions," ``plan sponsor," and ``Required by law" to Sec. 164.103.

5. Breach (Sec. 164.304)

Comment: One commenter asked that ``breach" be defined.

Response: The term ``breach" has been deleted and therefore not defined. Instead, we define the term ``security incident," which better describes the types of situations we were referring to as breaches.

6. Facility (Sec. 164.304)

This new term has been added as a result of changing the name of the ``physical access control" standard to ``facility access control." This change was made based on comments indicating that the original term was not descriptive. We have defined the term ``facility" as the physical premises and interior and exterior of a building.

7. Security Incident (Sec. 164.304)

Comment: We received comments asking that this term be defined.

Response: This final rule defines ``Security incident" in Sec. 164.304 as ``the attempted or successful unauthorized access, use, disclosure, modification, or destruction of information or interference with system operations in an information system."

8. System (Sec. 164.304)

Comment: One commenter asked that ``system" be defined.

Response: This final rule defines ``system," in the context of an information system, in Sec. 164.304 as ``an interconnected set of information resources under the same direct management control that shares common functionality. A system normally includes hardware, software, information, data, applications, communications, and people."

9. Workstation (Sec. 164.304)

Comment: One commenter expressed concern that the use of the term ``workstation" implied limited applicability to fixed devices (such as terminals), excluding laptops and other portable devices.

Response: We have added a definition of the term ``workstation" to clarify that portable devices are also included. This final rule defines workstation as ``an electronic computing device, for example, a laptop or desktop computer, or any other device that performs similar functions, and electronic media stored in its immediate environment."

10. Definitions Not Adopted

Several definitions in the proposed <strong>regulations</strong> text and glossary are not adopted as definitions in the final rule: ``participant," ``contingency plan," ``risk," ``role-based access control," and ``user-based access control." The terms ``participant," ``role-based access control," and ``user-based access control" are not used in this final rule and thus are not defined. ``Risk" is not defined as its meaning is generally understood. While we do not define the term, we address ``contingency plan" as a standard in Sec. 164.308(a)(7) below.

a. Comment: We received comments requesting that we define the following terms: ``token" and ``documentation."

Response: These terms were defined in Addendum 2 of the proposed rule. In this final rule, we do not adopt a definition for ``token" because it is not used in the final rule. ``Documentation" is discussed in Sec. 164.316 below.

b. Comment: We received several comments that ``small" and ``rural" should be defined as those terms apply

[[Page 8341]]

to providers. We received an equal number of comments stating that there is no need to define these terms. One commenter stated that definitions for these terms would be necessary only if special exemptions existed for small and rural providers. Several commenters suggested initiation of a study to determine limitations and potential barriers small and rural providers will have in implementing these <strong>regulations</strong>.

Response: The statute requires that we address the needs of small and rural providers. We believe that we have done this through the provisions, which require the risk assessment and the response to be assessment based on the needs and capabilities of the entity. This scalability concept takes the needs of those providers into account and eliminates any need to define those terms.

c. Comment: In the proposed rule, we proposed the following definition for the term ``Access control": ``A method of restricting access to resources, allowing only privileged entities access. Types of access control include, among others, mandatory access control, discretionary access control, time-of-day, classification, and subject-object separation." One commenter believed the proposed definition is too restrictive and requested revision of the definition to read: ``Access control refers to a method of restricting access to resources, allowing access to only those entities which have been specifically granted the desired access rights." Another commenter wanted the definition expanded to include partitioned rule-based access control (PRBAC).

Response: We agree with the commenter who suggested that the definition as proposed seemed too restrictive. In this case, as in many others, a number of commenters believed the examples given in the proposed rule provided the only acceptable compliance actions. As previously noted, in order to clarify that the examples listed were not to be considered all-inclusive, we have generalized the proposed requirements in this final rule. In this case, we have also generalized the requirements and placed the substantive provisions governing access control at Sec. 164.308(a)(4), Sec. 164.310(a)(1), and Sec. 164.312(a)(1). With respect to PRBAC, the access control standard does not exclude this control, and entities should adopt it if appropriate to their circumstances.

D. General Rules (Sec. 164.306)

In the proposed rule, we proposed to cover all health information maintained or transmitted in electronic form by a covered entity. We proposed to adopt, in Sec. 142.308, a nation-wide security standard that would require covered entities to implement security measures that would be technology-neutral and scalable, and yet integrate all the components of security (administrative procedures, physical safeguards, technical security services, and technical security mechanisms) that must be in place to preserve health information confidentiality, integrity, and availability (three basic elements of security). Since no comprehensive, scalable, and technology-neutral set of standards currently exists, we proposed to designate a new standard, which would define the security requirements to be fulfilled.

The proposed rule proposed to define the security standard as a set of scalable, technology-neutral requirements with implementation features that providers, plans, and clearinghouses would have to include in their operations to ensure that health information pertaining to an individual that is electronically maintained or electronically transmitted remains safeguarded. The proposed rule would have required that each affected entity assess its own security needs and risks and devise, implement, and maintain appropriate security to address its own unique security needs. How individual security requirements would be satisfied and which technology to use would be business decisions that each entity would have to make.

In the final rule we adopt this basic framework. In Sec. 164.306, we set forth general rules pertaining to the security standards. In paragraph (a), we describe the general requirements. Paragraph (a) generally reflects section 1173(d)(2) of the Act, but makes explicit the connection between the security standards and the privacy standards (see Sec. 164.306(a)(3)). In Sec. 164.306(a)(1), we provide that the security standards apply to all electronic protected health information the covered entity creates, receives, maintains, or transmits. In paragraph (b)(1), we provide explicitly for the scalability of this rule by discussing the flexibility of the standards, and paragraph (b)(2) of Sec. 164.306 discusses various factors covered entities must consider in complying with the standards.

The provisions of Sec. 164.306(c) provide the framework for the security standards, and establish the requirement that covered entities must comply with the standards. The administrative, physical, and technical safeguards a covered entity employs must be reasonable and appropriate to accomplish the tasks outlined in paragraphs (1) through (4) of Sec. 164.306(a). Thus, an entity's risk analysis and risk management measures required by Sec. 164.308(a)(1) must be designed to lead to the implementation of security measures that will comply with Sec. 164.306(a).

It should be noted that the implementation of reasonable and appropriate security measures also supports compliance with the privacy standards, just as the lack of adequate security can increase the risk of violation of the privacy standards. If, for example, a particular safeguard is inadequate because it routinely permits reasonably anticipated uses or disclosures of electronic protected health information that are not permitted by the Privacy Rule, and that could have been prevented by implementation of one or more security measures appropriate to the scale of the covered entity, the covered entity would not only be violating the Privacy Rule, but would also not be in compliance with Sec. 164.306(a)(3) of this rule.

Paragraph (d) of Sec. 164.306 establishes two types of implementation specifications, required and addressable. It provides that required implementation specifications must be met. However, with respect to implementation specifications that are addressable, Sec. 164.306(d)(3) specifies that covered entities must assess whether an implementation specification is a reasonable and appropriate safeguard in its environment, which may include consideration of factors such as the size and capability of the organization as well as the risk. If the organization determines it is a reasonable and appropriate safeguard, it must implement the specification. If an addressable implementation specification is determined not to be a reasonable and appropriate answer to a covered entity's security needs, the covered entity must do one of two things: implement another equivalent measure if reasonable and appropriate; or if the standard can otherwise be met, the covered entity may choose to not implement the implementation specification or any equivalent alternative measure at all. The covered entity must document the rationale behind not implementing the implementation specification. See the detailed discussion in section II.A.3.

Paragraph (e) of Sec. 164.306 addresses the requirement for covered entities to maintain the security measures

[[Page 8342]]

implemented by reviewing and modifying the measures as needed to continue the provision of reasonable and appropriate protections, for example, as technology moves forward, and as new threats or vulnerabilities are discovered.

1. Scope of Health Information Covered by the Rule (Sec. 164.306(a))

We proposed to cover health information maintained or transmitted by a covered entity in electronic form. We have modified, by narrowing, the scope of health information to be safeguarded under this rule from that which was proposed. The statute requires the privacy standards to cover individually identifiable health information. The Privacy Rule covers all individually identifiable information except for: (1) Education records covered by the Family and Educational Rights and Privacy Act (FERPA); (2) records described in 20 U.S.C. 1232g(a)(4)(B)(iv); and (3) employment records. (see the Privacy Rule at 65 FR 82496. See also 67 FR 53191 through 53193). The scope of information covered in the Privacy Rule is referred to as ``protected health information." Based upon the comments we received, we align the requirements of the Security and Privacy Rules with regard to the scope of information covered, in order to eliminate confusion and ease implementation. Thus, this final rule requires protection of the same scope of information as that covered by the Privacy Rule, except that it only covers that information if it is in electronic form.

We note that standards for the security of all health information or protected health information in nonelectronic form may be proposed at a later date.

a. Comment: One commenter stated that the rule should apply to aggregate information that is not identifiable to an individual. In contrast, another commenter asked that health information used for statistical analysis be exempted if the covered entity may reasonably expect that the removed information cannot be used to re-identify an individual.

Response: As a general proposition, any electronic protected health information received, created, maintained, or transmitted by a covered entity is covered by this final rule. We agree with the second commenter that certain information, from which identifiers have been stripped, does not come within the purview of this final rule. Information that is de-identified, as defined in the Privacy Rule at Sec. 164.502(d) and Sec. 164.514(a), is not ``individually identifiable" within the meaning of these rules and, thus, does not come within the definition of ``protected health information." It accordingly is not covered by this final rule. For a full discussion of the issues of de-identification and re-identification of individually identifiable health information see 65 FR 82499 and 82708 through 82712
and 67 FR 53232 through 53234.

b. Comment: Several commenters asked whether systems that determine
eligibility of clients for insurance coverage under broad categories such as medical coverage groups are considered health information. One commenter asked that we specifically exclude eligibility information from the standards.

Response: We cannot accept the latter suggestion. Eligibility information will typically be individually identifiable, and much eligibility information will also contain health information. If the information is ``individually identifiable" and is ``health information," (with three very specific exceptions noted in the general discussion above) and it is in electronic form, it is covered by the security standards if maintained or transmitted by a covered entity.

c. Comment: Several commenters requested clarification as to whether the standards apply to identifiable health information in paper form. Some commenters believed the rule should be applicable to paper; others argued that it should apply to all confidential, identifiable health information.

Response: While we agree that protected health information in paper or other form also should have appropriate security protections, the proposed rule proposing the security standards proposed to apply those standards to health information in electronic form only. We are, accordingly, not extending the scope in this final rule.

We may establish standards to secure protected health information in other media in a future rule, in accordance with our statutory authority to do so. See discussion, supra, responding to a comment on the definition of ``health information" and ``individually identifiable health information."

d. Comment: The proposed rule would have excluded ``telephone voice
response" and ``faxback" systems from the security standards, and we specifically solicited comments on that issue. A number of commenters agreed that telephone voice response and faxback should be excluded from the regulation, suggesting that the privacy standards rather than the security standards should apply. Others wanted those systems included, on the grounds that inclusion is necessary for consistency and in keeping with the intent of the Act. Still others specifically

wanted personal computer-fax transmissions included. One commenter asked for clarification of when we would cover faxes, and another commenter asked why we were excluding them. Several commenters suggested that the other security requirements provide for adequate security of these systems.

Response: In light of these comments, we have decided that telephone voice response and ``faxback" (that is, a request for information from a computer made via voice or telephone keypad input with the requested information returned as a fax) systems fall under this rule because they are used as input and output devices for computers, not because they have computers in them. Excluding these features would provide a huge loophole in any system concerned with security of the information contained and/or processed therein. It should be noted that employment of telephone voice response and/or faxback systems will generally require security protection by only one of the parties involved, and not the other. Information being transmitted via a telephone (either by voice or a DTMP tone pad) is not in electronic form (as defined in the first paragraph of the definition of ``electronic media") before transmission and therefore is not subject to the Security Rule. Information being returned via a telephone voice response system in response to a telephone request is data that is already in electronic form and stored in a computer. This latter transmission does require protection under the Security Rule.

Although most recently made electronic devices contain microprocessors (a form of computer) controlled by firmware (an unchangeable form of computer program), we intend the term ``computer" to include only software programmable computers, for example, personal computers, minicomputers, and mainframes. Copy machines, fax machines, and telephones, even those that contain memory and can produce multiple copies for multiple people are not intended to be included in the term ``computer." Therefore, because ``paper-to-paper" faxes, person-to-person telephone calls, video teleconferencing, or messages left on voice-mail were not in electronic form before the transmission, those activities are not covered by this rule. See also the definition of ``electronic media" at Sec. 160.103.

[[Page 8343]]

We note that this guidance differs from the guidance regarding the applicability of the Transactions Rule to faxback and voice response systems. HHS has stated that faxback and voice response systems are not required to follow the standards mandated in the Transactions Rule. This new guidance refers only to this rule.

e. Comment: One commenter asked whether there is a need to implement special security practices to address the shipping and receiving of health information and asked that we more fully explain our expectations and solutions in the final rules.

Response: If the handling of electronic protected health information involves shipping and receiving, appropriate measures must be taken to protect the information. However, specific solutions are not provided within this rule, as discussed in section III.A.3 of this final rule. The device and media controls standard under Sec. 164.310(d)(1) addresses this situation.

f. Comment: One commenter wanted the ``HTML" statement reworded to eliminate a specific exemption for HTML from the regulation.

Response: The Transactions Rule did not adopt the proposed exemption for HTML. The use of HTML or any other electronic protocol is not exempt from the security standards. Generally, if protected health information is contained in any form of electronic transmission, it must be appropriately safeguarded.

g. Comment: One commenter asked to what degree ``family history" is considered health information under this rule and what protections apply to family members included in a patient's family history.

Response: Any health-related ``family history" contained in a patient's record that identifies a patient, including a person other than the patient, is individually identifiable health information and, to the extent it is also electronic protected health information, must be afforded the security protections.

h. Comment: Two commenters asked that the rule prohibit re-identification of de-identified data. In contrast, several commenters asked that we identify a minimum list or threshold of specific re-identification data elements (for example, name, city, and ZIP) that would fall under this final rule so that, for example, the rule would not affect numerous systems, for example, network adequacy and population-based clinical analysis databases. One commenter asked that we establish a means to use re-identified information if the entity already has access to the information or is authorized to have access.

Response: The issue of re-identification is addressed in the Privacy Rule at Sec. 164.502(d) and Sec. 164.514(c). The reader is referred to those sections and the related discussion in the preamble to the Privacy Rule (65 FR 82712) and the preamble to the Privacy Modifications (67 FR 53232 through 53234) for a full discussion of the issues of re-identification. We note that once information in the possession (or constructive possession) of a covered entity is re-identified and meets the definition of electronic protected health information, the security standards apply.

2. Technology-Neutral Standards

Comment: Many commenters expressed support for our efforts to develop standards for the security of health information. A number of comments were made in support of the technology-neutral approach of the proposed rule. For example, one commenter stated, ``By avoiding prescription of the specific technologies health care entities should use to meet the law's requirements, you are opening the door for industry to apply innovation. Technologies that don't currently exist or are impractical today could, in the near future, enhance health information security while minimizing the overall cost." Several other commenters stated that the requirements should be general enough to withstand changes to technology without becoming obsolete. One commenter anticipates no problems with meeting the standards.

In contrast, one commenter suggested that whenever possible, specific technology recommendations should provide sufficient detail to promote systems interoperability and decrease the tendency toward adoption of multiple divergent standards. Several commenters stated that by letting each organization determine its own rules, the rules impose procedural burdens without any substantive benefit to security.

Response: The overwhelming majority of comments supported our position. We do not believe it is appropriate to make the standards technology-specific because technology is simply moving too fast, for example, the increased use and sophistication of internet-enabled hand held devices. We believe that the implementation of these rules will promote the security of electronic protected health information by (1) providing integrity and confidentiality; (2) allowing only authorized individuals access to that information; and (3) ensuring its availability to those authorized to access the information. The standards do not allow organizations to make their own rules, only their own technology choices.

3. Miscellaneous Comments

a. Comment: Some commenters stated that the requirements and implementation features set out in the proposed rule were not specific enough to be considered standards, and that the actual standards are delegated to the discretion of the covered entities, at the expense of medical record privacy. Several commenters stated that it was inappropriate to balance the interests of those seeking to use identifiable medical information without patient consent against the interest of patients. Several other commenters believe that allowing covered entities to make their own decisions about the adequacy and balance of security measures undermined patient confidentiality interests, and stated that the proposed rule did not appear to adequately consider patient concerns and viewpoints.

Response: Again, the overwhelming majority of commenters supported our approach. This final rule sets forth requirements with which covered entities must comply and labels those requirements as standards and implementation specifications. Adequate implementation of this final rule by covered entities will ensure that the electronic protected health information in a covered entity's care will be as protected as is feasible for that entity.

We disagree that covered entities are given complete discretion to determine their security polices under this rule, resulting in effect, in no standards. While cost is one factor a covered identity may consider in determining whether to implement a particular implementation specification, there is nonetheless a clear requirement that adequate security measures be implemented, see 45 CFR 164.306(b).
Cost is not meant to free covered entities from this responsibility.

b. Comment: Several commenters requested we withdraw the

<strong>regulations</strong>, citing resource shortages due to Y2K preparation, upcoming privacy legislation, and/or the ``excessive micro-management'' contained in the rules. One commenter stated that, to insurers, these rules were onerous, not necessary, and not justified as cost-effective, as they already have effective practices for computer security and are subject to rigorous State laws for the safeguarding of health information. Another

[[Page 8344]]

commenter stated that these rules would adversely affect a provider's practice environment.

Response: The HIPAA statute requires us to promulgate a rule adopting security standards for health information. Resource concerns due to Y2K should no longer be an issue. Covered entities will have 2 years (or, in the case of small health plans, 3 years) from the adoption of this final rule in which to comply. Concerns relative to effective and compliance dates and the Privacy Rule are discussed under Sec. 164.318, Compliance dates for initial implementation, below and at 65 FR 82751 through 82752.

We disagree that these standards will adversely affect a provider's practice environment. The scalability of the standards allows each covered entity to implement security protections that are appropriate to its specific needs, risks, and environments. These protections are necessary to maintain the confidentiality, integrity, and availability of patient data. A covered entity that lacks adequate protections risks inadvertent disclosure of patient data, with resulting loss of public trust, and potential legal action. For example, a covered entity with poor facility access controls and procedures would be susceptible to hacking of its databases. A provider with appropriate security protections already in place would only need to ensure that the protections are documented and are reassessed periodically to ensure that they continue to be appropriate and are actually being implemented. Our decision to classify many implementation specifications as addressable, rather than mandatory, provides even more flexibility to covered entities to develop cost-effective solutions. We believe that insurers who already have effective security programs in place will have met many of the requirements of this regulation.

c. Comment: One commenter believes the rule is arbitrary and capricious in its requirements without any justification that they will significantly improve the security of medical records and with the likelihood that their implementation may actually increase the vulnerability of the data. The commenter noted that the data backup requirements increase access to data and that security awareness training provides more information to employees.

Response: The standards are based on generally accepted security procedures, existing industry standards and guidelines, and recommendations contained in the National Research Council's 1997 report For The Record: Protecting Electronic Health Information, Chapter 6. We also consulted extensively with experts in the field of security throughout the health care industry. The standards are consistent with generally accepted security principles and practices that are already in widespread use.

Data backup need not result in increased access to that data. Backups should be stored in a secure location with controlled access. The appropriate secure location and access control will vary, based upon the security needs of the covered entity. For example, a procedure as simple as locking backup diskettes in a safe place and restricting who has access to the key may be suitable for one entity, whereas another may need to store backed-up information off-site in a secure computer facility. The information provided in security awareness training heightens awareness of security anomalies and helps to prevent security incidents.

d. Comment: Several commenters suggested that the proposed rule appears to reflect the Medicare program's perspective on security risks and solutions, and that it should be noted that not all industry segments share all the same risks as Medicare. One commenter stated that as future proposed rules are drafted, we should solicit input from those most significantly affected, for example, providers, plans, and clearinghouses.

Others stated that Medicaid agencies were not sufficiently involved in the discussions and debate. Still another stated that States would be unable to perform some basic business functions if all the standards are not designed to meet their needs.

Response: We believe that the standards are consistent with common industry practices and equitable, and that there has been adequate consultation with interested parties in the development of the standards. These standards are the result of an intensive process of public consultation. We consulted with the National Uniform Billing Committee, the National Uniform Claim Committee, the American Dental Association, and the Workgroup for Electronic Data Interchange, in the course of developing the proposed rule. Those organizations were specifically named in the Act to advise the Secretary, and their membership is drawn from the full spectrum of industry segments. In addition, the National Committee on Vital and Health Statistics (NCVHS), an independent advisory group to the Secretary, held numerous public hearings to obtain the views of interested parties. Again, many segments of the health care industry, including provider groups, health plans, clearinghouses, vendors, and government programs participated actively. The NCVHS developed recommendations to the Secretary, which were relied upon as we developed the proposed rule. Finally, we note that the opportunity to comment was available to all during the public comment period.

e. Comment: One commenter stated that there is a need to ensure the confidentiality of risk analysis information that may contain sensitive information.

Response: The information included in a risk analysis would not be subject to the security standards if it does not include electronic protected health information. We agree that risk analysis data could contain sensitive information, just as other business information can be sensitive. Covered entities may wish to develop their own business rules regarding access to and protections for risk analysis data.

f. Comment: One commenter expressed concern over the statement in the preamble of the proposed rule (63 FR 43250) that read: ``No one item is considered to be more important than another.'' The commenter suggested that security management should be viewed as most critical and perhaps what forms the foundation for all other security actions.

Response: The majority of comments received on this subject requested that we prioritize the standards. In response, we have regrouped the standards and implementation specifications in what we believe is a logical order within each of three categories: ``Administrative safeguards,'' ``Physical safeguards,'' and ``Technical safeguards.'' In this final rule, we order the standards in such a way that the ``Security management process'' is listed first under the ``Administrative safeguards'' section, as we believe this forms the foundation on which all of the other standards depend. The determination of the specific security measures to be implemented to comply with the standards will, in large part, be dependent upon completion of the implementation specifications within the security management process standard (see Sec. 164.308(a)(1)). We emphasize, however, that an entity implementing these standards may choose to implement them in any order, as long as the standards are met.

g. Comment: One commenter stated that there is a need for requirements concerning organizational practices (for example, education, training, and security and confidentiality policies), as

[[Page 8345]]

well as technical practices and procedures.

Response: We agree. Section 164.308 of this final rule describes administrative safeguards that address these topics. Section 164.308 requires covered entities to implement standards and required implementation specifications, as well as consider and implement, when appropriate and reasonable, addressable implementation specifications. For example, the security management process standard requires implementation of a risk analysis, risk management, a sanction policy, and an information system activity review. The information access management standard requires consideration, and implementation where appropriate and reasonable, of access authorization and access establishment and modification policies and procedures. Other areas addressed are assigned security responsibility, workforce security,

security awareness and training, security incident procedures, contingency planning, business associate contracts, and evaluation.

h. Comment: One commenter stated that internal and external security requirements should be separated and dealt with independently.

Response: The presentation of the standards within this final rule could have been structured in numerous ways, including by addressing separate internal and external security standards. We chose the current structure as we considered it a logical breakout for purposes of display within this final rule. Under our structure a covered entity may apply a given standard to internal activities and to external activities. Had we displayed separately the standards for internal security and the standards for external security, we would have needed to describe a number of the standards twice, as many apply to both internal and external security. However, a given entity may address the standards in whatever order it chooses, as long as the standards are met.

i. Comment: Two commenters stated that the standards identified in Addendum 3 of the proposed rule may not all have matured to implementation readiness.

Response: Addendum 3 of the proposed rule cross-referred individual requirements on the matrix to existing industry standards of varying levels of maturity. Addendum 3 was intended to show what we evaluated in searching for existing industry standards that could be adopted on a national level. No one standard was found to be comprehensive enough to be adopted, and none were proposed as the standards to be met under the Security Rule.

j. Comment: One commenter suggested we include a revised preamble in the final publication. Another questioned how clarification of points in the preamble will be handled if the preamble is not part of the final regulation.

Response: Preambles to proposed rules are not republished in the final rule. The preamble in this final rule contains summaries of the information presented in the preamble of the proposed rule, summaries of the comments received during the public comment period, and responses to questions and concerns raised in those comments and a summary of changes made. Additional clarification will be provided by HHS on an ongoing basis through written documents and postings on HHS's websites.

k. Comment: One commenter asked that we clarify that no third party can require implementation of more security features than are required in the final rule, for example, a third party could not require encryption but may choose to accept it if the other party so desires.

Response: The security standards establish a minimum level of security to be met by covered entities. It is not our intent to limit the level of security that may be agreed to between trading partners or others above this floor.

l. Comment: One commenter asked how privacy legislation would affect these rules. The commenter inquired whether covered entities will have to reassess and revise actions already taken in the spirit of compliance with the security <strong>regulations</strong>.

Response: We cannot predict if or how future legislation may affect the rules below. At present, the privacy standards at subpart E of 42 CFR part 164 have been adopted, and this final rule is compatible with them.

m. Comment: One commenter stated that a data classification policy, that is a method of assigning sensitivity ratings to specific pieces of data, should be part of the final <strong>regulations</strong>.

Response: We did not adopt such a policy because this final rule requires a floor of protection of all electronic protected health information. A covered entity has the option to exceed this floor. The sensitivity of information, the risks to and vulnerabilities of electronic protected health information and the means that should be employed to protect it are business determinations and decisions to be made by each covered entity.

n. Comment: One commenter stated that this proposed rule conflicts with previously stated rules that acceptable ``standards'' must have been developed by ANSI-recognized Standards Development Organizations (SDOs).

Response: In general, HHS is required to adopt standards developed by ANSI-accredited SDOs when such standards exist. The currently existing security standards developed by ANSI-recognized SDOs are targeted to specific technologies and/or activities. No existing security standard, or group of standards, is technology-neutral, scaleable to the extent required by HIPAA, and broad enough to be adopted in this final rule. Therefore, this final rule adopts standards under section 1172(c)(2)(B) of the Act, which permits us to develop standards when no industry standards exist.

o. Comment: One commenter stated that this regulation goes beyond the scope of the law, unjustifiably extending into business practices, employee policies, and facility security.

Response: We do not believe that this regulation goes beyond the scope of the law. The law requires HHS to adopt standards for reasonable and appropriate security safeguards concerning such matters as compliance by the officers and employees of covered entities, protection against reasonably anticipated unauthorized uses and disclosures of health information, and so on. Such standards will inevitably address the areas the commenter pointed to.

The intent of this regulation is to provide standards for the protection of electronic protected health information in accordance with the Act. In order to do this, covered entities are required to implement administrative, physical, and technical safeguards. Those entities must ensure that data are protected, to the extent feasible, from inappropriate access, modification, dissemination, and destruction. As noted above, however, this final rule has been modified to increase flexibility as to how this protection is accomplished.

p. Comment: One commenter stated that all sections regarding confidentiality and privacy should be removed, since they do not belong in this regulation.

Response: As the discussion in section III.A above of this final rule makes clear, the privacy and security standards are very closely related. Section 1173(d)(2) of the Act specifically mentions ``confidentiality'' and authorizes uses and disclosures of information as part of what security safeguards must address. Thus, we cannot omit all references to confidentiality and privacy in discussions of the security standards.

[[Page 8346]]

However, we have relocated material that relates to both security and privacy (including definitions) to the general section of part 164.

q. Comment: One commenter asked that data retention be addressed more specifically, since this will become a significant issue over time. It is recommended that a national work group be convened to address this issue.

Response: The commenter's concern is noted. While the documentation relating to Security Rule implementation must be retained for a period of 6 years (see Sec. 164.316(b)(2)), it is not within the scope of this final rule to address data retention time frames for administrative or clinical records.

r. Comment: One commenter stated that requiring provider practices to develop policies, procedures, and training programs and to implement record keeping and documentation systems would be tremendously resource-intensive and increase the costs of health care.

Response: We expect that many of the standards of this final rule are already being met in one form or another by covered entities. For example, as part of normal business operations, health care providers already take measures to protect the health information in their keeping. Health care providers already keep records, train their employees, and require employees to follow office policies and procedures. Similarly, health plans are already frequently required by State law to keep information confidential. While revisions to a practice's or plan's current activities may be necessary, the development of entirely new systems or procedures may not be necessary.

s. Comment: One commenter stated that there is no system for which risk has been eliminated and expressed concern over phrases such as covered entities must ``assure that electronic health information pertaining to an individual remains secure.''

Response: We agree with the commenter that there is no such thing as a totally secure system that carries no risks to security. Furthermore, we believe the Congress' intent in the use of the word ``ensure'' in section 1173(d) of the Act was to set an exceptionally high goal for the security of electronic protected health information. However, we note that the Congress also recognized that some trade-offs would be necessary, and that ``ensuring'' protection did not mean providing protection, no matter how expensive. See section 1173(d)(1)(A)(ii) of the Act. Therefore, when we state that a covered entity must ensure the safety of the information in its keeping, we intend that a covered entity take steps, to the best of its ability, to protect that information. This will involve establishing a balance between the information's identifiable risks and vulnerabilities, and the cost of various protective measures, and will also be dependent upon the size, complexity, and capabilities of the covered entity, as provided in Sec. 164.306(b).

E. Administrative Safeguards (Sec. 164.308)

We proposed that measures taken to comply with the rule be appropriate to protect the health information in a covered entity's care. Most importantly, we proposed to require that both the measures taken and documentation of those measures be kept current, that is, reviewed and updated periodically to continue appropriately to protect the health information in the care of covered entities. We would have required the documentation to be made available to those individuals responsible for implementing the procedure.

We proposed a number of administrative requirements and supporting implementation features, and required documentation for those administrative requirements and implementation features.

In this final rule, we have placed these administrative standards in Sec. 164.308. We have reordered them, deleted much of the detail of the proposed requirements, as discussed below, and omitted two of the proposed sets of requirements (system configuration requirements and a requirement for a formal mechanism for processing records) as discussed in paragraph 10 of the discussion of Sec. 164.308 of section III.E. of this preamble. Otherwise, the basic elements of the administrative safeguards are adopted in this final rule as proposed.

1. Security Management Process (Sec. 164.308(a)(1)(i))

We proposed the establishment of a formal security management process to involve the creation, administration, and oversight of policies to address the full range of security issues and to ensure the prevention, detection, containment, and correction of security violations. This process would include implementation features consisting of a risk analysis, risk management, and sanction and security policies.

We also proposed, in a separate requirement under administrative procedures, an internal audit, which would be an in-house review of the records of system activity (for example, logins, file accesses, and security incidents) maintained by an entity.

In this final rule, risk analysis, risk management, and sanction policy are adopted as required implementation specifications although some of the details are changed, and the proposed internal audit requirement has been renamed as ``information system activity review'' and incorporated here as an additional implementation specification.

a. Comment: Three commenters asked that this requirement be deleted. Two commenters cited this requirement as a possible burden. Several commenters asked that the implementation features be made optional.

Response: This standard and its component implementation specifications form the foundation upon which an entity's necessary security activities are built. See NIST SP 800-30, ``Risk Management Guide for Information Technology Systems,'' chapters 3 and 4, January 2002. An entity must identify the risks to and vulnerabilities of the information in its care before it can take effective steps to eliminate or minimize those risks and vulnerabilities. Some form of sanction or punishment activity must be instituted for noncompliance. Indeed, we question how the statutory requirement for safeguards ``to ensure compliance * * * by a [covered entity's] officers and employees'' could be met without a requirement for a sanction policy. See section 1176(d)(2)(C) of the Act. Accordingly, implementation of these specifications remains mandatory. However, it is important to note that covered entities have the flexibility to implement the standard in a manner consistent with numerous factors, including such things as, but not limited to, their size, degree of risk, and environment. We have deleted the implementation specification calling for an organizational security policy, as it duplicated requirements of the security management and training standard.

We note that the implementation specification for a risk analysis at Sec. 164.308(a)(1)(ii)(A) does not specifically require that a covered entity perform a risk analysis often enough to ensure that its security measures are adequate to provide the level of security required by Sec. 164.306(a). In the proposed rule, an assurance of adequate security was framed as a requirement to keep security measures ``current.'' We continue to believe that security measures must remain current, and have added regulatory language in Sec. 164.306(e) as a more precise way of communicating that security measures

[[Page 8347]]

in general that must be periodically reassessed and updated as needed.

The risk analysis implementation specification contains other terms that merit explanation. Under Sec. 164.308(a)(1)(ii)(A), the risk analysis must look at risks to the covered entity's electronic protected health information. A thorough and accurate risk analysis would consider ``all relevant losses'' that would be expected if the security measures were not in place. ``Relevant losses'' would include losses caused by unauthorized uses and disclosures and loss of data integrity that would be expected to occur absent the security measures.

b. Comment: Relative to the development of an entity's sanction policy, one commenter asked that we describe the sanction penalties for breach of security. Another suggested establishment of a standard to which one's conduct could be held and adoption of mitigating circumstances so that the fact that a person acted in good faith would be a factor that could be used to reduce or otherwise minimize any sanction imposed. Another commenter suggested sanction activities not be implemented before the full implementation and testing of all electronic transaction standards.

Response: The sanction policy is a required implementation specification because--(1) the statute requires covered entities to have safeguards to ensure compliance by officers and employees; (2) a negative consequence to noncompliance enhances the likelihood of compliance; and (3) sanction policies are recognized as a usual and necessary component of an adequate security program. The type and severity of sanctions imposed, and for what causes, must be determined by each covered entity based upon its security policy and the relative severity of the violation.

c. Comment: Commenters requested the definitions of ``risk analysis'' and ``breach.''

Response: ``Risk analysis'' is defined and described in the specification of the security management process standard, and is discussed in the preamble discussion of Sec. 164.308(a)(1)(ii)(A) of this final rule. The term breach is no longer used and is, therefore, not defined.

d. Comment: One commenter asked whether all health information is considered equally ``sensitive,'' the thought being that, in determining risk, an entity may consider the loss of a smaller amount of extraordinarily sensitive data to be more significant than the loss of a larger amount of routinely collected data. The commenter stated that common reasoning would suggest that the smaller amount of data would be considered more sensitive.

Response: All electronic protected health information must be protected at least to the degree provided by these standards. If an entity desires to protect the information to a greater degree than the risk analysis would indicate, it is free to do so.

e. Comment: One commenter asked that we add ``threat assessment'' to this requirement.

Response: We have not done this because we view threat assessment as an inherent part of a risk analysis; adding it would be redundant.

f. Comment: We proposed a requirement for internal audit, the in-house review of the records of system activity (for example, logins, file accesses, and security incidents) maintained by an entity. Several commenters wanted this requirement deleted. One suggested the audit trail requirement should not be mandatory, while another stated that internal audits would be unnecessary if physical security requirements are implemented.

A number of commenters asked that we clarify the nature and scope of what an internal audit covers and what the audit time frame should be. Several commenters offered further detail concerning what should and should not be required in an internal audit for security purposes. One commenter stated that ongoing intrusion detection should be included in this requirement. Another wanted us to specify the retention times for archived audit logs.

Several commenters had difficulty with the term ``audit'' and suggested we change the title of the requirement to ``logging and violation monitoring."

A number of commenters stated this requirement could result in an undue burden and would be economically unfeasible.

Response: Our intent for this requirement was to promote the periodic review of an entity's internal security controls, for example, logs, access reports, and incident tracking. The extent, frequency, and nature of the reviews would be determined by the covered entity's security environment. The term ``internal audit" apparently, based on the comments received, has certain rigid formal connotations we did not intend. We agree that the implementation of formal internal audits could prove burdensome or even unfeasible, to some covered entities due to the cost and effort involved. However, we do not want to overlook the value of internal reviews. Based on our review of the comments and the text to which they refer, it is clear that this requirement should be renamed for clarity and that it should actually be an implementation specification of the security management process rather than an independent standard. We accordingly remove ``internal audit" as a separate requirement and add ``information system activity review" under the security management process standard as a mandatory implementation specification.

2. Assigned Security Responsibility (Sec. 164.308(a)(2))

We proposed that the responsibility for security be assigned to a specific individual or organization to provide an organizational focus and importance to security, and that the assignment be documented. Responsibilities would include the management and supervision of (1) the use of security measures to protect data, and (2) the conduct of personnel in relation to the protection of data.

In this final rule, we clarify that the final responsibility for a covered entity's security must be assigned to one official. The requirement for documentation is retained, but is made part of Sec. 164.316 below. This policy is consistent with the analogous policy in the Privacy Rule, at 45 CFR 164.530(a), and the same considerations apply. See 65 FR 82744 through 87445. The same person could fill the role for both security and privacy.

a. Comment: Commenters were concerned that delegation of assigned security responsibility, especially in large organizations, needs to be to more than a single individual. Commenters believe that a large health organization's security concerns would likely cross many departmental boundaries requiring group responsibility.

Response: The assigned security responsibility standard adopted in this final rule specifies that final security responsibility must rest with one individual to ensure accountability within each covered entity. More than one individual may be given specific security responsibilities, especially within a large organization, but a single individual must be designated as having the overall final responsibility for the security of the entity's electronic protected health information. This decision also aligns this rule with the final Privacy Rule provisions concerning the Privacy Official.

b. Comment: One commenter disagreed with placing assigned security responsibility as part of physical safeguards. The commenter suggested that assigned security responsibility should be included under the Administrative Procedures.

[[Page 8348]]

Response: Upon review of the matrix and <strong>regulations</strong> text, we agree with the commenter, because this requirement involves an administrative decision at the highest levels of who should be responsible for ensuring security measures are implemented and maintained. Assigned security responsibility has been removed from ``Physical safeguards" and is now located under ``Administrative safeguards" at Sec. 164.308.

3. Workforce Security (Sec. 164.308(a)(3)(i))

We proposed implementation of a number of features for personnel security, including ensuring that maintenance personnel are supervised by a knowledgeable person, maintaining a record of access authorizations, ensuring that operating and maintenance personnel have proper access authorization, establishing personnel clearance procedures, establishing and maintaining personnel security policies and procedures, and ensuring that system users have proper training.

In this final rule, to provide clarification and reduce duplication, we have combined the ``Assure supervision of maintenance personnel by authorized, knowledgeable person" implementation feature and the ``Operating, and in some cases, maintenance personnel have proper access authorization" feature into one addressable implementation specification titled ``Authorization and/or supervision."

In a related, but separate, requirement entitled ``Termination procedures," we proposed implementation features for the ending of an employee's employment or an internal or external user's access. These features would include things such as changing combination locks, removal from access lists, removal of user account(s), and the turning in of keys, tokens, or cards that allow access.

In this final rule, ``Termination procedures" has been made an addressable implementation specification under ``Workforce security." This is addressable because in certain circumstances, for example, a solo physician practice whose staff consists only of the physician's spouse, formal procedures may not be necessary.

The proposed ``Personnel security policy/procedure" and ``record of access authorizations" implementation features have been removed from this final rule, as they have been determined to be redundant. Implementation of the balance of the ``Workforce security" implementation specifications and the other standards contained within this final rule will result in assurance that all personnel with access to electronic protected health information have the required access authority as well as appropriate clearances.

a. Comment: The majority of comments concerned the supervision of maintenance personnel by an authorized knowledgeable person. Commenters stated this would not be feasible in smaller settings. For example, the availability of technically knowledgeable persons to ensure this supervision would be an issue. We were asked to either reword this implementation feature or delete it.

Response: We agree that a ``knowledgeable" person may not be available to supervise maintenance personnel. We have accordingly modified this implementation specification so that, in this final rule, we are adopting an addressable implementation specification titled, ``Authorization and/or supervision," requiring that workforce members, for example, operations and maintenance personnel, must either be supervised or have authorization when working with electronic protected health information or in locations where it resides (see Sec. 164.308(a)(3)(ii)(A)). Entities can decide on the feasibility of meeting this specification based on their risk analysis.

b. Comment: The second largest group of comments requested assurance that, with regard to the proposed ``Personnel clearance procedure" implementation feature, having appropriate clearances does not mean performing background checks on everyone. We were asked to delete references to ``clearance" and use the term ``authorization" in its place.

Response: We agree with the commenters concerning background checks. This feature was not intended to be interpreted as an absolute requirement for background checks. We retain the use of the term ``clearance," however, because we believe that it more accurately conveys the screening process intended than does the term ``authorization." We have attempted to clarify our intent in the language of Sec. 164.308(a)(3)(ii)(B), which now reads, ``Implement procedures to determine that the access of a workforce member to electronic protected health information is appropriate." The need for and extent of a screening process is normally based on an assessment of risk, cost, benefit, and feasibility as well as other protective measures in place. Effective personnel screening processes may be applied in a way to allow a range of implementation, from minimal procedures to more stringent procedures based on the risk analysis performed by the covered entity. So long as the standard is met and the underlying standard of Sec. 164.306(a) is met, covered entities have choices in how they meet these standards. To clarify the intent of this provision, we retitle the implementation specification ``Workforce clearance procedure."

c. Comment: One commenter asked that we expand the implementation features to include the identification of the restrictions that should be placed on members of the workforce and others.

Response: We have not adopted this comment in the interest of maintaining flexibility as discussed in Sec. 164.306. Restrictions would be dependent upon job responsibilities, the amount and type of supervision required and other factors. We note that a covered entity should consider in this regard the applicable requirements of the Privacy Rule (see, for example, Sec. 164.514(d)(2) (relating to minimum necessary requirements), and Sec. 164.530(c) (relating to safeguards).

Comment: One commenter believes that the proposed ``Personnel security'' requirement was reasonable, since an administrative determination of trustworthiness is needed before allowing access to sensitive information. Two commenters asked that we delete the requirement entirely. A number of commenters requested that we delete the implementation features. Another commenter stated that all the implementation features may not be applicable or even appropriate to a given entity and should be so qualified.

Response: While we do not believe this requirement should be eliminated, we agree that all the implementation specifications may not be applicable or even appropriate to a given entity. For example, a personal clearance may not be reasonable or appropriate for a small provider whose only assistant is his or her spouse. The implementation specifications are not mandatory, but must be addressed. This final rule has been changed to reflect this approach (see Sec. 164.308(a)(3)(ii)(B)).

e. Comment: The majority of commenters on the ``Termination procedures'' requirement asked that it be made optional, stating that it may not be applicable or even appropriate in all circumstances and should be so qualified or posed as guidelines. A number of commenters stated that the requirement should be deleted. One commenter stated that much of the material covered under the ``Termination procedures'' requirement is already covered in ``Information access control.'' A number of commenters stated that this requirement

[[Page 8349]]

was too detailed and some of the requirements excessive.

Response: Based upon the comments received, we agree that termination procedures should not be a separate standard; however, consideration of termination procedures remains relevant for any covered entity with employees, because of the risks associated with the potential for unauthorized acts by former employees, such as acts of retribution or use of proprietary information for personal gain. We further agree with the reasoning of the commenters who asked that these procedures be made optional; therefore, ``Termination procedures'' is now reflected in this final rule as an addressable implementation specification. We also removed reference to all specific termination activities, for example, changing locks, because, although the activities may be considered appropriate for some covered entities, they may not be reasonable for others.

f. Comment: One commenter asked whether human resource employee termination policies and procedures must be documented to show the types of security breaches that would result in termination.

Response: Policies and procedures implemented to adhere to this standard must be documented (see Sec. 164.316 below). The purpose of termination procedure documentation under this implementation specification is not to detail when or under which circumstances an employee should be terminated. This information would more appropriately be part of the entity's sanction policy. The purpose of termination procedure documentation is to ensure that termination procedures include security-unique actions to be followed, for example, revoking passwords and retrieving keys when a termination occurs.

4. Information Access Management (Sec. 164.308(a)(4))

We proposed an ``information access control'' requirement for establishment and maintenance of formal, documented policies and procedures defining levels of access for all personnel authorized to access health information, and how access is granted and modified. In Sec. 164.308(a)(4)(ii)(B) and (C) below, the proposed implementation features are made addressable specifications. We have added in Sec. 164.308(a)(4)(ii)(A), a required implementation specification to isolate health care clearinghouse functions to address the provisions of section 1173(d)(1)(B) of the Act which related to this area.

a. Comment: One commenter asked that the requirement be deleted, expressing the opinion that this requirement goes beyond ``reasonable boundaries'' into regulating common business practices. In contrast, another asked that we expand this requirement to identify participating parties and access privileges relative to specific data elements.

Response: We disagree that this requirement improperly imposes upon business functions. Restricting access to those persons and entities with a need for access is a basic tenet of security. By this mechanism, the risk of inappropriate disclosure, alteration, or destruction of information is minimized. We cannot, however, specifically identify participating parties and access privileges relative to data elements within this regulation. These will vary depending upon the entity, the needs within the user community, the system in which the data resides, and the specific data being accessed. This standard is consistent with Sec. 164.514(d) in the Privacy Rule (minimum necessary requirements for use and disclosure of protected health information), and is, therefore, being retained.

b. Comment: Several commenters asked that we not mandate the implementation features, but leave them as optional, a suggested means of compliance. The commenters noted that this might make the rules more
scalable and flexible, since this approach would allow providers to implement safeguards that best addressed their needs. Along this line, one commenter expressed the belief that each organization should implement features deemed necessary based on its own risk assessment.

Response: While the information access management standard in this final rule must be met, we agree that the implementation specifications at Sec. 164.308(a)(4)(ii)(B) and (C) should not be mandated but posed as a suggested means of compliance, which must be addressed. These specifications may not be applicable to all entities based on their size and degree of automation. A fully automated covered entity spanning multiple locations and involving hundreds of employees may determine it has a need to adopt a formal policy for access authorization, while a small provider may decide that a desktop standard operating procedure will meet the specifications. The final rule has been revised accordingly.

c. Comment: Clarification was requested concerning the meaning of "formal."

Response: The word ``formal'' has caused considerable concern among
commenters, as it was thought ``formal'' carried the connotation of a rigidly defined structure similar to what might be found in the Department of Defense instructions. As used in the proposed rule, this word was not intended to convey such a strict structure. Rather, it was meant to convey that documentation should be an official organizational statement as opposed to word-of-mouth or cryptic notes scratched on a notepad. While documentation is still required (see Sec. 164.316), to alleviate confusion, the word ``formal'' has been deleted.

d. Comment: One commenter asked that we clarify that this requirement relates to both the establishment of policies for the access control function and to access control (the implementation of those policies).

Response: ``Information access management'' does address both the establishment of access control policies and their implementation. We use the term ``implement'' to clarify that the procedures must be in use, and we believe that the requirement to implement policies and procedures requires, as an antecedent condition, the establishment or adaptation of those policies and procedures.

5. Security Awareness and Training (Sec. 164.308(a)(5)(i))

We proposed, under the requirement ``Training,'' that security training be required for all staff, including management. Training would include awareness training for all personnel, periodic security reminders, user education concerning virus protection, user education in the importance of monitoring login success/failure, and how to report discrepancies, and user education in password management.

In this final rule, we adopt this proposed requirement in modified form. For the standard ``Security awareness and training,'' in Sec. 164.308(a)(5), we require training of the workforce as reasonable and appropriate to carry out their functions in the facility. All proposed training features have been combined as implementation specifications under this standard. Specific implementation specifications relative to content are addressable. The ``Virus protection'' implementation feature has been renamed ``protection from malicious software,'' because we did not intend by the nomenclature to exclude coverage of malicious acts that might not come within the prior term, such as worms.

a. Comment: One commenter believes that security awareness training for all

[[Page 8350]]

system users would be too difficult to do in a large organization.
Response: We disagree with the commenter. Security awareness training is a critical activity, regardless of an organization's size. This feature would typically become part of an entity's overall training program (which would include privacy and other information technology items as well). For example, the Government Information Systems Reform ACT (GISRA) of 2000 requires security awareness training as part of Federal agencies' information security programs, including Federal covered entities, such as the Medicare program. In addition, National Institute of Standards and Technology (NIST) SP 800-16, Information Technology Security Training Requirements, A role and performance base model, April 1998, provides an excellent source of information and guidance on this subject and is targeted at industry as well as government activities. We also note that covered entities must have discretion in how they implement the requirement, so they can incorporate this training in other existing activities. One approach would be to require this training as part of employee orientation.

b. Comment: A number of commenters asked that this requirement be made optional or used as a guideline only. Several commenters stated that this requirement is too specific and is burdensome. Several asked that the implementation features be removed.

Several others stated that this requirement is not appropriate for agents or contractors. One commenter asked how to apply this requirement to outsiders having access to data. Another asked if this requirement included all subcontractor staff. Others stated that contracts, signed by entities such as consultants, that address training should be sufficient.

Response: Security training remains a requirement because of its criticality; however, we have revised the implementation specifications to indicate that the amount and type of training needed will be dependent upon an entity's configuration and security risks. Business associates must be made aware of security policies and procedures, whether through contract language or other means. Covered entities are not required to provide training to business associates or anyone else that is not a member of their workforce.

c. Comment: Several commenters questioned why security awareness training appeared in two places, under ``Physical safeguards" as well as ``Administrative safeguards." Others questioned the appropriateness of security awareness training under ``Physical safeguards."

Response: We reviewed the definitions of the proposed ``Awareness training for all personnel" (``Administrative safeguards") implementation feature and the proposed ``Security awareness training" (``Physical safeguards") requirement. We agree that, to avoid confusion and eliminate redundancy, security awareness and training should appear in only one place. We believe the appropriate location for it is under ``Administrative safeguards," as such training is essentially an administrative function.

d. Comment: Several commenters objected to the blanket requirement for security awareness training of individuals who may be on site for a limited time period (for example, a single day).

Response: Each individual who has access to electronic protected health information must be aware of the appropriate security measures to reduce the risk of improper access, uses, and disclosures. This requirement does not mean lengthy training is appropriate in every instance; there are alternative methods to inform individuals of security responsibilities (for example, provisions of pamphlets or copies of security policies, and procedures).

e. Comment: One commenter asked that ``training" be changed to ``orientation."

Response: We believe the term ``training," as presented within this rule is the more appropriate term. The rule does not contemplate a one-time type of activity as connoted by ``orientation," but rather an on-going, evolving process as an entity's security needs and procedures change.

f. Comment: Several commenters asked how often training should be conducted and asked for a definition of ``periodic," as it appears in the proposed implementation feature ``Periodic security reminders." One asked if the training should be tailored to job need.

Response: Amount and timing of training should be determined by each covered entity; training should be an on-going, evolving process in response to environmental and operational changes affecting the security of electronic protected health information. While initial training must be carried out by the compliance date, we provide flexibility for covered entities to construct training programs. Training can be tailored to job need if the covered entity so desires.

6. Security Incident Procedures (Sec. 164.308(a)(6))

We proposed a requirement for implementation of accurate and current security incident procedures: formal, documented report and response procedures so that security violations would be reported and handled promptly. We adopt this standard in the final rule, along with an implementation specification for response and reporting, since documenting and reporting incidents, as well as responding to incidents are an integral part of a security program.

a. Comment: Several commenters asked that we further define the scope of a breach of security. Along this same line, another commenter stated that the proposed security incident procedures were too vague as stated. We were asked to specify what a security incident would be, what the internal chain for reporting procedures would be, and what should be included in the documentation (for example, hardware/ software, personnel responses).

Response: We define a security incident in Sec. 164.304. Whether a specific action would be considered a security incident, the specific process of documenting incidents, what information should be contained in the documentation, and what the appropriate response should be will be dependent upon an entity's environment and the information involved.

An entity should be able to rely upon the information gathered in complying with the other security standards, for example, its risk assessment and risk management procedures and the privacy standards, to determine what constitutes a security incident in the context of its business operations.

b. Comment: One commenter asked what types of incidents must be reported to outside entities. Another commented that we clarify that incident reporting is internal.

Response: Internal reporting is an inherent part of security incident procedures. This regulation does not specifically require any incident reporting to outside entities. External incident reporting is dependent upon business and legal considerations.

c. Comment: One commenter stated that network activity should be included here.

Response: We see no reason to exclude network activity under this requirement. Improper network activity should be treated as a security incident, because, by definition, it represents an improper instance of access to or use of information.

[[Page 8351]]

d. Comment: One commenter stated that this requirement should address suspected misuse also.

Response: We agree that security incidents include misuse of data; therefore, this requirement is addressed.

e. Comment: Several commenters asked that this requirement be deleted. One commenter asked that we delete the implementation features.

Response: As indicated above, we have adopted the proposed standard and combined the implementation specifications.

7. Contingency Plan (Sec. 164.308(a)(7)(i))

We proposed that a contingency plan must be in effect for responding to system emergencies. The plan would include an applications and data criticality analysis, a data backup plan, a disaster recovery plan, an emergency mode operation plan, and testing and revision procedures.

In this final rule, we make the implementation specifications for testing and revision procedures and an applications and data criticality analysis addressable, but otherwise require that the contingency features proposed be met.

a. Comment: Several commenters suggested the contingency plan requirement be deleted. Several thought that this aspect of the proposed regulation went beyond its intended scope. Another believed that more discussion and development is needed before developing regulatory guidance on contingency plans. Others wanted this to be an optional requirement. In contrast, one commenter requested more guidance concerning contingency planning. Still others wanted to require that a contingency plan be in place but stated that we should not regulate its contents. One comment stated that data backup, disaster recovery, and emergency mode operation should not be part of this requirement.

Response: A contingency plan is the only way to protect the availability, integrity, and security of data during unexpected negative events. Data are often most exposed in these events, since the usual security measures may be disabled, ignored, or not observed.

Each entity needs to determine its own risk in the event of an emergency that would result in a loss of operations. A contingency plan may involve highly complex processes in one processing site, or simple manual processes in another. The contents of any given contingency plan will depend upon the nature and configuration of the entity devising it.

While the contingency plan standard must be met, we agree that the proposed testing and revision implementation feature should be an addressable implementation specification in this final rule. Dependent upon the size, configuration, and environment of a given covered entity, the entity should decide if testing and revision of all parts of a contingency plan should be done or if there are more reasonable alternatives. The same is true for the proposed applications and data criticality analysis implementation feature. We have revised the final rule to reflect this approach.

b. Comment: One commenter believed that adhering to this requirement could prove burdensome. Another stated that testing of certain parts of a contingency plan would be burdensome, and even infeasible, for smaller entities.

Response: Without contingency planning, a covered entity has no assurance that its critical data could survive an emergency situation. Recent events, such as September 11, 2001, illustrate the importance of such planning. Contingency planning will be scalable based upon, among other factors, office configuration, and risk assessment. However, in response to the scalability issue raised by the commenter, we have made the testing and revision implementation specification addressable (see Sec. 164.308(a)(7)(ii)).

c. Comment: Two commenters considered a 2-year implementation time frame for this requirement inadequate for large health plans. Another commenter stated that implementation of measures against natural disaster would be too big an issue for this regulation.

Response: The statute sets forth the compliance dates for the initial standards. The statute requires that compliance with initial standards is not later than 2 years after adoption of the standards for all covered entities except small health plans for which the compliance date is not later than 3 years after adoption.

The final rule calls for covered entities to consider how natural disasters could damage systems that contain electronic protected health information and develop policies and procedures for responding to such situations. We consider this to be a reasonable precautionary step to take since in many cases the risk would be deemed to be low.

d. Comment: A commenter requested clarification of the term ``Emergency mode'' with regard to the proposed ``Emergency mode operation plan'' implementation feature.

Response: We have clarified the ``Emergency mode operations plan'' to show that it only involves those critical business processes that must occur to protect the security of electronic protected health information during and immediately after a crisis situation.

8. Evaluation (Sec. 164.308(a)(8))

We proposed that certification would be required and could be performed internally or by an external accrediting agency. We solicited input on appropriate mechanisms to permit an independent assessment of compliance. We were particularly interested in input from those engaging in health care electronic data interchange (EDI), as well as independent certification and auditing organizations addressing issues of documentary evidence of steps taken for compliance; need for, or desirability of, independent verification, validation, and testing of system changes; and certifications required for off-the-shelf products used to meet the requirements of this regulation. We also solicited comments on the extent to which obtaining external certification would create an undue burden on small or rural providers.

In this final rule, we require covered entities to periodically conduct an evaluation of their security safeguards to demonstrate and document their compliance with the entity's security policy and the requirements of this subpart. Covered entities must assess the need for a new evaluation based on changes to their security environment since their last evaluation, for example, new technology adopted or responses to newly recognized risks to the security of their information.

a. Comment: We received several comments that certification should be performed externally. A larger group of commenters preferred self-certification. The majority of the comments, however, were to the effect that external certification should be encouraged but not mandated.

A number of commenters thought that mandating external certification would create an undue financial burden, regardless of the size of the entity being certified. One commenter stated that external certification would not place an undue burden on a small or rural provider.

Response: Evaluation by an external entity is a business decision to be left to each covered entity. Evaluation is required under Sec. 164.308(a)(8), but a covered entity may comply with this standard either by using its own workforce or an external accreditation agency, which would be acting as a business associate. External evaluation may be too costly an option for small entities.

[[Page 8352]]

b. Comment: Several commenters stated that the certification should cover all components of the proposed rule, not just the information systems.

Response: We agree. We have revised this section to reflect that evaluation would be both technical and nontechnical components of security.

c. Comment: A number of commenters expressed a desire for the creation of certification guides or models to complement the rule.

Response: We agree that creation of compliance guidelines or models for different business environments would help in the implementation and evaluation of HIPAA security requirements and we encourage professional associations and others to do so. We may develop technical assistance materials, but do not intend to create certification criteria because we do not have the resources to address the large number of different business environments.

d. Comment: Some commenters asked how certification is possible without specifying the level of risk that is permissible.

Response: The level of risk that is permissible is specified by Sec. 164.306(a). How such risk is managed will be determined by a covered entity through its security risk analysis and the risk mitigation activities it implements in order to ensure that the level of security required by Sec. 164.306 is provided.

e. Comment: Several commenters requested creation of a list of Federally ``certified'' security software and off-the-shelf products. Several others stated that this request was not feasible. Regarding certification of off-the-shelf products, one commenter thought this should be encouraged, but not mandated; several thought this would be an impractical endeavor.

Response: While we will not assume the task of certifying software and off-the-shelf products for the reason described above, we have noted with interest that other Government agencies such as the National Institute of Standards and Technology (NIST) are working towards that end. The health care industry is encouraged to monitor the activity of NIST and provide comments and suggestions when requested (see <A HREF="http://frwebgate.access.gpo.gov/cgi-bin/leaving.cgi?from=leavingFR.html&log=linklog&to=http://www.niap.nist.gov">http://www.niap.nist.gov</A>.
).

f. Comment: One commenter stated, ``With HCFA's publishing of these
HIPAA standards, and their desire to retain the final responsibility for determining violations and imposing penalties of the statute, it also seems appropriate for HCFA to also provide certifying services to ensure security compliance.''

Response: In view of the enormous number and variety of covered entities, we believe that evaluation can best be handled through the marketplace, which can develop more usable and targeted evaluation instruments and processes.

8. Business Associate Contracts or Other Arrangements (Sec. 164.308(b)(1))

In the proposed rule Sec. 142.308(a)(2) ``Chain of trust'' requirement, we proposed that covered entities be required to enter into a chain of trust partner agreement with their business partners, in which the partners would agree to electronically exchange data and protect the integrity, confidentiality, and availability of the data exchanged. This standard has been modified from the proposed requirement to reflect, in Sec. 164.308(b)(1) ``Business associate contracts and other arrangements," the business associate structure put in place by the Privacy Rule.

In this final rule, covered entities must enter into a contract or other arrangement with persons that meet the definition of business associate in Sec. 160.103. The covered entity must obtain satisfactory assurances from the business associate that it will appropriately safeguard the information in accordance with these standards (see Sec. 164.314(a)(1)).

The comments received on the proposed chain of trust partner agreements are discussed in section 2 ``Business associate contracts and other arrangements" of the discussion of Sec. 164.314 below.

9. Proposed Requirements Not Adopted in This Final Rule

a. Security Configuration Management

We proposed that an organization would be required to implement measures, practices, and procedures regarding security configuration management. They would be coordinated and integrated with other system configuration management practices for the security of information systems. These would include documentation, hardware and/or software installation and maintenance review and testing for security features, inventory procedures, security testing, and virus checking.

Comment: Several commenters asked that the entire requirement be deleted. Several others asked that the inventory and virus checking implementation features be removed as they believe those features are not germane to security configuration management. A number of commenters requested that security testing be deleted because this implementation feature is too detailed, unreasonable, impractical, and beyond the scope of the legislation. Others stated that the testing would be very complex and expensive. Others wanted more clarification of what we intend by security testing, and how much would be enough. A number of commenters asked that all of the implementation features be deleted. Others asked that the implementation features be made optional. Several commenters wanted to know the scope of organizational integration required. Several others asked if what we meant by Security Configuration Management was change or version control.

Response: Upon review, this requirement appears unnecessary because it is redundant of other requirements we are adopting in this rule. A covered entity will have addressed the activities described by the features under this proposed requirement by virtue of having implemented the risk analysis, risk management measures, sanction policies, and information systems criticality review called for under the security management process. The proposed documentation implementation feature has been made a separate standard (see Sec. 164.316). As a result, the Security Configuration Management requirement is not adopted in this final rule.

b. Formal Mechanism for Processing Records

The proposed rule proposed requiring a formal mechanism for processing records, and documented policies and procedures for the routine and nonroutine receipt, manipulation, storage, dissemination, transmission, and/or disposal of health information. This requirement has not been adopted in the final rule.

Comment: Several commenters thought this requirement concerned the regulation of formal procedures for how an entity does business and stated that such procedures should not be regulated. Others asked for additional clarification of what is meant by this requirement. One commenter thought the requirement too ambiguous and asked for clarification as to whether we meant such things as ``the proper handling of storage media, databases, transmissions," or ``the clinical realm of processes."

Two commenters asked how extensive this requirement would be and whether systems' user manuals and policies and procedures for handling health information would suffice and what level of detail would be expected.

[[Page 8353]]

Several thought this requirement could result in a significant resource and monetary burden to develop and maintain formal procedures. Two asked for an explanation of the benefit to be derived from this requirement.

One asked that covered entities be required to document processes that create a security risk only and suggested that a risk assessment would determine the need for this documentation.

Response: We agree with the commenters that the standard is ambiguous, and upon review, is unnecessary because the remaining standards, for example, device and media controls, provide adequate safeguards. Accordingly, this requirement is not adopted in this final rule.

F. Physical Safeguards (Sec. 164.310)

We proposed requirements and implementation features for documented physical safeguards to guard data integrity, confidentiality, and availability. We proposed to require safeguards in the following areas: Assigned security responsibility; media controls; physical access controls; policies and guidelines on workstation use; a secure workstation location; and security awareness training. A number of specific implementation features were proposed under the media controls and physical access controls requirements.

In Sec. 164.310 of this final rule, most of the proposed implementation features are adopted as addressable implementation specifications. The proposed requirements for the assigned security responsibility and security awareness training requirements are relocated in Sec. 164.308.

1. General Comments

a. Comment: Several commenters made suggestions to modify the language to more clearly describe ``Physical safeguards."

Response: In response to comments, we have revised the definition of ``Physical safeguards" to read as follows: ``Physical safeguards are security measures to protect a covered entity's electronic information systems and related buildings and equipment, from natural and environmental hazards, and unauthorized intrusion."

b. Comment: One commenter was concerned that electronic security systems could not be used in lieu of physical security systems.

Response: This final rule does not preclude the use of electronic security systems in lieu of, or in combination with, physical security systems to meet a ``Physical safeguard" standard.

2. Facility Access Controls (Sec. 164.310(a)(1))

We proposed, under the ``Physical access controls" requirement, formal, documented policies and procedures for limiting physical access to an entity while ensuring that properly authorized access is allowed. These controls would include the following implementation features: disaster recovery, emergency mode operation, equipment control (into and out of site), a facility security plan, procedures for verifying access authorizations before physical access, maintenance records, need-to-know procedures for personnel access, sign-in for visitors and escort, if appropriate, and testing and revision.

In Sec. 164.310(a)(2) below, we combine and restate these as addressable implementation specifications. These are contingency operations, facility security plan, access control and validation procedures, and maintenance records.

a. Comment: Many commenters were concerned because the proposed language would require implementation of all physical access control features. Other commenters were concerned that the language did not allow entities to use the results of their risk assessment and risk management process to arrive at the appropriate solutions for them.

Response: We agree that implementation of all implementation specifications may not be appropriate in all situations. While the facility access controls standard must be met, we agree that the implementation specifications should not be required in all circumstances, but should be addressable. In this final rule, all four implementation specifications are addressable.

We have also determined, based on ``level of detail" comments requesting consolidation of the list of implementation features, that the proposed implementation feature ``Equipment control (into and out of site)" was redundant. ``Equipment control" is already covered under the ``Device and media controls" standard at Sec. 164.310(d)(1). Accordingly, we have eliminated it as a separate implementation specification.

b. Comment: One commenter raised the issue of a potential conflict of authority between those having access to the data and those responsible for checking and maintaining access controls.

Response: Any potential conflicts should be identified, addressed, and resolved in the policies and procedures developed according to the standards under Sec. 164.308.

c. Comment: Several commenters questioned whether ``Physical Access Controls" was a descriptive phrase to describe a technology to be used, or whether the phrase referred to a facility.

Response: We agree that the term ``Physical" may be misleading; to remove any confusion, the requirement is reflected in this final rule as a standard titled ``Facility access controls." We believe this is a more precise term to describe that the standard, and its associated implementation specifications, is applicable to an entity's business location or locations.

d. Comment: Several commenters requested that the disaster recovery and emergency mode operations features be moved to ``Administrative safeguards." Other commenters recommended that disaster recovery and emergency mode operations should be replaced by, and included in, a ``Contingency Operations" implementation feature.

Response: The ``Administrative safeguards" section addresses the contingency planning that must be done to contend with emergency situations. The placement of the disaster recovery and emergency mode operations implementation specifications in the ``Physical safeguards" section is also appropriate, however, because ``Physical safeguards" defines the physical operations (processes) that provide access to the facility to implement the associated plans, developed under Sec. 164.308. We agree, however, that the term ``contingency operations" better describes, and would include, disaster recovery and emergency mode operations, and have modified the regulation text accordingly (see Sec. 164.310(a)(1)).

e. Comment: Commenters were concerned about having to address in their facility security plan the exterior/interior security of a building when they are one of many occupants rather than the sole occupant. Additional commenters were concerned that the responsibility for physical security of the building could not be delegated to a third party when the covered entity shares the building with other offices.

Response: The facility security plan is an addressable implementation specification. However, the covered entity retains responsibility for considering facility security even where it shares space within a building with other organizations. Facility security measures taken by a third party must be considered and documented in the covered entity's facility security plan, when appropriate.

[[Page 8354]]

3. Workstation Use (Sec. 164.310(b))

We proposed policy and guidelines on workstation use that included documented instructions/procedures delineating the proper functions to be performed and the manner in which those functions are to be performed (for example, logging off before leaving a workstation unattended) to maximize the security of health information. In this final rule, we adopt this standard.

Comment: One commenter was concerned most people may be misled by the use of ``terminal" as an example in the definition of workstation. The concern was that the standard only addresses ``fixed location devices," while in many instances the workstation has become a laptop computer.

Response: For clarity, we have added the definition of ``workstation" to Sec. 164.304 and deleted the word ``terminal" from the description of workstation use in Sec. 164.310(b).

4. Workstation Security (Sec. 164.310(c))

We proposed that each organization would be required to put in place physical safeguards to restrict access to information. In this final rule, we retain the general requirement for a secure workstation.

Comment: Comments were directed toward the example profiled in the definition of a secure workstation location. It was believed that what constitutes a secure workstation location must be dependent upon the entity's risk management process.

Response: We agree that what constitutes an appropriate solution to a covered entity's workstation security issues is dependent on the entity's risk analysis and risk management process. Because many commenters incorrectly interpreted the examples as the required and only solution for securing the workstation location, we have modified the <strong>regulations</strong> text description to generalize the requirement (see Sec. 164.310(c)). Also, for clarity, the title ``Secure workstation location" has been changed to ``Workstation security" (see also the definition of ``Workstation" at Sec. 164.304).

5. Device and Media Controls (Sec. 164.310(d)(1))

We proposed that covered entities have media controls in the form of formal, documented policies and procedures that govern the receipt and removal of hardware and/or software (for example, diskettes and tapes) into and out of a facility. Implementation features would have included ``Access control," ``Accountability" (tracking mechanism), ``Data backup," ``Data storage," and ``Disposal."

In this final rule, we adopt most of these provisions as addressable implementation specifications and add a specification for media re-use. We change the name from ``Media controls" to ``Device and media controls" to more clearly reflect that this standard concerns hardware as well as electronic media. The proposed ``Access control" implementation feature has been removed, as it is addressed as part of other standards (see section III.C.12.c of this preamble).

a. Comment: One commenter was concerned about the exclusion of removable media devices from examples of physical types of hardware and/or software.

Response: The media examples used were not intended to represent all possible physical types of hardware and/or software. Removable media devices, although not specifically listed, are not intended to be excluded.

b. Comment: Comments were made that the issue of equipment re-use or recycling of media containing mass storage was not addressed in ``Media controls."

Response: We agree that equipment re-use or recycling should be addressed, since this equipment may contain electronic protected health information. The ``Device and media controls" standard is accordingly expanded to include a required implementation specification that addresses the re-use of media (see Sec. 164.310(d)(2)(ii)).

c. Comment: Several commenters asked for a definition of the term ``facility," as used in the proposed ``Media controls" requirement description. Commenters were unclear whether we were talking about a corporate entity or the physical plant.

Response: The term ``facility" refers to the physical premises and the interior and exterior of a building(s). We have added this definition to Sec. 164.304.

d. Comment: Several commenters believe the ``Media controls" implementation features are too onerous and should be deleted.

Response: While the ``Device and media controls" standard must be met, we believe, based upon further review, that implementation of all specifications would not be necessary in every situation, and might even be counter-productive in some situations. For example, small providers would be unlikely to be involved in large-scale moves of equipment that would require systematic tracking, unlike, for example, large health care providers or health plans. We have, therefore, reclassified the ``Accountability and data backup" implementation specification as addressable to provide more flexibility in meeting the standard.

e. Comment: One commenter was concerned about the accountability impact of audit trails on system resources and the pace of system services.

Response: The proposed audit trail implementation feature appears as the addressable ``Accountability" implementation specification. The name change better reflects the purpose and intended scope of the implementation specification. This implementation specification does not address audit trails within systems and/or software. Rather it requires a record of the actions of a person relative to the receipt and removal of hardware and/or software into and out of a facility that are traceable to that person. The impact of maintaining accountability on system resources and services will depend upon the complexity of the mechanism to establish accountability. For example, the appropriate mechanism for a given entity may be manual, such as receipt and removal restricted to specific persons, with logs kept. Maintaining accountability in such a fashion should have a minimal, if any, effect on system resources and services.

f. Comment: A commenter was concerned about the resource expenditure (system and fiscal) for total e-mail backup and wanted a clarification of the extensiveness of data backup.

Response: The data an entity needs to backup, and which operations should be used to carry out the backup, should be determined by the entity's risk analysis and risk management process. The data backup plan, which is part of the required contingency plan (see Sec.

164.308(a)(7)(ii)(A)), should define exactly what information is needed to be retrievable to allow the entity to continue business ``as usual'' in the face of damage or destruction of data, hardware, or software. The extent to which e-mail backup would be needed would be determined through that analysis.

G. Technical Safeguards (Sec. 164.312)

We proposed five technical security services requirements with supporting implementation features: Access control; Audit controls; Authorization control; Data authentication; and Entity authentication. We also proposed specific technical security mechanisms for data transmitted over a communications network, Communications/network controls with supporting implementation features; Integrity controls; Message authentication; Access controls;

[[Page 8355]]

Encryption; Alarm; Audit trails; Entity authentication; and Event reporting.

In this final rule, we consolidate these provisions into Sec. 164.312. That section now includes standards regarding access controls, audit controls, integrity (previously titled data authentication), person or entity authentication, and transmission security. As discussed below, while certain implementation specifications are required, many of the proposed security implementation features are now addressable implementation specifications. The function of authorization control has been incorporated into the information access management standard under Sec. 164.308, Administrative safeguards.

1. Access Control (Sec. 164.312(a)(1))

In the proposed rule, we proposed to require that the access controls requirement include features for emergency access procedures and provisions for context-based, role-based, and/or user-based access; we also proposed the optional use of encryption as a means of providing access control. In this final rule, we require unique user identification and provision for emergency access procedures, and retain encryption as an addressable implementation specification. We also make ``Automatic logoff'' an addressable implementation specification. ``Automatic logoff'' and ``Unique user identification'' were formerly implementation features under the proposed ``Entity authentication'' (see Sec. 164.312(d)).

a. Comment: Some commenters believe that in specifying ``Context,'' ``Role,'' and ``User'' based controls, use of other controls would effectively be excluded, for example, ``Partition rule-based access controls,'' and the development of new access control technology.

Response: We agree with the commenters that other types of access controls should be allowed. There was no intent to limit the implementation features to the named technologies and this final rule has been reworded to make it clear that use of any appropriate access control mechanism is allowed. Proposed implementation features titled ``Context-based access,'' ``Role-based access,'' and ``User-based access'' have been deleted and the access control standard at Sec. 164.312(a)(1) states the general requirement.

b. Comment: A large number of comments were received objecting to the identification of ``Automatic logoff'' as a mandatory implementation feature. Generally the comments asked that we not be so specific and allow other forms of inactivity lockout, and that this type of feature be made optional, based more on the particular configuration in use and a risk assessment/analysis.

Response: We agree with the comments that mandating an automatic logoff is too specific. This final rule has been written to clarify that the proposed implementation feature of automatic logoff now appears as an addressable access control implementation specification and also permits the use of an equivalent measure.

c. Comment: We received comments asking that encryption be deleted as an implementation feature and stating that encryption is not required for ``data at rest.''

Response: The use of file encryption is an acceptable method of denying access to information in that file. Encryption provides confidentiality, which is a form of control. The use of encryption, for the purpose of access control of data at rest, should be based upon an entity's risk analysis. Therefore, encryption has been adopted as an addressable implementation specification in this final rule.

d. Comment: We received one comment stating that the proposed implementation feature ``Procedure for emergency access,'' is not access control and recommending that emergency access be made a separate requirement.

Response: We believe that emergency access is a necessary part of access controls and, therefore, is properly a required implementation specification of the ``Access controls'' standard. Access controls will still be necessary under emergency conditions, although they may be very different from those used in normal operational circumstances. For example, in a situation when normal environmental systems, including electrical power, have been severely damaged or rendered inoperative due to a natural or man-made disaster, procedures should be established beforehand to provide guidance on possible ways to gain access to needed electronic protected health information.

2. Audit Controls (Sec. 164.312(b))

We proposed that audit control mechanisms be put in place to record and examine system activity. We adopt this requirement in this final rule.

a. Comment: We received a comment stating that ``Audit controls'' should be an implementation feature rather than the standard, and suggesting that we change the title of the standard to ``Accountability,'' and provide additional detail to the audit control implementation feature.

Response: We do not adopt the term ``Accountability'' in this final rule because it is not descriptive of the requirement, which is to have the capability to record and examine system activity. We believe that it is appropriate to specify audit controls as a type of technical safeguard. Entities have flexibility to implement the standard in a manner appropriate to their needs as deemed necessary by their own risk analyses. For example, see NIST Special Publication 800-14, Generally Accepted Principles and Practices for Securing Information Technology Systems and NIST Special Publication 800-33, Underlying Technical Models for Information Technology Security.

b. Comment: One commenter recommended that this final rule state that audit control mechanisms should be implemented based on the findings of an entity's risk assessment and risk analysis. The commenter asserted that audit control mechanisms should be utilized only when appropriate and necessary and should not adversely affect system performance.

Response: We support the use of a risk assessment and risk analysis to determine how intensive any audit control function should be. We believe that the audit control requirement should remain mandatory, however, since it provides a means to assess activities regarding the electronic protected health information in an entity's care.

c. Comment: One commenter was concerned about the interplay of State and Federal requirements for auditing of privacy data and requested additional guidance on the interplay of privacy rights, laws, and the expectation for audits under the rule.

Response: In general, the security standards will supercede any contrary provision of State law. Security standards in this final rule establish a minimum level of security that covered entities must meet. We note that covered entities may be required by other Federal law to adhere to additional, or more stringent security measures. Section 1178(a)(2) of the statute provides several exceptions to this general rule. With regard to protected health information, the preemption of State laws and the relationship of the Privacy Rule to other Federal laws is discussed in the Privacy Rule beginning at 65 FR 82480; the preemption provisions of the rule are set out at 45 CFR part 160, subpart B.

It should be noted that although the Privacy Rule does not incorporate a requirement for an ``audit trail'' function, it does call for providing an accounting of certain disclosures of protected health information to an

[[Page 8356]]

individual upon request. There has been a tendency to assume that this Privacy Rule requirement would be satisfied via some sort of process involving audit trails. We caution against assuming that the Security Rule's requirement for an audit capability will satisfy the Privacy Rule's requirement regarding accounting for disclosures of protected health information. The two rules cover overlapping, but not identical information. Further, audit trails are typically used to record uses within an electronic information system, while the Privacy Rule requirement for accounting applies to certain disclosures outside of the covered entity (for example, to public health authorities).

3. Integrity (Sec. 164.312(c)(1))

We proposed under the ``Data authentication" requirement, that each organization be required to corroborate that data in its possession have not been altered or destroyed in an unauthorized manner and provided examples of mechanisms that could be used to accomplish this task. We adopt the proposed requirement for data authentication in the final rule as an addressable implementation specification ``Mechanism to authenticate data," under the ``Integrity" standard.

a. Comment: We received a large number of comments requesting clarification of the ``Data authentication" requirement. Many of these comments suggested that the requirement be called ``Data integrity" instead of ``Data authentication." Others asked for guidance regarding just what ``data" must be authenticated. A significant number of commenters indicated that this requirement would put an extraordinary burden on large segments of the health care industry, particularly when legacy systems are in use. Requests were received to make this an ``optional" requirement, based on an entity's risk assessment and analysis.

Response: We adopt the suggested ``integrity" terminology because it more clearly describes the intent of the standard. We retain the meaning of the term ``Data authentication" under the addressable implementation specification ``Mechanism to authenticate data," and provide an example of a potential means to achieve data integrity.

Error-correcting memory and magnetic disc storage are examples of the built-in data authentication mechanisms that are ubiquitous in hardware and operating systems today. The risk analysis process will address what data must be authenticated and should provide answers appropriate to the different situations faced by the various health care entities implementing this regulation.

Further, we believe that this standard will not prove difficult to implement, since there are numerous techniques available, such as processes that employ digital signature or check sum technology to accomplish the task.

b. Comment: We received numerous comments suggesting that ``Double keying" be deleted as a viable ``Data authentication" mechanism, since this practice was generally associated with the use of punched cards.

Response: We agree that the process of ``Double keying" is outdated. This final rule omits any reference to ``Double keying."

4. Person or Entity Authentication (Sec. 164.312(d))

We proposed that an organization implement the requirement for ``Entity authentication", the corroboration that an entity is who it claims to be. ``Automatic logoff" and ``Unique user identification" were specified as mandatory features, and were to be coupled with at least one of the following features: (1) A ``biometric" identification system; (2) a ``password" system; (3) a ``personal identification number"; and (4) ``telephone callback," or a ``token" system that uses a physical device for user identification.

In this final rule, we provide a general requirement for person or entity authentication without the specifics of the proposed rule.

Comment: We received comments from a number of organizations requesting that the implementation features for entity authentication be either deleted in their entirety or at least be made optional. On the other hand, comments were received requesting that the use of digital signatures and soft tokens be added to the list of implementation features.

Response: We agree with the commenters that many different mechanisms may be used to authenticate entities, and this final rule now reflects this fact by not incorporating a list of implementation specifications, in order to allow covered entities to use whatever is reasonable and appropriate. ``Digital signatures" and ``soft tokens" may be used, as well as many other mechanisms, to implement this standard.

The proposed mandatory implementation feature, ``Unique user identification," has been moved from this standard and is now a required implementation specification under ``Access control" at Sec. 164.312(a)(1). ``Automatic logoff" has also been moved from this standard to the ``Access control" standard and is now an addressable implementation specification.

5. Transmission Security (Sec. 164.312(e)(1))

Under ``Technical Security Mechanisms to Guard Against Unauthorized Access to Data that is Transmitted Over a Communications Network," we proposed that ``Communications/network controls" be required to protect the security of health information when being transmitted electronically from one point to another over open networks, along with a combination of mandatory and optional implementation features. We proposed that some form of encryption must be employed on ``open" networks such as the Internet or dial-up lines.

In this final rule, we adopt integrity controls and encryption, as addressable implementation specifications.

a. Comment: We received a number of comments asking for overall clarification as well as a definition of terms used in this section. A definition for the term ``open networks" was the most requested action, but there was a general expression of dislike for the manner in which we approached this section, with some comments suggesting that the entire section be rewritten. A significant number of comments were received on the question of encryption requirements when dial-up lines were to be employed as a means of connectivity. The overwhelming majority strongly urged that encryption not be mandatory when using any transmission media other than the Internet, but rather be considered optional based on individual entity risk assessment/analysis. Many comments noted that there are very few known breaches of security over dial-up lines and that nonjudicious use of encryption can adversely affect processing times and become both financially and technically burdensome. Only one commenter suggested that ``most" external traffic should be encrypted.

Response: In general, we agree with the commenters who asked for clarification and revision. This final rule has been significantly revised to reflect a much simpler and more direct requirement. The term ``Communications/network controls" has been replaced with ``Transmission security" to better reflect the requirement that, when electronic protected health information is transmitted from one point to another, it must be protected in a manner commensurate with the associated risk.

[[Page 8357]]

We agree with the commenters that switched, point-to-point connections, for example, dial-up lines, have a very small probability of interception.

Thus, we agree that encryption should not be a mandatory requirement for transmission over dial-up lines. We also agree with commenters who mentioned the financial and technical burdens associated with the employment of encryption tools. Particularly when considering situations faced by small and rural providers, it became clear that there is not yet available a simple and interoperable solution to encrypting e-mail communications with patients. As a result, we decided to make the use of encryption in the transmission process an addressable implementation specification. Covered entities are encouraged, however, to consider use of encryption technology for transmitting electronic protected health information, particularly over the internet.

As business practices and technology change, there may arise situations where electronic protected health information being transmitted from a covered entity would be at significant risk of being accessed by unauthorized entities. Where risk analysis showed such risk to be significant, we would expect covered entities to encrypt those transmissions, if appropriate, under the addressable implementation specification for encryption.

We do not use the term ``open network" in this final rule because its meaning is too broad. We include as an addressable implementation specification the requirement that transmissions be encrypted when appropriate based on the entity's risk analysis.

b. Comment: We received comments requesting that the implementation features be deleted or made optional. Three commenters asked that the requirement for an alarm be deleted.

Response: This final rule has been revised to reflect deletion of the following implementation features: (1) The alarm capability; (2)

audit trail; (3) entity authentication; and (4) event reporting. These features were associated with a proposed requirement for ``Communications/network controls" and have been deleted since they are normally incorporated by telecommunications providers as part of network management and control functions that are included with the provision of network services. A health care entity would not expect to be responsible for these technical telecommunications features. ``Access controls" has also been deleted from the implementation features since the consideration of the use of encryption will satisfy the intent of this feature. We retain as addressable implementation specifications two features: (1) ``Integrity controls" and ``encryption". ``Message authentication" has been deleted as an implementation feature because the use of data authentication codes (called for in the ``integrity controls" implementation specification) satisfies the intent of ``Message authentication."

c. Comment: A number of comments were received asking that this final rule establish a specific (or at least a minimum) cryptographic algorithm strength. Others recommended that the rule not specify an encryption strength since technology is changing so rapidly. Several commenters requested guidelines and minimum encryption standards for the Internet. Another stated that, since an example was included (small or rural providers for example), the government should feel free to name a specific encryption package. One commenter stated that the requirement for encryption on the Internet should reference the ``CMS Internet Security Policy."

Response: We remain committed to the principle of technology neutrality and agree with the comment that rapidly changing technology makes it impractical and inappropriate to name a specific technology. Consistent with this principle, specification of an algorithm strength or specific products would be inappropriate. Moreover, rapid advances in the success of ``brute force" cryptanalysis techniques suggest that any minimum specification would soon be outmoded. We maintain that it is much more appropriate for this final rule to state a general requirement for encryption protection when necessary and depend on covered entities to specify technical details, such as algorithm types and strength. Because ``CMS Internet Security Policy" is the policy of a single organization and applies only to information sent to CMS, and not between all covered entities, we have not referred to it here.

d. Comment: The proposed definition of ``Integrity controls" generated comments that asked that the word ``validity" be changed to ``Integrity." Commenters were concerned about the ability of an entity to ensure that information was ``valid."

Response: We agree with the commenters about the meaning of the word ``validity" in the context of the proposed definition of ``Integrity controls." We have named ``integrity controls" as an implementation specification in this final rule to require mechanisms to ensure that electronically transmitted information is not improperly modified without detection (see Sec. 164.312(c)(1)).

e. Comment: Three commenters asked for clarification and guidance regarding the unsolicited electronic receipt of health information in an unsecured manner, for example, when the information was submitted by a patient via e-mail over the Internet. Commenters asked for guidance as to what was their obligation to protect data received in this manner.

Response: The manner in which electronic protected health information is received by a covered entity does not affect the requirement that security protection must subsequently be afforded to that information by the covered entity once that information is in possession of the covered entity.

6. Proposed Requirements Not Adopted in This Final Rule

a. Authorization Control

We proposed, under ``Technical Security Services to Guard Data Integrity, Confidentiality, and Availability," that a mechanism be required for obtaining consent for the use and disclosure of health information using either ``Role-based access" or ``User-based access" controls. In this final rule, we do not adopt this requirement.

Comment: We received a large number of comments regarding use of the word ``consent." It was pointed out that this could be construed to mean patient consent to the use or disclosure of patient information, which would make this a privacy issue, rather than one of security. Other comments suggested deletion of the requirement in its entirety. We received a comment asking for clarification about the distinction between ``Access control" and ``Authorizations."

Response: These requirements were intended to address authorization of workforce members and others for the use and disclosure of health information, not patient consent. Upon reviewing the differences between ``Access control" and ``Authorization control," we found it to be unnecessary to retain ``Authorization control" as a separate requirement. Both the access control and the authorization control proposed requirements involved implementation of types of automated access controls, that is, role-based access and user-based access. It can be argued that the process of managing access involves allowing and restricting access to those individuals that have been authorized to access the data. The intent of the proposed authorization control implementation feature is now

[[Page 8358]]

incorporated in the access authorization implementation specification under the information access management standard in Sec. 164.308(a)(4). Under the information access management standard, a covered entity must implement, if appropriate and reasonable to its situation, policies and procedures first to authorize a person to access electronic protected health information and then to actually establish such access. These policies and procedures will enable entities to follow the Privacy Rule minimum necessary requirements, which provide when persons should have access to information.

H. Organizational Requirements (Sec. 164.314)

We proposed that each health care clearinghouse must comply with the security standards to ensure all health information and activities are protected from unauthorized access. If the clearinghouse is part of a larger organization, then unauthorized access by the larger organization must be prevented. We also proposed that parties processing data through a third party would be required to enter into a chain of trust partner agreement, a contract in which the parties agree to electronically exchange data and to protect the transmitted data in accordance with the security standards.

In this final rule, we have adopted the concepts of hybrid and affiliated entities, as previously defined in Sec. 164.504, and now defined in Sec. 164.103, and business associates as defined in Sec. 160.103, to be consistent with the Privacy Rule. General organizational requirements related to affiliated covered entities and hybrid entities are now contained in a new Sec. 164.105. The proposed chain of trust partner agreement has been replaced by the standards for business associate contracts or other arrangements and the standards for group health plans. Consistent with the statute and the policy of the Privacy Rule, this final rule does not require noncovered entities to comply with the security standards.

1. Health Care Clearinghouses

The proposed rule proposed that if a health care clearinghouse were part of a larger organization, it would be required to ensure that all health information pertaining to an individual is protected from unauthorized access by the larger organization; this statement closely tracked the statutory language in section 1173(d)(1)(B) of the Act. Since the point of the statutory language is to ensure that health care information in the possession of a health care clearinghouse is not inappropriately accessed by the larger organization of which it is a part, this final rule implements the statutory language through the information access management provision of Sec. 164.308(a)(4)(ii)(A).

The final rule, at Sec. 164.105, makes the health care component and affiliated entity standards of the Privacy Rule applicable to the security standards. Therefore, we have not changed those standards substantively. In pertaining to the Privacy Rule, we have simply moved them to a new location in part 164. Any differences between Sec. 164.105 and Sec. 164.504(a) through (d) reflects the addition of requirements specific to the security standards.

The health care component approach was developed in response to extensive comment received principally on the Privacy Rule. See 65 FR 82502 through 82503 and 82637 through 82640 for a discussion of the policy concerns underlying the health care component approach. Since the security standards are intended to support the protection of electronic information protected by the Privacy Rule, it makes sense to incorporate organizational requirements that parallel those required of covered entities by the Privacy Rule. This policy will also minimize the burden of complying with both rules.

a. Comment: Relative to the following preamble statement (63 FR 43258): ``If the clearinghouse is part of a larger organization, then security must be imposed to prevent unauthorized access by the larger organization." One commenter asked what is considered to be ``the larger organization." For example, if a clearinghouse function occurs in a department of a larger business entity, will the regulation cover all internal electronic communication, such as e-mail, within the larger business and all external electronic communication, such as e-mail with its owners?

Response: The ``larger organization" is the overall business entity that a clearinghouse would be part of. Under the Security Rule, the larger organization must assure that the health care clearinghouse function has instituted measures to ensure only that electronic protected health information that it processes is not improperly accessed by unauthorized persons or other entities, including the larger organization. Internal electronic communication within the larger organization will not be covered by the rule if it does not involve the clearinghouse, assuming that it has designated health care components, of which the health care clearinghouse is one. External communication must be protected as sent by the clearinghouse, but need not be protected once received.

b. Comment: One commenter asked that the first sentence in Sec. 142.306(b) of the proposed rule, ``If a health care clearinghouse is part of a larger organization, it must assure all health information is protected from unauthorized access by the larger organization" be expanded to read, ``If a health care clearinghouse or any other health care entity is part of a larger organization . . ."

Response: The Act specifically provides, at section 1173(d)(1)(B), that the Secretary must adopt standards to ensure that a health care clearinghouse, if part of a larger organization, has policies and security procedures to protect information from unauthorized access by the larger organization.

Health care providers and health plans are often part of larger organizations that are not themselves health care providers or health plans. The security measures implemented by health plans and covered health care providers should protect electronic protected health information in circumstances such as the one identified by the commenter. Therefore, we agree with the comment that the requirement should be expanded as suggested by the commenter. In this final rule, those components of a hybrid entity that are designated as health care components must comply with the security standards and protect against unauthorized access with respect to the other components of the larger entity in the same way as they must deal with separate entities.

2. Business Associate Contracts and Other Arrangements

We proposed that parties processing data through a third party would be required to enter into a chain of trust partner agreement, a contract in which the parties agree to electronically exchange data and to protect the transmitted data. This final rule narrows the scope of agreements required. It essentially tracks the provisions in Sec. 164.502(e) and Sec. 164.504(e) of the Privacy Rule, although appropriate modifications have been made in this rule to the required elements of the contract.

In this final rule, a contract between a covered entity and a business associate must provide that the business associate must--(1) implement safeguards that reasonably and appropriately protect the confidentiality, integrity, and availability of the electronic protected health information that it creates,

[[Page 8359]]

receives, maintains, or transmits on behalf of the covered entity; (2) ensure that any agent, including a subcontractor, to whom it provides this information agrees to implement reasonable and appropriate safeguards; (3) report to the covered entity any security incident of which it becomes aware; (4) make its policies and procedures, and documentation required by this subpart relating to such safeguards, available to the Secretary for purposes of determining the covered entity's compliance with this subpart; and (5) authorize termination of the contract by the covered entity if the covered entity determines that the business associate has violated a material term of the contract.

When a covered entity and its business associate are both governmental entities, an ``other arrangement" is sufficient. The covered entity is in compliance with this standard if it enters into a memorandum of understanding with the business associate that contains terms that accomplish the objectives of the above-described business associate contract. However, the covered entity may omit from this memorandum the termination authorization required by the business associate contract provisions if this authorization is inconsistent with the statutory obligations of the covered entity or its business associate. If other law (including <strong>regulations</strong> adopted by the covered entity or its business associate) contains requirements applicable to the business associate that accomplish the objectives of the above-described business associate contract, a contract or agreement is not required. If a covered entity enters into other arrangements with another governmental entity that is a business associate, such arrangements may omit provisions equivalent to the termination authorization required by the business associate contract, if inconsistent with the statutory obligation of the covered entity or its business associate.

If a business associate is required by law to perform a function or activity on behalf of a covered entity or to provide a service described in the definition of business associate in Sec. 160.103 of this subchapter to a covered entity, the covered entity may permit the business associate to receive, create, maintain, or transmit electronic protected health information on its behalf to the extent necessary to comply with the legal mandate without meeting the requirements of the above-described business associate contract, provided that the covered entity attempts in good faith to obtain satisfactory assurances as required by the above described business associate contract and documents the attempt and the reasons that these assurances cannot be obtained.

We have added a standard for group health plans that parallels the provisions of the Privacy Rule. It became apparent during the course of the security and privacy rulemaking that our original chain of trust approach was both overly broad in scope and failed to address appropriately the circumstances of certain covered entities, particularly the ERISA group health plans. These latter considerations and the solutions arrived at in the Privacy Rule are described in detail in the Privacy Rule at 65 FR 82507 through 82509. Because the purpose of the security standards is in part to reinforce privacy protections, it makes sense to align the organizational policies of the two rules. This decision should also make compliance less burdensome for covered entities than would a decision to have different organizational requirements for the two sets of rules.

Thus, we have added at Sec. 164.314(b) a standard for group health plan that tracks the standard at Sec. 164.504(f) very closely. The purpose of these provisions is to ensure that, except when the electronic protected health information disclosed to a plan sponsor is summary health information or enrollment or disenrollment information as provided for by Sec. 164.504(f), group health plan documents provide that the plan sponsor will reasonably and appropriately safeguard electronic protected health information created, received, maintained or transmitted to or by the plan sponsor on behalf of the group health plan. The plan documents of the group health plan must be amended to incorporate provisions to require the plan sponsor to implement reasonable and appropriate safeguards to protect the confidentiality, integrity, and availability of the electronic protected health information that it creates, receives, maintains, or transmits on behalf of the group health plan; ensure that the adequate separation required by Sec. 164.504(f)(2)(iii) is supported by reasonable and appropriate security measures; ensure that any agents, including a subcontractor, to whom it provides this information agrees to implement reasonable and appropriate safeguards to protect the information; report to the group health plan any security incident of which it becomes aware; and make its policies and procedures and documentation relating to these safeguards available to the Secretary for purposes of determining the group health plan's compliance with this subpart.

a. Comment: Several commenters expressed confusion concerning the applicability of proposed Sec. 142.104 to security.

Response: The proposed preamble included language generally applicable to most of the proposed standards under HIPAA. Proposed Sec. 142.104 concerned general requirements for health plans relative to processing transactions. We proposed that plans could not refuse to conduct a transaction as a standard transaction, or delay or otherwise adversely affect a transaction on the grounds that it was a standard transaction; health information transmitted and received in connection with a transaction must be in the form of standard data elements; and plans conducting transactions through an agent must ensure that the agent met all the requirements that applied to the health plan. Except for the statement that a plan's agent (``business associate" in the final rule) must meet the requirements (which would include security) that apply to the health plan, this proposed section did not pertain to the security standards and was addressed in the Transaction Rule.

b. Comment: The majority of comments concerned proposed rule language stating ``the same level of security will be maintained at all links in the chain * * *" Commenters believed the current language will have an adverse impact on one of the security standard's basic premises, which is scalability. It was requested that the language be changed to indicate that, while appropriate security must be maintained, all partners do not need to maintain the same level of security.

A number of commenters expressed some confusion concerning their responsibility for the security of information once it has passed from their control to their trading partner's control, and so on down the trading partner chain. Requests were made that we clarify that chain of trust partner agreements were really between two parties, and that, if a trading partner agreement has been entered into, any given partner would not be responsible, or liable, for the security of data once it is out of his or her control.

In line with this concern, several commenters were concerned that they would have some responsibility to ensure the level of security maintained by their trading partner.

Several commenters believe a chain of trust partner agreement should not be a security requirement. One commenter stated that because covered entities must already conform to the regulation

[[Page 8360]]

requirements, a ``chain of trust" agreement does not add to overall security. Compliance with the regulation should be sufficient.

Response: We believe the commenters are correct that the rule as proposed would--(1) not allow for scalability; and (2) would lead an entity to believe it is responsible, and liable, for making sure all entities down the line maintain the same level of security. The confusion here seems to come from the phrase ``same level of security." Our intention was that each trading partner would maintain reasonable and appropriate safeguards to protect the information. We did not mean that partners would need to implement the same security technology or measures and procedures.

We have replaced the proposed ``Chain of trust" standard with a standard for ``Business associate contracts and other arrangements."

When another entity is acting as a business associate of a covered entity, we require the covered entity to require the other entity to protect the electronic protected health information that it creates, receives, maintains or transmits on the covered entity's behalf. The level of security afforded particular electronic protected health information should not decrease just because the covered entity has made the business decision to entrust a business associate with using or disclosing that information in connection with the performance of certain functions instead of doing those functions itself. Thus, the rule below requires covered entities to require their business associates to implement certain safeguards and take other measures to ensure that the information is safeguarded (see Sec. 164.308(b)(1) and Sec. 164.314(a)(1)).

The specific requirements of Sec. 164.314(a)(1) are drawn from the analogous requirements at 45 CFR 164.504(e) of the Privacy Rule, although they have been adapted to reflect the objectives and context of the security standards. Compare, in particular, 45 CFR 164.504(e)(2)(ii) with Sec. 164.314(a)(1). We have not imported all of the requirements of 45 CFR 164.504(e), however, as many have no clear analog in the security context (see, for example, 45 CFR 164.504(e)(2)(i) regarding permitted and required uses and disclosures made by a business associate). HHS had previously committed to reconciling its security and privacy policies regarding business associates (see 65 FR 82643). The close relationship of many of the organizational requirements in section 164.314 with the analogous requirements of the Privacy Rule should facilitate the implementation and coordination of security and privacy policies and procedures by covered entities.

In contrast, when another entity is not acting as a business associate for the covered entity, but rather is acting in the capacity of some other sort of trading partner, we do not require the covered entity to require the other entity to adopt particular security measures, as previously proposed. This policy is likewise consistent with the general approach of the Privacy Rule (see the discussion in the Privacy Rule at 65 FR 82476). The covered entity is free to negotiate security arrangements with its non-business associate trading partners, but this rule does not require it to do so.

A similar approach underlies Sec. 164.314(b) below. These provisions are likewise drawn from, and intended to support, the analogous privacy protections provided for by 45 CFR 164.504(f) (see the discussion of Sec. 164.504(f) of the Privacy Rule at 65 FR 82507 through 82509, and 82646 through 82648). As with the business associate
contract provisions, however, they are imported and adapted only to the extent they make sense in the security context. Thus, for example, the requirement at Sec. 164.504(f)(2)(ii)(C) prohibits the plan documents from permitting disclosure of protected health information to the plan sponsor for employment-related purposes. As this prohibition goes entirely to the permissibility of a particular type of disclosure, it has no analog in Sec. 164.314(b).

c. Comment: Several commenters stated that if security features are determined by agreements established between ``trading partners," as stated in the proposed <strong>regulations</strong>, there should be some guidelines or
boundaries for those agreements so that extreme or unusual provisions are not permitted.

Response: This final rule sets a baseline, or minimum level, of security measures that must be taken by a covered entity and stipulates that a business associate must also implement reasonable and appropriate safeguards. This final rule does not, however, prohibit a covered entity from employing more stringent security measures or from requiring a business associate to employ more stringent security measures. A covered entity may determine that, in order to do business with it, a business associate must also employ equivalent measures. This would be a business decision and would not be governed by the provisions of this rule. Security mechanisms relative to the transmission of electronic protected health information between entities may need to be agreed upon by both parties in order to successfully complete the transmission. However, the determination of the specific transmission mechanisms and the specific security features to be implemented remains a business decision.

d. Comment: Several commenters asked whether existing contracts could be used to meet the requirement for a trading partner agreement, or does the rule require entry into a new contract specific to this purpose. Also, the commenters want to know about those whose working
agreements do not involve written contractual agreement: Do they now need to set up formal agreements and incur the additional expense that would entail?

Response: This final rule requires written agreements between covered entities and business associates. New contracts do not have to be entered into specifically for this purpose, if existing written contracts adequately address the applicable requirements (or can be amended to do so).

e. Comment: Several commenters asked whether covered entities are responsible for the security of all individual health information sent to them, or only information sent by chain of trust partners. They also asked if they can refuse to process standard transactions sent to them in an unsecured fashion. In addition, they inquired if they can refuse to send secured information in standard transactions to entities not required by law to secure the information. One commenter asked if there is a formula for understanding in any particular set of relationships where the ultimate responsibility for compliance with the standards would lie.

Response: Pursuant to the Transactions Rule, if a health plan receives an unsecured standard transaction, it may not refuse to process that transaction simply because it was sent in an unsecured manner. The health plan is not responsible under this rule, for how the transaction was sent to it (unless the transmission was made by a business associate, in which case different considerations apply); however, once electronic protected health information is in the possession of a covered entity, the covered entity is responsible for the security of the electronic protected health information received. The covered entity must implement technical security mechanisms to guard against unauthorized access to electronic protected health information that is transmitted over an electronic communication network. In addition, the rule requires the transmitting

[[Page 8361]]

covered entity to obtain written assurance from a business associate receiving the transmission that it will provide an adequate level of protection to the information. For the business associate provisions, see Sec. 164.308(b) and Sec. 164.314(a) of this final rule.

f. Comment: One commenter asked what security standards a vendor having access to a covered entity's health information during development, testing, and repair must meet and wanted to know whether the rule anticipates having a double layer of security compliance (one at the user level and one at the vendor level). If so, the commenter believes this will cause duplication of work.

Response: In the situation described, the vendor would be acting as a business associate. The covered entity must require the business associate to implement reasonable and appropriate security protections of electronic protected health information. This requirement, however, does not impose detailed requirements for how that level of protection must be achieved. The resulting flexibility should permit entities and their business associates to adapt their security safeguards in ways that make sense in their particular environments.

g. Comment: A number of commenters requested sample contract language or models of contracts. We also received one comment that suggested that we should not dictate the contents of contracted agreements.

Response: We will consider developing sample contract language as part of our guideline development.

I. Policies and Procedures and Documentation Requirements (Sec. 164.316)

We proposed requiring documented policies and procedures for the routine and nonroutine receipt, manipulation, storage, dissemination, transmission, and/or disposal of health information. We proposed that the documentation be reviewed and updated periodically.

We have emphasized throughout this final rule the scalability allowed by the security standards. This final rule requires covered entities to implement policies and procedures that are reasonably designed, taking into account the size and type of activities of the covered entity that relate to electronic protected health information, and requires that the policies and procedures must be documented in written form, which may be in electronic form. This final rule also provides that a covered entity may change its policies and procedures at any time, provided that it documents and implements the changes in accordance with the applicable requirements. Covered entities must also document designations, for example, of affiliation between covered entities (see Sec. 164.105(b)), and other actions, as required by other provisions of the subpart.

1. Comment: One commenter wanted development of written policies regarding such things as confidentiality and privacy rights for access to medical records, and approval of research by a review board when appropriate.

Response: These issues are covered in the Privacy Rule (65 FR 82462) (see, in particular, Sec. 164.512(i), Sec. 164.524, and Sec. 164.530(i)).

2. Comment: One commenter asked if standards will override agreements that require others to maintain hardcopy documentation (for example, signature on file) and no longer require submitters to maintain hardcopy documentation.

Response: The security standards will require a minimum level of documentation of security practices. Any agreements between trading partners for the exchange of electronic protected health information that impose additional documentation requirements will not be overridden by this final rule.

3. Comment: One commenter stated that there should be a requirement to document only applications deemed necessary by an applications and data criticality assessment.

Response: Electronic protected health information must be afforded security protection under this rule regardless of what application it resides in. The measures taken to protect that information must be documented.

4. Comment: One commenter asked how detailed the documentation must be. Another commenter asked what ``kept current'' meant.

Response: Documentation must be detailed enough to communicate the security measures taken and to facilitate periodic evaluations pursuant to Sec. 164.308(a)(8). While the term ``current'' is not in the final rule, this concept has been adopted in the requirement that documentation must be updated as needed to reflect security measures currently in effect.

5. Comment: We received one comment concerning review and updating of implementing documentation suggesting that ``periodically'' be changed to ``at least annually.''

Response: We believe that the requirement should remain as written, in order to allow individual entities to establish review and update cycles as deemed necessary. The need for review and update will vary dependent upon a given entity's size, configuration, environment, operational changes, and the security measures implemented.

J. Compliance Dates for Initial Implementation (Sec. 164.318)

We proposed that how the security standard would be implemented by each covered entity would be dependent upon industry trading partner agreements for electronic transmissions. Covered entities would be able to adapt the security matrix to meet business needs. We suggested that requirements of the security standard may be implemented earlier than the compliance date. However, we would require implementation to be complete by the applicable compliance date, which is 24 months after adoption of the standard, and 36 months after adoption of the standard for small health plans, as provided by the Act. In the proposed rule, we suggested that an entity choosing to convert from paper to standard EDI transactions, before the effective date of the security standard, consider implementing the security standard at the same time.

In this final rule the dates by which entities must be in compliance with the standards are called ``compliance dates,'' consistent with our practice in the Transactions, Privacy, and Employer Identifier Rules. Section 164.318 in this final rule is also organized consistent with the format of those rules. The substantive requirements, which are statutory, remain unchanged.

Many of the comments received concerning effective dates and compliance dates, including the compliance dates for modifications of standards, were addressed in the Transactions Rule. Those that were not addressed in that publication are presented below.

1. Comment: A number of commenters expressed support for the effective dates of the rules and stated that they should not be delayed. In contrast, one commenter stated that we should delay this rule to allow for an open consensus building debate to occur concerning security. One commenter asked that the rule be delayed until after implementation of the ICD-CM changes.

A number of comments were received expressing the opinion that the security regulation should not be published until either the Congress has enacted legislation governing standards with respect to the privacy of individually identifiable health information, or the Secretary of HHS has promulgated final <strong>regulations</strong> containing these standards. One commenter stated, ``we find

[[Page 8362]]

ourselves in the difficult position of reacting to proposed rules setting the standards for how information should be physically and electronically protected, without having reached agreement on the larger issues of consent for and disclosure of individual medical information.''

Response: The effective date of the final rule is 60 days after this final rule is published in the Federal Register. The statute sets forth the compliance dates for the standards. Covered entities must comply with this final rule no later than 24 months (36 months for small plans) after the effective date.

The final Privacy Rule has already been published. We note that numerous comments concerning the timing of the adoption of privacy and security standards were also received in the privacy rulemaking and are discussed in the Privacy Rule at 65 FR 82752.

2. Comment: One commenter asked that proposed Sec. 142.312 be rewritten to separate the effective dates for the Security Rule and the Transactions Rule.

Response: The proposed rule incorporated general language applicable to all the proposed Administrative Simplification standards. Language concerning standards other than Security is not included in Sec. 164.318. Because this final rule is adopted after the Transactions Rule was adopted, the compliance dates for the security standards differ from those for the transactions standards. Comments concerning general effective dates were addressed in the Transactions Rule. Comments specific to the security standards are addressed here.

3. Comment: Several commenters suggested that we not allow early implementation of the Security Rules. A number of others asked that we allow, but not require, early implementation by willing trading partners. Another commenter suggested that early implementation by willing trading partners be allowed as long as the data content transmitted is equal to that required by statute. Another commenter requested that it be stipulated that entities cannot implement less than 1 year from the date of this final rule and then only after successful testing, and that a ``start testing by'' date be defined.

Response: Whether or not to implement before the compliance date is a business decision that each covered entity must make. Moreover, the vast majority of the standards address internal policies and procedures that can be implemented at any time without any impact on trading partners.

4. Comment: One commenter asked us to establish a research site or test laboratory for a trial implementation.

Response: The concept of a ``trial implementation'' that would have widespread relevance is inconsistent with our basic principles of flexibility, scalability, and technology-neutrality.

5. Comment: One commenter stated that the 2-year time frame for implementation of a contingency plan is too short for health plans that serve multiple regions of the country.

Response: The Congress mandated that entities must be in compliance 2 years from the initial standard's adoption date (3 years for small plans).

K. Appendix

The proposed rule contained three addenda. Addendum 1 set out in matrix form the proposed requirements and related implementation features of the proposed rule. Addendum 2 set out in list form a glossary of terms with citations to the sources of those terms. Addendum 3 identified and mapped areas of overlap in the proposed security standard and implementation features.

This final rule retains only the first proposed addendum, the matrix, as an appendix, that is modified to reflect the changes in the administrative, physical, and technical safeguard portions of the rule below. Numerous terms in the glossary now appear in the rule below, typically (but not always) as definitions.

1. Comment: Over two-thirds of the comments received on this topic asked that the matrix be incorporated into the final rule. One commenter asked that a simplified version be made part of the final rule. Six commenters wanted it kept in this final rule as an addendum. One commenter stated that it should be in an appendix to the rule, while others stated that it should not be included in this final rule.

Response: Since a significant majority of commenters requested retention of the matrix, it has been incorporated into this final rule as an appendix. The matrix displays, in tabular form, the administrative, physical, and technical safeguard standards and relating implementation specifications described in this final rule in Sec. 164.308, Sec. 164.310, and Sec. 164.312. It should be noted that the requirements of Sec. 164.105, Sec. 164.314, and Sec. 164.316 are not presented in the matrix.

2. Comment: A large majority of commenters stated that the glossary located in Addendum 2 of the proposed rule should be included as part of the final rule. Several commenters asked that it be incorporated into the definitions section of the final rule. One commenter stated that the glossary should not be part of this final rule.

Response: The terms defined in the glossary in Addendum 2 of the proposed rule are found throughout this final rule, either as part of the text of Sec. 164.306 through Sec. 164.312 or under Sec. 164.304, as appropriate. We included only terms relevant to the particular standards and implementation specifications being adopted.

3. Comment: Several commenters requested that the mapped matrix located in Addendum 3 of the proposed rule be included in this final rule, either as part of the rule or as an addendum, while others stated that it should not be part of this final rule. Several commenters cited items to be added to the mapped matrix.

Response: The mapped matrix was merely a snapshot of current standards and guidelines that the implementation team was able to obtain for review during the development of the security and electronic signature requirements and was provided in the proposed rule as background material. Since this matrix has not been fully populated or kept up-to-date, it is not being published as part of this final rule. Where relevant, we do reference various standards and guidelines indicated in the matrix in this preamble.

L. Miscellaneous Issues

1. Preemption

The statute requires generally that the security standards supersede contrary provisions of State law including State law requiring medical or health plan records to be maintained or transmitted in written rather than electronic formats. The statute provides certain exceptions to the general rule; section 1178(a)(2) of the Act identifies conditions under which an exception applies. The proposed rule did not provide for a process for making exception determinations; rather, a process was proposed in the privacy rulemaking and was adopted with the Privacy Rule (see part 160, subpart B). This process applies to exception determinations for all of the Administrative Simplification rules, including this rule.

a. Comment: Several commenters stated that the proposed rule does not include substantive protections for the privacy rights of patients' electronic medical records, while the rule attempts to preempt State privacy laws with respect to these records. Comments stated that, by omitting a clarification of State privacy law applicability, the proposed rule creates confusion. They believe that the rule must contain

[[Page 8363]]

express and specific exemptions of State laws with respect to medical privacy.

Response: The Privacy Rule establishes standards for the rights of patients in regard to the privacy of their medical records and for the allowable uses and disclosures of protected health information. The identified concerns were discussed in the Privacy Rule (see 65 FR 82587 through 82588). The security standards do not specifically address privacy but will safeguard electronic protected health information against unauthorized access or modification.

b. Comment: One commenter asked how these <strong>regulations</strong> relate to confidentiality laws, which vary from State to State.

Response: It is difficult to respond to this question in the abstract without the benefit of reference to a specific State statute. However, in general, these security standards will preempt contrary State laws. Per section 1178(a)(2) of the Act, this general rule would not hold if the Secretary determines that a contrary provision of State law is necessary for certain identified purposes to prevent fraud and abuse; to ensure appropriate State regulation of insurance and health plans; for State reporting on health care delivery costs; or if it addresses controlled substances. See 45 CFR part 160 subpart B. In such case, the contrary provision of State law would preempt a Federal provision of these security standards. State laws that are related but not contrary to this final rule, will not be affected.

Section 1178 of the Act also limits the preemptive effect of the Federal requirements on certain State laws other than where the Secretary makes certain determinations. Section 1178(b) of the Act provides that State laws for reporting of disease and other conditions and for public health surveillance, investigation, or intervention are not invalidated or limited by the Administrative Simplification rules. Section 1178(c) of the Act provides that the Federal requirements do not limit States' abilities to require that health plans report or provide access to certain information.

c. Comment: Several commenters stated that allowing State law to establish additional security restrictions conflicts with the purpose of the Federal rule and/or would make implementation very difficult. One commenter asked for clarification as to whether additional requirements tighter than the requirements outlined in the proposed rule may be imposed.

Response: The general rule is that the security standards in this final rule supersede contrary State law. Only where the Secretary has granted an exception under section 1178(a)(2)(A) of the Act, or in situations under section 1178(b) or (c) of the Act, will the general rule not hold true. Covered entities may be required to adhere to stricter State-imposed security measures that are not contrary to this final rule.

2. Enforcement

The proposed rule did not contain specific enforcement provisions. This final rule likewise does not contain specific enforcement provisions; it is expected that enforcement provisions applicable to all Administrative Simplification rules will be proposed in a future rulemaking.

a. Comment: One commenter voiced support for the proposed rule's approach. Another stated that the process is poorly defined. One commenter stated that fines should be eliminated, or the scope of activity subject to fines should be more narrowly defined.

While a number of commenters were of the opinion that HHS must retain enforcement responsibility, stating that it would be unconstitutional to give it to a private entity, several others stated that it may not be practical for HHS to retain the responsibility for determining violations and imposing penalties specified by the statute. A concern was voiced over HHS's ability to fairly and consistently apply the rules due to budget constraints. Several commenters support industry solutions to enforcement with some level of government involvement. One commenter recommended a single audit process using accrediting bodies already in place. Another stated that entities providing accreditation services should not be involved in enforcement as this would result in a conflict of interest.

Clarification was requested, including the use of examples, concerning what constitutes a violation, and how a penalty applies to a ``person." Commenters asked if the term ``person" referred to the people responsible for the system and how penalties would apply to corporations and other entities.

Response: It is expected that enforcement of HIPAA standards will be addressed in <strong>regulations</strong> to be issued at a later date.

b. Comment: Several commenters stated that enforcement of the security standards will be arbitrarily delegated to private businesses that compete with physicians and with each other.

Response: These comments are premature for the reasons stated above.

3. Comment Period

The comment period on the proposed rule was 60 days.

Comment: We received comments suggesting that significant changes to the standards could occur in the final rule as a result of changes made in response to comments. The commenter believes such changes could adversely affect payers and providers, and suggested that the rule should be republished as a proposed rule with a new comment period to allow additional comments concerning any changes. A ``work-in-progress" approach was also suggested, to give all stakeholders time to read, analyze, and comment upon evolving versions of a particular proposed rule.

Response: We have not accepted these suggestions. The numerous comments received were thoughtful, analytical, detailed, and addressed every area of the proposed rule. This response to the proposed rule indicates that the public had ample time to read, analyze, and comment upon the proposed rule. If we were to treat the rule as a ``work-in-progress" and issue evolving versions, allowing for comments to each version, we would never implement the statute and achieve administrative simplification as directed by the Congress.

M. Proposed Impact Analysis

The preamble to the Transactions Rule contains comments and responses on the impact of all the administrative simplification standards in general except privacy. Comments and responses specific to the relative impact of implementing this final rule are presented below.

a. Comment: Several commenters stated that the proposed security standards are complex, costly, administratively burdensome, and could result in decreased use of EDI. One commenter stated that this rule runs counter to the explicit intent of Administrative Simplification that requires, ``any standard adopted under this part shall be consistent with the objective of reducing the administrative costs of providing and paying for health care."

Several commenters expressed concern that there was no cost benefit analysis provided for these proposed <strong>regulations</strong>, stating that, faced with increasingly limited resources, it is essential that a security standards cost/benefit analysis for all health care trading partners be provided. Another said an independent cost estimate by the General Accounting Office (GAO) should be performed on these rules and

[[Page 8364]]

HHS cost estimates should be publicized for comparison purposes.

Still another commenter stated that HHS must provide accurate public sector implementation cost figures and provide funds to offset the cost burden.

One commenter asked for cost benefit evaluations to understand the relationship between competing technologies, levels of security and potential threats to be guarded against. These would demonstrate the costs and the benefits to be gained for both large and small organizations and would provide an understanding of how the levels of security vary by organization size and what the inducements and support available to facilitate adoption are. One commenter suggested that we establish a workgroup to more fully assess the costs and provide Federal funds to offset implementation costs.

One commenter noted a seeming disconnect between two statements in the preamble. Section A, Security standards, states, ``no individual small entity is expected to experience direct costs that exceed benefits as a result of this rule." In contrast, section E, Factors in establishing the security standards reads, ``We cannot estimate the per-entity cost of implementation because there is no information available regarding the extent to which providers', plans', and clearinghouses' current security practices are deficient."

Response: We are unable to estimate, of the nation's 2 million-plus health plans and 1 million-plus providers that conduct electronic transactions, the number of entities that would require new or modified security safeguards and procedures beyond what they currently have in place. Nor are we able to estimate the number of entities that neither conduct electronic transactions nor maintain individually identifiable electronic health information but may become covered entities at some future time. As we are unable to estimate the number of entities and what measures are or are not already in place, or what specific implementation will be chosen to meet the requirements of the regulation, we are also unable to estimate the cost to those entities.

However, the use of electronic technology to maintain or transmit health information results in many new and potentially large risks. These risks represent expected costs, both monetary and social. Leaving risk assessment up to individual entities will minimize the impact and ensure that security effort is proportional to security risk.

As discussed earlier, the security requirements are both scalable and technically flexible. We have made significant changes to this final rule, reducing the number of required implementation features and providing for greater flexibility in satisfaction of the requirements. In other words, we have focused more on what needs to be done and less on how it should be accomplished.

We have removed the statement regarding the extent of costs versus benefits for small entities.

b. Comment: One commenter stated that on page 43262 of the proposed rule, it indicate that complexity of conversion to the security standards would be affected by the choice to use a clearinghouse. The commenter stated that this choice would have little effect on implementation of security standards. Another commenter stated that the complexity (and cost) of the conversion to meet the security standards is affected by far more than just the ``volume of claims health plans process electronically and the desire to transmit the claims or to use the services of a VAN or clearinghouse'' as is stated on page 43262. Because the security standards apply to internal systems as well as to transactions between entities, a number of additional factors must be considered, for example, modification of existing security mechanisms, legacy systems, architecture, and culture.

Response: We agree. We have modified the Regulatory Impact Analysis section to take into account that there are other factors involved, such as the architecture and technology limitations of existing systems.

c. Comment: One commenter stated that States will need 90 percent funding of development and implementation, without the burden of an advanced planning documents requirement, from us for this costly process to succeed. Any new operational obligation should be 100 percent funded. Also human resource obligations will be significant. Some States believe they will have difficulty obtaining the budget funds for the State share of the costs. State Medicaid agencies, as purchasers, may also face paying the implementation costs of health care providers, clearinghouses, and health plans in the form of higher rates.

Response: The statute does not authorize any new or special funding for implementation of the <strong>regulations</strong>. Medicaid system changes, simply because they are ``HIPAA related'' do not automatically qualify for 90 percent Federal funding participation. As with any systems request, the usual rules will be applied to determine funding eligibility for State HIPAA initiatives. Nevertheless, HHS recognizes that there are significant issues regarding the funding and implementation of HIPAA by Medicaid State agencies, and intends to address them through normal channels of communication with States.

d. Comment: One commenter stated that the proposed rule does not establish how the security standards will contribute to reduced cost for providers. One commenter expected the unintended result of this regulation will be impediment of EDI growth and perhaps even a decline in EDI use by providers. Another stated that the proposed rule actively discourages physician EDI participation by suggesting a fallback to paper processing for those unable to meet the cost of highly complex security compliance.

Response: Ensuring the integrity of an electronic message, its delivery to the correct person, and its confidentiality must be an integral part of conducting electronic commerce. We believe that the consistent application of the measures provided in this rule will actually encourage use of EDI because it will provide increased confidence in the reliability and confidentiality of health information to all parties involved. Also, the implementation of these security requirements will reduce the potential overall cost of risk to a greater extent than additional security controls will increase costs. Put another way, the potential cost of not reasonably addressing security risks could substantially exceed the cost of compliance.

e. Comment: One commenter stated that the implementation impact of the technical safeguards is clearly understated for physicians who use digitally-based equipment that has been in place for some time. The commenter believes that the rule will likely have greatest impact on the installed base of digital systems, including imaging modalities and other medical devices that store or transmit patient information because software for legacy systems will likely require retrofitting or replacement to come into compliance. The commenter believes that this is a negative impact and would outweigh any benefits derived from the potential risk of security breaches. The commenter recommended compliance for digital imaging devices be extended by an additional 3 years to allow time to upgrade systems and defray the associated costs.

Response: Compliance dates for the initial implementation of the initial standards are statutorily prescribed; therefore, we are unable to allow additional time outside of the statutory timeframes for compliance.

f. Comment: A commenter stated that, as a new regulatory mandate, HIPAA

[[Page 8365]]

costs must be factored into any base year calculations for the proposed prospective payment system. Without an adjustment, this will be another regulatory mandate that comes at the cost of patient care.

Response: Costs included in the prospective payment system are legislatively mandated. The Congress did not direct the inclusion of HIPAA costs into the system, so they are not included. However, the Department believes that the HIPAA standards will provide savings to the provider community over the next 10 years.

g. Comment: One commenter suggested that we include requirements for how a compliant business could dually operate--(1) in a HIPAA compliant manner; and (2) in their former noncompliant manner in order to accommodate doing business with other organizations that are not yet compliant.

Response: The statute imposes a 2-year implementation period between the adoption of the initial standards and the date by which covered entities (except small health plans) must be in compliance. An entity may come into compliance at any point in time during the 2 years. Therefore, the rule does not require a covered entity to comply before the established compliance date. Those entities that come into compliance before the 2-year deadline should decide how best to deal with entities that are not yet compliant. Further, we note that, generally speaking, compliance by a covered entity with these security rules will not hinge on compliance by other entities.

h. Comment: One commenter stated that privacy legislation could impose significant changes to written policies and procedures on authorization, access to health information, and how sensitive information is disclosed to others. The commenter believes these changes could mean the imposition of security requirements different from those contained in the proposed rule, and money spent complying with the security provisions could be ill spent if significant new requirements result from the privacy legislation.

Response: The privacy standards at subpart E of 42 CFR part 164 are now in effect, and this final rule is compatible with them. If, in the future, the Congress passes a law whose provisions differ from these standards, the standards would have to be modified.

i. Comment: One commenter stated that the private sector should develop educational tools or models in order to assist physicians, other providers, and health plans to comply with the security <strong>regulations</strong>.

Response: We agree. The health care industry is striving to do this. HHS is also considering provider outreach and education activities.

IV. Provisions of the Final Regulation

We have made the following changes to the provisions of the August 12, 1998 proposed rule. Specifically, we have--

[sbull] Changed the CFR part from 142 to 164.

[sbull] Removed information throughout the document pertaining to electronic signature standards. Electronic signature standards will be published in a separate final rule.

[sbull] Replaced the word ``requirement,'' when referring to a standard, with ``standard.'' Replaced ``Implementation feature'' with ``Implementation specification.''

[sbull] Made minor modifications to the text throughout the document for purposes of clarity.

[sbull] Modified numerous implementation features so that they are now addressable rather than mandatory.

[sbull] Removed the word ``formal'' when referring to documentation.

[sbull] Revised the phrase ``health information pertaining to an individual'' to ``electronic protected health information.''

[sbull] Added the following definitions to Sec. 160.103: ``Disclosure,'' ``Electronic protected health information,'' ``Electronic media,'' ``Organized health care arrangement,'' and ``Use.''

[sbull] Removed proposed Sec. 142.101 as this information is

conveyed in Sec. 160.101 and Sec. 160.102 of the Privacy Rule (65 FR 82798). Removed proposed Sec. 142.102 as it is redundant.

[sbull] Removed the following definitions from proposed Sec. 142.103 since they are pertinent to other administrative simplification <strong>regulations</strong> and are defined elsewhere: code set, health care clearinghouse, health care provider, health information, health plan, medical care, small health plan, standard, and transaction.

[sbull] Moved the following definitions from Sec. 164.501 to Sec. 164.103 (proposed Sec. 142.103): `` ``Plan sponsor'' and ``Protected health information.'' Added definitions of ``Covered functions'' and ``Required by law.''

[sbull] Removed proposed Sec. 142.104, ``General requirements for health plans,'' and proposed Sec. 142.105, ``Compliance using a health care clearinghouse,'' since these sections are not pertinent to the security standards.

[sbull] Removed proposed Sec. 142.106, ``Effective dates of a modification to a standard or implementation specification,'' since this information is covered in the ``Standards for Electronic Transactions'' final rule (65 FR 50312).

[sbull] Moved proposed Sec. 142.302 to Sec. 164.302. Changed the section heading from ``Applicability and scope'' to ``Applicability.'' Modified language to state that covered entities must comply with the security standards.

[sbull] Moved proposed Sec. 142.304 to Sec. 164.304. Modified language to remove definitions of words and concepts not used in this final rule: ``Access control,'' ``Contingency plan,'' ``Participant,'' ``Role-based access control,'' ``Token,'' and ``User-based access.''

[sbull] Moved proposed Sec. 142.304 to Sec. 164.304. Modified language to add definitions requested by commenters; previously published in Addendum 2 but not in the draft regulation itself; or necessitated by the change of scope to electronic protected health information and alignment with the Privacy Rule to include: ``Administrative safeguards,'' ``Availability,'' ``Confidentiality,'' ``Data,'' ``Data authentication Code,'' ``Integrity,'' ``Electronic protected health information,'' ``Facility,'' ``Information System,'' ``Security or security measures,'' ``Security incident,'' ``Technical safeguards,'' ``User,'' and ``Workstation.''

[sbull] Moved definitions related to privacy from Sec. 164.504 to new Sec. 164.103: ``Common control,'' ``Common ownership,'' ``Health care component,'' ``Hybrid entity.''

[sbull] Moved proposed Sec. 142.306, ``Rules for the security Standard,'' to Sec. 164.306. Modified language to more clearly state the general requirements of the final rule relative to the standards and implementation specifications contained therein. Retitled the section as ``Security standards: General Rules.''

[sbull] Moved proposed Sec. 142.308 to Sec. 164.308. Where this section was proposed to contain all of the security standards in paragraphs (a) through (d), it now encompasses the Administrative safeguards.

[sbull] Moved and reorganized proposed Sec. 142.308 (a) through (d) requirements to Sec. 164.308, Sec. 164.310, and Sec. 164.312.

[sbull] Moved proposed Sec. 142.308(a)(1), ``Certification,'' to Sec. 164.308(a)(8). Modified language to indicate both technical and nontechnical evaluation is involved and renamed ``Evaluation''.

[sbull] Moved proposed Sec. 142.308(a)(2), ``Chain of trust,'' to Sec. 164.308(b)(1), renamed to ``Business associate contracts and other arrangements,'' and revised language to redefine who must enter into a contract under this rule for the protection of electronic protected health information.

[sbull] Moved proposed Sec. 142.308(a)(3), ``Contingency plan,'' to

[[Page 8366]]

Sec. 164.308(a)(7)(i). Modified language to state that two implementation specifications, ``Applications and data criticality analysis'' and ``Testing and revision procedures,'' are addressable.

[sbull] Removed ``Formal mechanism for processing records'' (proposed Sec. 142.308(a)(4)) since this requirement was determined to be in part intrusive into business functions and in part redundant.

[sbull] Moved proposed Sec. 142.308(a)(5), ``Information access control,'' to Sec. 164.308(a)(4)(i) and renamed as ``Information access management.'' Removed the word ``formal'' from description. Modified language to state that two implementation specifications (``Access Authorization'' and Access Establishment and Modification'') are addressable.

[sbull] Moved proposed Sec. 142.308(a)(6), ``Internal audit,'' to Sec. 164.308(a)(1)(ii)(D) as an implementation specification under the ``Security management process'' standard since this was determined to be a more logical placement of this item. Retitled, for clarity, ``Information system activity review.''

[sbull] Moved proposed Sec. 142.308(a)(7), ``Personnel security,'' to Sec. 164.308(a)(3)(i) and retitled ``Workforce security.'' Modified language to state that implementation specifications are addressable.

[sbull] Combined proposed Sec. 142.308(a)(7)(i), and Sec. 142.308(a)(7)(iii) (``Assuring supervision of maintenance personnel by an authorized, knowledgeable person'' and ``Assuring that operations and maintenance personnel have proper access authorization,'') under Sec. 164.308(a)(3)(ii)(A) and renamed to ``Authorization and/or supervision.'' Modified description for clarity.

[sbull] Moved proposed Sec. 142.308(a)(7)(iv), ``Personnel clearance procedure,'' to Sec. 164.308(a)(3)(ii)(B), renamed to ``Workforce clearance procedure,'' and modified description for clarity.

[sbull] Removed proposed Sec. 142.308(a)(7)(v), ``Personnel security policies and procedures,'' as this feature was determined to require redundant effort.

[sbull] Removed proposed Sec. 142.308(a)(7)(vi), ``Security awareness training.'' Information concerning this subject has been incorporated under Sec. 164.308(a)(5)(i), ``Security awareness and training.''

[sbull] Removed proposed Sec. 142.308(a)(8), ``Security configuration management,'' and all implementation features, except ``Documentation'' (hardware and/or software installation, Inventory, Security testing, and Virus checking), since this requirement was determined to be redundant. ``Documentation'' has been made a discrete standard at Sec. 164.316.

[sbull] Moved proposed Sec. 142.308(a)(9), ``Security incident procedures,'' to Sec. 164.308(a)(6)(i) and reworded for clarity. Combined ``Report procedures'' and ``Response procedures'' features into a single required implementation specification, named ``Response and Reporting'' at Sec. 164.308(a)(6)(ii).

[sbull] Moved proposed Sec. 142.308(a)(10), ``Security management process,'' to Sec. 164.308(a)(1).

[sbull] Moved proposed Sec. 142.308(a)(10)(i), ``Risk analysis,'' to Sec. 164.308(a)(1)(ii)(A).

[sbull] Moved proposed Sec. 142.308(a)(10)(ii), ``Risk management,'' to Sec. 164.308(a)(1)(ii)(B).

[sbull] Moved proposed Sec. 142.308(a)(10)(iii), ``Sanction policy,'' to Sec. 164.308(a)(1)(ii)(C).

[sbull] Removed proposed Sec. 142.308(a)(10)(iv), ``Security policy,'' since this requirement was determined to be redundant.

[sbull] Moved proposed Sec. 142.308(a)(11), ``Termination,'' to Sec. 164.308(a)(3)(ii)(C) as an addressable implementation specification under the ``Workforce security'' standard, and renamed as ``Termination procedures''. Removed ``Termination'' implementation features (changing locks, removal from access lists, removal of user accounts, turning in of keys, tokens, or cards) since these were determined to be too specific.

[sbull] Moved proposed Sec. 142.308(a)(12), ``Training,'' to Sec. 164.308(a)(5)(i) and renamed as ``Security awareness and training.'' Language modified to incorporate all training information under this one standard. Revised and made addressable all implementation specifications under this standard.

[sbull] Moved proposed Sec. 142.308(b), ``Physical safeguards to guard data integrity, confidentiality and availability,'' to Sec. 164.310 and renamed as ``Physical safeguards.'' Removed specific reference to locks and keys.

[sbull] Moved proposed Sec. 142.308(b)(1), ``Assigned security responsibility requirement,'' to Sec. 164.308(a)(2) since this has been determined to be an administrative procedure. Modified language to
clarify that responsibility could be assigned to more than one individual.

[sbull] Moved proposed Sec. 142.308(b)(2), ``Media controls,'' to Sec. 164.310(d)(1) and renamed as ``Device and media controls.'' Removed the word ``formal.'' Added ``Media re-use'' as a required implementation specification at Sec. 164.310(d)(2)(ii).

[sbull] Removed proposed Sec. 142.308(b)(2)(i), ``Access control," implementation feature as it was determined to be redundant.
[sbull] Moved proposed Sec. 142.308(b)(2)(ii), ``Accountability" implementation feature to Sec. 164.310(d)(2)(iii), and made it an addressable implementation specification.
[sbull] Combined proposed Sec. 142.308(b)(2)(iii), ``Data backup," implementation feature with proposed Sec. 142.308(b)(2)(iv), ``Data storage" implementation feature, renamed as ``Data backup and storage", moved to Sec. 164.310(d)(2)(iv), and made it an addressable implementation specification.
[sbull] Moved proposed Sec. 142.308(b)(2)(v), ``Data disposal," implementation feature to Sec. 164.310(d)(2)(i) and made it a required implementation specification.
[sbull] Moved proposed Sec. 142.308(b)(3),``Physical access controls," to Sec. 164.310(a)(1) and renamed as ``Facility access controls." Removed word ``formal."
[sbull] Moved proposed Sec. 142.308(b)(3)(i), ``Disaster recovery," implementation feature to Sec. 164.310(a)(2)(i). It is now part of the ``Contingency operations" implementation specification.
[sbull] Moved proposed Sec. 142.308(b)(3)(ii), ``Emergency mode operations," implementation feature to Sec. 164.310(a)(2)(i). It is now part of the ``Contingency operations" implementation specification.
[sbull] Removed proposed Sec. 142.308(b)(3)(iii), ``Equipment control (into and out of site)," as this information is now covered under Sec. 164.310(d)(1), ``Device and media controls."
[sbull] Moved proposed Sec. 142.308(b)(3)(iv), ``A facility security plan," to Sec. 164.310(a)(2)(ii).
[sbull] Moved proposed Sec. 142.308(b)(3)(v), ``Procedure for verifying access authorizations," to Sec. 164.310(a)(2)(iii) and renamed as ``Access control and validation procedures." Removed the word ``formal" from text.
[sbull] Moved proposed Sec. 142.308(b)(3)(vi), ``Maintenance records," to Sec. 164.310(a)(2)(iv).
[sbull] Moved proposed Sec. 142.308(b)(3)(vii), ``Need to know procedures for personnel access," to sect; 164.310(a)(2)(iii) and renamed as ``Access control and validation procedures."
[sbull] Moved proposed Sec. 142.308(b)(3)(viii), ``Procedures to sign in visitors and provide escort, if appropriate," to Sec. 164.310(a)(2)(iii) and renamed as ``Access control and validation procedures."

[[Page 8367]]

[sbull] Moved proposed Sec. 142.308(b)(3)(ix), ``Testing and revision," to Sec. 164.310(a)(2)(iii) and renamed as ``Access control and validation procedures."
[sbull] Moved proposed Sec. 142.308(b)(4), ``Policy and guidelines on workstation use," to Sec. 164.310(b) and renamed as ``Workstation use."
[sbull] Moved proposed Sec. 142.308(b)(5), ``Secure work station location," to Sec. 164.310(c) and renamed as ``Workstation security."
[sbull] Removed proposed Sec. 142.308(b)(6), ``Security awareness training," as a separate requirement. This requirement has been incorporated under Sec. 164.308(a)(5)(i), ``Security awareness and training."
[sbull] Combined and moved proposed Sec. 142.308(c) and Sec. 142.308(d), ``Technical security services to guard data integrity, confidentiality and availability" and ``Technical security mechanisms," to Sec. 164.312 and renamed as ``Technical safeguards."
[sbull] Removed proposed Sec. 142.308(c)(1) since it is no longer pertinent.
[sbull] Moved proposed Sec. 142.308(c)(1)(i), ``Access control," to Sec. 164.312(a)(1).
[sbull] Moved proposed Sec. 142.308(c)(1)(i)(A), ``Procedure for emergency access," to Sec. 164.312(a)(2)(ii), and renamed as ``Emergency access procedures."
[sbull] Removed proposed Sec. 142.308(c)(1)(i)(B).
[sbull] Removed proposed Sec. 142.308(c)(1)(i)(B)(1), ``Context-based access," Sec. 142.308(c)(1)(i)(B)(2), ``Role-based access," and Sec. 142.308(c)(1)(i)(B)(3), ``User-based access," since these features were deemed too specific and were perceived as the only options permissible.
[sbull] Moved proposed Sec. 142.308(c)(1)(i)(C), ``Optional use of encryption," to Sec. 164.312(a)(2)(iv) and retitled ``Encryption and decryption."
[sbull] Moved proposed Sec. 142.308(c)(1)(ii), ``Audit controls," to Sec. 164.312(b).
[sbull] Removed proposed Sec. 142.308(c)(1)(iii), ``Authorization control," and all implementation features (Role-based access, User-based access) since this function has been incorporated into Sec. 164.308(a)(4), ``Information access management."
[sbull] Moved proposed Sec. 142.308(c)(1)(iv), ``Data authentication," to Sec. 164.312(c)(1), and retitled as ``Integrity." Reworded part of description and placed in Sec. 164.312(c)(2), ``Mechanism to authenticate data," a new, addressable implementation specification. Removed reference to double keying.
[sbull] Moved proposed Sec. 142.308(c)(1)(v), ``Entity authentication," to Sec. 164.312(d) and retitled as ``Person or entity authentication."
[sbull] Moved proposed Sec. 142.308(c)(1)(v)(A), ``Automatic logoff," to Sec. 164.312(a)(2)(iii).
[sbull] Moved proposed Sec. 142.308(c)(1)(v)(B), ``Unique user identification," to Sec. 164.312(a)(2)(i).
[sbull] Removed proposed Sec. 142.308(c)(1)(v)(C) since text is no longer pertinent.
[sbull] Removed proposed Sec. 142.308(c)(1)(v)(C)(2), ``Password," as too specific.
[sbull] Removed proposed Sec. 142.308(c)(1)(v)(C)(3), ``PIN," as too specific.
[sbull] Removed proposed Sec. 142.308(c)(1)(v)(C)(4), ``Telephone callback," as too specific.
[sbull] Removed proposed Sec. 142.308(c)(1)(v)(C)(5), ``Token," as too specific.
[sbull] Removed proposed Sec. 142.308(c)(2), as no longer relevant.
[sbull] Moved proposed Sec. 142.308(d)(1), ``Communications or network controls," to Sec. 164.312(e)(1) and renamed as ``Transmission security."
[sbull] Removed proposed Sec. 142.308(d)(1)(i), since it is no longer pertinent.
[sbull] Moved proposed Sec. 142.308(d)(1)(i)(A), ``Integrity controls," to Sec. 164.312(e)(2)(i) and reworded for clarity.
[sbull] Removed proposed Sec. 142.308(d)(1)(i)(B), ``Message authentication," since this subject is now covered under Sec. 164.312(e)(2)(i), ``Integrity controls."
[sbull] Removed proposed Sec. 142.308(d)(1)(ii) text since it is no longer pertinent.
[sbull] Removed proposed Sec. 142.308(d)(1)(ii)(A), ``Access controls."
[sbull] Moved proposed Sec. 142.308(d)(1)(ii)(B), ``Encryption," to Sec. 164.312(e)(2)(ii) and reworded to enhance flexibility and scalability.
[sbull] Removed proposed Sec. 142.308(d)(2) text regarding: ``Network controls," and all implementation features (``Alarm," ``Audio trail," ``Entity authentication," ``Event reporting").
[sbull] Removed proposed Sec. 142.310, ``Electronic signature," and all subheadings. This section will be issued as a separate future regulation.
[sbull] Moved proposed Sec. 142.310 ``Electronic signature Standard," to Sec. 164.310. Where this section was proposed to contain the electronic signature standard, it now encompasses the ``Physical safeguards."
[sbull] Moved proposed Sec. 142.312, ``Effective date of the implementation of the security and electronic signature standards," to Sec. 164.318 and retitled as ``Compliance dates for the initial implementation of the security standards." Reworded and retitled subsections.
[sbull] Added Sec. 164.105, ``Organizational requirements," with two standards, ``Health care component and ``Affiliated covered entities" with related implementation specifications.
[sbull] Added Sec. 164.310(d)(2)(ii), ``Media re-use procedures," implementation specification.
[sbull] Added Sec. 164.312, ``Technical safeguards," encompassing the combined technical services and technical mechanisms standards (proposed Sec. 142.308(c) and (d)).
[sbull] Added Sec. 164.314, ``Organizational requirements."

[sbull] Added Sec. 164.314(a)(1), ``Business associate contracts or other arrangements" standard and related implementation specifications.
[sbull] Added Sec. 164.314(b)(1), ``Requirements for group health plans" standard and related implementation specifications.
[sbull] Added Sec. 164.316, ``Policies and procedures and documentation requirements."
[sbull] Added Sec. 164.316(a), ``Policies and procedures" standard.
[sbull] Added Sec. 164.316(b)(1), ``Documentation" standard and related implementation specifications.
[sbull] Added Sec. 164.318, ``Compliance dates for the initial implementation of the security standards."
[sbull] Renamed Addendum 1 as Appendix A.
[sbull] Removed Addendum 2. Definitions of terms used in this final rule are now incorporated into Sec. 164.103 and Sec. 164.304, or within the rule itself.
[sbull] Removed Addendum 3.

V. Collection of Information Requirements

Under the Paperwork Reduction Act of 1995 (PRA), we are required to provide 30-day notice in the Federal Register and solicit public comment before a collection of information requirement is submitted to the Office of Management and Budget (OMB) for review and approval. In order to fairly evaluate whether an information collection should be approved by OMB, section 3506(c)(2)(A) of the Paperwork Reduction Act of 1995 (PRA) requires that we solicit comment on the following issues:
[sbull] The need for the information collection and its usefulness in carrying out the proper functions of our agency.
[sbull] The accuracy of our estimate of the information collection burden.
[sbull] The quality, utility, and clarity of the information to be collected.

[[Page 8368]]

[sbull] Recommendations to minimize the information collection burden on the affected public, including automated collection techniques.
As discussed below, we are soliciting comment on the recordkeeping requirements, as referenced in Sec. 164.306, Sec. 164.308, Sec. 164.310, Sec. 164.314, and Sec. 164.316 of this document.

Section 164.306 Security Standards: General Rules

Under paragraph (d), a covered entity must, if implementing the implementation specification is not reasonable and appropriate, document why it would not be reasonable and appropriate to implement the implementation specification.
We estimate that 75,000 entities will be affected by this requirement and that they will have to create documentation 3 times for this requirement. We estimate each instance of documentation will take .25 hours, for a one-time total burden of 56,250 hours.

Section 164.308 Administrative Safeguards

Under this section, a covered entity must document known security incidents and their outcomes.
We estimate that there will be 50 known incidents annually and that it will take 8 hours to document this requirement, for an annual burden of 400 hours.
This section further requires that each entity have a contingency plan, with specified components.
We estimate that there will be 60,000 entities affected by this requirement and that it will take each entity 8 hours to comply, for a total one-time burden of 480,000 hours.
This section also requires that the written contract or other arrangement with a business associate document the satisfactory assurances that the business associate will appropriately safeguard the information through a written contract or other arrangement with the business associate that meets the applicable requirements of Sec. 164.314(a).
We believe that the burden associated with this requirement is not subject to the PRA. It is good business practice for entities to document their arrangements via written contracts and as such is usual and customary among the entities subject to them. A burden associated with a requirement conducted in the normal course of business is exempt from the PRA as defined in 5 CFR 1320.3(b)(2).

Section 164.310 Physical Safeguards

This section requires that a covered entity implement policies and procedures to document repairs and modifications to the physical components of a facility that are related to security (for example, hardware, walls, doors, and locks).
We believe that 15,500 entities will have to repair or modify physical components, most of which will need to be done in the first year of implementation. In the following years, we estimate that 500 entities will need to make repairs or modifications. We estimate that it will take 10 minutes to document each repair or modification for a burden of 2,583 hours the first year and 83 hours annually subsequently.
This section requires that a covered entity create a retrievable, exact copy of electronic protected health information, where needed, before movement of equipment.
We believe that the burden associated with this requirement is not subject to the PRA. It is good business practice for entities to backup their data files, and as such is usual and customary among the entities subject to them. A burden associated with a requirement conducted in the normal course of business is exempt from the PRA as defined in 5 CFR 1320.3(b)(2).

Section 164.314 Organizational Requirements

This section requires that a covered entity report to the Secretary problems with a business associate's pattern of an activity or practice of the business associate that constitute a material breach or violation of the business associate's obligation under the contract or other arrangement if it is not feasible to terminate the contract or arrangement.
We believe that 10 entities will need to comply with this reporting requirement and that it will take them 60 minutes to comply with this requirement for an annual burden of 10 hours.
This section also requires that a covered entity may, if a business associate is required by law to perform a function or activity on behalf of a covered entity or to provide a service described in the definition of business associate as specified in Sec. 160.103 of this subchapter to a covered entity, permit the business associate to create, receive, maintain, or transmit electronic protected health information on its behalf to the extent necessary to comply with the legal mandate without meeting the requirements of paragraph (a)(2)(i) of this section, provided that the covered entity attempts in good faith to obtain satisfactory assurances as required by paragraph (a)(2)(ii)(A) of this section, and documents the attempt and the reasons that these assurances cannot be obtained.
We believe that this situation will affect 20 entities and that it will take 60 minutes to document attempts to obtain assurances and the reasons they cannot be obtained for an annual burden of 20 hours.
This section further requires that business associate contracts or other arrangements and group health plans must require the business entity and plan sponsor, respectively, to report to the covered entity any security incident of which it becomes aware.
We believe that the burden associated with this requirement is not subject to the PRA. It is good business practice for entities to document their agreements via written contracts, and as such is usual and customary among the entities subject to them. A burden associated with a requirement conducted in the normal course of business is exempt

from the PRA as defined in 5 CFR 1320.3(b)(2).

Section 164.316 Policies and Procedures and Documentation Requirements

Paragraph (b)(1), Standard: Documentation, of this section requires a covered entity to--

(i) Maintain the policies and procedures implemented to comply with this subpart in written (which may be electronic) form; and

(ii) If an action, activity, assessment, or designation is required by this subpart to be documented, maintain a written (which may be electronic) record of the action, activity, assessment, or designation.

We estimate that it will take the 4,000,000 entities covered by this final rule 16 hours to document their policies and procedures, for a total one-time burden of 64,000,000 hours.

The total annual burden of the information collection requirements contained in this final rule is 64,539,264 hours. These information collection requirements will be submitted to OMB for review under the PRA and will not become effective until approved by OMB.

If you comment on these information collection and recordkeeping requirements, please mail copies directly to the following:

Centers for Medicare and Medicaid Services, Office of Strategic Operations and Regulatory Affairs, <strong>Regulations</strong> Development and
Issuances Group, Attn: Reports

[[Page 8369]]

Clearance Officer, 7500 Security Boulevard, Baltimore, MD 21244-1850, Attn: Julie Brown, CMS-0049-F; and
Office of Information and Regulatory Affairs, Office of Management and Budget, Room 10235, New Executive Office Building, Washington, DC 20503, Attn: Brenda Aguilar, CMS Desk Officer.

IV. Regulatory Impact Analysis

A. Overall Impact

We have examined the impacts of this rule as required by Executive Order 12866 (September 1993, Regulatory Planning and Review), the Regulatory Flexibility Act (RFA) (September 16, 1980, Pub. L. 96-354), section 1102(b) of the Social Security Act, the Unfunded Mandates Reform Act of 1995 (Pub. L. 104-4), and Executive Order 13132.

Executive Order 12866 (as amended by Executive Order 13258, which merely reassigns responsibility of duties) directs agencies to assess all costs and benefits of available regulatory alternatives and, if regulation is necessary, to select regulatory approaches that maximize net benefits (including potential economic, environmental, public health and safety effects, distributive impacts, and equity). A regulatory impact analysis (RIA) must be prepared for major rules with economically significant effects ($100 million or more in any 1 year). Although we cannot determine the specific economic impact of the standards in this final rule (and individually each standard may not have a significant impact), the overall impact analysis makes clear that, collectively, all the standards will have a significant impact of over $100 million on the economy. Because this rule affects over 2 million entities, a requirement as low as $50 per entity would render this rule economically significant. This rule requires each of these entities to engage in, for example, at least some risk assessment activity; thus, this rule is almost certainly economically significant even though we do not have an estimate of the marginal impact of the additional security standards. However, the standards adopted in this rule are considerably more flexible than those anticipated in the overall impact analysis. Therefore, their implementation costs should be lower than those assumed in the impact analysis.

The RFA requires agencies to analyze options for regulatory relief of small businesses. For purposes of the RFA, small entities include small businesses, nonprofit organizations, and government agencies. Most hospitals and most other providers and suppliers are small entities, either by nonprofit status or by having revenues of $6 million to $29 million in any 1 year. While each standard may not have a significant impact on a substantial number of small entities, the combined effects of all the standards are likely to have a significant effect on a substantial number of small entities. Although we have certified this rule as having a significant impact, we have previously discussed the impact of small entities in the RFA published as part of the August 17, 2000 final regulation for the Standards for Electronic Transactions (65 FR 50312), on pages 50359 through 50360. That analysis
included the impact of the set of HIPAA standards
<strong>regulations</strong>
(transactions and code sets, identifiers, and security). Although we discussed the impact on small entities in the previous analysis, we would like to discuss how this final rule has been structured to minimize the impact on small entities, compared to the proposed rule.

The proposed rule mandated 69 implementation features for all entities. A large number of commenters indicated that mandating such a large number would be burdensome for all entities. As a result, we have restructured this final rule to permit greater flexibility. While all standards must be met, we are now only requiring 13 implementation specifications. The remainder of the implementation specifications is ``addressable.'' For addressable specifications, an entity decides whether each specification is a reasonable and appropriate security measure to apply within its particular security framework. This decision is based on a variety of factors, for example, the entity's risk analysis, what measures are already in place, the particular interest to small entities, and the cost of implementation.

Based on the decision, an entity can--(1) implement the specification if reasonable and appropriate; (2) implement an alternative security measure to accomplish the purposes of the standard; or (3) not implement anything if the specification is not reasonable and appropriate and the standard can still be met.

This approach will provide flexibility for all entities, and especially small entities that would be most concerned about the cost and complexity of the security standards. Small entities can look at the addressable implementation specifications and tailor their compliance based on their risks and capabilities of addressing those risks.

The required risk analysis is also a tool to allow flexibility for entities in meeting the requirements of this final rule. The risk analysis requirement is designed to allow entities to look at their own operations and determine the security risks involved. The degree of response is determined by the risks identified. We assume that smaller entities, who deal with smaller amounts of information would have smaller physical facilities, smaller work forces, and therefore, would assume less risk. The smaller amount of risk involved means that the response to that risk can be developed on a smaller scale than that for larger organizations.

Individuals and States are not included in the definition of a small entity. However, the security standards will affect small entities, such as providers and health plans, and vendors in much the same way as they affect any larger entities. Small providers who conduct electronic transactions and small health plans must meet the provisions of this regulation and implement the security standards. A more detailed analysis of the impact on small entities is part of the impact analysis published on August 17, 2000 (65 FR 50312), which provided the impact for all of the HIPAA standards, except privacy. As we discussed above, the scalability factor of the standards means that the requirements placed upon small providers and plans would be consistent with the complexity of their operations. Therefore, small providers and plans with appropriate security processes in place would need to do relatively little in order to comply with the standards. Moreover, small plans will have an additional year to come into compliance.

In addition, section 1102(b) of the Act requires us to prepare a regulatory impact analysis if a rule may have a significant impact on the operations of a substantial number of small rural hospitals. This analysis must conform to the provisions of section 604 of the RFA. For purposes of section 1102(b) of the Act, we define a small rural hospital as a hospital that is located outside of a Metropolitan Statistical Area and has fewer than 100 beds. While this rule may have a significant impact on small rural hospitals, the impact should be minimized by the scalability factors of the standards, as discussed above in the impact on all small entities. In addition, we have previously discussed the impact of small entities in the RIA published as part of the August 17, 2000 final regulation for the Standards for Electronic Transactions.

Section 202 of the Unfunded Mandates Reform Act (UMRA) of 1995

[[Page 8370]]

also requires that agencies assess anticipated costs and benefits before issuing any rule that may result in expenditure in any 1 year by State, local, or tribal governments, in the aggregate, or by the private sector, of $110 million. We estimate that implementation of all the standards will require the expenditure of more than $110 million by the private sector. Therefore, the rule establishes a Federal private sector mandate and is a significant regulatory action within the meaning of section 202 of UMRA (2 U.S.C. 1532). We have included the statements to address the anticipated effects of these rules under section 202.

These standards also apply to State and local governments in their roles as health plans or health care providers. Because these entities, in their roles as health plans or providers, must implement the requirements in these rules, the rules impose unfunded mandates on them. Further discussion of this issue can be found in the previously published impact analysis for all standards (65 FR 50360 through 50361).

The anticipated benefits and costs of the security standards, and other issues raised in section 202 of the UMRA, are addressed in the analysis below, and in the combined impact analysis. In addition, as required under section 205 of the UMRA (2 U.S.C. 1535), having considered a reasonable number of alternatives as outlined in the preamble to this rule, HHS has concluded that this final rule is the most cost-effective alternative for implementation of HHS's statutory objective of administrative simplification.

Executive Order 13132 establishes certain requirements that an agency must meet when it promulgates a proposed rule (and subsequent final rule) that imposes substantial direct requirement costs on State and local governments, preempts State law, or otherwise has Federalism implications. The proposed rule was published before the enactment of Executive Order 13132 of August 4, 1999, Federalism (published in the Federal Register on August 10, 1999 (64 FR 43255)), which required meaningful and timely input by State and local officials in the development of rules that have Federalism implications). However, we received and considered comments on the proposed rule from State agencies and from entities who conduct transactions with State agencies. Several of the comments referred to the costs that will result from implementation of the HIPAA standards. As we stated in the impact analysis, we are unable to estimate the cost of implementing security features as implementation needs will vary dependent upon a risk assessment and upon what is already in place. However, the previously referenced impact analysis in the August 17, 2000 final rule (65 FR 50312) showed that Administrative Simplification costs will be offset by future savings.

In complying with the requirements of part C of title XI, the Secretary established interdepartmental implementation teams who consulted with appropriate State and Federal agencies and private organizations. These external groups consisted of the National Committee on Vital and Health Statistics (NCVHS) Subcommittee on Standards and Security, the Workgroup for Electronic Data Interchange (WEDI), the National Uniform Claim Committee (NUCC), the National Uniform Billing Committee (NUBC), and the American Dental Association (ADA). The teams also received comments on the proposed regulation from a variety of organizations, including State Medicaid agencies and other Federal agencies.

B. Anticipated Effects

The analysis in the August 2000, Transaction Rule included the expected costs and benefits of the administrative simplification <strong>regulations</strong> related to electronic systems for 10 years. Although only the electronic transaction standards were promulgated in the transaction rule, HHS expected affected parties to make systems compliance investments collectively because the <strong>regulations</strong> are so integrated. Moreover, the data available to us were also based on the collective requirements of this regulation. It is not feasible to identify the incremental technological and computer costs for each regulation. Although HHS is issuing rules under HIPAA sequentially, affected entities and vendors are bundling services, that is, they have been anticipating the various needs and are designing relatively comprehensive systems as they develop hardware and software. For example, a vendor developing a system for electronic billing would also anticipate and include security features, even in the absence of any regulation. Moreover, a draft of the security rule was first published in 1998. Even though the final is different (and less burdensome), vendors had a reasonable indication of the direction policy would go. Thus, in preparing the electronic transaction rule, we recognized and included costs that might theoretically be associated with security or other HIPPA rules. Hence, some of the ``costs'' of security have already been accounted for in the Standards for Electronic Transactions cost estimate (45 CFR parts 160 and 162), which was published in the Federal Register on August 17, 2000 (65 FR 50312).

This analysis showed that the combined impact of the Administrative Simplification standards is expected to save the industry $29.9 billion over 10 years. We are including in each subsequent rule an impact analysis that is specific to the standard or standards in that rule, but the impact analysis will assess only the incremental cost of implementing a given standard over another. Thus, the following discussion contains the impact analysis for the marginal costs of the security standards in this final rule.

The following describes the specific impacts that relate to the security standards. The security of electronic protected health information is, and has been for some time, a basic business requirement that health care entities ignore at their peril. Instances of ``hacking'' and other security violations may be widely publicized, and can seriously damage an institution's community standing. Appropriate security protections are crucial for encouraging the growth and use of electronic data interchange. The synergistic effect of the employment of the security standards will enhance all aspects of HIPAA's Administrative Simplification requirements. In addition, it is important to recognize that security is not a one-time project, but rather an on-going, dynamic process.

C. Changes From the 1998 Impact Analysis

The overall impact analysis for Administrative Simplification was first published on May 7, 1998 (63 FR 25320) in the proposed rule for the National Provider Identifier standard (45 CFR part 142), the first of the proposed Administrative Simplification rules. That impact analysis was based on the industry situation at that time, used statistics which were current at that time, and assumed that all of the HIPAA standards would be implemented at roughly the same time, which would permit software changes to be made less expensively. While the original impact analysis represented our best information at that time, we realize that the state of the industry, and of security technology, has changed since 1998. We discuss several of those changes and how they affect the impact of this regulation.

1. Changes in Technology

The state of technology for health care security has changed since 1998. New

[[Page 8371]]

technologies to protect information have been developed over the past several years. As a result, HHS has consulted with the Gartner Group, a leading technology assessment organization, regarding what impact these changes in the industry might have on the expected impact of this regulation. The Gartner analysis indicated that the cost of meeting the requirements of a reasonable interpretation of the security rule in

2002 is probably less than 10 percent higher in 2002 than it was in 1998. This increase is mainly driven by more active threats and increased personnel costs offsetting decreases in technology costs over the past 4 years. However, spending by companies who have anticipated the security rule or who have independently made business decisions to implement security policies and procedures as good business practice(s) has already occurred, and probably will cancel out the increased costs of implementation. Therefore, Gartner expects the cost of complying with the HIPAA security standards to be about the same now as it was in 1998.

2. Synchronizing Standards

The timelines for the implementation of the initial HIPAA standards (transactions, identifiers, and security) are no longer closely synchronized. However, we do not believe that this lack of synchronization will have a significant impact on the cost of implementing security. The analysis provided by the Gartner group indicated that implementing security standards is being viewed by entities as a separate task from implementing the transaction standards, and that this is not having a significant impact on costs. As with other HIPAA standards, most current entities will have a 2-year implementation period before compliance with the standards is required. Covered entities will develop their own implementation schedules, and may phase in various security measures over that time period.

3. Relationship to Privacy Standards

The publication of the final Privacy Rules (45 CFR parts 160 and 164) on December 28, 2000 in the Federal Register (65 FR 82462) and on August 14, 2002 (67 FR 53182) has affected the impact of this regulation significantly. Covered entities must implement the privacy standards by April 14, 2003 (April 14, 2004 for small health plans). The implementation of privacy standards reduces the cost of implementing the security standards in two significant areas.

First, we have made substantial efforts to ensure that the many requirements in the security standards parallel those for privacy, and can easily be satisfied using the solutions for privacy. Administrative requirements like the need for written policies, responsible officers, and business associate agreements that are already required by the Privacy Rule can also serve to meet the security standards without significant additional cost. The analysis of data flows and data uses that covered entities are doing so as to comply with the Privacy Rule should also serve as the starting point for parallel analysis required by this final rule.

Second, it is likely that covered entities will meet a number of the requirements in the security standards through the implementation of the privacy requirements. For example, in order to comply with the Privacy Rule requirements to make reasonable efforts to limit the access of members of the work force to specified categories of protected health information, covered entities may implement some of the administrative, physical, and technical safeguards that the entity's risk analysis and assessment would require under the Security Rule. E-mail authentication procedures put into place for privacy protection may also meet the security standards, thereby eliminating the need for additional investments to meet these standards. As a result, covered entities that have moved forward in implementing the privacy standards are also implementing security measures at the same time. Since the proposed security standards proposed rule represents the most authoritative guidance now available on the nature of these standards, some entities have been using them to develop their security measures. Those entities should face minimal incremental costs in implementing the final version of these standards.

We are unable to quantify these overlaps, but we believe they may reduce the cost of implementing these security standards. The analysis provided to the HHS by the Gartner Group also stated that compliance with the Privacy Rule will have a moderate effect on the cost of compliance with the Security Rule, reducing it slightly.

4. Sensitivity to Security Concerns as a Result of September 11, 2001

In our discussions with the Gartner Group, they indicated that they saw little evidence of increased security awareness in health care organizations as a result of the events of September 11, 2001. However, a survey conducted by Phoenix Health Systems in the winter of 2002 showed that 65 percent of the respondents to the survey (hospitals, payers, vendors, and clearinghouses) have moderately to greatly increased their attention on overall security. If these organizations have already made investments in security that meet some of the requirements of this rule, it will reduce their added costs of compliance. However, HHS can make no clear statement of the impact of this attention.

D. Guiding Principles for Standard Selection

The implementation teams charged with designating standards under the statute have defined, with significant input from the health care industry, a set of common criteria for evaluating potential standards. These criteria are based on direct specifications in the HIPAA, the purpose of the law, and principles that support the regulatory philosophy set forth in the E.O. 12866 of September 30, 1993, and the Paperwork Reduction Act of 1995. In order to be designated as such, a standard should do the following:

[sbull] Improve the efficiency and effectiveness of the health care system by leading to cost reductions for or improvements in benefits from electronic health care transactions. This principle supports the regulatory goals of cost-effectiveness and avoidance of burden.

[sbull] Meet the needs of the health data standards user community, particularly health care providers, health plans, and health care clearinghouses. This principle supports the regulatory goal of cost-effectiveness.

[sbull] Be consistent and uniform with the other HIPAA standards (that is, their data element definitions and codes, and their privacy and security requirements) and, secondarily, with other private and public sector health data standards. This principle supports the regulatory goals of consistency and avoidance of incompatibility, and it establishes a performance objective for the standard.

[sbull] Have low additional development and implementation costs relative to the benefits of using the standard. This principle supports the regulatory goals of cost-effectiveness and avoidance of burden.

[sbull] Be supported by an ANSI-accredited standards developing organization or other private or public organization that would ensure continuity and efficient updating of the standard over time. This principle supports the regulatory goal of predictability.

[sbull] Have timely development, testing, implementation, and updating procedures to achieve administrative simplification benefits faster. This

[[Page 8372]]

principle establishes a performance objective for the standard.

[sbull] Be technologically independent of the computer platforms and transmission protocols used in health transactions, except when they are explicitly part of the standard. This principle establishes a performance objective for the standard and supports the regulatory goal of flexibility.

[sbull] Be precise and unambiguous but as simple as possible. This principle supports the regulatory goals of predictability and simplicity.

[sbull] Keep data collection and paperwork burdens on users as low as is feasible. This principle supports the regulatory goals of cost-effectiveness and avoidance of duplication and burden.

[sbull] Incorporate flexibility to adapt more easily to changes in the health care infrastructure (for example, new services, organizations, and provider types) and information technology. This principle supports the regulatory goals of flexibility and encouragement of innovation.

We assessed a wide variety of security standards and guidelines against the principles listed above, with the overall goal of achieving the maximum benefit for the least cost. As we stated in the proposed rule, we found that no single standard for security exists that encompasses all the requirements that were listed in the law. However, we believe that the standards we are adopting in this final rule collectively accomplish these goals.

E. Affected Entities

1. Health Care Providers

Covered health care providers may incur implementation costs for establishing or updating their security systems. The majority of costs to implement the security standard (purchase and installation of appropriate computer hardware and software, and physical safeguards) would generally be incurred in the initial implementation period for the specific requirements of the security standard. Health care providers that do not conduct electronic transactions for which standards have been adopted are not affected by these <strong>regulations</strong>.

2. Health Plans

All health plans, as the term is defined in regulation at 45 CFR 160.103, must comply with these security standards. In addition, health plans that engage in electronic health care transactions may have to modify their systems to meet the security standards. Health plans that maintain electronic health information may also have to modify their systems to meet the security standards. This conversion would have a one-time cost impact on Federal, State, and private plans alike.

We recognize that this conversion process has the potential to cause business disruption of some health plans. However, health plans would be able to schedule their implementation of the security standards and other standards in a way that best fits their needs, as long as they meet the deadlines specified in the HIPAA law and <strong>regulations</strong>. Moreover, small plans (many of which are employer-
sponsored) will have an additional year in which to achieve compliance. Small health plans are defined at 45 CFR 160.103 as health plans with annual receipts of $5 million or less.

3. Clearinghouses

All health care clearinghouses must meet the requirements of this regulation. Health care clearinghouses would face effects similar to those experienced by health care providers and health plans. However, because clearinghouses represent one way in which providers and plans can achieve compliance, the clearinghouses' costs of complying with these standards would probably be passed along to those entities, to be shared over the entire customer base.

4. System Vendors

Systems vendors that provide computer software applications to health care providers and other billers of health care services would likely be affected. These vendors would have to develop software solutions that would allow health plans, providers, and other users of electronic transactions to protect these transactions and the information in their databases from unauthorized access to their systems. Their costs would also probably be passed along to their customer bases.

F. Factors in Establishing the Security Standard

1. General Effect

In assessing the impact of these standards, it is first necessary to focus on the general nature of the standards, their scalability, and the fact that they are not dependent upon specific technologies. These factors will make it possible for covered entities to implement them with the least possible impact on resources. Because there is no national security standard in widespread use throughout the industry, adopting any of the candidate standards would require most health care providers, health plans, and health care clearinghouses to at least conduct an assessment of how their current security measures conform to the new standards. However, we assume that most, if not all, covered entities already have at least some rudimentary security measures in place. Covered entities that identify gaps in their current measures would need to establish or revise their security precautions.

It is also important to note that the standards specify what goals are to be achieved, but give the covered entity some flexibility to determine how to meet those goals. This is different from the transaction standards, where all covered entities must use the exact same implementation guide. With respect to security, covered entities will be able to blend security processes now in place with new processes. This should significantly reduce compliance costs.

Based on our analysis and comments received, the security standards adopted in this rule do not impose a greater burden on the industry than the options we did not select, and they present significant advantages in terms of universality and flexibility.

We understand that some large health plans, health care providers, and health care clearinghouses that currently exchange health information among trading partners may already have security systems and procedures in place to protect the information from unauthorized access. These entities may not incur significant costs to meet the security standards. Large entities that have sophisticated security systems in place may only need minor revisions or updates to their systems to meet the security standards, or indeed, may not need to make any changes in their systems.

While small providers are not likely to have implemented sophisticated security measures, they are also not as likely to need them as larger covered entities. The scalability principle allows providers to adopt measures that are appropriate to their own circumstances.

2. Complexity of Conversion

The complexity of the conversion to the security standards could be significantly affected by the volume of transactions that covered entities transmit and process electronically and the desire to transmit directly or to use the services of a Value Added Network (VAN) or a clearinghouse. If a VAN or clearinghouse is used, some of the conversion activities would be carried out by that organization, rather than by the covered entity. This would simplify conversion for the covered entity, but makes the covered entity dependent on the success of its business associate. The architecture, and specific technology

[[Page 8373]]

limitations of existing systems could also affect the complexity of the conversion (for example, certain practice management software that does
not contain password protection will require a greater conversion effort than software that has a password protection option already built into it).

3. Cost of Conversion

Virtually all providers, health plans, and clearinghouses that transmit or store data electronically have already implemented some security measures and will need to assess existing security, identify areas of risk, and implement additional measures in order to come into compliance with the standards adopted in this rule. We cannot estimate the per-entity cost of implementation because there is no information available regarding the extent to which providers', plans', and clearinghouses' current security practices are deficient. Moreover, some security solutions are almost cost-free to implement (for example, reminding employees not to post passwords on their monitors), while others are not.

Affected entities will have many choices regarding how they will implement security. Some may choose to assess security using in-house staff, while others will use consultants. Practice management software vendors may also provide security consultation services to their customers. Entities may also choose to implement security measures that require hardware and/or software purchases at the time they do routine equipment upgrades.

The security standards we adopt in this rule were developed with considerable input from the health care industry, including providers, health plans, clearinghouses, vendors, and standards organizations. Industry members strongly advocated the flexible approach we adopt in this rule, which permits each affected entity to develop cost-effective security measures appropriate to their particular needs. We believe that this approach will yield the lowest implementation cost to industry while ensuring that electronic protected health information is safeguarded.

All of the nation's health plans (over 2 million) and providers (over 600,000) will need to conduct some level of gap analysis to assess current procedures against the standards. However, we cannot estimate the number of covered entities that would have to implement additional security systems and procedures to meet the adopted standards. Also, we are not able to estimate the number of providers that do not conduct electronic transactions today but may choose to do so at some future time (these would be entities that send and receive paper transactions and maintain paper records and thus would not be affected). We believe that the security standards represent the minimum necessary for adequate protection of health information in an electronic format and as such should be implemented by all covered entities. As discussed earlier in this preamble, the security requirements are both scalable and technically flexible; and while the law requires each health plan that is not a small plan to comply with the security and electronic signature requirements no later than 24 months after the effective date of the final rule, small plans will be allowed an additional 12 months to comply.

Since we are unable to estimate the number of entities that may need to make changes to meet the security standards, we are also unable to estimate the cost for those entities. However, we believe that the cost of establishing security systems and procedures is a portion of the costs associated with converting to the administrative simplification standards that are required under HIPAA, which are estimated in the previously referenced impact analysis.

This discussion on conversion costs relates only to health plans, health care providers, and health care clearinghouses that are required to implement the security standards. The cost of implementing security systems and procedures for entities that do not transmit, receive, or maintain health information electronically is not a cost imposed by the rule, and thus, is not included in our estimates.

G. Alternatives Considered

In developing this final rule, the Department considered some alternatives. One alternative was to not issue a final rule. However, this would not meet the Department's obligations under the HIPAA statute. It would also leave the health industry without a set of standards for protecting the security of health information. The vast majority of commenters supported our efforts in developing a set of standards. Thus, we concluded that not publishing a final rule was not in the best interests of the industry and not in the best interests of persons whose medical information will be protected by these measures.

A second alternative was to publish the final rule basically unchanged from the proposed rule. Although most commenters supported the approach of the proposed rule, there were significant objections to the number of required specifications, concerns about the scope of certain requirements, duplication and ambiguity of some requirements, and the overall complexity of the approach. Based on those comments, it was clear that revisions had to be made. In addition, the proposed rule was developed before the Privacy Rule requirements were developed. Thus, it did not allow for any alignment of requirements between the Privacy and Security standards.

As a result, the Department determined that an approach that modified the proposed rule and aligned the requirements with the Privacy standards was the preferred alternative.

V. Federalism

Executive Order 13132 of August 4, 1999, Federalism, published in the Federal Register on August 10, 1999 (64 FR 43255), requires us to ensure meaningful and timely input by State and local officials in the development of rules that have Federalism implications. Although the proposed rule for security standards was published before the enactment of this Executive Order, the Department consulted with State and local officials as part of an outreach program in the process of developing the proposed regulation. The Department received comments on the proposed rule from State agencies and from entities that conduct transactions with State agencies. Many of these comments were concerned with the burden that the proposed security standards would place on their organizations. In response to those comments, we have modified the security standards to make them more flexible and less burdensome.

In complying with the requirements of part C of Title XI, the Secretary established an interdepartmental team who consulted with appropriate State and Federal agencies and private organizations. These external groups included the NCVHS Workgroup on Standards and Security, the Workgroup for Electronic Data Interchange, the National Uniform Claim Committee, and the National Uniform Billing Committee. Most of these groups have State officials as members. We also received comments on the proposed regulation from these organizations.

In accordance with the provisions of Executive Order 12866, this rule has been reviewed by the Office of Management and Budget.

List of Subjects

45 CFR Part 160

Electronic transactions, Employer benefit plan, Health, Health care, Health facilities, Health insurance, Health

[[Page 8374]]

records, Medicaid, Medical research, Medicare, Privacy, Reporting and record keeping requirements.

45 CFR Part 162

Administrative practice and procedure, Health facilities, Health insurance, Hospitals, Medicaid, Medicare, report and recordkeeping requirement.

45 CFR Part 164

Administrative practice and procedure, Health facilities, Health insurance, Hospitals, Medicaid, Medicare, Electronic Information System, Security, Report and recordkeeping requirement.

For the reasons set forth in the preamble, the Department of Health and Human Services amends title 45, subtitle A, subchapter C, parts 160, 162, and 164 as set forth below:

PART 160--GENERAL ADMINISTRATIVE REQUIREMENTS

1. The authority citation for part 160 continues to read as follows:

Authority: Sec. 1171 through 1179 of the Social Security Act, (42 U.S.C. 1320d-1329d-8) as added by sec. 262 of Pub. L. 104-191, 110 Stat. 2021-2031 and sec. 264 of Pub. L. 104-191 (42 U.S.C. 1320d-2(note)).

2. In Sec. 160.103, the definitions of ``disclosure", ``electronic media", ``electronic protected health information," ``individual," ``organized health care arrangement", ``protected health information," and ``use" are added in alphabetical order to read as follows:

Sec. 160.103 Definitions.

* * * * *

Disclosure means the release, transfer, provision of, access to, or divulging in any other manner of information outside the entity holding the information.

* * * * *

Electronic media means:

(1) Electronic storage media including memory devices in computers (hard drives) and any removable/transportable digital memory medium, such as magnetic tape or disk, optical disk, or digital memory card; or

(2) Transmission media used to exchange information already in electronic storage media. Transmission media include, for example, the internet (wide-open), extranet (using internet technology to link a business with information accessible only to collaborating parties), leased lines, dial-up lines, private networks, and the physical

movement of removable/transportable electronic storage media. Certain transmissions, including of paper, via facsimile, and of voice, via telephone, are not considered to be transmissions via electronic media, because the information being exchanged did not exist in electronic form before the transmission.

Electronic protected health information means information that comes within paragraphs (1)(i) or (1)(ii) of the definition of protected health information as specified in this section.

* * * * *

Individual means the person who is the subject of protected health information.

* * * * *

Organized health care arrangement means:

(1) A clinically integrated care setting in which individuals typically receive health care from more than one health care provider;

(2) An organized system of health care in which more than one covered entity participates and in which the participating covered entities:

(i) Hold themselves out to the public as participating in a joint arrangement; and

(ii) Participate in joint activities that include at least one of the following:

(A) Utilization review, in which health care decisions by participating covered entities are reviewed by other participating covered entities or by a third party on their behalf;

(B) Quality assessment and improvement activities, in which treatment provided by participating covered entities is assessed by other participating covered entities or by a third party on their behalf; or

(C) Payment activities, if the financial risk for delivering health care is shared, in part or in whole, by participating covered entities through the joint arrangement and if protected health information created or received by a covered entity is reviewed by other participating covered entities or by a third party on their behalf for the purpose of administering the sharing of financial risk.

(3) A group health plan and a health insurance issuer or HMO with respect to such group health plan, but only with respect to protected health information created or received by such health insurance issuer or HMO that relates to individuals who are or who have been participants or beneficiaries in such group health plan;

(4) A group health plan and one or more other group health plans each of which are maintained by the same plan sponsor; or

(5) The group health plans described in paragraph (4) of this definition and health insurance issuers or HMOs with respect to such group health plans, but only with respect to protected health information created or received by such health insurance issuers or HMOs that relates to individuals who are or have been participants or beneficiaries in any of such group health plans.

Protected health information means individually identifiable health information:

(1) Except as provided in paragraph (2) of this definition, that is:

(i) Transmitted by electronic media;

(ii) Maintained in electronic media; or

(iii) Transmitted or maintained in any other form or medium.

(2) Protected health information excludes individually identifiable health information in:

(i) Education records covered by the Family Educational Rights and Privacy Act, as amended, 20 U.S.C. 1232g;

(ii) Records described at 20 U.S.C. 1232g(a)(4)(B)(iv); and

(iii) Employment records held by a covered entity in its role as employer.

* * * * *

Use means, with respect to individually identifiable health information, the sharing, employment, application, utilization, examination, or analysis of such information within an entity that maintains such information.

* * * * *

PART 162--ADMINISTRATIVE REQUIREMENTS

1. The authority citation for part 162 is revised to read as follows:

Authority: Secs. 1171 through 1179 of the Social Security Act (42 U.S.C. 1320d-1320d-8), as added by sec. 262 of Pub. L. 104-191, 110 Stat. 2021-2031, and sec. 264 of Pub. L. 104-191, 110 Stat. 2033-2034 (42 U.S.C. 1320d-2 (note)).

Sec. 162.103 [Amended]

2. In Sec. 162.103, the definition of ``electronic media" is removed.

PART 164--SECURITY AND PRIVACY

1. The authority citation for part 164 is revised to read as follows:

Authority: Secs. 1171 through 1179 of the Social Security Act (42 U.S.C. 1320d-1320d-8), as added by sec. 262 of Pub. L. 104-191, 110 Stat. 2021-2031, and 42 U.S.C. 1320d-2 and 1320d-4, sec. 264 of Pub. L. 104-191, 110 Stat. 2033-2034 (42 U.S.C. 1320d-2 (note)).

2. A new Sec. 164.103 is added to read as follows:

Sec. 164.103 Definitions.

As used in this part, the following terms have the following meanings:

Common control exists if an entity has the power, directly or indirectly,

[[Page 8375]]

significantly to influence or direct the actions or policies of another entity.

Common ownership exists if an entity or entities possess an ownership or equity interest of 5 percent or more in another entity.

Covered functions means those functions of a covered entity the performance of which makes the entity a health plan, health care provider, or health care clearinghouse.

Health care component means a component or combination of components of a hybrid entity designated by the hybrid entity in accordance with Sec. 164.105(a)(2)(iii)(C).

Hybrid entity means a single legal entity:

(1) That is a covered entity;

(2) Whose business activities include both covered and non-covered functions; and

(3) That designates health care components in accordance with paragraph Sec. 164.105(a)(2)(iii)(C).

Plan sponsor is defined as defined at section 3(16)(B) of ERISA, 29 U.S.C. 1002(16)(B).

Required by law means a mandate contained in law that compels an entity to make a use or disclosure of protected health information and that is enforceable in a court of law. Required by law includes, but is not limited to, court orders and court-ordered warrants; subpoenas or summons issued by a court, grand jury, a governmental or tribal inspector general, or an administrative body authorized to require the production of information; a civil or an authorized investigative demand; Medicare conditions of participation with respect to health care providers participating in the program; and statutes or

<strong>regulations</strong> that require the production of information, including statutes or <strong>regulations</strong> that require such information if payment is sought under a government program providing public benefits.

3. Section 164.104 is revised to read as follows:

Sec. 164.104 Applicability.

(a) Except as otherwise provided, the standards, requirements, and implementation specifications adopted under this part apply to the following entities:

(1) A health plan.

(2) A health care clearinghouse.

(3) A health care provider who transmits any health information in electronic form in connection with a transaction covered by this subchapter.

(b) When a health care clearinghouse creates or receives protected health information as a business associate of another covered entity, or other than as a business associate of a covered entity, the clearinghouse must comply with Sec. 164.105 relating to organizational requirements for covered entities, including the designation of health care components of a covered entity.

4. A new Sec. 164.105 is added to read as follows:

Sec. 164.105 Organizational requirements.

(a)(1) Standard: Health care component. If a covered entity is a hybrid entity, the requirements of subparts C and E of this part, other than the requirements of this section, Sec. 164.314, and Sec. 164.504, apply only to the health care component(s) of the entity, as specified in this section.

(2) Implementation specifications:

(i) Application of other provisions. In applying a provision of subparts C and E of this part, other than the requirements of this section, Sec. 164.314, and Sec. 164.504, to a hybrid entity:

(A) A reference in such provision to a ``covered entity" refers to a health care component of the covered entity;

(B) A reference in such provision to a ``health plan," ``covered health care provider," or ``health care clearinghouse," refers to a health care component of the covered entity if such health care component performs the functions of a health plan, health care provider, or health care clearinghouse, as applicable;

(C) A reference in such provision to ``protected health information" refers to protected health information that is created or received by or on behalf of the health care component of the covered entity; and

(D) A reference in such provision to ``electronic protected health information" refers to electronic protected health information that is created, received, maintained, or transmitted by or on behalf of the health care component of the covered entity.

(ii) Safeguard requirements. The covered entity that is a hybrid entity must ensure that a health care component of the entity complies with the applicable requirements of this section and subparts C and E of this part. In particular, and without limiting this requirement, such covered entity must ensure that:

(A) Its health care component does not disclose protected health information to another component of the covered entity in circumstances in which subpart E of this part would prohibit such disclosure if the health care component and the other component were separate and distinct legal entities;

(B) Its health care component protects electronic protected health information with respect to another component of the covered entity to the same extent that it would be required under subpart C of this part to protect such information if the health care component and the other component were separate and distinct legal entities;

(C) A component that is described by paragraph (a)(2)(iii)(C)(2) of this section does not use or disclose protected health information that it creates or receives from or on behalf of the health care component in a way prohibited by subpart E of this part;

(D) A component that is described by paragraph (a)(2)(iii)(C)(2) of this section that creates, receives, maintains, or transmits electronic protected health information on behalf of the health care component is in compliance with subpart C of this part; and

(E) If a person performs duties for both the health care component in the capacity of a member of the workforce of such component and for another component of the entity in the same capacity with respect to that component, such workforce member must not use or disclose protected health information created or received in the course of or incident to the member's work for the health care component in a way prohibited by subpart E of this part.

(iii) Responsibilities of the covered entity. A covered entity that is a hybrid entity has the following responsibilities:

(A) For purposes of subpart C of part 160 of this subchapter, pertaining to compliance and enforcement, the covered entity has the responsibility of complying with subpart E of this part.

(B) The covered entity is responsible for complying with Sec. 164.316(a) and Sec. 164.530(i), pertaining to the implementation of policies and procedures to ensure compliance with applicable requirements of this section and subparts C and E of this part, including the safeguard requirements in paragraph (a)(2)(ii) of this section.

(C) The covered entity is responsible for designating the components that are part of one or more health care components of the covered entity and documenting the designation in accordance with paragraph (c) of this section, provided that, if the covered entity designates a health care component or components, it must include any component that would meet the definition of covered entity if it were a separate legal entity. Health care component(s) also may include a component only to the extent that it performs:

(1) Covered functions; or

(2) Activities that would make such component a business associate of a

[[Page 8376]]

component that performs covered functions if the two components were separate legal entities.

(b)(1) Standard: Affiliated covered entities. Legally separate covered entities that are affiliated may designate themselves as a single covered entity for purposes of subparts C and E of this part.

(1) Implementation specifications:

(i) Requirements for designation of an affiliated covered entity.

(A) Legally separate covered entities may designate themselves (including any health care component of such covered entity) as a single affiliated covered entity, for purposes of subparts C and E of this part, if all of the covered entities designated are under common ownership or control.

(B) The designation of an affiliated covered entity must be documented and the documentation maintained as required by paragraph (c) of this section.

(ii) Safeguard requirements. An affiliated covered entity must ensure that:

(A) The affiliated covered entity's creation, receipt, maintenance, or transmission of electronic protected health information complies with the applicable requirements of subpart C of this part;

(B) The affiliated covered entity's use and disclosure of protected health information comply with the applicable requirements of subpart E of this part; and

(C) If the affiliated covered entity combines the functions of a health plan, health care provider, or health care clearinghouse, the affiliated covered entity complies with Sec. 164.308(a)(4)(ii)(A) and Sec. 164.504(g), as applicable.

(c)(1) Standard: Documentation. A covered entity must maintain a written or electronic record of a designation as required by paragraphs (a) or (b) of this section.

(2) Implementation specification: Retention period. A covered entity must retain the documentation as required by paragraph (c)(1) of this section for 6 years from the date of its creation or the date when it last was in effect, whichever is later.

5. A new subpart C is added to part 164 to read as follows:

Subpart C--Security Standards for the Protection of Electronic Protected Health Information

Sec.
164.302 Applicability.
164.304 Definitions.
164.306 Security standards: General rules.
164.308 Administrative safeguards.
164.310 Physical safeguards.
164.312 Technical safeguards.
164.314 Organizational requirements.
164.316 Policies and procedures and documentation requirements.
164.318 Compliance dates for the initial implementation of the security standards.

Appendix A to Subpart C of Part 164--Security Standards: Matrix

Authority: 42 U.S.C. 1320d-2 and 1320d-4.

Sec. 164.302 Applicability.

A covered entity must comply with the applicable standards, implementation specifications, and requirements of this subpart with respect to electronic protected health information.

Sec. 164.304 Definitions.

As used in this subpart, the following terms have the following meanings:

Access means the ability or the means necessary to read, write, modify, or communicate data/information or otherwise use any system resource. (This definition applies to ``access'' as used in this subpart, not as used in subpart E of this part.)

Administrative safeguards are administrative actions, and policies and procedures, to manage the selection, development, implementation, and maintenance of security measures to protect electronic protected health information and to manage the conduct of the covered entity's workforce in relation to the protection of that information.

Authentication means the corroboration that a person is the one claimed.

Availability means the property that data or information is accessible and useable upon demand by an authorized person.

Confidentiality means the property that data or information is not made available or disclosed to unauthorized persons or processes.

Encryption means the use of an algorithmic process to transform data into a form in which there is a low probability of assigning meaning without use of a confidential process or key.

Facility means the physical premises and the interior and exterior of a building(s).

Information system means an interconnected set of information resources under the same direct management control that shares common functionality. A system normally includes hardware, software, information, data, applications, communications, and people.

Integrity means the property that data or information have not been altered or destroyed in an unauthorized manner.

Malicious software means software, for example, a virus, designed to damage or disrupt a system.

Password means confidential authentication information composed of a string of characters.

Physical safeguards are physical measures, policies, and procedures to protect a covered entity's electronic information systems and related buildings and equipment, from natural and environmental hazards, and unauthorized intrusion.

Security or Security measures encompass all of the administrative, physical, and technical safeguards in an information system.

Security incident means the attempted or successful unauthorized access, use, disclosure, modification, or destruction of information or interference with system operations in an information system.

Technical safeguards means the technology and the policy and procedures for its use that protect electronic protected health information and control access to it.

User means a person or entity with authorized access.

Workstation means an electronic computing device, for example, a laptop or desktop computer, or any other device that performs similar functions, and electronic media stored in its immediate environment.

Sec. 164.306 Security standards: General rules.

(a) General requirements. Covered entities must do the following:

(1) Ensure the confidentiality, integrity, and availability of all electronic protected health information the covered entity creates, receives, maintains, or transmits.

(2) Protect against any reasonably anticipated threats or hazards to the security or integrity of such information.

(3) Protect against any reasonably anticipated uses or disclosures of such information that are not permitted or required under subpart E of this part.

(4) Ensure compliance with this subpart by its workforce.

(b) Flexibility of approach.

(1) Covered entities may use any security measures that allow the covered entity to reasonably and appropriately implement the standards and implementation specifications as specified in this subpart.

(2) In deciding which security measures to use, a covered entity must take into account the following factors:

(i) The size, complexity, and capabilities of the covered entity.

[[Page 8377]]

(ii) The covered entity's technical infrastructure, hardware, and software security capabilities.

(iii) The costs of security measures.

(iv) The probability and criticality of potential risks to electronic protected health information.

(c) Standards. A covered entity must comply with the standards as provided in this section and in Sec. 164.308, Sec. 164.310, Sec. 164.312, Sec. 164.314, and Sec. 164.316 with respect to all electronic protected health information.

(d) Implementation specifications.

In this subpart:

(1) Implementation specifications are required or addressable. If an implementation specification is required, the word ``Required'' appears in parentheses after the title of the implementation specification. If an implementation specification is addressable, the word ``Addressable'' appears in parentheses after the title of the implementation specification.

(2) When a standard adopted in Sec. 164.308, Sec. 164.310, Sec. 164.312, Sec. 164.314, or Sec. 164.316 includes required implementation specifications, a covered entity must implement the implementation specifications.

(1) When a standard adopted in Sec. 164.308, Sec. 164.310, Sec. 164.312, Sec. 164.314, or Sec. 164.316 includes addressable implementation specifications, a covered entity must--

(i) Assess whether each implementation specification is a reasonable and appropriate safeguard in its environment, when analyzed with reference to the likely contribution to protecting the entity's electronic protected health information; and

(ii) As applicable to the entity--

(A) Implement the implementation specification if reasonable and

appropriate; or
(B) If implementing the implementation specification is not reasonable and appropriate--
(1) Document why it would not be reasonable and appropriate to implement the implementation specification; and
(2) Implement an equivalent alternative measure if reasonable and appropriate.
(e) Maintenance. Security measures implemented to comply with standards and implementation specifications adopted under Sec. 164.105 and this subpart must be reviewed and modified as needed to continue provision of reasonable and appropriate protection of electronic protected health information as described at Sec. 164.316.

Sec. 164.308 Administrative safeguards.

(a) A covered entity must, in accordance with Sec. 164.306:
(1)(i) Standard: Security management process. Implement policies and procedures to prevent, detect, contain, and correct security violations.
(ii) Implementation specifications:
(A) Risk analysis (Required). Conduct an accurate and thorough assessment of the potential risks and vulnerabilities to the confidentiality, integrity, and availability of electronic protected health information held by the covered entity.
(B) Risk management (Required). Implement security measures sufficient to reduce risks and vulnerabilities to a reasonable and appropriate level to comply with Sec. 164.306(a).
(C) Sanction policy (Required). Apply appropriate sanctions against workforce members who fail to comply with the security policies and procedures of the covered entity.
(D) Information system activity review (Required). Implement procedures to regularly review records of information system activity, such as audit logs, access reports, and security incident tracking reports.
(2) Standard: Assigned security responsibility. Identify the security official who is responsible for the development and implementation of the policies and procedures required by this subpart for the entity.
(3)(i) Standard: Workforce security. Implement policies and procedures to ensure that all members of its workforce have appropriate access to electronic protected health information, as provided under paragraph (a)(4) of this section, and to prevent those workforce members who do not have access under paragraph (a)(4) of this section from obtaining access to electronic protected health information.
(ii) Implementation specifications:
(A) Authorization and/or supervision (Addressable). Implement procedures for the authorization and/or supervision of workforce members who work with electronic protected health information or in locations where it might be accessed.
(B) Workforce clearance procedure (Addressable). Implement procedures to determine that the access of a workforce member to electronic protected health information is appropriate.
(C) Termination procedures (Addressable). Implement procedures for terminating access to electronic protected health information when the employment of a workforce member ends or as required by determinations made as specified in paragraph (a)(3)(ii)(B) of this section.
(4)(i) Standard: Information access management. Implement policies and procedures for authorizing access to electronic protected health information that are consistent with the applicable requirements of subpart E of this part.
(ii) Implementation specifications:
(A) Isolating health care clearinghouse functions (Required). If a health care clearinghouse is part of a larger organization, the clearinghouse must implement policies and procedures that protect the electronic protected health information of the clearinghouse from unauthorized access by the larger organization.
(B) Access authorization (Addressable). Implement policies and procedures for granting access to electronic protected health information, for example, through access to a workstation, transaction, program, process, or other mechanism.
(C) Access establishment and modification (Addressable). Implement policies and procedures that, based upon the entity's access authorization policies, establish, document, review, and modify a user's right of access to a workstation, transaction, program, or process.
(5)(i) Standard: Security awareness and training. Implement a security awareness and training program for all members of its workforce (including management).
(ii) Implementation specifications. Implement:
(A) Security reminders (Addressable). Periodic security updates.
(B) Protection from malicious software (Addressable). Procedures for guarding against, detecting, and reporting malicious software.
(C) Log-in monitoring (Addressable). Procedures for monitoring log-in attempts and reporting discrepancies.
(D) Password management (Addressable). Procedures for creating, changing, and safeguarding passwords.
(6)(i) Standard: Security incident procedures. Implement policies and procedures to address security incidents.
(ii) Implementation specification: Response and Reporting (Required). Identify and respond to suspected or known security incidents; mitigate, to the extent practicable, harmful effects of security incidents that are known to the covered entity; and document security incidents and their outcomes.
(7)(i) Standard: Contingency plan. Establish (and implement as needed) policies and procedures for responding to an emergency or other occurrence (for example, fire, vandalism, system failure, and natural disaster) that damages systems that contain electronic protected health information.
(ii) Implementation specifications:

[[Page 8378]]

(A) Data backup plan (Required). Establish and implement procedures to create and maintain retrievable exact copies of electronic protected health information.
(B) Disaster recovery plan (Required). Establish (and implement as needed) procedures to restore any loss of data.
(C) Emergency mode operation plan (Required). Establish (and implement as needed) procedures to enable continuation of critical business processes for protection of the security of electronic protected health information while operating in emergency mode.
(D) Testing and revision procedures (Addressable). Implement procedures for periodic testing and revision of contingency plans.
(E) Applications and data criticality analysis (Addressable). Assess the relative criticality of specific applications and data in support of other contingency plan components.
(8) Standard: Evaluation. Perform a periodic technical and nontechnical evaluation, based initially upon the standards implemented under this rule and subsequently, in response to environmental or operational changes affecting the security of electronic protected health information, that establishes the extent to which an entity's security policies and procedures meet the requirements of this subpart.
(b)(1) Standard: Business associate contracts and other arrangements. A covered entity, in accordance with Sec. 164.306, may permit a business associate to create, receive, maintain, or transmit electronic protected health information on the covered entity's behalf only if the covered entity obtains satisfactory assurances, in accordance with Sec. 164.314(a) that the business associate will appropriately safeguard the information.
(2) This standard does not apply with respect to--
(i) The transmission by a covered entity of electronic protected health information to a health care provider concerning the treatment of an individual.
(ii) The transmission of electronic protected health information by a group health plan or an HMO or health insurance issuer on behalf of a group health plan to a plan sponsor, to the extent that the requirements of Sec. 164.314(b) and Sec. 164.504(f) apply and are met; or
(iii) The transmission of electronic protected health information from or to other agencies providing the services at Sec. 164.502(e)(1)(ii)(C), when the covered entity is a health plan that is a government program providing public benefits, if the requirements of Sec. 164.502(e)(1)(ii)(C) are met.
(3) A covered entity that violates the satisfactory assurances it

provided as a business associate of another covered entity will be in noncompliance with the standards, implementation specifications, and requirements of this paragraph and Sec. 164.314(a).

(4) Implementation specifications: Written contract or other arrangement (Required). Document the satisfactory assurances required by paragraph (b)(1) of this section through a written contract or other arrangement with the business associate that meets the applicable requirements of Sec. 164.314(a).

Sec. 164.310 Physical safeguards.

A covered entity must, in accordance with Sec. 164.306:

(a)(1) Standard: Facility access controls. Implement policies and procedures to limit physical access to its electronic information systems and the facility or facilities in which they are housed, while ensuring that properly authorized access is allowed.

(2) Implementation specifications:

(i) Contingency operations (Addressable). Establish (and implement as needed) procedures that allow facility access in support of restoration of lost data under the disaster recovery plan and emergency mode operations plan in the event of an emergency.

(ii) Facility security plan (Addressable). Implement policies and procedures to safeguard the facility and the equipment therein from unauthorized physical access, tampering, and theft.

(iii) Access control and validation procedures (Addressable). Implement procedures to control and validate a person's access to facilities based on their role or function, including visitor control, and control of access to software programs for testing and revision.

(iv) Maintenance records (Addressable). Implement policies and procedures to document repairs and modifications to the physical components of a facility which are related to security (for example, hardware, walls, doors, and locks).

(b) Standard: Workstation use. Implement policies and procedures that specify the proper functions to be performed, the manner in which those functions are to be performed, and the physical attributes of the surroundings of a specific workstation or class of workstation that can access electronic protected health information.

(c) Standard: Workstation security. Implement physical safeguards for all workstations that access electronic protected health information, to restrict access to authorized users.

(d)(1) Standard: Device and media controls. Implement policies and procedures that govern the receipt and removal of hardware and electronic media that contain electronic protected health information into and out of a facility, and the movement of these items within the facility.

(2) Implementation specifications:

(i) Disposal (Required). Implement policies and procedures to address the final disposition of electronic protected health information, and/or the hardware or electronic media on which it is stored.

(ii) Media re-use (Required). Implement procedures for removal of electronic protected health information from electronic media before the media are made available for re-use.

(iii) Accountability (Addressable). Maintain a record of the movements of hardware and electronic media and any person responsible therefore.

(iv) Data backup and storage (Addressable). Create a retrievable, exact copy of electronic protected health information, when needed, before movement of equipment.

Sec. 164.312 Technical safeguards.

A covered entity must, in accordance with Sec. 164.306:

(a)(1) Standard: Access control. Implement technical policies and procedures for electronic information systems that maintain electronic protected health information to allow access only to those persons or software programs that have been granted access rights as specified in Sec. 164.308(a)(4).

(2) Implementation specifications:

(i) Unique user identification (Required). Assign a unique name and/or number for identifying and tracking user identity.

(ii) Emergency access procedure (Required). Establish (and implement as needed) procedures for obtaining necessary electronic protected health information during an emergency.

(iii) Automatic logoff (Addressable). Implement electronic procedures that terminate an electronic session after a predetermined time of inactivity.

(iv) Encryption and decryption (Addressable). Implement a mechanism to encrypt and decrypt electronic protected health information.

(b) Standard: Audit controls. Implement hardware, software, and/or procedural mechanisms that record and examine activity in information systems that contain or use electronic protected health information.

(c)(1) Standard: Integrity. Implement policies and procedures to protect

[[Page 8379]]

electronic protected health information from improper alteration or destruction.

(2) Implementation specification: Mechanism to authenticate electronic protected health information (Addressable). Implement electronic mechanisms to corroborate that electronic protected health information has not been altered or destroyed in an unauthorized manner.

(d) Standard: Person or entity authentication. Implement procedures to verify that a person or entity seeking access to electronic protected health information is the one claimed.

(e)(1) Standard: Transmission security. Implement technical security measures to guard against unauthorized access to electronic protected health information that is being transmitted over an electronic communications network.

(2) Implementation specifications:

(i) Integrity controls (Addressable). Implement security measures to ensure that electronically transmitted electronic protected health information is not improperly modified without detection until disposed of.

(ii) Encryption (Addressable). Implement a mechanism to encrypt electronic protected health information whenever deemed appropriate.

Sec. 164.314 Organizational requirements.

(a)(1) Standard: Business associate contracts or other arrangements.

(i) The contract or other arrangement between the covered entity and its business associate required by Sec. 164.308(b) must meet the requirements of paragraph (a)(2)(i) or (a)(2)(ii) of this section, as applicable.

(ii) A covered entity is not in compliance with the standards in Sec. 164.502(e) and paragraph (a) of this section if the covered entity knew of a pattern of an activity or practice of the business associate that constituted a material breach or violation of the business associate's obligation under the contract or other arrangement, unless the covered entity took reasonable steps to cure the breach or end the violation, as applicable, and, if such steps were unsuccessful--

(A) Terminated the contract or arrangement, if feasible; or

(B) If termination is not feasible, reported the problem to the Secretary.

(2) Implementation specifications (Required).

(i) Business associate contracts. The contract between a covered entity and a business associate must provide that the business associate will--

(A) Implement administrative, physical, and technical safeguards that reasonably and appropriately protect the confidentiality, integrity, and availability of the electronic protected health information that it creates, receives, maintains, or transmits on behalf of the covered entity as required by this subpart;

(B) Ensure that any agent, including a subcontractor, to whom it provides such information agrees to implement reasonable and appropriate safeguards to protect it;

(C) Report to the covered entity any security incident of which it becomes aware;

(D) Authorize termination of the contract by the covered entity, if the covered entity determines that the business associate has violated a material term of the contract.

(ii) Other arrangements.

(A) When a covered entity and its business associate are both governmental entities, the covered entity is in compliance with paragraph (a)(1) of this section, if--

(1) It enters into a memorandum of understanding with the business associate that contains terms that accomplish the objectives of paragraph (a)(2)(i) of this section; or

(2) Other law (including <strong>regulations</strong> adopted by the covered entity
or its business associate) contains requirements applicable to the business associate that accomplish the objectives of paragraph (a)(2)(i) of this section.

(B) If a business associate is required by law to perform a function or activity on behalf of a covered entity or to provide a service described in the definition of business associate as specified in Sec. 160.103 of this subchapter to a covered entity, the covered entity may permit the business associate to create, receive, maintain, or transmit electronic protected health information on its behalf to the extent necessary to comply with the legal mandate without meeting the requirements of paragraph (a)(2)(i) of this section, provided that the covered entity attempts in good faith to obtain satisfactory assurances as required by paragraph (a)(2)(ii)(A) of this section, and documents the attempt and the reasons that these assurances cannot be obtained.

(C) The covered entity may omit from its other arrangements authorization of the termination of the contract by the covered entity, as required by paragraph (a)(2)(i)(D) of this section if such authorization is inconsistent with the statutory obligations of the covered entity or its business associate.

(b)(1) Standard: Requirements for group health plans. Except when the only electronic protected health information disclosed to a plan sponsor is disclosed pursuant to Sec. 164.504(f)(1)(ii) or (iii), or as authorized under Sec. 164.508, a group health plan must ensure that its plan documents provide that the plan sponsor will reasonably and appropriately safeguard electronic protected health information created, received, maintained, or transmitted to or by the plan sponsor on behalf of the group health plan.

(2) Implementation specifications (Required). The plan documents of the group health plan must be amended to incorporate provisions to require the plan sponsor to--

(i) Implement administrative, physical, and technical safeguards that reasonably and appropriately protect the confidentiality, integrity, and availability of the electronic protected health information that it creates, receives, maintains, or transmits on behalf of the group health plan;

(ii) Ensure that the adequate separation required by Sec. 164.504(f)(2)(iii) is supported by reasonable and appropriate security measures;

(iii) Ensure that any agent, including a subcontractor, to whom it provides this information agrees to implement reasonable and appropriate security measures to protect the information; and

(iv) Report to the group health plan any security incident of which it becomes aware.

Sec. 164.316 Policies and procedures and documentation requirements.

A covered entity must, in accordance with Sec. 164.306:

(a) Standard: Policies and procedures. Implement reasonable and appropriate policies and procedures to comply with the standards, implementation specifications, or other requirements of this subpart, taking into account those factors specified in Sec. 164.306(b)(2)(i), (ii), (iii), and (iv). This standard is not to be construed to permit or excuse an action that violates any other standard, implementation specification, or other requirements of this subpart. A covered entity may change its policies and procedures at any time, provided that the changes are documented and are implemented in accordance with this subpart.

(b)(1) Standard: Documentation.

(i) Maintain the policies and procedures implemented to comply with this subpart in written (which may be electronic) form; and

(ii) If an action, activity or assessment is required by this subpart to be documented, maintain a written (which may be electronic) record of the action, activity, or assessment.

(2) Implementation specifications:

[[Page 8380]]

(i) Time limit (Required). Retain the documentation required by paragraph (b)(1) of this section for 6 years from the date of its creation or the date when it last was in effect, whichever is later.

(ii) Availability (Required). Make documentation available to those persons responsible for implementing the procedures to which the documentation pertains.

(iii) Updates (Required). Review documentation periodically, and update as needed, in response to environmental or operational changes affecting the security of the electronic protected health information.

Sec. 164.318 Compliance dates for the initial implementation of the security standards.

(a) Health plan.

(1) A health plan that is not a small health plan must comply with the applicable requirements of this subpart no later than April 20, 2005.

(2) A small health plan must comply with the applicable requirements of this subpart no later than April 20, 2006.

(b) Health care clearinghouse. A health care clearinghouse must comply with the applicable requirements of this subpart no later than April 20, 2005.

(c) Health care provider. A covered health care provider must comply with the applicable requirements of this subpart no later than April 20, 2005.

Appendix A to Subpart C of Part 164--Security Standards: Matrix

----

Implementation
Specifications
Standards Sections
(R)=Required,
(A)=Addressable

Administrative Safeguards

Security Management Process............................ 164.308(a)(1) Risk
Analysis (R)
.... Risk
Management (R)
.... Sanction Policy
(R)
.... Information
System

Activity Review (R)
Assigned Security Responsibility....................... 164.308(a)(2) (R)
Workforce Security.................................... 164.308(a)(3) Authorization and/or
Supervision (A)
.... Workforce Clearance
Procedure
.... Termination Procedures
(A)
Information Access Management......................... 164.308(a)(4) Isolating Health
care
Clearinghouse Function
(R)
.... Access Authorization (A)
.... Access Establishment and
Modification (A)
Security Awareness and Training........................ 164.308(a)(5) Security Reminders
(A)
.... Protection from
Malicious Software (A)
.... Log-in Monitoring (A)
.... Password Management (A)
Security Incident Procedures........................... 164.308(a)(6) Response and
Reporting
(R)
Contingency Plan...................................... 164.308(a)(7) Data Backup Plan (R)
.... Disaster Recovery Plan
(R)
.... Emergency Mode Operation
Plan (R)
.... Testing and Revision
Procedure (A)
.... Applications and Data
Criticality Analysis
(A)
Evaluation.. 164.308(a)(8) (R)
Business Associate Contracts and Other Arrangement..... 164.308(b)(1) Written
Contract or
Other Arrangement (R)

Physical Safeguards

Facility Access Controls.............................. 164.310(a)(1) Contingency Operations
(A)
.... Facility Security Plan
(A)
.... Access Control and
Validation Procedures
(A)
.... Maintenance Records (A)
Workstation Use....................................... 164.310(b) (R)
Workstation Security.................................. 164.310(c) (R)
Device and Media Controls............................. 164.310(d)(1) Disposal (R)
.... Media Re-use (R)
.... Accountability (A)
.... Data Backup and Storage
(A)

Technical Safeguards (see Sec. 164.312)

Access Control.. 164.312(a)(1) Unique User
Identification (R)
.... Emergency Access
Procedure (R)
.... Automatic Logoff (A)
.... Encryption and
Decryption (A)
Audit Controls.. 164.312(b) (R)
Integrity... 164.312(c)(1)
Mechanism to
Authenticate
Electronic
Protected Health
Information (A)
Person or Entity Authentication....................... 164.312(d)
(R)
Transmission Security................................. 164.312(e)(1)
Integrity Controls (A)
.... Encryption (A)

[[Page 8381]]

Sec. 164.500 [Amended]

6. Sec. In 164.500(b)(1)(iv), remove the words ``including the designation of health care components of a covered entity''.

Sec. 165.501 [Amended]

7. In Sec. 164.501, the definitions of the following terms are removed: Covered functions, Disclosure, Individual, Organized health care arrangement, Plan sponsor Protected health information, Required by law, and Use.

Sec. 164.504 [Amended]

8. In Sec. 164.504, the following changes are made:
a. The definitions of the following terms are removed: Common control, Common ownership, Health care component, and Hybrid entity.
b. Paragraphs (b) through (d) are removed and reserved.

Authority: Sections 1173 and 1175 of the Social Security Act (42 U.S.C. 1329d-2 and 1320-4).

Dated: January 13, 2003.
Tommy G. Thompson,
Secretary.
[FR Doc. 03-3877 Filed 2-13-03; 8:45 am]
BILLING CODE 4120-01-P

</PRE>

STANDARDS FOR PRIVACY OF
INDIVIDUALLY IDENTIFIABLE HEALTH INFORMATION
[45 CFR Parts 160 and 164]

Introduction

This guidance explains and answers questions about key elements of the requirements of the HIPAA *Standards for Privacy of Individually Identifiable Health Information* (the Privacy Rule). The Department of Health and Human Services (HHS) published the Privacy Rule on December 28, 2000, and adopted modifications of the Rule on August 14, 2002.

The Privacy Rule (45 CFR Part 160 and Subparts A and E of Part 164) provides the first comprehensive Federal protection for the privacy of health information. All segments of the health care industry have expressed support for the objective of enhanced patient privacy in the health care system. The Privacy Rule, as modified, is carefully balanced to provide strong privacy protections that do not interfere with patient access to, or the quality of, health care delivery.

The guidance that follows is meant to communicate as clearly as possible the privacy policies contained in the Privacy Rule. For a particular segment in the Privacy Rule, the guidance will provide a brief explanation of the segment and how the Rule works, followed by "Frequently Asked Questions" about that provision. The guidance does not address all of the relevant provisions in the Rule, although we anticipate adding segments in the future as we develop guidance on more Privacy Rule standards. We will also be adding to the "Frequently Asked Questions" on an ongoing basis as new questions arise. HHS plans to work expeditiously to address these additional questions to facilitate understanding of the Rule and to encourage voluntary compliance with its requirements. However, for a full understanding of one's rights and responsibilities under the Rule, it is important to consult the Rule itself.

<u>The Privacy Rule Standards Addressed</u>

General Overview
Incidental Uses and Disclosures (45 CFR 164.502(a))
Minimum Necessary (45 CFR 164.502(b), 164.514(d))
Personal Representatives (45 CFR 164.502(g))
Business Associates (45 CFR 164.502(e), 164.504(e), 164.532(d) and (e))
Uses and Disclosures for Treatment, Payment, and Health Care Operations (45 CFR 164.506)
Marketing (45 CFR 164.501, 164.508(a))
Public Health (45 CFR 164.512(b))
Research (45 CFR 164.501, 164.508, 164.512(i), 164.514(e), 164.528, 164.532)
Workers' Compensation Laws (45 CFR 164.512(*l*))
Notice (45 CFR 164.520)
Government Access (45 CFR Part 160, Subpart C, 164.512(f))
Miscellaneous FAQs

GENERAL OVERVIEW OF STANDARDS FOR PRIVACY OF INDIVIDUALLY IDENTIFIABLE HEALTH INFORMATION
[*45 CFR Part 160 and Subparts A and E of Part 164*]

The following overview provides answers to general questions regarding the *Standards for Privacy of Individually Identifiable Health Information* (the Privacy Rule), promulgated by the Department of Health and Human Services (HHS).

To improve the efficiency and effectiveness of the health care system, the Health Insurance Portability and Accountability Act (HIPAA) of 1996, Public Law 104-191, included "Administrative Simplification" provisions that required HHS to adopt national standards for electronic health care transactions. At the same time, Congress recognized that advances in electronic technology could erode the privacy of health information. Consequently, Congress incorporated into HIPAA provisions that mandated the adoption of Federal privacy protections for individually identifiable health information.

In response to the HIPAA mandate, HHS published a final regulation in the form of the Privacy Rule in December 2000, which became effective on April 14, 2001. This Rule set national standards for the protection of health information, as applied to the three types of covered entities: health plans, health care clearinghouses, and health care providers who conduct certain health care transactions electronically. By the compliance date of April 14, 2003 (April 14, 2004, for small health plans), covered entities must implement standards to protect and guard against the misuse of individually identifiable health information. Failure to timely implement these standards may, under certain circumstances, trigger the imposition of civil or criminal penalties.

Secretary Tommy Thompson called for an additional opportunity for public comment on the Privacy Rule to ensure that the Privacy Rule achieves its intended purpose without adversely affecting the quality of, or creating new barriers to, patient care. After careful consideration of these comments, in March 2002 HHS published proposed modifications to the Rule, to improve workability and avoid unintended consequences that could have impeded patient access to delivery of quality health care. Following another round of public comment, in August 2002, the Department adopted as a final Rule the modifications necessary to ensure that the Privacy Rule worked as intended.

The Privacy Rule establishes, for the first time, a foundation of Federal protections for the privacy of protected health information. The Rule does not replace Federal, State, or other law that grants individuals even greater privacy protections, and covered entities are free to retain or adopt more protective policies or practices.

<u>GENERAL OVERVIEW</u>

<u>Frequently Asked Questions</u>

Q:What does the HIPAA Privacy Rule do?

A: Most health plans and health care providers that are covered by the new Rule must comply with the new requirements by April 14, 2003.

The HIPAA Privacy Rule for the first time creates national standards to protect individuals' medical records and other personal health information.

•It gives patients more <u>control</u> over their health information.

•It sets <u>boundaries</u> on the use and release of health records.

•It establishes appropriate safeguards that health care providers and others must achieve to protect the privacy of health information.

•It holds violators accountable, with civil and criminal penalties that can be imposed if they violate patients' privacy rights

•And it strikes a balance when public responsibility supports disclosure of some forms of data – for example, to protect public health.

For patients – it means being able to make informed choices when seeking care and reimbursement for care based on how personal health information may be used.

It enables patients to find out how their information may be used, and about certain disclosures of their information that have been made.

It generally limits release of information to the minimum reasonably needed for the purpose of the disclosure.

It generally gives patients the right to examine and obtain a copy of their own health records and request corrections.

It empowers individuals to control certain uses and disclosures of their health information.

Q: Why is the HIPAA Privacy Rule needed?

A: In enacting HIPAA, Congress mandated the establishment of Federal standards for the privacy of individually identifiable health information. When it comes to personal information that moves across hospitals, doctors' offices, insurers or third party payers, and State lines, our country has relied on a patchwork of Federal and State laws. Under the patchwork of laws existing prior to adoption of HIPAA and the Privacy Rule, personal health information could be distributed—without either notice or authorization—for reasons that had nothing to do with a patient's medical treatment or health care reimbursement. For example, unless otherwise forbidden by State or local law, without the Privacy Rule patient information held by a health plan could, without the patient's permission, be passed on to a lender who could then deny the patient's application for a home mortgage or a credit card, or to an employer who could use it in personnel decisions. The Privacy Rule establishes a Federal floor of safeguards to protect the confidentiality of medical information. State laws which provide stronger privacy protections will continue to apply over and above the new Federal privacy standards.

Health care providers have a strong tradition of safeguarding private health information. However, in today's world, the old system of paper records in locked filing cabinets is not enough. With information broadly held and transmitted electronically, the Rule provides clear standards for the protection of personal health information.

Q: Generally, what does the HIPAA Privacy Rule require the average provider or health plan to do?

A: For the average health care provider or health plan, the Privacy Rule requires activities, such as:

•Notifying patients about their privacy rights and how their information can be used.

•Adopting and implementing privacy procedures for its practice, hospital, or plan.

•Training employees so that they understand the privacy procedures.

•Designating an individual to be responsible for seeing that the privacy procedures are adopted and followed.

•Securing patient records containing individually identifiable health information so that they are not readily available to those who do not need them.

Responsible health care providers and businesses already take many of the kinds of steps required by the Rule to protect patients' privacy. Covered entities of all types and sizes are required to comply with the Privacy Rule. To ease the burden of complying with the new requirements, the Privacy Rule gives needed flexibility for providers and plans to create their own privacy procedures, tailored to fit their size and needs. The scalability of the Rule provides a more efficient and appropriate means of safeguarding protected health information than would any single standard. For example,

•The privacy official at a small physician practice may be the office manager, who will have other non-privacy related duties; the privacy official at a large health plan may be a full-time position, and may have the regular support and advice of a privacy staff or board.

•The training requirement may be satisfied by a small physician practice's providing each new member of the workforce with a copy of its privacy policies and documenting that new members have reviewed the policies; whereas a large health plan may provide training through live instruction, video presentations, or interactive software programs.

•The policies and procedures of small providers may be more limited under the Rule than those of a large hospital or health plan, based on the volume of health information maintained and the number of interactions with those within and outside of the health care system.

Q: Who must comply with these new HIPAA privacy standards?

A: As required by Congress in HIPAA, the Privacy Rule covers:

•Health plans

•Health care clearinghouses

•Health care providers who conduct certain financial and administrative transactions electronically. These electronic transactions are those for which standards have been adopted by the Secretary under HIPAA, such as electronic billing and fund transfers.

These entities (collectively called "covered entities") are bound by the new privacy standards even if they contract with others (called "business associates") to perform some of their essential functions. The law does not give the Department of Health and Human Services (HHS) the authority to regulate other types of private businesses or public agencies through this regulation. For example, HHS does not have the authority to regulate employers, life insurance companies, or public agencies that deliver social security or welfare benefits. See the fact sheet and frequently asked questions on this web site about the standards on "Business Associates" for a more detailed discussion of the covered entities' responsibilities when they engage others to perform essential functions or services for them.

Q: When will covered entities have to meet these HIPAA privacy standards?

A: As Congress required in HIPAA, most covered entities have until April 14, 2003 to come into compliance with these standards, as modified by the August, 2002 final Rule. Small health plans will have an additional year – until April 14, 2004 – to come into compliance.

The Department of Health and Human Services (HHS) Office for Civil Rights (OCR) is providing assistance to help covered entities prepare to comply with the Rule. For example, OCR maintains a web site with helpful information, such as the Guidance, Frequently Asked Questions, sample "business associate" contract provisions, significant reference documents, and other technical assistance information for consumers and the health care industry, at http://www.hhs.gov/ocr/hipaa/.

Q: What were the major modifications to the HIPAA Privacy Rule that the Department of Health and Human Services (HHS) adopted in August 2002?

A: Based on the information received through public comments, testimony at public hearings, meetings at the request of industry and other stakeholders, as well as other communications, HHS identified a number of areas in which the Privacy Rule, as issued in December 2000, would have had potential unintended effects on health care quality or access. As a result, HHS proposed modifications that would maintain strong protections for the privacy of individually identifiable health information, address the unintended negative effects of the Privacy Rule on health care quality or access to health care, and relieve unintended administrative burdens created by the Privacy Rule.

Final modifications to the Rule were adopted on August 14, 2002. Among other things, the modifications addressed the following aspects of the Privacy Rule:

•Uses and disclosures for treatment, payment and health care operations, including eliminating the requirement for the individual's consent for these activities;

•The notice of privacy practices that covered entities must provide to patients;

•Uses and disclosures for marketing purposes;

•Minimum necessary uses and disclosures;

•Parents as the personal representatives of unemancipated minors;

•Uses and disclosures for research purposes; and

•Transition provisions, including business associate contracts.

In addition to these key areas, the modifications included changes to certain other provisions where necessary to clarify the Privacy Rule, and a list of technical corrections intended as editorial or typographical corrections to the Privacy Rule.

For more information about the final modifications to the Privacy Rule, see the Fact Sheet entitled, *Modifications to the Standards for Privacy of Individually Identifiable Health Information – Final Rule*. This Fact Sheet can be found at http://www.hhs.gov/news/press/2002pres/20020809.html.

Q: Why was the consent requirement eliminated from the HIPAA Privacy Rule, and how will it affect individuals' privacy protections?

A: The consent requirement created the unintended effect of preventing health care providers from providing timely, quality health care to individuals in a variety of circumstances. The most troubling and pervasive problem was that health care providers would not have been able to use or disclose protected health information for treatment, payment, or health care operations purposes prior to the initial face-to-face encounter with the patient, which is routinely done to provide timely access to quality health care. The following are some examples of how the consent requirement would have posed barriers to health care:

•Pharmacists would not have been able to fill a prescription, search for potential drug interactions, determine eligibility, or verify coverage before the individual arrived at the pharmacy to pick up the prescription if the individual had not already provided consent under the Privacy Rule.

•Hospitals would not have been able to use information from a referring physician to schedule and prepare for procedures before the individual presented at the hospital for such procedure, or the patient would have had to make a special trip to the hospital to sign the consent form.

•Providers who do not provide treatment in person (such as a provider prescribing over the telephone) may have been unable to provide care because they would have had difficulty obtaining prior written consent to use protected health information at the first service delivery.

•Emergency medical providers were concerned that, even if a situation was urgent, they would have had to try to obtain consent to comply with the Privacy Rule, even if that would be inconsistent with the appropriate practice of emergency medicine.

•Emergency medical providers were also concerned that the requirement that they attempt to obtain consent as soon as reasonably practicable after an emergency would have required significant efforts and administrative burden which might have been viewed as harassing by patients, because these providers typically do not have ongoing relationships with individuals.

To eliminate such barriers to health care, mandatory consent was replaced with the voluntary consent provision that permits health care providers to obtain consent for treatment, payment and healthcare operations, at their option, and enables them to obtain consent in a manner that does not disrupt needed treatment. Although consent is no longer mandatory, the Rule still affords individuals the opportunity to engage in important discussions regarding the use and disclosure of their health information through the strengthened notice requirement, while allowing activities that are essential to quality health care to occur unimpeded. These modifications will ensure that the Rule protects patient privacy as intended without harming consumers' access to care or the quality of that care. Further, the individual's right to request restrictions on the use or disclosure of his or her protected health information is retained in the Rule as modified.

Q: Did the final modifications to the HIPAA Privacy Rule alter the compliance date(s) for covered entities?

A: No. The compliance dates for the Privacy Rule, as modified, remain April 14, 2003, for most health plans, covered health care providers, and health care clearinghouses, and April 14, 2004, for small health plans. Under HIPAA, compliance with a modification to an existing standard or implementation specification is required by a date set by the Secretary, but not earlier than 180 days from the adoption of the modification. By publishing the modifications to the Privacy Rule in August 2002, the original compliance date of April 2003 is maintained for the entire Rule, as modified.

Q: Will the Department of Health and Human Services (HHS) make future changes to the HIPAA Privacy Rule and, if so, how will these changes be made?

A: Under HIPAA, HHS has the authority to modify the privacy standards as the Secretary may deem appropriate. However, a standard can be modified only once in a 12-month period.

As a general rule, future modifications to the Privacy Rule must be made in accordance with the Administrative Procedure Act (APA). HHS will comply with the APA by publishing proposed rule changes, if any, in the *Federal Register* through a Notice of Proposed Rulemaking and will invite comment from the public. After reviewing and addressing those comments, HHS will issue a modified final rule.

INCIDENTAL USES AND DISCLOSURES
[*45 CFR 164.502(a)(1)(iii)*]

Background

Many customary health care communications and practices play an important or even essential role in ensuring that individuals receive prompt and effective health care. Due to the nature of these communications and practices, as well as the various environments in which individuals receive health care or other services from covered entities, the potential exists for an individual's health information to be disclosed incidentally. For example, a hospital visitor may overhear a provider's confidential conversation with another provider or a patient, or may glimpse a patient's information on a sign-in sheet or nursing station whiteboard. The HIPAA Privacy Rule is not intended to impede these customary and essential communications and practices and, thus, does not require that all risk of incidental use or disclosure be eliminated to satisfy its standards. Rather, the Privacy Rule permits certain incidental uses and disclosures of protected health information to occur when the covered entity has in place reasonable safeguards and minimum necessary policies and procedures to protect an individual's privacy.

How the Rule Works

General Provision. The Privacy Rule permits certain incidental uses and disclosures that occur as a by-product of another permissible or required use or disclosure, as long as the covered entity has applied *reasonable safeguards* and implemented the *minimum necessary standard*, where applicable, with respect to the primary use or disclosure. See 45 CFR 164.502(a)(1)(iii). An incidental use or disclosure is a secondary use or disclosure that cannot reasonably be prevented, is limited in nature, and that occurs as a result of another use or disclosure that is permitted by the Rule. However, an incidental use or disclosure is not permitted if it is a by-product of an underlying use or disclosure which violates the Privacy Rule.

Reasonable Safeguards. A covered entity must have in place appropriate administrative, technical, and physical safeguards that protect against uses and disclosures not permitted by the Privacy Rule, as well as that limit incidental uses or disclosures. See 45 CFR 164.530(c). It is not expected that a covered entity's safeguards guarantee the privacy of protected health information from any and all potential risks. Reasonable safeguards will vary from covered entity to covered entity depending on factors, such as the size of the covered entity and the nature of its business. In implementing reasonable safeguards, covered entities should analyze their own needs and circumstances, such as the nature of the protected health information it holds, and assess the potential risks to patients' privacy. Covered entities should also take into account the potential effects on patient care and may consider other issues, such as the financial and administrative burden of implementing particular safeguards.

Many health care providers and professionals have long made it a practice to ensure reasonable safeguards for individuals' health information – for instance:

By speaking quietly when discussing a patient's condition with family members in a waiting room or other public area;

By avoiding using patients' names in public hallways and elevators, and posting signs to remind employees to protect patient confidentiality;

By isolating or locking file cabinets or records rooms; or

By providing additional security, such as passwords, on computers maintaining personal information.

Protection of patient confidentiality is an important practice for many health care and health information management professionals; covered entities can build upon those codes of conduct to develop the reasonable safeguards required by the Privacy Rule.

Minimum Necessary. Covered entities also must implement reasonable minimum necessary policies and procedures that limit how much protected health information is used, disclosed, and requested for certain purposes. These minimum necessary policies and procedures also reasonably must limit who within the entity has access to protected health information, and under what conditions, based on job responsibilities and the nature of the business. The minimum necessary standard does not apply to disclosures, including oral disclosures, among health care providers for treatment purposes. For example, a physician is not required to apply the minimum necessary standard when discussing a patient's medical chart information with a specialist at another hospital. See 45 CFR 164.502(b) and 164.514(d), and the fact sheet and frequently asked questions on this web site about the minimum necessary standard, for more information.

An incidental use or disclosure that occurs as a result of a failure to apply reasonable safeguards or the minimum necessary standard, where required, is not permitted under the Privacy Rule.

For example:

The minimum necessary standard requires that a covered entity limit who within the entity has access to protected health information, based on who needs access to perform their job duties. If a hospital employee is allowed to have routine, unimpeded access to patients' medical records, where such access is not necessary for the hospital employee to do his job, the hospital is not applying the minimum necessary standard. Therefore, any incidental use or disclosure that results from this practice, such as another worker overhearing the hospital employee's conversation about a patient's condition, would be an unlawful use or disclosure under the Privacy Rule.

INCIDENTAL USES AND DISCLOSURES

Frequently Asked Questions

Q: Can health care providers engage in confidential conversations with other providers or with patients, even if there is a possibility that they could be overheard?

A: Yes. The HIPAA Privacy Rule is not intended to prohibit providers from talking to each other and to their patients. Provisions of this Rule requiring covered entities to implement reasonable safeguards that reflect their particular circumstances and exempting treatment disclosures from certain requirements are intended to ensure that providers' primary consideration is the appropriate treatment of their patients. The Privacy Rule recognizes that oral communications often must occur freely and quickly in treatment settings. Thus, covered entities are free to engage in communications as required for quick, effective, and high quality health care. The Privacy Rule also recognizes that overheard communications in these settings may be unavoidable and allows for these incidental disclosures.

For example, the following practices are permissible under the Privacy Rule, if reasonable precautions are taken to minimize the chance of incidental disclosures to others who may be nearby:

Health care staff may orally coordinate services at hospital nursing stations.

Nurses or other health care professionals may discuss a patient's condition over the phone with the patient, a provider, or a family member.

A health care professional may discuss lab test results with a patient or other provider in a joint treatment area.

A physician may discuss a patients' condition or treatment regimen in the patient's semi-private room.

Health care professionals may discuss a patient's condition during training rounds in an academic or training institution.

A pharmacist may discuss a prescription with a patient over the pharmacy counter, or with a physician or the patient over the phone.

In these circumstances, reasonable precautions could include using lowered voices or talking apart from others when sharing protected health information. However, in an emergency situation, in a loud emergency room, or where a patient is hearing impaired, such precautions may not be practicable. Covered entities are free to engage in communications as required for quick, effective, and high quality health care.

Q: Does the HIPAA Privacy Rule require hospitals and doctors' offices to be retrofitted, to provide private rooms, and soundproof walls to avoid any possibility that a conversation is overheard?

A: No, the Privacy Rule does not require these types of structural changes be made to facilities.

Covered entities must have in place appropriate administrative, technical, and physical safeguards to protect the privacy of protected health information. This standard requires that covered entities make reasonable efforts to prevent uses and disclosures not permitted by the Rule. The Department does not consider facility restructuring to be a requirement under this standard.

For example, the Privacy Rule does not require the following types of structural or systems changes:

Private rooms.

Soundproofing of rooms.

Encryption of wireless or other emergency medical radio communications which can be intercepted by scanners.

Encryption of telephone systems.

Covered entities must implement reasonable safeguards to limit incidental, and avoid prohibited, uses and disclosures. The Privacy Rule does not require that all risk of protected health information disclosure be eliminated. Covered entities must review their own practices and determine what steps are reasonable to safeguard their patient information. In determining what is reasonable, covered entities should assess potential risks to patient privacy, as well as consider such issues as the potential effects on patient care, and any administrative or financial burden to be incurred from implementing particular safeguards. Covered entities also may take into consideration the steps that other prudent health care and health information professionals are taking to protect patient privacy.

Examples of the types of adjustments or modifications to facilities or systems that may constitute reasonable safeguards are:

Pharmacies could ask waiting customers to stand a few feet back from a counter used for patient counseling.

In an area where multiple patient-staff communications routinely occur, use of cubicles, dividers, shields, curtains, or similar barriers may constitute a reasonable safeguard. For example, a large clinic intake area may reasonably use cubicles or shield-type dividers, rather than separate rooms, or providers could add curtains or screens to areas where discussions often occur between doctors and patients or among professionals treating the patient.

Hospitals could ensure that areas housing patient files are supervised or locked.

Q: May physician's offices or pharmacists leave messages for patients at their homes, either on an answering machine or with a family member, to remind them of appointments or to inform them that a prescription is ready? May providers continue to mail appointment or prescription refill reminders to patients' homes?

A: Yes. The HIPAA Privacy Rule permits health care providers to communicate with patients regarding their health care. This includes communicating with patients at their homes, whether through the mail or by phone or in some other manner. In addition, the Rule does not prohibit covered entities from leaving messages for patients on their answering machines. However, to reasonably safeguard the individual's privacy, covered entities should take care to limit the amount of information disclosed on the answering machine. For example, a covered entity might want to consider leaving only its name and number and other information necessary to confirm an appointment, or ask the individual to call back.

A covered entity also may leave a message with a family member or other person who answers the phone when the patient is not home. The Privacy Rule permits covered entities to disclose limited information to family members, friends, or other persons regarding an individual's care, even when the individual is not present. However, covered entities should use professional judgment to assure that such disclosures are in the best interest of the individual and limit the information disclosed. See 45 CFR 164.510(b)(3).

In situations where a patient has requested that the covered entity communicate with him in a confidential manner, such as by alternative means or at an alternative location, the covered entity must accommodate that request, if reasonable. For example, the Department considers a request to receive mailings from the covered entity in a closed envelope rather than by postcard to be a reasonable request that should be accommodated. Similarly, a request to receive mail from the covered entity at a post office box rather than at home, or to receive calls at the office rather than at home are also considered to be reasonable requests, absent extenuating circumstances. See 45 CFR 164.522(b).

Q: May physicians offices use patient sign-in sheets or call out the names of their patients in their waiting rooms?

A: Yes. Covered entities, such as physician's offices, may use patient sign-in sheets or call out patient names in waiting rooms, so long as the information disclosed is appropriately limited. The HIPAA Privacy Rule explicitly permits the incidental disclosures that may result from this practice, for example, when other patients in a waiting room hear the identity of the person whose name is called, or see other patient names on a sign-in sheet. However, these incidental disclosures are permitted only when the covered entity has implemented reasonable safeguards and the minimum necessary standard, where appropriate. For example, the sign-in sheet may not display medical information that is not necessary for the purpose of signing in (e.g., the medical problem for which the patient is seeing the physician). See 45 CFR 164.502(a)(1)(iii).

Q: Are physicians and doctor's offices prohibited from maintaining patient medical charts at bedside or outside of exam rooms, or from engaging in other customary practices where the potential exists for patient information to be incidentally disclosed to others?

A: No. The HIPAA Privacy Rule does not prohibit covered entities from engaging in common and important health care practices; nor does it specify the specific measures that must be applied to protect an individual's privacy while engaging in these practices. Covered entities must implement reasonable safeguards to protect an individual's privacy. In addition, covered entities must reasonably restrict how much information is used and disclosed, where appropriate, as well as who within the entity has access to protected health information. Covered entities must evaluate what measures make sense in their environment and tailor their practices and safeguards to their particular circumstances.

For example, the Privacy Rule does not prohibit covered entities from engaging in the following practices, where reasonable precautions have been taken to protect an individual's privacy:

•Maintaining patient charts at bedside or outside of exam rooms, displaying patient names on the outside of patient charts, or displaying patient care signs (e.g., "high fall risk" or "diabetic diet") at patient bedside or at the doors of hospital rooms.

Possible safeguards may include: reasonably limiting access to these areas, ensuring that the area is supervised, escorting non-employees in the area, or placing patient charts in their holders with identifying information facing the wall or otherwise covered, rather than having health information about the patient visible to anyone who walks by.

•Announcing patient names and other information over a facility's public announcement system.

Possible safeguards may include: limiting the information disclosed over the system, such as referring the patients to a reception desk where they can receive further instructions in a more confidential manner.

•Use of X-ray lightboards or in-patient logs, such as whiteboards, at a nursing station.

Possible safeguards may include: if the X-ray lightboard is in an area generally not accessible by the public, or if the nursing station whiteboard is not readily visible to the public, or any other safeguard which reasonably limits incidental disclosures to the general public.

The above examples of possible safeguards are not intended to be exclusive. Covered entities may engage in any practice that reasonably safeguards protected health information to limit incidental uses and disclosures.

Q: A clinic customarily places patient charts in the plastic box outside an exam room. It does not want the record left unattended with the patient, and physicians want the record close by for fast review right before they walk into the exam room. Will the HIPAA Privacy Rule allow the clinic to continue this practice?

A: Yes, the Privacy Rule permits this practice as long as the clinic takes reasonable and appropriate measures to protect the patient's privacy. The physician or other health care professionals use the patient charts for treatment purposes. Incidental disclosures to others that might occur as a result of the charts being left in the box are permitted, if the minimum necessary and reasonable safeguards requirements are met. See 45 CFR 164.502(a)(1)(iii). As the purpose of leaving the chart in the box is to provide the physician with access to the medical information relevant to the examination, the minimum necessary requirement would be satisfied. Examples of measures that could be reasonable and appropriate to safeguard the patient chart in such a situation would be limiting access to certain areas, ensuring that the area is supervised, escorting non-employees in the area, or placing the patient chart in the box with the front cover facing the wall rather than having protected health information about the patient visible to anyone who walks by. Each covered entity must evaluate what measures are reasonable and appropriate in its environment. Covered entities may tailor measures to their particular circumstances. See 45 CFR 164.530(c).

Q: A hospital customarily displays patients' names next to the door of the hospital rooms that they occupy. Will the HIPAA Privacy Rule allow the hospital to continue this practice?

A: The Privacy Rule explicitly permits certain incidental disclosures that occur as a by-product of an otherwise permitted disclosure—for example, the disclosure to other patients in a waiting room of the identity of the person whose name is called. In this case, disclosure of patient names by posting on the wall is permitted by the Privacy Rule, if the use or disclosure is for treatment (for example, to ensure that patient care is provided to the correct individual) or health care operations purposes (for example, as a service for patients and their families). The disclosure of such information to other persons (such as other visitors) that will likely also occur due to the posting is an incidental disclosure.

Incidental disclosures are permitted only to the extent that the covered entity has applied reasonable and appropriate safeguards and implemented the minimum necessary standard, where appropriate. See 45 CFR 164.502(a)(1)(iii). In this case, it would appear that the disclosure of names is the minimum necessary for the purposes of the permitted uses or disclosures described above, and there do not appear to be additional safeguards that would be reasonable to take in these circumstances. However, each covered entity must evaluate what measures are reasonable and appropriate in its environment. Covered entities may tailor measures to their particular circumstances.

Q: May mental health practitioners or other specialists provide therapy to patients in a group setting where other patients and family members are present?

A: Yes. Disclosures of protected health information in a group therapy setting are treatment disclosures and, thus, may be made without an individual's authorization. Furthermore, the HIPAA Privacy Rule generally permits a covered entity to disclose protected health information to a family member or other person involved in the individual's care. Where the individual is present during the disclosure, the covered entity may disclose protected health information if it is reasonable to infer from the circumstances that the individual does not object to the disclosure. Absent countervailing circumstances, the individual's agreement to participate in group therapy or family discussions is a good basis for inferring the individual's agreement.

Q: Are covered entities required to document incidental disclosures permitted by the HIPAA Privacy Rule, in an accounting of disclosures provided to an individual?

A: No. The Privacy Rule includes a specific exception from the accounting standard for incidental disclosures permitted by the Rule. See 45 CFR 164.528(a)(1).

Q: Do the HIPAA Privacy Rule's provisions permitting certain incidental uses and disclosures apply only to treatment situations or discussions among health care providers?

A: No. The provisions apply universally to incidental uses and disclosures that result from any use or disclosure permitted under the Privacy Rule, and not just to incidental uses and disclosures resulting from treatment communications, or only to communications among health care providers or other medical staff. For example:

A provider may instruct an administrative staff member to bill a patient for a particular procedure, and may be overheard by one or more persons in the waiting room.

A health plan employee discussing a patient's health care claim on the phone may be overheard by another employee who is not authorized to handle patient information.

If the provider and the health plan employee made reasonable efforts to avoid being overheard and reasonably limited the information shared, an incidental use or disclosure resulting from such conversations would be permissible under the Rule.

Q: Is a covered entity required to prevent any incidental use or disclosure of protected health information?

A: No. The HIPAA Privacy Rule does not require that all risk of incidental use or disclosure be eliminated to satisfy its standards. Rather, the Rule requires only that covered entities implement reasonable safeguards to limit incidental uses or disclosures. See 45 CFR 164.530(c)(2).

MINIMUM NECESSARY
[*45 CFR 164.502(b), 164.514(d)*]

Background

The minimum necessary standard, a key protection of the HIPAA Privacy Rule, is derived from confidentiality codes and practices in common use today. It is based on sound current practice that protected health information should not be used or disclosed when it is not necessary to satisfy a particular purpose or carry out a function. The minimum necessary standard requires covered entities to evaluate their practices and enhance safeguards as needed to limit unnecessary or inappropriate access to and disclosure of protected health information. The Privacy Rule's requirements for minimum necessary are designed to be sufficiently flexible to accommodate the various circumstances of any covered entity.

How the Rule Works

The Privacy Rule generally requires covered entities to take reasonable steps to limit the use or disclosure of, and requests for, protected health information to the minimum necessary to accomplish the intended purpose. The minimum necessary standard does not apply to the following:

Disclosures to or requests by a health care provider for treatment purposes.

Disclosures to the individual who is the subject of the information.

Uses or disclosures made pursuant to an individual's authorization.

Uses or disclosures required for compliance with the Health Insurance Portability and Accountability Act (HIPAA) Administrative Simplification Rules.

Disclosures to the Department of Health and Human Services (HHS) when disclosure of information is required under the Privacy Rule for enforcement purposes.

Uses or disclosures that are required by other law.

The implementation specifications for this provision require a covered entity to develop and implement policies and procedures appropriate for its own organization, reflecting the entity's business practices and workforce. While guidance cannot anticipate every question or factual application of the minimum necessary standard to each specific industry context, where it would be generally helpful we will seek to provide additional clarification on this issue in the future. In addition, the Department will continue to monitor the workability of the minimum necessary standard and consider proposing revisions, where appropriate, to ensure that the Rule does not hinder timely access to quality health care.

Uses and Disclosures of, and Requests for, Protected Health Information. For uses of protected health information, the covered entity's policies and procedures must identify the persons or classes of persons within the covered entity who need access to the information to carry out their job duties, the categories or types of protected health information needed, and conditions appropriate to such access. For example, hospitals may implement policies that permit doctors, nurses, or others involved in treatment to have access to the entire medical record, as needed. Case-by-case review of each use is not required. Where the entire medical record is necessary, the covered entity's policies and procedures must state so explicitly and include a justification.

For routine or recurring requests and disclosures, the policies and procedures may be standard protocols and must limit the protected health information disclosed or requested to that which is the minimum necessary for that particular type of disclosure or request. Individual review of each disclosure or request is not required.

For non-routine disclosures and requests, covered entities must develop reasonable criteria for determining and limiting the disclosure or request to only the minimum amount of protected health information necessary to accomplish the purpose of a non-routine disclosure or request. Non-routine disclosures and requests must be reviewed on an individual basis in accordance with these criteria and limited accordingly.

Of course, where protected health information is disclosed to, or requested by, health care providers for treatment purposes, the minimum necessary standard does not apply.

Reasonable Reliance. In certain circumstances, the Privacy Rule permits a covered entity to rely on the judgment of the party requesting the disclosure as to the minimum amount of information that is needed. Such reliance must be reasonable under the particular circumstances of the request. This reliance is permitted when the request is made by:

A public official or agency who states that the information requested is the minimum necessary for a purpose permitted under 45 CFR 164.512 of the Rule, such as for public health purposes (45 CFR 164.512(b)).

Another covered entity.

A professional who is a workforce member or business associate of the covered entity holding the information and who states that the information requested is the minimum necessary for the stated purpose.

A researcher with appropriate documentation from an Institutional Review Board (IRB) or Privacy Board.

The Rule does not require such reliance, however, and the covered entity always retains discretion to make its own minimum necessary determination for disclosures to which the standard applies.

MINIMUM NECESSARY

Frequently Asked Questions

Q: How are covered entities expected to determine what is the minimum necessary information that can be used, disclosed, or requested for a particular purpose?

A: The HIPAA Privacy Rule requires a covered entity to make reasonable efforts to limit use, disclosure of, and requests for protected health information to the minimum necessary to accomplish the intended purpose. To allow covered entities the flexibility to address their unique circumstances, the Rule requires covered entities to make their own assessment of what protected health information is reasonably necessary for a particular purpose, given the characteristics of their business and workforce, and to implement policies and procedures accordingly. This is not an absolute standard and covered entities need not limit information uses or disclosures to those that are absolutely needed to serve the purpose. Rather, this is a reasonableness standard that calls for an approach consistent with the best practices and guidelines already used by many providers and plans today to limit the unnecessary sharing of medical information.

The minimum necessary standard requires covered entities to evaluate their practices and enhance protections as needed to limit unnecessary or inappropriate access to protected health information. It is intended to reflect and be consistent with, not override, professional judgment and standards. Therefore, it is expected that covered entities will utilize the input of prudent professionals involved in health care activities when developing policies and procedures that appropriately limit access to personal health information without sacrificing the quality of health care.

Q: Won't the HIPAA Privacy Rule's minimum necessary restrictions impede the delivery of quality health care by preventing or hindering necessary exchanges of patient medical information among health care providers involved in treatment?

A: No. Disclosures for treatment purposes (including requests for disclosures) between health care providers are explicitly exempted from the minimum necessary requirements.

Uses of protected health information for treatment are not exempt from the minimum necessary standard. However, the Privacy Rule provides the covered entity with substantial discretion with respect to how it implements the minimum necessary standard, and appropriately and reasonably limits access to identifiable health information within the covered entity. The Rule recognizes that the covered entity is in the best position to know and determine who in its workforce needs access to personal health information to perform their jobs. Therefore, the covered entity may develop role-based access policies that allow its health care providers and other employees, as appropriate, access to patient information, including entire medical records, for treatment purposes.

Q: Do the HIPAA Privacy Rule's minimum necessary requirements prohibit medical residents, medical students, nursing students, and other medical trainees from accessing patients' medical information in the course of their training?

A: No. The definition of "health care operations" in the Privacy Rule provides for "conducting training programs in which students, trainees, or practitioners in areas of health care learn under supervision to practice or improve their skills as health care providers." Covered entities can shape their policies and procedures for minimum necessary uses and disclosures to permit medical trainees access to patients' medical information, including entire medical records.

Q: Must the HIPAA Privacy Rule's minimum necessary standard be applied to uses or disclosures that are authorized by an individual?

A: No. Uses and disclosures that are authorized by the individual are exempt from the minimum necessary requirements. For example, if a covered health care provider receives an individual's authorization to disclose medical information to a life insurer for underwriting purposes, the provider is permitted to disclose the information requested on the authorization without making any minimum necessary determination. The authorization must meet the requirements of 45 CFR 164.508.

Q: Are providers required to make a minimum necessary determination to disclose to Federal or State agencies, such as the Social Security Administration (SSA) or its affiliated State agencies, for individuals' applications for Federal or State benefits?

A: No. These disclosures must be authorized by an individual and, therefore, are exempt from the HIPAA Privacy Rule's minimum necessary requirements. Furthermore, use of the provider's own authorization form is not required. Providers can accept an agency's authorization form as long as it meets the requirements of 45 CFR 164.508 of the Privacy Rule. For example, disclosures to SSA (or its affiliated State agencies) for purposes of determining eligibility for disability benefits are currently made subject to an individual's completed SSA authorization form. After the compliance date, the current process may continue subject only to modest changes in the SSA authorization form to conform to the requirements in 45 CFR 164.508.

Q: Doesn't the HIPAA Privacy Rule's minimum necessary standard conflict with the HIPAA transactions standards?

A: No, because the Privacy Rule exempts from the minimum necessary standard any uses or disclosures that are required for compliance with the applicable requirements of the transactions standards, including disclosures of all data elements that are required or situationally required in those transactions. See 45 CFR 164.502(b)(2)(vi). However, covered entities have significant discretion as to the information included in the transactions as optional data elements. Therefore, the minimum necessary standard does apply to the optional data elements. The transactions standard adopted for the outpatient pharmacy sector is an example of a standard that uses optional data elements. The health plan, or payer, currently specifies which of the optional data elements are needed for payment of its particular pharmacy claims. The health plan or its business associates must apply the minimum necessary standard when requesting this information. In this example, a pharmacist may reasonably rely on the health plan's request for information as the minimum necessary for the intended disclosure. For example, as part of a routine protocol, the name of the individual may be requested by the payer as the minimum necessary to validate the identity of the claimant or for drug interaction or other patient safety reasons.

Q: Does the HIPAA Privacy Rule strictly prohibit the use, disclosure, or request of an entire medical record? If not, are case-by-case justifications required each time an entire medical record is disclosed?

A: No. The Privacy Rule does not prohibit the use, disclosure, or request of an entire medical record; and a covered entity may use, disclose, or request an entire medical record without a case-by-case justification, if the covered entity has documented in its policies and procedures that the entire medical record is the amount reasonably necessary for certain identified purposes. For uses, the policies and procedures would identify those persons or classes of person in the workforce that need to see the entire medical record and the conditions, if any, that are appropriate for such access. Policies and procedures for routine disclosures and requests and the criteria used for non-routine disclosures and requests would identify the circumstances under which disclosing or requesting the entire medical record is reasonably necessary for particular purposes.

The Privacy Rule does not require that a justification be provided with respect to each distinct medical record.

Finally, no justification is needed in those instances where the minimum necessary standard does not apply, such as disclosures to or requests by a health care provider for treatment purposes or disclosures to the individual who is the subject of the protected health information.

Q: A provider might have a patient's medical record that contains older portions of a medical record that were created by another or previous provider. Will the HIPAA Privacy Rule permit a provider who is a covered entity to disclose a complete medical record even though portions of the record were created by other providers?

A: Yes, the Privacy Rule permits a provider who is a covered entity to disclose a complete medical record including portions that were created by another provider, assuming that the disclosure is for a purpose permitted by the Privacy Rule, such as treatment.

Q: In limiting access, are covered entities required to completely restructure existing workflow systems, including redesigning office space and upgrading computer systems, in order to comply with the HIPAA Privacy Rule's minimum necessary requirements?

A: No. The basic standard for minimum necessary uses requires that covered entities make reasonable efforts to limit access to protected health information to those in the workforce that need access based on their roles in the covered entity.

The Department generally does not consider facility redesigns as necessary to meet the reasonableness standard for minimum necessary uses. However, covered entities may need to make certain adjustments to their facilities to minimize access, such as isolating and locking file cabinets or records rooms, or providing additional security, such as passwords, on computers maintaining personal information.

Covered entities should also take into account their ability to configure their record systems to allow access to only certain fields, and the practicality of organizing systems to allow this capacity. For example, it may not be reasonable for a small, solo practitioner who has largely a paper-based records system to limit access of employees with certain functions to only limited fields in a patient record, while other employees have access to the complete record. In this case, appropriate training of employees may be sufficient. Alternatively, a hospital with an electronic patient record system may reasonably implement such controls, and therefore, may choose to limit access in this manner to comply with the Privacy Rule.

Q: Is a covered entity required to apply the HIPAA Privacy Rule's minimum necessary standard to a disclosure of protected health information it makes to another covered entity?

A: Covered entities are required to apply the minimum necessary standard to their own requests for protected health information. One covered entity may reasonably rely on another covered entity's request as the minimum necessary, and then does not need to engage in a separate minimum necessary determination. See 45 CFR 164.514(d)(3)(iii). However, if a covered entity does not agree that the amount of information requested by another covered entity is reasonably necessary for the purpose, it is up to both covered entities to negotiate a resolution of the dispute as to the amount of information needed. Nothing in the Privacy Rule prevents a covered entity from discussing its concerns with another covered entity making a request, and negotiating an information exchange that meets the needs of both parties. Such discussions occur today and may continue after the compliance date of the Privacy Rule.

Q: May a covered entity accept documentation of an external Institutional Review Board's (IRB) waiver of authorization for purposes of reasonably relying on the request as the minimum necessary?

A: Yes. The HIPAA Privacy Rule explicitly permits a covered entity to reasonably rely on a researcher's documentation of an Institutional Review Board (IRB) or Privacy Board waiver of authorization pursuant to 45 CFR 164.512(i) that the information requested is the minimum necessary for the research purpose. See 45 CFR 164.514(d)(3)(iii). This is true regardless of whether the documentation is obtained from an external IRB or Privacy Board or from one that is associated with the covered entity.

Q: Are business associates required to restrict their uses and disclosures to the minimum necessary? May a covered entity reasonably rely on a request from a covered entity's business associate as the minimum necessary?

A: A covered entity's contract with a business associate may not authorize the business associate to use or further disclose the information in a manner that would violate the HIPAA Privacy Rule if done by the covered entity. See 45 CFR 164.504(e)(2)(i). Thus, a business associate contract must limit the business associate's uses and disclosures of, as well as requests for, protected health information to be consistent with the covered entity's minimum necessary policies and procedures. Given that a business associate contract must limit a business associate's requests for protected health information on behalf of a covered entity to that which is reasonably necessary to accomplish the intended purpose, a covered entity is permitted to reasonably rely on such requests from a business associate of another covered entity as the minimum necessary.

PERSONAL REPRESENTATIVES

[*45 CFR 164.502(g)*]

Background

The HIPAA Privacy Rule establishes a foundation of Federally-protected rights which permit individuals to control certain uses and disclosures of their protected health information. Along with these rights, the Privacy Rule provides individuals with the ability to access and amend this information, and the right to an accounting of certain disclosures. The Department recognizes that there may be times when individuals are legally or otherwise incapable of exercising their rights, or simply choose to designate another to act on their behalf with respect to these rights. Under the Rule, a person authorized (under State or other applicable law, e.g., tribal or military law) to act on behalf of the individual in making health care related decisions is the individual's "personal representative." Section 164.502(g) provides when, and to what extent, the personal representative must be treated as the individual for purposes of the Rule. In addition to these formal designations of a personal representative, the Rule at 45 CFR 164.510(b) addresses situations in which persons are involved in the individual's health care but are not expressly authorized to act on the individual's behalf.

How the Rule Works

General Provisions. Except as otherwise provided in 45 CFR 164.502(g), the Privacy Rule requires covered entities to treat an individual's personal representative as the individual with respect to uses and disclosures of the individual's protected health information, as well as the individual's rights under the Rule.

The personal representative stands in the shoes of the individual and has the ability to act for the individual and exercise the individual's rights. For instance, covered entities must provide the individual's personal representative with an accounting of disclosures in accordance with 45 CFR 164.528, as well as provide the personal representative access to the individual's protected health information in accordance with 45 CFR 164.524 to the extent such information is relevant to such representation. In addition to exercising the individual's rights under the Rule, a personal representative may also authorize disclosures of the individual's protected health information.

In general, the scope of the personal representative's authority to act for the individual under the Privacy Rule derives from his or her authority under applicable law to make health care decisions for the individual. Where the person has broad authority to act on the behalf of a living individual in making decisions related to health care, such as a parent with respect to a minor child or a legal guardian of a mentally incompetent adult, the covered entity must treat the personal representative as the individual for all purposes under the Rule, unless an exception applies. (See below with respect to abuse, neglect or endangerment situations, and the application of State law in the context of parents and minors). Where the authority to act for the individual is limited or specific to particular health care decisions, the personal representative is to be treated as the individual only with respect to protected health information that is relevant to the representation. For example, a person with an individual's limited health care power of attorney regarding only a specific treatment, such as use of artificial life support, is that individual's personal representative only with respect to protected health information that relates to that health care decision. The covered entity should not treat that person as the individual for other purposes, such as to sign an authorization for the disclosure of protected health information for marketing purposes. Finally, where the person has authority to act on the behalf of a deceased individual or his estate, which does not have to include the authority to make decisions related to health care, the covered entity must treat the personal representative as the individual for all purposes under the Rule. State or other law should be consulted to determine the authority of the personal representative to receive or access the individual's protected health information.

Who Must Be Recognized as the Individual's Personal Representative. The following chart displays who must be recognized as the personal representative for a category of individuals:

If the Individual Is:	The Personal Representative Is:
An Adult or An Emancipated Minor	A person with legal authority to make health care decisions on behalf of the individual *Examples*: Health care power of attorney; Court appointed legal guardian; General power of attorney
An Unemancipated Minor	A parent, guardian, or other person acting *in loco parentis* with legal authority to make health care decisions on behalf of the minor child *Exceptions*: See parents and minors discussion below.
Deceased	A person with legal authority to act on behalf of the decedent or the estate (not restricted to health care decisions) *Examples*: Executor of the estate; Next of kin or other family member; Durable power of attorney

Parents and Unemancipated Minors. The Privacy Rule defers to State or other applicable laws that address the ability of a parent, guardian, or other person acting *in loco parentis* (collectively, "parent") to obtain health information about a minor child. In most cases under the Rule, the parent is the personal representative of the minor child and can exercise the minor's rights with respect to protected health information, because the parent usually has the authority to make health care decisions about his or her minor child. Regardless of whether a parent is the personal representative, the Privacy Rule permits a covered entity to disclose to a parent, or provide the parent with access to, a minor child's protected health information when and to the extent it is expressly permitted or required by State or other laws (including relevant case law). Likewise, the Privacy Rule prohibits a covered entity from disclosing a minor child's protected health information to a parent, or providing a parent with access to, such information when and to the extent it is expressly prohibited under State or other laws (including relevant case law). Thus, State and other applicable law governs when such law explicitly requires, permits, or prohibits the disclosure of, or access to, the health information about a minor child.

The Privacy Rule specifies three circumstances in which the parent is not the "personal representative" with respect to certain health information about his or her minor child. These exceptions generally track the ability of certain minors to obtain specified health care without parental consent under State or other laws, or standards of professional practice. In these situations, the parent does not control the minor's health care decisions, and thus under the Rule, does not control the protected health information related to that care. The three exceptional circumstances when a parent is not the minor's personal representative are:

When State or other law does not require the consent of a parent or other person before a minor can obtain a particular health care service, and the minor consents to the health care service;

Example: A State law provides an adolescent the right to obtain mental health treatment without the consent of his or her parent, and the adolescent consents to such treatment without the parent's consent.

When a court determines or other law authorizes someone other than the parent to make treatment decisions for a minor;

Example: A court may grant authority to make health care decisions for the minor to an adult other than the parent, to the minor, or the court may make the decision(s) itself.

When a parent agrees to a confidential relationship between the minor and the physician.

Example: A physician asks the parent of a 16-year-old if the physician can talk with the child confidentially about a medical condition and the parent agrees.

Even in these exceptional circumstances, where the parent is not the "personal representative" of the minor, the Privacy Rule defers to State or other laws that require, permit, or prohibit the covered entity to disclose to a parent, or provide the parent access to, a minor child's protected health information. Further, in these situations, if State or other law is silent or unclear concerning parental access to the minor's protected health information, a covered entity has discretion to provide or deny a parent with access to the minor's health information, if doing so is consistent with State or other applicable law, and provided the decision is made by a licensed health care professional in the exercise of professional judgment.

Abuse, Neglect, and Endangerment Situations. When a physician or other covered entity reasonably believes that an individual, including an unemancipated minor, has been or may be subjected to domestic violence, abuse or neglect by the personal representative, or that treating a person as an individual's personal representative could endanger the individual, the covered entity may choose not to treat that person as the individual's personal representative, if in the exercise of professional judgment, doing so would not be in the best interests of the individual. For example, if a physician reasonably believes that disclosing information about an incompetent elderly individual to the individual's personal representative would endanger that individual, the Privacy Rule permits the physician to decline to make such disclosure.

PERSONAL REPRESENTATIVES

Frequently Asked Questions

Q. Does the HIPAA Privacy Rule change the way in which an individual can grant another person health care power of attorney?

A. No. Nothing in the Privacy Rule changes the way in which an individual grants another person power of attorney for health care decisions. State law (or other law) regarding health care powers of attorney continue to apply. The intent of the provisions regarding personal representatives was to complement, not interfere with or change, current practice regarding health care powers of attorney or the designation of other personal representatives. Such designations are formal, legal actions which give others the ability to exercise the rights of, or make treatment decisions related to, an individual. The Privacy Rule provisions regarding personal representatives generally grant persons, who have authority to make health care decisions for an individual under other law, the ability to exercise the rights of that individual with respect to health information.

Q. If someone has health care power of attorney for an individual, can they obtain access to that individual's medical record?

A. Yes, an individual that has been given a health care power of attorney will have the right to access the medical records of the individual related to such representation to the extent permitted by the HIPAA Privacy Rule at 45 CFR 164.524. However, when a physician or other covered entity reasonably believes that an individual, including an unemancipated minor, has been or may be subjected to domestic violence, abuse or neglect by the personal representative, or that treating a person as an individual's personal representative could endanger the individual, the covered entity may choose not to treat that person as the individual's personal representative, if in the exercise of professional judgment, doing so would not be in the best interests of the individual.

Q. Can the personal representative of an adult or emancipated minor obtain access to the individual's medical record?

A. The HIPAA Privacy Rule treats an adult or emancipated minor's personal representative as the individual for purposes of the Rule regarding the health care matters that relate to the representation, including the right of access under 45 CFR 164.524. The scope of access will depend on the authority granted to the personal representative by other law. If the personal representative is authorized to make health care decisions, generally, then the personal representative may have access to the individual's protected health information regarding health care in general. On the other hand, if the authority is limited, the personal representative may have access only to protected health information that may be relevant to making decisions within the personal representative's authority. For example, if a personal representative's authority is limited to authorizing artificial life support, then the personal representative's access to protected health information is limited to that information which may be relevant to decisions about artificial life support.

There is an exception to the general rule that a covered entity must treat an adult or emancipated minor's personal representative as the individual. Specifically, the Privacy Rule does not require a covered entity to treat a personal representative as the individual if, in the exercise of professional judgment, it believes doing so would not be in the best interest of the individual because of a reasonable belief that the individual has been or may be subject to domestic violence, abuse or neglect by the personal representative, or that doing so would otherwise endanger the individual. This exception applies to adults and both emancipated and unemancipated minors who may be subject to abuse or neglect by their personal representatives.

Q: How can family members of a deceased individual obtain the deceased individual's protected health information that is relevant to their own health care?

A: The HIPAA Privacy Rule recognizes that a deceased individual's protected health information may be relevant to a family member's health care. The Rule provides two ways for a surviving family member to obtain the protected health information of a deceased relative. First, disclosures of protected health information for treatment purposes—even the treatment of another individual—do not require an authorization; thus, a covered entity may disclose a decedent's protected health information, without authorization, to the health care provider who is treating the surviving relative. Second, a covered entity must treat a deceased individual's legally authorized executor or administrator, or a person who is otherwise legally authorized to act on the behalf of the deceased individual or his estate, as a personal representative with respect to protected health information relevant to such representation. Therefore, if it is within the scope of such personal representative's authority under other law, the Rule permits the personal representative to obtain the information or provide the appropriate authorization for its disclosure.

Q: Does the HIPA Privacy Rule address when a person may not be the appropriate person to control an individual's protected health information?

A: Generally, no. The Rule defers to State and other laws that address the fitness of a person to act on an individual's behalf. However, a covered entity does not have to treat a personal representative as the individual when it reasonably believes, in the exercise of professional judgment, the individual is subject to domestic violence, abuse or neglect by the personal representative, or doing so would otherwise endanger the individual.

Q: Does a power of attorney given to a person for purposes other than health care, such as a power of attorney to close on real estate, authorize that person to access an individual's health information as that individual's personal representative?

A: No. Except with respect to decedents, a covered entity must treat a personal representative as the individual only when that person has authority under other law to act on the individual's behalf on matters related to health care. A power of attorney that does not include decisions related to health care in its scope would not authorize the holder to exercise the individual's rights under the HIPAA Privacy Rule. Further, a covered entity does not have to treat a personal representative as the individual if, in the exercise of professional judgment, it believes doing so would not be in the best interest of the individual because of a reasonable belief that the individual has been or may be subject to domestic violence, abuse or neglect by the personal representative, or that doing so would otherwise endanger the individual.

With respect to personal representatives of deceased individuals, the Privacy Rule requires a covered entity to treat the personal representative as the individual as long as the person has the authority under law to act for the decedent or the estate. The power of attorney would have to be valid after the individual's death to qualify the holder as the personal representative of the decedent.

Q: May adults with mental retardation control their protected health information if they are able to authorize uses and disclosures of their protected health information?

A: Individuals may control their protected health information under the HIPAA Privacy Rule to the extent State or other law permits them to act on their own behalf. Further, even if an individual is deemed incompetent under State or other law to act on his or her own behalf, covered entities may decline a request by a personal representative for protected health information if the individual objects to the disclosure (or for any other reason), and the disclosure is merely permitted, but not required, under the Rule.

However, covered entities must make disclosures that are required under the Rule (i.e., disclosures to the Secretary under subpart C of part 160 regarding enforcement of the Rule, and to the individual under 45 CFR 164.524 and 164.528 with respect to the individual's right of access to his or her protected health information and an accounting of disclosures, respectively). Consequently, with respect to the individual's right of access to protected health information and for an accounting of disclosures, covered entities must provide the individual's personal representative access to the individual's protected health information or an accounting of disclosures upon the request of the personal representative, unless the covered entity, in the exercise of professional judgment, believes doing so would not be in the best interest of the individual because of a reasonable belief that the individual may be subject to domestic violence, abuse or neglect by the personal representative, or that doing so would otherwise endanger the individual. The Rule allows a specified time period before a covered entity must act on such a request; and during this interim period, an individual and his personal representative will have an opportunity to resolve any dispute they may have concerning the request.

Q: How does a covered entity identify an individual's personal representative?

A: State or other law determines who is authorized to act on an individual's behalf, thus the Privacy Rule does not address how personal representatives should be identified. Covered entities should continue to identify personal representatives the same way they have in the past. However, the HIPAA Privacy Rule does require covered entities to verify a personal representative's authority in accordance with 45 CFR 164.514(h).

Q. Does the HIPAA Privacy Rule allow parents the right to see their children's medical records?

A. Yes, the Privacy Rule generally allows a parent to have access to the medical records about his or her child, as his or her minor child's personal representative when such access is not inconsistent with State or other law.

There are three situations when the parent would not be the minor's personal representative under the Privacy Rule. These exceptions are: (1) when the minor is the one who consents to care and the consent of the parent is not required under State or other applicable law; (2) when the minor obtains care at the direction of a court or a person appointed by the court; and (3) when, and to the extent that, the parent agrees that the minor and the health care provider may have a confidential relationship. However, even in these exceptional situations, the parent may have access to the medical records of the minor related to this treatment when State or other applicable law requires or permits such parental access. Parental access would be denied when State or other law prohibits such access. If State or other applicable law is silent on a parent's right of access in these cases, the licensed health care provider may exercise his or her professional judgment to the extent allowed by law to grant or deny parental access to the minor's medical information.

Finally, as is the case with respect to all personal representatives under the Privacy Rule, a provider may choose not to treat a parent as a personal representative when the provider reasonably believes, in his or her professional judgment, that the child has been or may be subjected to domestic violence, abuse or neglect, or that treating the parent as the child's personal representative could endanger the child.

Q: If a child receives emergency medical care without a parent's consent, can the parent get all information about the child's treatment and condition?

A: Generally, yes. Even though the parent did not consent to the treatment in this situation, the parent would be the child's personal representative under the HIPAA Privacy Rule. This would not be so when the parent does not have authority to act for the child (e.g., parental rights have been terminated), when expressly prohibited by State or other applicable law, or when the covered entity, in the exercise of professional judgment, believes that providing such information would not be in the best interest of the individual because of a reasonable belief that the individual may be subject to abuse or neglect by the personal representative, or that doing so would otherwise endanger the individual.

Q: Does the HIPAA Privacy Rule provide rights for children to be treated without parental consent?

A: No. The Privacy Rule does not address consent to treatment, nor does it preempt or change State or other laws that address consent to treatment. The Rule addresses access to, and disclosure of, health information, not the underlying treatment.

Q. When an individual reaches the age of majority or becomes emancipated, who controls the protected health information concerning health care services rendered while the individual was an unemancipated minor?

A: The individual who is the subject of the protected health information can exercise all rights granted by the HIPAA Privacy Rule with respect to all protected health information about him or her, including information obtained while the individual was an unemancipated minor consistent with State or other law. Generally, the parent would no longer be the personal representative of his or her child once the child reaches the age of majority or becomes emancipated, and therefore, would no longer control the health information about his or her child. Of course, any individual can have a personal representative – which may include a parent – who can exercise rights on his or her behalf.

Q. May a psychologist continue his practice to notify a parent before treating his or her minor child, even though the minor child is able to consent to such health care under State law?

A. The HIPAA Privacy Rule would defer to State or other applicable law that addresses the disclosure of health information to a parent about a minor child. If the minor child is permitted, under State law, to consent to such health care without the consent of her parent and does consent to such care, the provider may notify the parent when the State law explicitly requires or permits the health provider to do so. If State law permits the minor child to consent to such health care without parental consent, but is silent on parental notification, the provider would need the child's permission to notify a parent.

BUSINESS ASSOCIATES
[*45 CFR 164.502(e), 164.504(e), 164.532(d) and (e)*]

Background

By law, the HIPAA Privacy Rule applies only to covered entities – health plans, health care clearinghouses, and certain health care providers. However, most health care providers and health plans do not carry out all of their health care activities and functions by themselves. Instead, they often use the services of a variety of other persons or businesses. The Privacy Rule allows covered providers and health plans to disclose protected health information to these "business associates" if the providers or plans obtain satisfactory assurances that the business associate will use the information only for the purposes for which it was engaged by the covered entity, will safeguard the information from misuse, and will help the covered entity comply with some of the covered entity's duties under the Privacy Rule. Covered entities may disclose protected health information to an entity in its role as a business associate *only* to help the covered entity carry out its health care functions – not for the business associate's independent use or purposes, except as needed for the proper management and administration of the business associate.

How the Rule Works

General Provision. The Privacy Rule requires that a covered entity obtain satisfactory assurances from its business associate that the business associate will appropriately safeguard the protected health information it receives or creates on behalf of the covered entity. The satisfactory assurances must be in writing, whether in the form of a contract or other agreement between the covered entity and the business associate.

What Is a "Business Associate?" A "business associate" is a person or entity that performs certain functions or activities that involve the use or disclosure of protected health information on behalf of, or provides services to, a covered entity.

A member of the covered entity's workforce is not a business associate.

A covered health care provider, health plan, or health care clearinghouse can be a business associate of another covered entity.

The Privacy Rule lists some of the functions or activities, as well as the particular services, that make a person or entity a business associate, if the activity or service involves the use or disclosure of protected health information. The types of functions or activities that may make a person or entity a business associate include payment or health care operations activities, as well as other functions or activities regulated by the Administrative Simplification Rules.

Business associate functions and activities include: claims processing or administration; data analysis, processing or administration; utilization review; quality assurance; billing; benefit management; practice management; and repricing.

Business associate services are: legal; actuarial; accounting; consulting; data aggregation; management; administrative; accreditation; and financial.

See the definition of "business associate" at 45 CFR 160.103.

Examples of Business Associates.

A third party administrator that assists a health plan with claims processing.

A CPA firm whose accounting services to a health care provider involve access to protected health information.

An attorney whose legal services to a health plan involve access to protected health information.

A consultant that performs utilization reviews for a hospital.

A health care clearinghouse that translates a claim from a non-standard format into a standard transaction on behalf of a health care provider and forwards the processed transaction to a payer.

An independent medical transcriptionist that provides transcription services to a physician.

A pharmacy benefits manager that manages a health plan's pharmacist network.

Business Associate Contracts. A covered entity's contract or other written arrangement with its business associate must contain the elements specified at 45 CFR 164.504(e). For example, the contract must:

Describe the permitted and required uses of protected health information by the business associate;

Provide that the business associate will not use or further disclose the protected health information other than as permitted or required by the contract or as required by law; and

Require the business associate to use appropriate safeguards to prevent a use or disclosure of the protected health information other than as provided for by the contract.

Where a covered entity knows of a material breach or violation by the business associate of the contract or agreement, the covered entity is required to take reasonable steps to cure the breach or end the violation, and if such steps are unsuccessful, to terminate the contract or arrangement. If termination of the contract or agreement is not feasible, a covered entity is required to report the problem to the Department of Health and Human Services (HHS) Office for Civil Rights (OCR).

Sample business associate contract language is available on the HHS OCR Privacy of Health Information website at http://www.hhs.gov/ocr/hipaa/contractprov.html.

Transition Provisions for Existing Contracts. Covered entities (other than small health plans) that have an existing contract (or other written agreement) with a business associate prior to October 15, 2002, are permitted to continue to operate under that contract for up to one additional year beyond the April 14, 2003 compliance date, provided that the contract is not renewed or modified prior to April 14, 2003. This transition period applies only to written contracts or other written arrangements. Oral contracts or other arrangements are not eligible for the transition period. Covered entities with contracts that qualify are permitted to continue to operate under those contracts with their business associates until April 14, 2004, or until the contract is renewed or modified, whichever is sooner, regardless of whether the contract meets the Rule's applicable contract requirements at 45 CFR 164.502(e) and 164.504(e). A covered entity must otherwise comply with the Privacy Rule, such as making only permissible disclosures to the business associate and permitting individuals to exercise their rights under the Rule.

See 45 CFR 164.532(d) and (e).

Exceptions to the Business Associate Standard. The Privacy Rule includes the following exceptions to the business associate standard. See 45 CFR 164.502(e). In these situations, a covered entity is not required to have a business associate contract or other written agreement in place before protected health information may be disclosed to the person or entity.

Disclosures by a covered entity to a health care provider for treatment of the individual.

For example:

<A hospital is not required to have a business associate contract with the specialist to whom it refers a patient and transmits the patient's medical chart for treatment purposes.

<A physician is not required to have a business associate contract with a laboratory as a condition of disclosing protected health information for the treatment of an individual.
<A hospital laboratory is not required to have a business associate contract to disclose protected health information to a reference laboratory for treatment of the individual.

Disclosures to a health plan sponsor, such as an employer, by a group health plan, or by the health insurance issuer or HMO that provides the health insurance benefits or coverage for the group health plan, provided that the group health plan's documents have been amended to limit the disclosures or one of the exceptions at 45 CFR 164.504(f) have been met.

The collection and sharing of protected health information by a health plan that is a public benefits program, such as Medicare, and an agency other than the agency administering the health plan, such as the Social Security Administration, that collects protected health information to determine eligibility or enrollment, or determines eligibility or enrollment, for the government program, where the joint activities are authorized by law.

<u>Other Situations in Which a Business Associate Contract Is NOT Required.</u>

When a health care provider discloses protected health information to a health plan for payment purposes, or when the health care provider simply accepts a discounted rate to participate in the health plan's network. A provider that submits a claim to a health plan and a health plan that assesses and pays the claim are each acting on its own behalf as a covered entity, and not as the "business associate" of the other.

With persons or organizations (e.g., janitorial service or electrician) whose functions or services do not involve the use or disclosure of protected health information, and where any access to protected health information by such persons would be incidental, if at all.

With a person or organization that acts merely as a conduit for protected health information, for example, the US Postal Service, certain private couriers, and their electronic equivalents.

Among covered entities who participate in an organized health care arrangement (OHCA) to make disclosures that relate to the joint health care activities of the OHCA.

Where a group health plan purchases insurance from a health insurance issuer or HMO. The relationship between the group health plan and the health insurance issuer or HMO is defined by the Privacy Rule as an OHCA, with respect to the individuals they jointly serve or have served. Thus, these covered entities are permitted to share protected health information that relates to the joint health care activities of the OHCA.

Where one covered entity purchases a health plan product or other insurance, for example, reinsurance, from an insurer. Each entity is acting on its own behalf when the covered entity purchases the insurance benefits, and when the covered entity submits a claim to the insurer and the insurer pays the claim.

To disclose protected health information to a researcher for research purposes, either with patient authorization, pursuant to a waiver under 45 CFR 164.512(i), or as a limited data set pursuant to 45 CFR 164.514(e). Because the researcher is not conducting a function or activity regulated by the Administrative Simplification Rules, such as payment or health care operations, or providing one of the services listed in the definition of "business associate" at 45 CFR 160.103, the researcher is not a business associate of the covered entity, and no business associate agreement is required.

When a financial institution processes consumer-conducted financial transactions by debit, credit, or other payment card, clears checks, initiates or processes electronic funds transfers, or conducts any other activity that directly facilitates or effects the transfer of funds for payment for health care or health plan premiums. When it conducts these activities, the financial institution is providing its normal banking or other financial transaction services to its customers; it is not performing a function or activity for, or on behalf of, the covered entity.

BUSINESS ASSOCIATES

<u>Frequently Asked Questions</u>

Q: Has the Secretary exceeded the HIPAA statutory authority by requiring "satisfactory assurances" for disclosures to business associates?

A: No. The Health Insurance Portability and Accountability Act of 1996 (HIPAA) gives the Secretary authority to directly regulate health plans, health care clearinghouses, and certain health care providers. It also grants the Department explicit authority to regulate the uses and disclosures of protected health information maintained and transmitted by covered entities. Therefore, the Department does have the authority to condition the disclosure of protected health information by a covered entity to a business associate on the covered entity's having a written contract with that business associate.

Q: Has the Secretary exceeded the HIPAA statutory authority by requiring "business associates" to comply with the Privacy Rule, even if that requirement is through a contract?

A: The HIPAA Privacy Rule does not "pass through" its requirements to business associates or otherwise cause business associates to comply with the terms of the Rule. The assurances that covered entities must obtain prior to disclosing protected health information to business associates create a set of contractual obligations far narrower than the provisions of the Rule, to protect information generally and help the covered entity comply with its obligations under the Rule.

Business associates, however, are not subject to the requirements of the Privacy Rule, and the Secretary cannot impose civil monetary penalties on a business associate for breach of its business associate contract with the covered entity, unless the business associate is itself a covered entity. For example, covered entities do not need to ask their business associates to agree to appoint a privacy officer, or develop policies and procedures for use and disclosure of protected health information.

Q: What are a covered entity's obligations under the HIPAA Privacy Rule with respect to protected health information held by a business associate during the contract transition period?

A: During the contract transition period, covered entities must observe the following responsibilities with respect to protected health information held by their business associates:

Make information available to the Secretary, including information held by a business associate, as necessary for the Secretary to determine compliance by the covered entity.

Fulfill an individual's rights to access and amend his or her protected health information contained in a designated record set, including information held by a business associate, if appropriate, and receive an accounting of disclosures by a business associate.

Mitigate, to the extent practicable, any harmful effect that is known to the covered entity of an impermissible use or disclosure of protected health information by its business associate.

Covered entities are required to ensure, in whatever reasonable manner deemed effective by the covered entity, the appropriate cooperation by their business associates in meeting these requirements during the transition period.

However, a covered entity is not required to obtain the satisfactory assurances required by the Privacy Rule from a business associate to which the transition period applies.

Of course, even during the transition period, covered entities still may only disclose protected health information to a business associate for a purpose permitted under the Rule and must apply the minimum necessary standard, as appropriate, to such disclosures.

Q: I have an existing contract with a business associate that will renew automatically before April 14, 2003. Does this automatic renewal mean I have to modify the contract by April 14, 2003, to make it compliant with the HIPAA Privacy Rule's business associate contract provisions or can I still take advantage of the transition period?

A: Evergreen or other contracts that renew automatically without any change in terms or other action by the parties and that exist by October 15, 2002, are eligible for the transition period. The automatic renewal of a contract itself does not terminate qualification for the transition period, or the transition period itself. Renewal or modification for the purposes of the transition provisions requires action by the parties involved. For example, an automatic inflation adjustment to the price of a contract does not trigger the end of the transition period, nor make the contract ineligible for the transition period if the adjustment occurs before April 14, 2003.

Q: Is a covered entity liable for, or required to monitor, the actions of its business associates?

A: No. The HIPAA Privacy Rule requires covered entities to enter into written contracts or other arrangements with business associates which protect the privacy of protected health information; but covered entities are not required to monitor or oversee the means by which their business associates carry out privacy safeguards or the extent to which the business associate abides by the privacy requirements of the contract. Nor is the covered entity responsible or liable for the actions of its business associates. However, if a covered entity finds out about a material breach or violation of the contract by the business associate, it must take reasonable steps to cure the breach or end the violation, and, if unsuccessful, terminate the contract with the business associate. If termination is not feasible (e.g., where there are no other viable business alternatives for the covered entity), the covered entity must report the problem to the Department of Health and Human Services Office for Civil Rights. See 45 CFR 164.504(e)(1).

With respect to business associates, a covered entity is considered to be out of compliance with the Privacy Rule if it fails to take the steps described above. If a covered entity is out of compliance with the Privacy Rule because of its failure to take these steps, further disclosures of protected health information to the business associate are not permitted. In cases where a covered entity is also a business associate, the covered entity is considered to be out of compliance with the Privacy Rule if it violates the satisfactory assurances it provided as a business associate of another covered entity.

Q: Instead of entering into a contract, can business associates self-certify or be certified by a third party as compliant with the HIPAA Privacy Rule?

A: No. A covered entity is required to enter into a contract or other written arrangement with a business associate that meets the requirements at 45 CFR 164.504(e).

Q: Are accreditation organizations business associates of the covered entities they accredit?

A: Yes. The HIPAA Privacy Rule explicitly defines organizations that accredit covered entities as business associates. See the definition of "business associate" at 45 CFR 160.103. Like other business associates, accreditation organizations provide a service to the covered entity which requires the sharing of protected health information. The business associate provisions may be satisfied by standard or model contract forms which could require little or no modification for each covered entity. As an alternative to the business associate contract, covered entities may disclose a limited data set of protected health information, not including direct identifiers, to an accreditation organization, subject to a data use agreement. See 45 CFR 164.514(e). If only a limited data set of protected health information is disclosed, the satisfactory assurances required of the business associate are satisfied by the data use agreement.

Q: Is a business associate contract required for a covered entity to disclose protected health information to a researcher?

A: No. Disclosures from a covered entity to a researcher for research purposes do not require a business associate contract, even in those instances where the covered entity has hired the researcher to perform research on the covered entity's own behalf. A business associate agreement is required only where a person or entity is conducting a function or activity regulated by the Administrative Simplification Rules on behalf of a covered entity, such as payment or health care operations, or providing one of the services listed in the definition of "business associate" at 45 CFR 160.103. However, the HIPAA Privacy Rule does not prohibit a covered entity from entering into a business associate contract with a researcher if the covered entity wishes to do so. Notwithstanding the above, a covered entity is only permitted to disclose protected health information to a researcher as permitted by Rule, that is, with an individual's authorization pursuant to 45 CFR 164.508, without an individual's authorization as permitted by 45 CFR 164.512(i), or as a limited data set provided that a data use agreement is in place as permitted by 45 CFR 164.514(e).

Q: When is a health care provider a business associate of another health care provider?

A: The HIPAA Privacy Rule explicitly excludes from the business associate requirements disclosures by a covered entity to a health care provider for treatment purposes. See 45 CFR 164.502(e)(1). Therefore, any covered health care provider (or other covered entity) may share protected health information with a health care provider for treatment purposes without a business associate contract. However, this exception does not preclude one health care provider from establishing a business associate relationship with another health care provider for some other purpose. For example, a hospital may enlist the services of another health care provider to assist in the hospital's training of medical students. In this case, a business associate contract would be required before the hospital could allow the health care provider access to patient health information.

Q: May a covered entity share protected health information directly with another covered entity's business associate?

A: Yes. If the HIPAA Privacy Rule permits a covered entity to share protected health information with another covered entity, the covered entity is permitted to make the disclosure directly to a business associate acting on behalf of that other covered entity.

Q: Are covered entities that engage in joint activities under an organized health care arrangement (OHCA) required to have business associate contracts with each other?

A: No. Covered entities that participate in an OHCA are permitted to share protected health information for the joint health care activities of the OHCA without entering into business associate contracts with each other. Of course, each such entity is independently required to observe its obligations under the HIPAA Privacy Rule with respect to protected health information.

Q: Is a business associate contract required with organizations or persons where inadvertent contact with protected health information may result – such as in the case of janitorial services?

A: A business associate contract is not required with persons or organizations whose functions, activities, or services do not involve the use or disclosure of protected health information, and where any access to protected health information by such persons would be incidental, if at all. Generally, janitorial services that clean the offices or facilities of a covered entity are not business associates because the work they perform for covered entities does not involve the use or disclosure of protected health information, and any disclosure of protected health information to janitorial personnel that occurs in the performance of their duties (such as may occur while emptying trash cans) is limited in nature, occurs as a by-product of their janitorial duties, and could not be reasonably prevented. Such disclosures are incidental and permitted by the HIPAA Privacy Rule. See 45 CFR 164.502(a)(1).

If a service is hired to do work for a covered entity where disclosure of protected health information is not limited in nature (such as routine handling of records or shredding of documents containing protected health information), it likely would be a business associate. However, when such work is performed under the direct control of the covered entity (e.g., on the covered entity's premises), the Privacy Rule permits the covered entity to treat the service as part of its workforce, and the covered entity need not enter into a business associate contract with the service.

Q: Is a physician required to have business associate contracts with technicians such as plumbers, electricians or photocopy machine repairmen who provide repair services in a physician's office?

A: No, plumbers, electricians and photocopy repair technicians do not require access to protected health information to perform their services for a physician's office, so they do not meet the definition of a "business associate". Under the HIPAA Privacy Rule, "business associates" are contractors or other non-workforce members hired to do the work of, or for, a covered entity that involves the use or disclosure of protected health information. See the definition of "business associate" at 45 CFR 160.103.

Any disclosure of protected health information to such technicians that occurs in the performance of their duties (such as may occur walking through or working in file rooms) is limited in nature, occurs as a by-product of their duties, and could not be reasonably prevented. Such disclosures are incidental and permitted by the Privacy Rule. See 45 CFR 164.502(a)(1).

Q. Are the following entities considered "business associates" under the HIPAA Privacy Rule: US Postal Service, United Parcel Service, delivery truck line employees and/or their management?

A: No, the Privacy Rule does not require a covered entity to enter into business associate contracts with organizations, such as the US Postal Service, certain private couriers and their electronic equivalents that act merely as conduits for protected health information. A conduit transports information but does not access it other than on a random or infrequent basis as necessary for the performance of the transportation service or as required by law. Since no disclosure is intended by the covered entity, and the probability of exposure of any particular protected health information to a conduit is very small, a conduit is not a business associate of the covered entity.

Q: Does the HIPAA Privacy Rule require a business associate to provide individuals with access to their protected health information or an accounting of disclosures, or an opportunity to amend protected health information?

A: The Privacy Rule regulates covered entities, not business associates. The Rule requires covered entities to include specific provisions in agreements with business associates to safeguard protected health information, and addresses how covered entities may share this information with business associates. Covered entities are responsible for fulfilling Privacy Rule requirements with respect to individual rights, including the rights of access, amendment, and accounting, as provided for by 45 CFR 164.524, 164.526, and 164.528. With limited exceptions, a covered entity is required to provide an individual access to his or her protected health information in a designated record set. This includes information in a designated record set of a business associate, unless the information held by the business associate merely duplicates the information maintained by the covered entity. Therefore, the Rule requires covered entities to specify in the business associate contract that the business associate must make such protected health information available if and when needed by the covered entity to provide an individual with access to the information. However, the Privacy Rule does not prevent the parties from agreeing through the business associate contract that the business associate will provide access to individuals, as may be appropriate where the business associate is the only holder of the designated record set, or part thereof.

Under 45 CFR 164.526, a covered entity must amend protected health information about an individual in a designated record set, including any designated record sets (or copies thereof) held by a business associate. Therefore, the Rule requires covered entities to specify in the business associate contract that the business associate must amend protected health information in such records (or copies) when requested by the covered entity. The covered entity itself is responsible for addressing requests from individuals for amendment and coordinating such requests with its business associate. However, the Privacy Rule also does not prevent the parties from agreeing through the contract that the business associate will receive and address requests for amendment on behalf of the covered entity.

Under 45 CFR 164.528, the Privacy Rule requires a covered entity to provide an accounting of certain disclosures, including certain disclosures by its business associate, to the individual upon request. The business associate contract must provide that the business associate will make such information available to the covered entity in order for the covered entity to fulfill its obligation to the individual. As with access and amendment, the parties can agree through the business associate contract that the business associate will provide the accounting to individuals, as may be appropriate given the protected health information held by, and the functions of, the business associate.

Q: Would a business associate contract in electronic form, with an electronic signature, satisfy the HIPAA Privacy Rule's business associate contract requirements?

A: Yes, assuming that the electronic contract satisfies the applicable requirements of State contract law. The Privacy Rule generally allows for electronic documents, including business associate contracts, to qualify as written documents for purposes of meeting the Rule's requirements. However, currently, no standards exist under HIPAA for electronic signatures. In the absence of specific standards, covered entities must ensure any electronic signature used will result in a legally binding contract under applicable State or other law.

Q: Do physicians with hospital privileges have to enter into business associate contracts with the hospital?

A: No. The hospital and such physicians participate in what the HIPAA Privacy Rule defines as an organized health care arrangement (OHCA). Thus, they may use and disclose protected health information for the joint health care activities of the OHCA without entering into a business associate agreement.

Q: Under the HIPAA Privacy Rule, may a covered entity contract with a business associate to create a limited data set the same way it can use a business associate to create de-identified data?

A: Yes. See 45 CFR 164.514(e)(3)(ii). For example, if a researcher needs county data, but the covered entity's data contains only the postal address of the individual, a business associate may be used to convert the covered entity's geographical information into that needed by the researcher. In addition, the covered entity may hire the intended recipient of the limited data set as the business associate for this purpose in accordance with the business associate requirements. That is, the covered entity may provide protected health information, including direct identifiers, to a business associate who is also the intended data recipient, to create a limited data set of the information responsive to the recipient's request. However, the data recipient, as a business associate, must agree to return or destroy the information that includes the direct identifiers once it has completed the conversion for the covered entity.

Q: I want to hire the intended recipient of a limited data set to also create the limited data set as my business associate. Can I combine the data use agreement and business associate contract?

A: Yes. A data use agreement can be combined with a business associate agreement into a single agreement that meets the requirements of both provisions of the HIPAA Privacy Rule. In the above situation, because the covered entity is providing the recipient with protected health information that includes direct identifiers, a business associate agreement would be required in addition to the data use agreement to protect the information. For example, the agreement must require that the recipient agree to return or destroy the information that includes the direct identifiers once it has completed the conversion for the covered entity.

Q: If the only protected health information a business associate receives is a limited data set, does the HIPAA Privacy Rule require the covered entity to enter into both a business associate agreement and data use agreement with the business associate?

A: No. Where a covered entity discloses only a limited data set to a business associate for the business associate to carry out a health care operations function, the covered entity satisfies the Rule's requirements that it obtain satisfactory assurances from its business associate with the data use agreement. For example, where a State hospital association receives only limited data sets of protected health information from its member hospitals for the purposes of conducting and sharing comparative quality analyses with these hospitals, the member hospitals need only have data use agreements in place with the State hospital association.

Q: Are business associates required to restrict their uses and disclosures to the minimum necessary? May a covered entity reasonably rely on a request from a covered entity's business associate as the minimum necessary?

A: A covered entity's contract with a business associate may not authorize the business associate to use or further disclose the information in a manner that would violate the HIPAA Privacy Rule if done by the covered entity. See 45 CFR 164.504(e)(2)(i). Thus, a business associate contract must limit the business associate's uses and disclosures of, as well as requests for, protected health information to be consistent with the covered entity's minimum necessary policies and procedures. Given that a business associate contract must limit a business associate's requests for protected health information on behalf of a covered entity to that which is reasonably necessary to accomplish the intended purpose, a covered entity is permitted to reasonably rely on such requests from a business associate of another covered entity as the minimum necessary.

Q: Is a physician or other provider considered to be a business associate of a health plan or other payer?

A: Generally, providers are not business associates of payers. For example, if a provider is a member of a health plan network and the only relationship between the health plan (payer) and the provider is one where the provider submits claims for payment to the plan, then the provider is not a business associate of the health plan. Each covered entity is acting on its own behalf when a provider submits a claim to a health plan, and when the health plan assesses and pays the claim. However, a business associate relationship could arise if the provider is performing another function on behalf of, or providing services to, the health plan (e.g., case management services) that meet the definition of "business associate" at 45 CFR 160.103.

Q: Is a health insurance issuer or HMO who provides health insurance or health coverage to a group health plan a business associate of the group health plan?

A: A health insurance issuer or HMO does not become a business associate simply by providing health insurance or health coverage to a group health plan. The relationship between the group health plan and the health insurance issuer or HMO is defined by the Privacy Rule as an organized health care arrangement (OHCA), with respect to the individuals they jointly serve or have served. Thus, these covered entities are permitted to share protected health information that relates to the joint health care activities of the OHCA. However, where a group health plan contracts with a health insurance issuer or HMO to perform functions or activities or to provide services that are in addition to or not directly related to the joint activity of providing insurance, the health insurance issuer or HMO may be a business associate with respect to those additional functions, activities, or services.

Q: Is a reinsurer a business associate of a health plan?

A: Generally, no. A reinsurer does not become a business associate of a health plan simply by selling a reinsurance policy to a health plan and paying claims under the reinsurance policy. Each entity is acting on its own behalf when the health plan purchases the reinsurance benefits, and when the health plan submits a claim to a reinsurer and the reinsurer pays the claim. However, a business associate relationship could arise if the reinsurer is performing a function on behalf of, or providing services to, the health plan that do not directly relate to the provision of the reinsurance benefits.

Q: Is a software vendor a business associate of a covered entity?

A: The mere selling or providing of software to a covered entity does not give rise to a business associate relationship if the vendor does not have access to the protected health information of the covered entity. If the vendor does need access to the protected health information of the covered entity in order to provide its service, the vendor would be a business associate of the covered entity. For example, a software company that hosts the software containing patient information on its own server or accesses patient information when troubleshooting the software function, is a business associate of a covered entity. In these examples, a covered entity would be required to enter into a business associate agreement before allowing the software company access to protected health information. However, when an employee of a contractor, like a software or information technology vendor, has his or her primary duty station on-site at a covered entity, the covered entity may choose to treat the employee of the vendor as a member of the covered entity's workforce, rather than as a business associate. See the definition of "workforce" at 45 CFR 160.103.

USES AND DISCLOSURES FOR TREATMENT, PAYMENT, AND HEALTH CARE OPERATIONS

[*45 CFR 164.506*]

Background

The HIPAA Privacy Rule establishes a foundation of Federal protection for personal health information, carefully balanced to avoid creating unnecessary barriers to the delivery of quality health care. As such, the Rule generally prohibits a covered entity from using or disclosing protected health information unless authorized by patients, except where this prohibition would result in unnecessary interference with access to quality health care or with certain other important public benefits or national priorities.

Ready access to treatment and efficient payment for health care, both of which require use and disclosure of protected health information, are essential to the effective operation of the health care system. In addition, certain health care operations—such as administrative, financial, legal, and quality improvement activities—conducted by or for health care providers and health plans, are essential to support treatment and payment. Many individuals expect that their health information will be used and disclosed as necessary to treat them, bill for treatment, and, to some extent, operate the covered entity's health care business. To avoid interfering with an individual's access to quality health care or the efficient payment for such health care, the Privacy Rule permits a covered entity to use and disclose protected health information, with certain limits and protections, for treatment, payment, and health care operations activities.

How the Rule Works

<u>What are Treatment, Payment, and Health Care Operations?</u> The core health care activities of "Treatment," "Payment," and "Health Care Operations" are defined in the Privacy Rule at 45 CFR 164.501.

"Treatment" generally means the provision, coordination, or management of health care and related services among health care providers or by a health care provider with a third party, consultation between health care providers regarding a patient, or the referral of a patient from one health care provider to another.

"Payment" encompasses the various activities of health care providers to obtain payment or be reimbursed for their services and of a health plan to obtain premiums, to fulfill their coverage responsibilities and provide benefits under the plan, and to obtain or provide reimbursement for the provision of health care.

In addition to the general definition, the Privacy Rule provides examples of common payment activities which include, but are not limited to:

<Determining eligibility or coverage under a plan and adjudicating claims;
<Risk adjustments;
<Billing and collection activities;
<Reviewing health care services for medical necessity, coverage, justification of charges, and the like;

<Utilization review activities; and

<Disclosures to consumer reporting agencies (limited to specified identifying information about the individual, his or her payment history, and identifying information about the covered entity).

"Health care operations" are certain administrative, financial, legal, and quality improvement activities of a covered entity that are necessary to run its business and to support the core functions of treatment and payment. These activities, which are limited to the activities listed in the definition of "health care operations" at 45 CFR 164.501, include:

<Conducting quality assessment and improvement activities, population-based activities relating to improving health or reducing health care costs, and case management and care coordination;

<Reviewing the competence or qualifications of health care professionals, evaluating provider and health plan performance, training health care and non-health care professionals, accreditation, certification, licensing, or credentialing activities;

<Underwriting and other activities relating to the creation, renewal, or replacement of a contract of health insurance or health benefits, and ceding, securing, or placing a contract for reinsurance of risk relating to health care claims;

<Conducting or arranging for medical review, legal, and auditing services, including fraud and abuse detection and compliance programs;

<Business planning and development, such as conducting cost-management and planning analyses related to managing and operating the entity; and

<Business management and general administrative activities, including those related to implementing and complying with the Privacy Rule and other Administrative Simplification Rules, customer service, resolution of internal grievances, sale or transfer of assets, creating de-identified health information or a limited data set, and fundraising for the benefit of the covered entity.

<u>General Provisions at 45 CFR 164.506.</u> A covered entity may, without the individual's authorization:

Use or disclose protected health information for its own treatment, payment, and health care operations activities.

For example:

<A hospital may use protected health information about an individual to provide health care to the individual and may consult with other health care providers about the individual's treatment.

<A health care provider may disclose protected health information about an individual as part of a claim for payment to a health plan.

<A health plan may use protected health information to provide customer service to its enrollees.

A covered entity may disclose protected health information for the treatment activities of any health care provider (including providers not covered by the Privacy Rule).

For example:

<A primary care provider may send a copy of an individual's medical record to a specialist who needs the information to treat the individual.

<A hospital may send a patient's health care instructions to a nursing home to which the patient is transferred.

A covered entity may disclose protected health information to another covered entity or a health care provider (including providers not covered by the Privacy Rule) for the payment activities of the entity that receives the information.

For example:

<A physician may send an individual's health plan coverage information to a laboratory who needs the information to bill for services it provided to the physician with respect to the individual.

<A hospital emergency department may give a patient's payment information to an ambulance service provider that transported the patient to the hospital in order for the ambulance provider to bill for its treatment services.

A covered entity may disclose protected health information to another covered entity for certain health care operation activities of the entity that receives the information if:

<Each entity either has or had a relationship with the individual who is the subject of the information, and the protected health information pertains to the relationship; and

<The disclosure is for a quality-related health care operations activity (i.e., the activities listed in paragraphs (1) and (2) of the definition of "health care operations" at 45 CFR 164.501) or for the purpose of health care fraud and abuse detection or compliance.

For example:

<A health care provider may disclose protected health information to a health plan for the plan's Health Plan Employer Data and Information Set (HEDIS) purposes, provided that the health plan has or had a relationship with the individual who is the subject of the information.

A covered entity that participates in an organized health care arrangement (OHCA) may disclose protected health information about an individual to another covered entity that participates in the OHCA for any joint health care operations of the OHCA.

For example:

<The physicians with staff privileges at a hospital may participate in the hospital's training of medical students.

Uses and Disclosures of Psychotherapy Notes. Except when psychotherapy notes are used by the originator to carry out treatment, or by the covered entity for certain other limited health care operations, uses and disclosures of psychotherapy notes for treatment, payment, and health care operations require the individual's authorization. See 45 CFR 164.508(a)(2).

Minimum Necessary. A covered entity must develop policies and procedures that reasonably limit its disclosures of, and requests for, protected health information for payment and health care operations to the minimum necessary. A covered entity also is required to develop role-based access policies and procedures that limit which members of its workforce may have access to protected health information for treatment, payment, and health care operations, based on those who need access to the information to do their jobs. However, covered entities are not required to apply the minimum necessary standard to disclosures to or requests by a health care provider for treatment purposes. See the fact sheet and frequently asked questions on this web site about the minimum necessary standard for more information.

Consent. A covered entity may voluntarily choose, but is not required, to obtain the individual's consent for it to use and disclose information about him or her for treatment, payment, and health care operations. A covered entity that chooses to have a consent process has complete discretion under the Privacy Rule to design a process that works best for its business and consumers.

A "consent" document is not a valid permission to use or disclose protected health information for a purpose that requires an "authorization" under the Privacy Rule (see 45 CFR 164.508), or where other requirements or conditions exist under the Rule for the use or disclosure of protected health information.

Right to Request Privacy Protection. Individuals have the right to request restrictions on how a covered entity will use and disclose protected health information about them for treatment, payment, and health care operations. A covered entity is not required to agree to an individual's request for a restriction, but is bound by any restrictions to which it agrees. See 45 CFR 164.522(a).

Individuals also may request to receive confidential communications from the covered entity, either at alternative locations or by alternative means. For example, an individual may request that her health care provider call her at her office, rather than her home. A *health care provider* must accommodate an individual's reasonable request for such confidential communications. A *health plan* must accommodate an individual's reasonable request for confidential communications, if the individual clearly states that not doing so could endanger him or her. See 45 CFR 164.522(b).

Notice. Any use or disclosure of protected health information for treatment, payment, or health care operations must be consistent with the covered entity's notice of privacy practices. A covered entity is required to provide the individual with adequate notice of its privacy practices, including the uses or disclosures the covered entity may make of the individual's information and the individual's rights with respect to that information. See the fact sheet and frequently asked questions on this web site about the notice standard for more information.

USES AND DISCLOSURES FOR TREATMENT, PAYMENT, AND HEALTH CARE OPERATIONS

Frequently Asked Questions

Q: My State requires consent to use or disclose health information. Does the HIPAA Privacy Rule take away this protection?

A: No. The Privacy Rule does not prohibit a covered entity from obtaining an individual's consent to use or disclose his or her health information and, therefore, presents no barrier to the entity's ability to comply with State law requirements.

Q: How does the HIPAA Privacy Rule change the laws concerning consent for treatment?

A: The Privacy Rule relates to uses and disclosures of protected health information, not to whether a patient consents to the health care itself. As such, the Privacy Rule does not affect informed consent for treatment, which is addressed by State law.

Q: Can a pharmacist use protected health information to fill a prescription that was telephoned in by a patient's physician without the patient's written consent if the patient is a new patient to the pharmacy?

A: Yes. The pharmacist is using the protected health information for treatment purposes, and the HIPAA Privacy Rule does not require covered entities to obtain an individual's consent prior to using or disclosing protected health information about him or her for treatment, payment, or health care operations.

Q: Can health care providers, such as a specialist or hospital, to whom a patient is referred for the first time, use protected health information to set up appointments or schedule surgery or other procedures without the patient's written consent?

A: Yes. The HIPAA Privacy Rule does not require covered entities to obtain an individual's consent prior to using or disclosing protected health information about him or her for treatment, payment, or health care operations.

Q: Are health care providers restricted from consulting with other providers about a patient's condition without the patient's written authorization?

A: No. Consulting with another health care provider about a patient is within the HIPAA Privacy Rule's definition of "treatment" and, therefore, is permissible. In addition, a health care provider (or other covered entity) is expressly permitted to disclose protected health information about an individual to a health care provider for that provider's treatment of the individual. See 45 CFR 164.506.

Q: Does the HIPAA Privacy Rule restrict pharmacists from giving advice about over-the-counter medicines to customers?

A: No. A pharmacist may provide advice to customers about over-the-counter medicines. The Privacy Rule permits a covered entity to disclose protected health information about an individual to the individual. See 45 CFR 164.502(a)(1)(i).

Q: Can a patient have a friend or family member pick up a prescription for her?

A: Yes. A pharmacist may use professional judgment and experience with common practice to make reasonable inferences of the patient's best interest in allowing a person, other that the patient, to pick up a prescription. See 45 CFR 164.510(b). For example, the fact that a relative or friend arrives at a pharmacy and asks to pick up a specific prescription for an individual effectively verifies that he or she is involved in the individual's care, and the HIPAA Privacy Rule allows the pharmacist to give the filled prescription to the relative or friend. The individual does not need to provide the pharmacist with the names of such persons in advance.

Q: What is the difference between "consent" and "authorization" under the HIPAA Privacy Rule?

A: The Privacy Rule permits, but does not require, a covered entity voluntarily to obtain patient consent for uses and disclosures of protected health information for treatment, payment, and health care operations. Covered entities that do so have complete discretion to design a process that best suits their needs.

By contrast, an "authorization" is required by the Privacy Rule for uses and disclosures of protected health information not otherwise allowed by the Rule. Where the Privacy Rule requires patient authorization, voluntary consent is not sufficient to permit a use or disclosure of protected health information unless it also satisfies the requirements of a valid authorization. An authorization is a detailed document that gives covered entities permission to use protected health information for specified purposes, which are generally other than treatment, payment, or health care operations, or to disclose protected health information to a third party specified by the individual. An authorization must specify a number of elements, including a description of the protected health information to be used and disclosed, the person authorized to make the use or disclosure, the person to whom the covered entity may make the disclosure, an expiration date, and, in some cases, the purpose for which the information may be used or disclosed. With limited exceptions, covered entities may not condition treatment or coverage on the individual providing an authorization.

Q: May a health care provider disclose protected health information to a health plan for the plan's Health Plan Employer Data and Information Set (HEDIS)?

A: Yes, the HIPAA Privacy Rule permits a provider to disclose protected health information to a health plan for the quality-related health care operations of the health plan, provided that the health plan has or had a relationship with the individual who is the subject of the information, and the protected health information requested pertains to the relationship. See 45 CFR 164.506(c)(4). Thus, a provider may disclose protected health information to a health plan for the plan's Health Plan Employer Data and Information Set (HEDIS) purposes, so long as the period for which information is needed overlaps with the period for which the individual is or was enrolled in the health plan.

Q: Does the HIPAA Privacy Rule permit a covered entity or its collection agency to communicate with parties other than the patient (e.g., spouses or guardians) regarding payment of a bill?

A: Yes. The Privacy Rule permits a covered entity, or a business associate acting on behalf of a covered entity (e.g., a collection agency), to disclose protected health information as necessary to obtain payment for health care, and does not limit to whom such a disclosure may be made. Therefore, a covered entity, or its business associate, may contact persons other than the individual as necessary to obtain payment for health care services. See 45 CFR 164.506(c) and the definition of "payment" at 45 CFR 164.501. However, the Privacy Rule requires a covered entity, or its business associate, to reasonably limit the amount of information disclosed for such purposes to the minimum necessary, as well as to abide by any reasonable requests for confidential communications and any agreed-to restrictions on the use or disclosure of protected health information. See 45 CFR 164.502(b), 164.514(d), and 164.522.

Q: Does the HIPAA Privacy Rule prevent reporting to consumer credit reporting agencies or otherwise create any conflict with the Fair Credit Reporting Act (FCRA)?

A: No. The Privacy Rule's definition of "payment" includes disclosures to consumer reporting agencies. These disclosures, however, are limited to the following protected health information about the individual: name and address; date of birth; social security number; payment history; and account number. In addition, disclosure of the name and address of the health care provider or health plan making the report is allowed. The covered entity may perform this payment activity directly, or may carry out this function through a third party, such as a collection agency, under a business associate arrangement.

The Privacy Rule permits uses and disclosures by the covered entity or its business associate as may be required by the Fair Credit Reporting Act (FCRA) or other law. Therefore, the Department does not believe there is a conflict between the Privacy Rule and legal duties imposed on data furnishers by FCRA.

Q: Does the HIPAA Privacy Rule prevent health plans and providers from using debt collection agencies? Does the Privacy Rule conflict with the Fair Debt Collection Practices Act?

A: The Privacy Rule permits covered entities to continue to use the services of debt collection agencies. Debt collection is recognized as a payment activity within the "payment" definition. See the definition of "payment" at 45 CFR 164.501. Through a business associate arrangement, the covered entity may engage a debt collection agency to perform this function on its behalf. Disclosures to collection agencies are governed by other provisions of the Privacy Rule, such as the business associate and minimum necessary requirements.

The Department is not aware of any conflict between the Privacy Rule and the Fair Debt Collection Practices Act. Where a use or disclosure of protected health information is necessary for the covered entity to fulfill a legal duty, the Privacy Rule would permit such use or disclosure as required by law.

Q: Are location information services of collection agencies, which are required under the Fair Debt Collection Practices Act, permitted under the HIPAA Privacy Rule?

A: "Payment" is broadly defined as activities by health plans or health care providers to obtain premiums or obtain or provide reimbursements for the provision of health care. The activities specified are by way of example and are not intended to be an exclusive listing. Billing, claims management, collection activities and related data processing are expressly included in the definition of "payment." See the definition of "payment" at 45 CFR 164.501. Obtaining information about the location of the individual is a routine activity to facilitate the collection of amounts owed and the management of accounts receivable, and, therefore, would constitute a payment activity. See 45 CFR 164.501. The covered entity and its business associate would also have to comply with any limitations placed on location information services by the Fair Debt Collection Practices Act.

Q: Does the HIPAA Privacy Rule permit an eye doctor to confirm a contact prescription received by a mail-order contact company?

A: Yes. The disclosure of protected health information by an eye doctor to a distributor of contact lenses for the purpose of confirming a contact lens prescription is a treatment disclosure, and is permitted under the Privacy Rule at 45 CFR 164.506.

Q: Does a physician need a patient's written authorization to send a copy of the patient's medical record to a specialist or other health care provider who will treat the patient?

A: No. The HIPAA Privacy Rule permits a health care provider to disclose protected health information about an individual, without the individual's authorization, to another health care provider for that provider's treatment of the individual. See 45 CFR 164.506 and the definition of "treatment" at 45 CFR 164.501.

Q: Is a hospital permitted to contact another hospital or health care facility, such as a nursing home, to which a patient will be transferred for continued care, without the patient's authorization?

A: Yes. The HIPAA Privacy Rule permits a health care provider to disclose protected health information about an individual, without the individual's authorization, to another health care provider for that provider's treatment or payment purposes, as well as to another covered entity for certain health care operations of that entity. See 45 CFR 164.506 and the definitions of "treatment," "payment," and "health care operations" at 45 CFR 164.501.

Q: When an ambulance service delivers a patient to a hospital, is it permitted to report its treatment of the patient and the patient's medical history to the hospital, without the patient's authorization?

A: Yes. The HIPAA Privacy Rule permits an ambulance service or other health care provider to disclose protected health information about an individual, without the individual's authorization, to another health care provider, such as a hospital, for that provider's treatment of the individual. See 45 CFR 164.506 and the definition of "treatment" at 45 CFR 164.501.

Q: How does the HIPAA Privacy Rule apply to professional liability insurance? Specifically, how can professional liability insurers continue to arrange for and maintain medical liability insurance for health care providers covered by the Rule?

A: The Privacy Rule permits a covered health care provider to disclose information for "health care operations" purposes, subject to certain requirements. Disclosures by a covered health care provider to a professional liability insurer or a similar entity for the purpose of obtaining or maintaining medical liability coverage or for the purpose of obtaining benefits from such insurance, including the reporting of adverse events, fall within "business management and general administrative activities" under the definition of "health care operations." Therefore, a covered health care provider may disclose individually identifiable health information to a professional liability insurer to the same extent as the provider is able to disclose such information for other health care operations purposes. See 45 CFR 164.502(a)(1)(ii) and the definition of "health care operations" at 45 CFR 164.501.

MARKETING
[*45 CFR 164.501, 164.508(a)(3)*]

Background

The HIPAA Privacy Rule gives individuals important controls over whether and how their protected health information is used and disclosed for marketing purposes. With limited exceptions, the Rule requires an individual's written authorization before a use or disclosure of his or her protected health information can be made for marketing. So as not to interfere with core health care functions, the Rule distinguishes marketing communications from those communications about goods and services that are essential for quality health care.

How the Rule Works

The Privacy Rule addresses the use and disclosure of protected health information for marketing purposes by:

•Defining what is "marketing" under the Rule;

•Excepting from that definition certain treatment or health care operations activities;

•Requiring individual authorization for all uses or disclosures of protected health information for marketing purposes with limited exceptions.

What is "Marketing"? The Privacy Rule defines "marketing" as making "a communication about a product or service that encourages recipients of the communication to purchase or use the product or service." Generally, if the communication is "marketing," then the communication can occur only if the covered entity first obtains an individual's "authorization." This definition of marketing has certain exceptions, as discussed below.

Examples of "marketing" communications requiring prior authorization are:

•A communication from a hospital informing former patients about a cardiac facility, that is not part of the hospital, that can provide a baseline EKG for $39, when the communication is not for the purpose of providing treatment advice.

•A communication from a health insurer promoting a home and casualty insurance product offered by the same company.

What Else is "Marketing"? Marketing also means: "An arrangement between a covered entity and any other entity whereby the covered entity discloses protected health information to the other entity, in exchange for direct or indirect remuneration, for the other entity or its affiliate to make a communication about its own product or service that encourages recipients of the communication to purchase or use that product or service." This part of the definition to marketing has no exceptions. The individual must authorize these marketing communications before they can occur.

Simply put, a covered entity may not sell protected health information to a business associate or any other third party for that party's own purposes. Moreover, covered entities may not sell lists of patients or enrollees to third parties without obtaining authorization from each person on the list.

For example, it is "marketing" when:

•A health plan sells a list of its members to a company that sells blood glucose monitors, which intends to send the plan's members brochures on the benefits of purchasing and using the monitors.

•A drug manufacturer receives a list of patients from a covered health care provider and provides remuneration, then uses that list to send discount coupons for a new anti-depressant medication directly to the patients.

What is NOT "Marketing"? The Privacy Rule carves out exceptions to the definition of marketing under the following three categories:

(1) A communication is not "marketing" if it is made to describe a health-related product or service (or payment for such product or service) that is provided by, or included in a plan of benefits of, the covered entity making the communication, including communications about:

<The entities participating in a health care provider network or health plan network;
<Replacement of, or enhancements to, a health plan; and
<Health-related products or services available only to a health plan enrollee that add value to, but are not part of, a plan of benefits.

This exception to the marketing definition permits communications by a covered entity about its own products or services.

For example, under this exception, it is not "marketing" when:

<A hospital uses its patient list to announce the arrival of a new specialty group (e.g., orthopedic) or the acquisition of new equipment (e.g., x-ray machine or magnetic resonance image machine) through a general mailing or publication.

<A health plan sends a mailing to subscribers approaching Medicare eligible age with materials describing its Medicare supplemental plan and an application form.

(2) A communication is not "marketing" if it is made for treatment of the individual.

For example, under this exception, it is not "marketing" when:

<A pharmacy or other health care provider mails prescription refill reminders to patients, or contracts with a mail house to do so.
<A primary care physician refers an individual to a specialist for a follow-up test or provides free samples of a prescription drug to a patient.

(3) A communication is not "marketing" if it is made for case management or care coordination for the individual, or to direct or recommend alternative treatments, therapies, health care providers, or settings of care to the individual.

For example, under this exception, it is not "marketing" when:

<An endocrinologist shares a patient's medical record with several behavior management programs to determine which program best suits the ongoing needs of the individual patient.

<A hospital social worker shares medical record information with various nursing homes in the course of recommending that the patient be transferred from a hospital bed to a nursing home.

For any of the three exceptions to the definition of marketing, the activity must otherwise be permissible under the Privacy Rule, and a covered entity may use a business associate to make the communication. As with any disclosure to a business associate, the covered entity must obtain the business associate's agreement to use the protected health information only for the communication activities of the covered entity.

<u>Marketing Authorizations and When Authorizations are NOT Necessary.</u> Except as discussed below, any communication that meets the definition of marketing is not permitted, unless the covered entity obtains an individual's authorization. To determine what constitutes an acceptable "authorization," see 45 CFR 164.508. If the marketing involves direct or indirect remuneration to the covered entity from a third party, the authorization must state that such remuneration is involved. See 45 CFR 164.508(a)(3).

A communication does not require an authorization, even if it is marketing, if it is in the form of a face-to-face communication made by a covered entity to an individual; or a promotional gift of nominal value provided by the covered entity.

For example, no prior authorization is necessary when:

•A hospital provides a free package of formula and other baby products to new mothers as they leave the maternity ward.

•An insurance agent sells a health insurance policy in person to a customer and proceeds to also market a casualty and life insurance policy as well.

MARKETING

<u>Frequently Asked Questions</u>

Q: Does the HIPAA Privacy Rule expand the ability of providers, plans, marketers and others to use my protected health information to market goods and services to me? Does the Privacy Rule make it easier for health care businesses to engage in door-to-door sales and marketing efforts?

A: No. The Privacy Rule's limitations on the use or disclosure of protected health information for marketing purposes do not exist in most States today. For example, the Rule requires patients' authorization for the following types of uses or disclosures of protected health information for marketing:

•Selling protected health information to third parties for their use and re-use. Thus, under the Rule, a hospital or other provider may not sell names of pregnant women to baby formula manufacturers or magazines without an authorization.

•Disclosing protected health information to outsiders for the outsiders' independent marketing use. Under the Rule, doctors may not provide patient lists to pharmaceutical companies for those companies' drug promotions without an authorization.

Without these Privacy Rule restrictions, these activities could occur with no authorization from the individual in most jurisdictions. In addition, if a State law provided additional limitations on disclosures of information for related activities, the Privacy Rule generally would not interfere with those laws.

Moreover, under the "business associate" provisions of the Privacy Rule, a covered entity may not give protected health information to a telemarketer, door-to-door salesperson, or other third party it has hired to make permitted communications (for example, about a covered entities' own goods and services) unless that third party has agreed by contract to use the information only for communicating on behalf of the covered entity. Without the Privacy Rule, there may be no restrictions on how third parties re-use information they obtain from health plans and providers. See the fact sheet and frequently asked questions on this web site about the business associate standard for more information.

Q: Can contractors (business associates) use protected health information to market to individuals for their own business purposes?

A: No. While covered entities may share protected health information with their contractors who meet the definition of "business associates" under the HIPAA Privacy Rule, that definition is limited to contractors that obtain protected health information to perform or assist in the performance of certain health care operations *on behalf of* covered entities. Thus, business associates, with limited exceptions, cannot use protected health information for their own purposes. Although, under the HIPAA statute, the Privacy Rule cannot govern contractors directly, the Rule does set clear parameters for how covered entities may contract with business associates. See 45 CFR 164.502(e) and 164.504(e), and the definition of "business associate" at 45 CFR 160.103.

Further, the Privacy Rule expressly prohibits health plans and covered health care providers from selling protected health information to third parties for the third party's own marketing activities, without authorization. So, for example, a pharmacist cannot, without patient authorization, sell a list of patients to a pharmaceutical company, for the pharmaceutical company to market its own products to the individuals on the list.

Q: Can telemarketers gain access to protected health information and call individuals to sell goods and services?

A: Under the HIPAA Privacy Rule, a covered entity can share protected health information with a telemarketer only if the covered entity has either obtained the individual's prior written authorization to do so, or has entered into a business associate relationship with the telemarketer for the purpose of making a communication that is not marketing, such as to inform individuals about the covered entity's own goods or services.

If the telemarketer is a business associate under the Privacy Rule, it must agree by contract to use the information only for communicating on behalf of the covered entity, and not to market its own goods or services (or those of another third party).

Q: When is an authorization required from the patient before a provider or health plan engages in marketing to that individual?

A: The HIPAA Privacy Rule expressly requires an authorization for uses or disclosures of protected health information for ALL marketing communications, except in two circumstances: (1) when the communication occurs in a face-to-face encounter between the covered entity and the individual; or (2) the communication involves a promotional gift of nominal value.

If the marketing communication involves direct or indirect remuneration to the covered entity from a third party, the authorization must state that such remuneration is involved.

Q: How can I distinguish between activities for treatment or health care operations versus marketing activities?

A: The overlap among common usages of the terms "treatment," "healthcare operations," and "marketing" is unavoidable. For instance, in recommending treatments, providers and health plans sometimes advise patients to purchase goods and services. Similarly, when a health plan explains to its members the benefits it provides, it too is encouraging the use or purchase of goods and services.

The HIPAA Privacy Rule defines these terms specifically, so they can be distinguished. For example, the Privacy Rule excludes treatment communications and certain health care operations activities from the definition of "marketing." If a communication falls under one of the definition's exceptions, the marketing rules do not apply. In these cases, covered entities may engage in the activity without first obtaining an authorization. See the fact sheet on this web site about marketing, as well as the definition of "marketing" at 45 CFR 164.501, for more information.

However, if a health care operation communication does not fall within one of these specific exceptions to the marketing definition, and the communication falls under the definition of "marketing," the Privacy Rule's provisions restricting the use or disclosure of protected health information for marketing purposes will apply. For these marketing communications, the individual's authorization is required before a covered entity may use or disclose protected health information.

Q: Do disease management, health promotion, preventive care, and wellness programs fall under the HIPAA Privacy Rule's definition of "marketing"?

A: Generally, no. To the extent the disease management or wellness program is operated by the covered entity directly or by a business associate, communications about such programs are not marketing because they are about the covered entity's own health-related services. So, for example, a hospital's Wellness Department could start a weight-loss program and send a flyer to all patients seen in the hospital over the past year who meet the definition of obese, even if those individuals were not specifically seen for obesity when they were in the hospital.

Moreover, a communication that merely promotes health in a general manner and does not promote a specific product or service from a particular provider does not meet the definition of "marketing." Such communications may include population-based activities in the areas of health education or disease prevention. Examples of general health promotional material include mailings reminding women to get an annual mammogram; mailings providing information about how to lower cholesterol, new developments in health care (e.g., new diagnostic tools), support groups, organ donation, cancer prevention, and health fairs.

Q: Is it "marketing" for a covered entity to describe products or services that are provided by the covered entity to its patients, or to describe products or services that are included in the health plan's plan of benefits to members of the health plan?

A: No. The HIPAA Privacy Rule excludes from the definition of "marketing" communications made to describe a covered entity's health-related product or service (or payment for such product or service) that is provided by, or included in a plan of benefits of, the covered entity making the communication. Thus, it would not be marketing for a physician who has developed a new anti-snore device to send a flyer describing it to all of her patients (whether or not each patient has actually sought treatment for snoring). Nor would it be marketing for an ophthalmologist or health plan to send existing patients or members discounts for eye-exams or eye-glasses available only to the patients and members. Similarly, it would not be marketing for an insurance plan to send its members a description of covered benefits, payment schedules, and claims procedures.

Q: Is it marketing for a covered entity to describe the entities participating in a health care provider network or a health plan network?

A: No. The HIPAA Privacy Rule excludes from the definition of "marketing," communications by a covered entity to describe the entities participating in a health care provider network or a health plan network. Thus, it would not be marketing for a health plan or insurer to mail its members or enrollees a list of health care providers in the health plan network or for an independent physicians association to send its patients a preferred provider list.

Q: Is it marketing for an insurance plan or health plan to send enrollees notices about changes, replacements, or improvements to existing plans?

A: No. The HIPAA Privacy Rule excludes from the definition of "marketing," communications about replacements of, or enhancements to, a health plan. Therefore, notices about changes in deductibles, co-pays and types of coverage, such as prescription drugs, are not marketing. Likewise, a notice to a family warning that a student reaching the age of majority on a parental policy will lose coverage, then offering continuation coverage, would not be considered marketing. Nor are special health care policies such as guaranteed issue products and conversion policies considered marketing. Similarly, notices from a health plan about its long term care benefits would not be considered marketing.

It would be considered marketing, however, for a health plan to send to its members promotional material about insurance products that are considered to be "excepted benefits" (described in section 2791(c)(1) of the Public Health Service Act), such as accident only policies. It would likewise be marketing for health plans to describe other lines of insurance, such as life insurance policies. Generally, such communications require authorizations.

Q: Can health plans communicate about health-related products or services to enrollees that add value to, but are not part of, a plan of benefits?

A: Yes. The provision of value-added items or services (VAIS) is a common practice, particularly for managed care organizations. Under the HIPAA Privacy Rule, communications may qualify under the marketing exception for a communication about a health plan's plan of benefits, even if the VAIS are not considered plan benefits for the Adjusted Community Rate purposes. To qualify for this exclusion, however, the VAIS must meet two conditions. First, they must be health-related. Therefore, discounts offered by Medicare + Choice or other managed care organizations for eyeglasses may be considered part of the plan's benefits, whereas discounts to attend movie theaters will not. Second, such items and services must demonstrably "add value" to the plan's membership and not merely be a pass-through of a discount or item available to the public at large.

So, a Medicare + Choice or other managed care organization could offer its members a special discount opportunity for eyeglasses and contact lenses without obtaining authorizations if the discount were only available through membership in the managed care organization. However, such communications would need an authorization if the members would be able to obtain such discounts directly from the eyeglass store. Similarly, a Medicare + Choice or other managed care organization could offer its members a special discount opportunity for a prescription drug card benefit or for a health/fitness club membership, which is not available to consumers on the open market. On the other hand, a Medicare+Choice or other managed care organization would need an authorization to notify its members of a discount to a movie theater available only to its members.

Q: Can a doctor or pharmacy be paid to make a prescription refill reminder without a prior authorization under the HIPAA Privacy Rule?

A: Yes. It is not marketing for a doctor to make a prescription refill reminder even if a third party pays for the communication. The prescription refill reminder is considered treatment. The communication is therefore excluded from the definition of marketing and does not require a prior authorization. Similarly, it is not marketing when a doctor or pharmacy is paid by a pharmaceutical company to recommend an alternative medication to patients. Communications about alternative treatments are excluded from the definition of marketing and do not require a prior authorization. The simple receipt of remuneration does not transform a treatment communication into a commercial promotion of a product or service.

Furthermore, covered entities may use a legitimate business associate to assist them in making such permissible communications. For instance, if a pharmacist that has been paid by a third party contracts with a mail house to send out prescription refill reminders to the pharmacist's patients, neither the mail house nor the pharmacist needs a prior authorization. However, a covered entity would require an authorization if it sold protected health information to a third party for the third party's marketing purposes.

Q: Are appointment reminders allowed under the HIPAA Privacy Rule without authorizations?

A: Yes, appointment reminders are considered part of treatment of an individual and, therefore, can be made without an authorization.

Q: What are examples of "alternative treatments" that are excepted from the HIPAA Privacy Rule's definition of "marketing"?

A: Alternative treatments are treatments that are within the range of treatment options available to an individual. For example, it would be an alternative treatment communication if a doctor, in response to an inquiry from a patient with skin rash about the range of treatment options, mails the patient a letter recommending that the patient purchase various ointments and medications described in brochures enclosed with the letter. Alternative treatment could also include alternative medicine. Thus, alternative treatments would include communications by a nurse midwife who recommends or sells vitamins and herbal preparations, dietary and exercise programs, massage services, music or other alternative types of therapy to her pregnant patients.

Q: Are prior authorizations required when a doctor or health plan distributes promotional gifts of nominal value?

A: No. In a specific exception, the HIPAA Privacy Rule allows covered entities to distribute items commonly known as promotional gifts of nominal value without prior authorization, even if such items are distributed with the intent of encouraging the receiver to buy the products or services. This authorization exception generally applies to items and services of a third party, whether or not they are health-related, or items and services of the covered entity that are not health-related. A covered doctor, for instance, may send patients items such as pens, note-pads, and cups embossed with a health plan's logo without prior authorization. Similarly, dentists may give patients free toothbrushes, floss and toothpaste.

Q: Are health care providers required to seek a prior authorization before discussing a product or service with a patient, or giving a product or service to a patient, in a face-to-face encounter?

A: No. In face-to-face encounters, the HIPAA Privacy Rule allows covered entities to give or discuss products or services, even when not health-related, to patients without a prior authorization. This exception prevents unnecessary intrusion into the doctor-patient relationship. Physicians may give out free pharmaceutical samples, regardless of their value. Similarly, hospitals may give infant supplies to new mothers. Moreover, the face-to-face exception would allow providers to leave general circulation materials in their offices for patients to pick up during office visits.

Q: Must insurance agents that are business associates of a health plan seek a prior authorization before talking to a customer in a face-to-face encounter about the insurance company's other lines of business?

A: No. In the specific case of face-to-face encounters, the HIPAA Privacy Rule allows health plans and their business associates to market both health and non-health insurance products to individuals.

Q: What effect do the "marketing" provisions of the HIPAA Privacy Rule have on Federal or State fraud and abuse statutes?

A: The Privacy Rule makes it clear that nothing in the marketing provisions of the Privacy Rule are to be construed as amending, modifying, or changing any rule or requirement related to any other Federal or State statutes or regulations, including specifically anti-kickback, fraud and abuse, or self-referral statutes or regulations, or to authorize or permit any activity or transaction currently proscribed by such statutes and regulations. Examples of such laws include the anti-kickback statute (section 1128B(b) of the Social Security Act), safe harbor regulations (42 CFR Parts 411 and 424), and HIPAA statute on self-referral (section 1128C of the Social Security Act). The definition of "marketing" is applicable solely to the Privacy Rule and the permissions granted by the Rule are only for a covered entity's use or disclosure of protected health information. In particular, although the Privacy Rule defines the term "marketing" to exclude communications to an individual to recommend, purchase, or use a product or service as part of the treatment of the individual or for case management or care coordination of that individual, such communication by a health care professional may violate the anti-kickback statute. Similar examples of pharmacist communications with patients relating to the marketing of products on behalf of pharmaceutical companies were identified by the Office of the Inspector General (OIG) as problematic in a 1994 Special Fraud Alert (December 19, 1994, 59 FR 65372). Other violations have involved home health nurses and physical therapists acting as marketers for durable medical equipment companies. Although a particular communication under the Privacy Rule may not require patient authorization because it is not "marketing," or may require patient authorization because it is "marketing" as the Rule defines it, the arrangement may nevertheless violate other statutes and regulations administered by the Department of Health and Human Services, Department of Justice, or other Federal or State agencies.

Q: May covered entities use information regarding specific clinical conditions of individuals in order to communicate about products or services for such conditions without a prior authorization?

A: Yes, if the communication is for the individual's treatment or for case management, care coordination, or the recommendation of alternative therapies. The HIPAA Privacy Rule permits the use of clinical information to the extent it is reasonably necessary for these communications. Similarly, population-based activities in the areas of health education or disease prevention are not considered marketing when they promote health in a general manner. Again clinical information may be used for such communications, such as in targeting a public education campaign.

Q: Are communications concerning information to beneficiaries about government programs or government-sponsored programs "marketing" under the HIPAA Privacy Rule?

A: No. Communications about government and government-sponsored programs do not fall within the definition of "marketing." There is no commercial component to communications about benefits available through public programs. Therefore, a covered entity is permitted to use and disclose protected health information to communicate about eligibility for such programs as Medicare, Medicaid, or the State Children's Health Insurance Program (SCHIP).

DISCLOSURES FOR PUBLIC HEALTH ACTIVITIES
[*45 CFR 164.512(b)*]

Background

The HIPAA Privacy Rule recognizes the legitimate need for public health authorities and others responsible for ensuring public health and safety to have access to protected health information to carry out their public health mission. The Rule also recognizes that public health reports made by covered entities are an important means of identifying threats to the health and safety of the public at large, as well as individuals. Accordingly, the Rule permits covered entities to disclose protected health information without authorization for specified public health purposes.

How the Rule Works

General Public Health Activities. The Privacy Rule permits covered entities to disclose protected health information, without authorization, to public health authorities who are legally authorized to receive such reports for the purpose of preventing or controlling disease, injury, or disability. This would include, for example, the reporting of a disease or injury; reporting vital events, such as births or deaths; and conducting public health surveillance, investigations, or interventions. See 45 CFR 164.512(b)(1)(i). Also, covered entities may, at the direction of a public health authority, disclose protected health information to a foreign government agency that is acting in collaboration with a public health authority. See 45 CFR 164.512(b)(1)(i). Covered entities who are also a public health authority may use, as well as disclose, protected health information for these public health purposes. See 45 CFR 164.512(b)(2).

A "public health authority" is an agency or authority of the United States government, a State, a territory, a political subdivision of a State or territory, or Indian tribe that is responsible for public health matters as part of its official mandate, as well as a person or entity acting under a grant of authority from, or under a contract with, a public health agency. See 45 CFR 164.501. Examples of a public health authority include State and local health departments, the Food and Drug Administration (FDA), the Centers for Disease Control and Prevention, and the Occupational Safety and Health Administration (OSHA).

Generally, covered entities are required reasonably to limit the protected health information disclosed for public health purposes to the minimum amount necessary to accomplish the public health purpose. However, covered entities are not required to make a minimum necessary determination for public health disclosures that are made pursuant to an individual's authorization, or for disclosures that are required by other law. See 45 CFR 164.502(b). For disclosures to a public health authority, covered entities may reasonably rely on a minimum necessary determination made by the public health authority in requesting the protected health information. See 45 CFR 164.514(d)(3)(iii)(A). For routine and recurring public health disclosures, covered entities may develop standard protocols, as part of their minimum necessary policies and procedures, that address the types and amount of protected health information that may be disclosed for such purposes. See 45 CFR 164.514(d)(3)(i).

Other Public Health Activities. The Privacy Rule recognizes the important role that persons or entities other than public health authorities play in certain essential public health activities. Accordingly, the Rule permits covered entities to disclose protected health information, without authorization, to such persons or entities for the public health activities discussed below.

•Child abuse or neglect. Covered entities may disclose protected health

information to report known or suspected child abuse or neglect, if the report is made to a public health authority or other appropriate government authority that is authorized by law to receive such reports. For instance, the social services department of a local government might have legal authority to receive reports of child abuse or neglect, in which case, the Privacy Rule would permit a covered entity to report such cases to that authority without obtaining individual authorization. Likewise, a covered entity could report such cases to the police department when the police department is authorized by law to receive such reports. See 45 CFR 164.512(b)(1)(ii). See also 45 CFR 512(c) for information regarding disclosures about adult victims of abuse, neglect, or domestic violence.

•Quality, safety or effectiveness of a product or activity regulated by the FDA. Covered entities may disclose protected health information to a person subject to FDA jurisdiction, for public health purposes related to the quality, safety or effectiveness of an FDA-regulated product or activity for which that person has responsibility. Examples of purposes or activities for which such disclosures may be made include, but are not limited to:

<Collecting or reporting adverse events (including similar reports regarding food and dietary supplements), product defects or problems (including problems regarding use or labeling), or biological product deviations;

<Tracking FDA-regulated products;
<Enabling product recalls, repairs, replacement or lookback (which includes locating and notifying individuals who received recalled or withdrawn products or products that are the subject of lookback); and
<Conducting post-marketing surveillance.

See 45 CFR 164.512(b)(1)(iii). The "person" subject to the jurisdiction of the FDA does not have to be a specific individual. Rather, it can be an individual or an entity, such as a partnership, corporation, or association. Covered entities may identify the party or parties responsible for an FDA-regulated product from the product label, from written material that accompanies the product (know as labeling), or from sources of labeling, such as the Physician's Desk Reference.

Persons at risk of contracting or spreading a disease. A covered entity may disclose protected health information to a person who is at risk of contracting or spreading a disease or condition if other law authorizes the covered entity to notify such individuals as necessary to carry out public health interventions or investigations. For example, a covered health care provider may disclose protected health information as needed to notify a person that (s)he has been exposed to a communicable disease if the covered entity is legally authorized to do so to prevent or control the spread of the disease. See 45 CFR 164.512(b)(1)(iv).

Workplace medical surveillance. A covered health care provider who provides a health care service to an individual at the request of the individual's employer, or provides the service in the capacity of a member of the employer's workforce, may disclose the individual's protected health information to the employer for the purposes of workplace medical surveillance or the evaluation of work-related illness and injuries to the extent the employer needs that information to comply with OSHA, the Mine Safety and Health Administration (MSHA), or the requirements of State laws having a similar purpose. The information disclosed must be limited to the provider's findings regarding such medical surveillance or work-related illness or injury. The covered health care provider must provide the individual with written notice that the information will be disclosed to his or her employer (or the notice may be posted at the worksite if that is where the service is provided). See 45 CFR 164.512(b)(1)(v).

DISCLOSURES FOR PUBLIC HEALTH ACTIVITIES

Frequently Asked Questions

Q: Must a health care provider or other covered entity obtain permission from a patient prior to notifying public health authorities of the occurrence of a reportable disease?

A: No. All States have laws that require providers to report cases of specific diseases to public health officials. The HIPAA Privacy Rule permits disclosures that are required by law. Furthermore, disclosures to public health authorities that are authorized by law to collect or receive information for public health purposes are also permissible under the Privacy Rule. In order to do their job of protecting the health of the public, it is frequently necessary for public health officials to obtain information about the persons affected by a disease. In some cases they may need to contact those affected in order to determine the cause of the disease to allow for actions to prevent further illness.

The Privacy Rule continues to allow for the existing practice of sharing protected health information with public health authorities that are authorized by law to collect or receive such information to aid them in their mission of protecting the health of the public. Examples of such activities include those directed at the reporting of disease or injury, reporting deaths and births, investigating the occurrence and cause of injury and disease, and monitoring adverse outcomes related to food (including dietary supplements), drugs, biological products, and medical devices. See the fact sheet and frequently asked questions on this web site about the public health provision for more information.

Q: Does the public health provision of the HIPAA Privacy Rule require covered entities to make public health disclosures?

A: No. The Privacy Rule's public health provision permits, but does not require, covered entities to make such disclosures. This provision is intended to allow covered entities to continue current voluntary reporting practices that are critically important to public health and safety. The Rule also permits covered entities to disclose protected health information when State or other law requires covered entities to make disclosures for public health purposes. For instance, many State laws require health care providers to report certain diseases, cases of child abuse, births, or deaths, and the Privacy Rule permits covered entities to disclose protected health information, without authorization, to make such reports. See the fact sheet and frequently asked questions on this web site about the public health provision for more information.

Q: May covered entities disclose facially identifiable protected health information, such as name, address, and social security number, for public health purposes?

A: Yes. The HIPAA Privacy Rule permits covered entities to disclose the amount and type of protected health information that is needed for public health purposes. In some cases, the disclosure will be required by other law, in which case, covered entities may make the required disclosure pursuant to 45 CFR 164.512(a) of the Rule. For disclosures that are not required by law, covered entities may disclose, without authorization, the information that is reasonably limited to that which is minimally necessary to accomplish the intended purpose of the disclosure. For routine or recurring public health disclosures, a covered entity may develop protocols as part of its minimum necessary policies and procedures to address the type and amount of information that may be disclosed for such purposes. Covered entities may also rely on the requesting public health authority's determination of the minimally necessary information. See the fact sheet and frequently asked questions on this web site about the public health and minimum necessary standards for more information.

Q: Does the HIPAA Privacy Rule's public health provision permit covered entities to disclose protected health information to authorities such as the National Institutes of Health (NIH)?

A: The definition of a "public health authority" requires that an agency's official mandate include the responsibility for public health matters. The mandate can be responsibility for public health matters, generally, or it can be for specific public health programs. Furthermore, an agency's official mandate does not have to be exclusively or primarily for public health. Therefore, to the extent a government agency has public health matters as part of its official mandate, it qualifies as a public health authority. For instance, various Department of Health and Human Service agencies, such as NIH and the Health Resources and Services Administration (HRSA), are authorized by law to assist the Secretary of Health and Human Services in carrying out the purposes of section 301 of the Public Health Service Act. Those agencies are public health authorities under the Rule, even if they have other non-public health mandates. To the extent a public health authority is authorized by law to collect or receive information for the public health purposes specified in the public health provision, covered entities may disclose protected health information to such public health authorities without authorization pursuant to the public health provision. See the fact sheet and frequently asked questions on this web site about the public health provision for more information.

Q: To whom may covered entities make public health disclosures regarding a product regulated by the Food and Drug Administration (FDA) when more than one person is identified on the product label?

A: Covered entities may identify persons responsible for an FDA-regulated product by using the product label, the literature that accompanies the product, or other sources of labeling, such as the Physician's Desk Reference. If multiple persons are named, covered entities may choose any of the persons named by these sources. See the fact sheet and frequently asked questions on this web site about the public health provision for more information.

Q: Is a covered entity permitted to disclose protected health information under the HIPAA Privacy Rule's public health provision when the link between an adverse event and a product regulated by the Food and Drug Administration (FDA) is only suspected?

A: Yes. In most instances when a covered entity makes an adverse event report to a person responsible for an FDA-regulated product, the covered entity will suspect, but not know, the product is the cause of the event. Determining whether the product is related to the adverse event almost always requires follow up with the covered entity which in turn may need further contact with the patient. FDA and product manufacturers receive a great deal of important information about the safety of regulated products from these reports. To limit such reports to those instances where the covered entity is convinced of the link between the product and the event would reduce the amount of useful safety, quality and effectiveness data available to the agency as well as to product manufacturers. This would limit significantly FDA's ability to protect the public health by helping to assure that only safe and effective products are marketed in the U.S. Accordingly, covered entities may disclose the minimum amount of protected health information that is reasonably necessary to report suspected adverse events associated with an FDA-regulated product. See the fact sheet and frequently asked questions on this web site about the public health and minimum necessary standards for more information.

Q: Does the HIPAA Privacy Rule's public health provision permit covered entities to disclose protected health information without authorization to a manufacturer of a product regulated by the Food and Drug Administration (FDA) for use by the manufacturer to assess the effectiveness of its marketing campaign?

A: No. The public health provision is intended to facilitate the flow of information that is essential to the FDA's public health mission. The provision does not permit covered entities to disclose protected health information to a manufacturer for the manufacturer's commercial purposes, or for any other non-public health purpose. For example, the Rule does not permit a covered entity to provide a drug manufacturer with a list of persons who prefer a different flavored cough syrup over the flavor of the manufacturer's product. Rather, this provision permits covered entities to disclose protected health information as necessary to continue current voluntary reporting of adverse events and similar reports that are necessary to ensure the quality, safety, or effectiveness of an FDA-regulated product. For instance, a covered entity would be permitted to report a concern to a drug manufacturer that its cough syrup might be unsafe based on the belief that a difference in the taste could be due to drug tampering or a manufacturing problem. Likewise, a covered health care provider would be permitted to disclose protected health information to a drug manufacturer to report that the failure of a patient's medical condition to improve may be due to the drug's ineffectiveness. In making such a report, the covered entity may disclose the protected health information that is reasonably necessary to achieve the purpose of the report. See the fact sheet and frequently asked questions on this web site about the public health and minimum necessary standards for more information.

Q: Does the HIPAA Privacy Rule's public health provision permit covered health care providers to disclose protected health information concerning the findings of pre-employment physicals, drug tests, or fitness-for-duty examinations to an individual's employer?

A: The public health provision permits covered health care providers to disclose an individual's protected health information to the individual's employer without authorization in very limited circumstances. First, the covered health care provider must provide the health care service to the individual at the request of the individual's employer or as a member of the employer's workforce. Second, the health care service provided must relate to the medical surveillance of the workplace or an evaluation to determine whether the individual has a work-related illness or injury. Third, the employer must have a duty under the Occupational Safety and Health Administration (OSHA), the Mine Safety and Health Administration (MSHA), or the requirements of a similar State law, to keep records on or act on such information. For example, OSHA requires employers to monitor employees' exposures to certain substances and to take specific actions when an employee's exposure level exceeds a specified limit. A covered entity which tests an individual for such an exposure level at the request of the individual's employer may disclose that test result to the employer without authorization.

Generally, pre-placement physicals, drug tests, and fitness-for-duty examinations are not performed for such purposes. However, to the extent such an examination is conducted at the request of the employer for the purpose of such workplace medical surveillance or work-related illness or injury, and the employer needs the information to comply with the requirements of OSHA, MSHA, or similar State law, the protected health information the employer needs to meet such legal obligation may be disclosed to the employer without authorization. Covered health care providers who make such disclosures must provide the individual with written notice that the information is to be disclosed to his or her employer (or by posting the notice at the worksite if the service is provided there).

When a health care service does not meet the above requirements, covered entities may not disclose an individual's protected health information to the individual's employer without an authorization, unless the disclosure is otherwise permitted without authorization by other provisions of the Rule. However, nothing in the Rule prohibits an employer from conditioning employment on an individual providing an authorization for the disclosure of such information.

RESEARCH

[*45 CFR 164.501, 164.508, 164.512(i)*]
[See also *45 CFR 164.514(e), 164.528, 164.532*]

Background

The HIPAA Privacy Rule establishes the conditions under which protected health information may be used or disclosed by covered entities for research purposes. Research is defined in the Privacy Rule as, "a systematic investigation, including research development, testing, and evaluation, designed to develop or contribute to generalizable knowledge." See 45 CFR 164.501. A covered entity may always use or disclose for research purposes health information which has been de-identified (in accordance with 45 CFR 164.502(d), and 164.514(a)-(c) of the Rule) without regard to the provisions below.

The Privacy Rule also defines the means by which individuals will be informed of uses and disclosures of their medical information for research purposes, and their rights to access information about them held by covered entities. Where research is concerned, the Privacy Rule protects the privacy of individually identifiable health information, while at the same time ensuring that researchers continue to have access to medical information necessary to conduct vital research. Currently, most research involving human subjects operates under the Common Rule (45 CFR Part 46, Subpart A) and/or the Food and Drug Administration's (FDA) human subject protection regulations (21 CFR Parts 50 and 56), which have some provisions that are similar to, but separate from, the Privacy Rule's provisions for research. These human subject protection regulations, which apply to most Federally-funded and to some privately funded research, include protections to help ensure the privacy of subjects and the confidentiality of information. The Privacy Rule builds upon these existing Federal protections. More importantly, the Privacy Rule creates equal standards of privacy protection for research governed by the existing Federal human subject regulations and research that is not.

<u>How the Rule Works</u>

In the course of conducting research, researchers may obtain, create, use, and/or disclose individually identifiable health information. Under the Privacy Rule, covered entities are permitted to use and disclose protected health information for research with individual authorization, or without individual authorization under limited circumstances set forth in the Privacy Rule.

<u>Research Use/Disclosure Without Authorization</u>. To use or disclose protected health information without authorization by the research participant, a covered entity must obtain one of the following:

•<u>Documented Institutional Review Board (IRB) or Privacy Board Approval</u>. Documentation that an alteration or waiver of research participants' authorization for use/disclosure of information about them for research purposes has been approved by an IRB or a Privacy Board. See 45 CFR 164.512(i)(1)(i). This provision of the Privacy Rule might be used, for example, to conduct records research, when researchers are unable to use de-identified information, and the research could not practicably be conducted if research participants' authorization were required.

A covered entity may use or disclose protected health information for research purposes pursuant to a waiver of authorization by an IRB or Privacy Board, provided it has obtained documentation of *all* of the following:

<Identification of the IRB or Privacy Board and the date on which the alteration or waiver of authorization was approved;
<A statement that the IRB or Privacy Board has determined that the alteration or waiver of authorization, in whole or in part, satisfies the three criteria in the Rule;
<A brief description of the protected health information for which use or access has been determined to be necessary by the IRB or Privacy Board;
<A statement that the alteration or waiver of authorization has been reviewed and approved under either normal or expedited review procedures; and
<The signature of the chair or other member, as designated by the chair, of the IRB or the Privacy Board, as applicable.

The following three criteria must be satisfied for an IRB or Privacy Board to approve a waiver of authorization under the Privacy Rule:

<The use or disclosure of protected health information involves no more than a minimal risk to the privacy of individuals, based on, at least, the presence of the following elements:

San adequate plan to protect the identifiers from improper use and disclosure;
San adequate plan to destroy the identifiers at the earliest opportunity consistent with conduct of the research, unless there is a health or research justification for retaining the identifiers or such retention is otherwise required by law; and
Sadequate written assurances that the protected health information will not be reused or disclosed to any other person or entity, except as required by law, for authorized oversight of the research project, or for other research for which the use or disclosure of protected health information would be permitted by this subpart;

<The research could not practicably be conducted without the waiver or alteration; and
<The research could not practicably be conducted without access to and use of the protected health information.

•<u>Preparatory to Research</u>. Representations from the researcher, either in writing or orally, that the use or disclosure of the protected health information is solely to prepare a research protocol or for similar purposes preparatory to research, that the researcher will not remove any protected health information from the covered entity, *and* representation that protected health information for which access is sought is necessary for the research purpose. See 45 CFR 164.512(i)(1)(ii). This provision might be used, for example, to design a research study or to assess the feasibility of conducting a study.

•<u>Research on Protected Health Information of Decedents</u>. Representations from the researcher, either in writing or orally, that the use or disclosure being sought is solely for research on the protected health information of decedents, that the protected health information being sought is necessary for the research, *and*, at the request of the covered entity, documentation of the death of the individuals about whom information is being sought. See 45 CFR 164.512(i)(1)(iii).

•<u>Limited Data Sets with a Data Use Agreement</u>. A data use agreement entered into by both the covered entity and the researcher, pursuant to which the covered entity may disclose a limited data set to the resercher for research, public health, or health care operations. See 45 CFR 164.514(e). A limited data set excludes specified direct identifiers of the individual or of relatives, employers, or household members of the individual. The data use agreement must:

<Establish the permitted uses and disclosures of the limited data set by the recipient, consistent with the purposes of the research, and which may not include any use or disclosure that would violate the Rule if done by the covered entity;
<Limit who can use or receive the data; and
<Require the recipient to agree to the following:

SNot to use or disclose the information other than as permitted by the data use agreement or as otherwise required by law;
SUse appropriate safeguards to prevent the use or disclosure of the information other than as provided for in the data use agreement;
SReport to the covered entity any use or disclosure of the information not provided for by the data use agreement of which the recipient becomes aware;
SEnsure that any agents, including a subcontractor, to whom the recipient provides the limited data set agrees to the same restrictions and conditions that apply to the recipient with respect to the limited data set; and
SNot to identify the information or contact the individual.

<u>Research Use/Disclosure With Individual Authorization</u>. The Privacy Rule also permits covered entities to use or disclose protected health information for research purposes when a research participant authorizes the use or disclosure of information about him or herself. Today, for example, a research participant's

authorization will typically be sought for most clinical trials and some records research. In this case, documentation of IRB or Privacy Board approval of a waiver of authorization is not required for the use or disclosure of protected health information.

To use or disclose protected health information with authorization by the research participant, the covered entity must obtain an authorization that satisfies the requirements of 45 CFR 164.508. The Privacy Rule has a general set of authorization requirements that apply to all uses and disclosures, including those for research purposes. However, several special provisions apply to research authorizations:

•Unlike other authorizations, an authorization for a research purpose may state that the authorization does not expire, that there is no expiration date or event, or that the authorization continues until the "end of the research study;" and

•An authorization for the use or disclosure of protected health information for research may be combined with a consent to participate in the research, or with any other legal permission related to the research study.

Accounting for Research Disclosures. In general, the Privacy Rule gives individuals the right to receive an accounting of certain disclosures of protected health information made by a covered entity. See 45 CFR 164.528. This accounting must include disclosures of protected health information that occurred during the six years prior to the individual's request for an accounting, or since the applicable compliance date (whichever is sooner), and must include specified information regarding each disclosure. A more general accounting is permitted for subsequent multiple disclosures to the same person or entity for a single purpose. See 45 CFR 164.528(b)(3). Among the types of disclosures that are exempt from this accounting requirement are:

•Research disclosures made pursuant to an individual's authorization;

•Disclosures of the limited data set to researchers with a data use agreement under 45 CFR 164.514(e).

In addition, for disclosures of protected health information for research purposes without the individual's authorization pursuant to 45 CFR164.512(i), and that involve at least 50 records, the Privacy Rule allows for a simplified accounting of such disclosures by covered entities. Under this simplified accounting provision, covered entities may provide individuals with a list of all protocols for which the patient's protected health information may have been disclosed under 45 CFR 164.512(i), as well as the researcher's name and contact information. Other requirements related to this simplified accounting provision are found in 45 CFR 164.528(b)(4).

Transition Provisions. Under the Privacy Rule, a covered entity may use and disclose protected health information that was created or received for research, either before or after the compliance date, if the covered entity obtained any one of the following prior to the compliance date:

•An authorization or other express legal permission from an individual to use or disclose protected health information for the research;

•The informed consent of the individual to participate in the research; or

•A waiver of informed consent by an IRB in accordance with the Common Rule or an exception under FDA's human subject protection regulations at 21 CFR 50.24.

However, if a waiver of informed consent was obtained prior to the compliance date, but informed consent is subsequently sought after the compliance date, the covered entity must obtain the individual's authorization as required at 45 CFR 164.508. For example, if there was a temporary waiver of informed consent for emergency research under the FDA's human subject protection regulations, and informed consent was later sought after the compliance date, individual authorization would be required before the covered entity could use or disclose protected health information for the research after the waiver of informed consent was no longer valid.

The Privacy Rule allows covered entities to rely on such express legal permission, informed consent, or IRB-approved waiver of informed consent, which they create or receive before the applicable compliance date, to use and disclose protected health information for specific research studies, as well as for future unspecified research that may be included in such permission.

RESEARCH

Frequently Asked Questions

Q:Will the HIPAA Privacy Rule hinder medical research by making doctors and others less willing and/or able to share with researchers information about individual patients?

A. We do not believe that the Privacy Rule will hinder medical research. Indeed, patients and health plan members should be more willing to authorize disclosures of their information for research and to participate in research when they know their information is protected. For example, in genetic studies conducted at the National Institutes of Health, nearly 32 percent of eligible people offered a test for breast cancer risk declined to take it. The overwhelming majority of those who refuse cite concerns about health insurance discrimination and loss of privacy as the reason. The Privacy Rule both permits important research and, at the same time, encourages patients to participate in research by providing much needed assurances about the privacy of their health information.

The Privacy Rule will require some covered health care providers and health plans to change their current practices related to documenting research uses and disclosures. It is possible that some covered health care providers and health plans may conclude that the Rule's requirements for research uses and disclosures are too burdensome and will choose to limit researchers' access to protected health information. We believe few providers will take this route, however, because the Common Rule includes similar, and more rigorous requirements, that have not impaired the willingness of researchers to undertake Federally-funded research. For example, unlike the Privacy Rule, the Common Rule requires an Institutional Review Board (IRB) review for all research proposals under its purview, even if informed consent is to be sought. The Privacy Rule requires documentation of IRB or Privacy Board approval only if patient authorization for the use or disclosure of protected health information for research purposes is to be altered or waived. See the fact sheet and frequently asked questions about the research provisions on this web site for more information about the Common Rule and Institutional Review and Privacy Boards.

Q: Are some of the criteria so subjective that inconsistent determinations may be made by Institutional Review Boards (IRB) and Privacy Boards reviewing similar or identical research projects?

A: Under the HIPAA Privacy Rule, IRBs and Privacy Boards need to use their judgment as to whether the waiver criteria have been satisfied. Several of the waiver criteria are closely modeled on the Common Rule's criteria for the waiver of informed consent and for the approval of a research study. Thus, it is anticipated that IRBs already have experience in making the necessarily subjective assessments of risks. While IRBs or Privacy Boards may reach different determinations, the assessment of the waiver criteria through this deliberative process is a crucial element in the current system of safeguarding research participants' privacy. The entire system of local IRBs is, in fact, predicated on a deliberative process that permits local IRB autonomy. The Privacy Rule builds upon this principle; it does not change it. Nonetheless, the Department will consider issuing guidance as necessary and appropriate to address concerns that may arise during implementation of these provisions. See the fact sheet and frequently asked questions about the research provisions on this web site for more information about the Common Rule and Institutional Review and Privacy Boards.

Q: Does the HIPAA Privacy Rule prohibit researchers from conditioning participation in a clinical trial on an authorization to use/disclose existing protected health information?

A: No. The Privacy Rule does not address conditions for enrollment in a research study. Therefore, the Privacy Rule in no way prohibits researchers from conditioning enrollment in a research study on the execution of an authorization for the use of pre-existing health information.

Q: Does the HIPAA Privacy Rule permit the creation of a database for research purposes through an Institutional Review Board (IRB) or Privacy Board waiver of individual authorization?

A: Yes. A covered entity may use or disclose protected health information without individuals' authorizations for the creation of a research database, provided the covered entity obtains documentation that an IRB or Privacy Board has determined that the specified waiver criteria were satisfied. Protected health information maintained by a covered entity in such a research database could be used or disclosed for future research studies as permitted by the Privacy Rule – that is, for future studies in which individual authorization has been obtained or where the Rule would permit research without an authorization, such as pursuant to an IRB or Privacy Board waiver. See the fact sheet and frequently asked questions about the research provisions on this web site for more information about Institutional Review and Privacy Boards.

Q: Can researchers continue to access existing databanks or repositories that are maintained by covered entities, even if those databases were created prior to the compliance date without patient permission or without a waiver of informed consent by an Institutional Review Board (IRB)?

A: Yes. Under the HIPAA Privacy Rule, covered entities may use or disclose protected health information from existing databases or repositories for research purposes either with individual authorization as required at 45 CFR 164.508, or with a waiver of individual authorization as permitted at 45 CFR 164.512(i). See the fact sheet and frequently asked questions about the research provisions on this web site for more information about Institutional Review Boards.

Q: How does the Rule help Institutional Review Boards (IRB) handle the additional responsibilities imposed by the HIPAA Privacy Rule?

A: Recognizing that some institutions may not have IRBs, or that some IRBs may not have the expertise needed to review research that requires consideration of risks to privacy, the Privacy Rule permits the covered entity to accept documentation of waiver of authorization from an alternative body called a Privacy Board– which could have fewer members, and members with different expertise than IRBs. See the fact sheet and frequently asked questions about the research provisions on this web site for more information about Institutional Review and Privacy Boards.

In addition, the Rule allows an IRB to use expedited review procedures as permitted by the Common Rule to review and approve requests for waiver of authorizations. Similarly, the Rule permits Privacy Boards to use an expedited review process when the research involves no more than a minimal privacy risk to the individuals. An expedited review process permits covered entities to accept documentation of waiver of authorization when only one or more members of the IRB or Privacy Board have conducted the review. See the fact sheet and frequently asked questions about the research provisions on this web site for more information about the Common Rule.

Q: By establishing new waiver criteria and authorization requirements, hasn't the HIPAA Privacy Rule, in effect, modified the Common Rule?

A: No. Where both the Privacy Rule and the Common Rule apply, both regulations must be followed. The Privacy Rule regulates only the content and conditions of the documentation that covered entities must obtain before using or disclosing protected health information for research purposes. See the fact sheet and frequently asked questions about the research provisions on this web site for more information about the Common Rule.

Q: Is documentation of Institutional Review Board (IRB) *and* Privacy Board approval required by the HIPAA Privacy Rule before a covered entity would be permitted to disclose protected health information for research purposes without an individual's authorization?

A: No. The HIPAA Privacy Rule requires documentation of waiver approval by either an IRB *or* a Privacy Board, not both. See the fact sheet and frequently asked questions about the research provisions on this web site for more information about Institutional Review and Privacy Boards.

Q: Does the HIPAA Privacy Rule require a covered entity to create an Institutional Review Board (IRB) or Privacy Board before using or disclosing protected health information for research?

A: No. The IRB or Privacy Board could be created by the covered entity or the recipient researcher, or it could be an independent board. See the fact sheet and frequently asked questions about the research provisions on this web site for more information about Institutional Review and Privacy Boards.

Q: What does the HIPAA Privacy Rule say about a research participant's right of access to research records or results?

A: With few exceptions, the Privacy Rule gives patients the right to inspect and obtain a copy of health information about themselves that is maintained by a covered entity or its business associate in a "designated record set." A designated record set is basically a group of records which a covered entity uses to make decisions about individuals, and includes a health care provider's medical records and billing records, and a health plan's enrollment, payment, claims adjudication, and case or medical management record systems. While it may be unlikely that a researcher would be maintaining a designated record set, any research records or results that are actually maintained by the covered entity as part of a designated record set would be accessible to research participants unless one of the Privacy Rule's permitted exceptions applies.

One of the permitted exceptions applies to protected health information created or obtained by a covered health care provider/researcher for a clinical trial. The Privacy Rule permits the individual's access rights in these cases to be suspended *while the clinical trial is in progress*, provided the research participant agreed to this denial of access when consenting to participate in the clinical trial. In addition, the health care provider/researcher must inform the research participant that the right to access protected health information will be reinstated at the conclusion of the clinical trial.

Q: Are the HIPAA Privacy Rule's requirements regarding patient access in harmony with the Clinical Laboratory Improvements Amendments of 1988 (CLIA)?

A: Yes. The Privacy Rule does not require clinical laboratories that are also covered health care providers to provide an individual access to information if CLIA prohibits them from doing so. CLIA permits clinical laboratories to provide clinical laboratory test records and reports only to "authorized persons," as defined primarily by State law. The individual who is the subject of the information is not always included as an authorized person. Therefore, the Privacy Rule includes an exception to individuals' general right to access protected health information about themselves if providing an individual such access would be in conflict with CLIA.

In addition, for certain research laboratories that are exempt from the CLIA regulations, the Privacy Rule does not require such research laboratories, if they are also a covered health care provider, to provide individuals with access to protected health information because doing so may result in the research laboratory losing its CLIA exemption.

Q: Do the HIPAA Privacy Rule's requirements for authorization and the Common Rule's requirements for informed consent differ?

A: Yes. Under the Privacy Rule, a patient's authorization is for the use and disclosure of protected health information for research purposes. In contrast, an individual's informed consent, as required by the Common Rule and the Food and Drug Administration's (FDA) human subjects regulations, is a consent to participate in the research study as a whole, not simply a consent for the research use or disclosure of protected health information. See the fact sheet and frequently asked questions about the research provisions on this web site for more information about the Common Rule. For this reason, there are important differences between the Privacy Rule's requirements for individual authorization, and the Common Rule's and FDA's requirements for informed consent. However, the Privacy Rule's authorization elements are compatible with the Common Rule's informed consent elements. Thus, both sets of requirements can be met by use of a single, combined form, which is permitted by the Privacy Rule. For example, the Privacy Rule allows the research authorization to state that the authorization will be valid until the conclusion of the research study, or to state that the authorization will not have an expiration date or event. This is compatible with the Common Rule's requirement for an explanation of the expected duration of the research subject's participation in the study. It should be noted that where the Privacy Rule, the Common Rule, and/or FDA's human subjects regulations are applicable, each of the applicable regulations will need to be followed.

Q: When is a researcher a covered health care provider under HIPAA?

A: A researcher is a covered health care provider if he or she furnishes health care services to individuals, including the subjects of research, and transmits any health information in electronic form in connection with a transaction covered by the Transactions Rule. See 45 CFR 160.102, 160.103. For example, a researcher who conducts a clinical trial that involves the delivery of routine health care, such as an MRI or liver function test, and transmits health information in electronic form to a third party payer for payment, would be a covered health care provider under the Privacy Rule. Researchers who provide health care to the subjects of research or other individuals would be covered health care providers even if they do not themselves electronically transmit information in connection with a HIPAA transaction, but have other entities, such as a hospital or billing service, conduct such electronic transactions on their behalf. For further assistance in determining covered entity status, see the "decision tool" at www.hhs.gov/ocr/hipaa/.

Q: When does a covered entity have discretion to determine whether a research component of the entity is part of their covered functions, and therefore, subject to the HIPAA Privacy Rule?

A: A covered entity that qualifies as a hybrid entity, meaning that the entity is a single legal entity that performs both covered and non-covered functions, may choose whether it wants to be a hybrid entity. If such a covered entity decides not to be a hybrid entity then it, and all of its components, are subject to the Privacy Rule in its entirety. Therefore, if a researcher is an employee or workforce member of a covered entity that has decided not to be a hybrid entity, the researcher is part of the covered entity and is, therefore, subject to the Privacy Rule.

If a covered entity decides to be a hybrid entity, it must define and designate as its health care component(s) those parts of the entity that engage in covered functions. "Covered functions" are those functions of a covered entity that make the entity a health plan, a health care provider, or a health care clearinghouse. Thus, research components of a hybrid entity that function as health care providers and engage in standard electronic transactions must be included in the hybrid entity's health care component(s), and be subject to the Privacy Rule.

However, research components that function as health care providers, but do not engage in standard electronic transactions may, but are not required to, be included in the health care component(s) of the hybrid entity. For example, a hybrid entity, such as a university, has the option to include or exclude a research laboratory, that functions as a health care provider but does not engage in electronic transactions, as part of the hybrid entity's health care component. If such a research laboratory is included in the hybrid entity's health care component, then the employees or workforce members of the laboratory must comply with the Privacy Rule. But if the research laboratory is excluded from the hybrid entity's health care component, the employees or workforce members of the laboratory are not subject to the Privacy Rule.

Q: If a research subject revokes his or her authorization to have protected health information used or disclosed for research, does the HIPAA Privacy Rule permit a researcher/covered health care provider to continue using the protected health information already obtained prior to the time the individual revoked his or her authorization?

A: Covered entities may continue to use and disclose protected health information that was obtained prior to the time the individual revoked his or her authorization, as necessary to maintain the integrity of the research study. An individual may not revoke an authorization to the extent the covered entity has acted in reliance on the authorization. For research uses and disclosures, this reliance exception at 45 CFR 164.508(b)(5)(i) permits the continued use and disclosure of protected health information already obtained pursuant to a valid authorization to the extent necessary to preserve the integrity of the research study. For example, the reliance exception would permit the continued use and disclosure of protected health information to account for a subject's withdrawal from the research study, as necessary to incorporate the information as part of a marketing application submitted to the Food and Drug Administration, to conduct investigations of scientific misconduct, or to report adverse events.

However, the reliance exception would not permit a covered entity to continue disclosing additional protected health information to a researcher or to use for its own research purposes information not already gathered at the time an individual withdraws his or her authorization.

Q: Can the preparatory research provision of the HIPAA Privacy Rule at 45 CFR 164.512(i)(1)(ii) be used to recruit individuals into a research study?

A: The preparatory research provision permits covered entities to use or disclose protected health information for purposes preparatory to research, such as to aid study recruitment. However, the provision at 45 CFR 164.512(i)(1)(ii) does not permit the researcher to remove protected health information from the covered entity's site. As such, a researcher who is an employee or a member of the covered entity's workforce could use protected health information to contact prospective research subjects. The preparatory research provision would allow such a researcher to identify prospective research participants for purposes of seeking their authorization to use or disclose protected health information for a research study. In addition, the Rule permits a covered entity to disclose protected health information to the individual who is the subject of the information. See 45 CFR 164.502(a)(1)(i). Therefore, covered health care providers and patients may continue to discuss the option of enrolling in a clinical trial without patient authorization, and without an Institutional Review Board (IRB) or Privacy Board waiver of the authorization. See the fact sheet and frequently asked questions about the research provisions on this web site for more information about Institutional Review and Privacy Boards. However, a researcher who is not a part of the covered entity may not use the preparatory research provision to contact prospective research subjects. Rather, the outside researcher could obtain contact information through a partial waiver of individual authorization by an IRB or Privacy Board as permitted at 45 CFR164.512(i)(1)(i). The IRB or Privacy Board waiver of authorization permits the partial waiver of authorization for the purposes of allowing a researcher to obtain protected health information as necessary to recruit potential research subjects. For example, even if an IRB does not waive informed consent and individual authorization for the study itself, it may waive such authorization to permit the disclosure of protected health information as necessary for the researcher to be able to contact and recruit individuals into the study.

Q: Does the HIPAA Privacy Rule require documentation of Institutional Review Board (IRB) or Privacy Board approval of an alteration or waiver of individual authorization before a covered entity may use or disclose protected health information for any of the following provisions: (1) for preparatory research at 45 CFR 164.512(i)(1)(ii), (2) for research on the protected health information of decedents at 45 CFR 164.512(i)(1)(iii), or (3) a limited data set with a data use agreement as stipulated at 45 CFR 164.514(e)?

A: No. Documentation of IRB or Privacy Board approval of an alteration or waiver of individual authorization is only needed before a covered entity may use or disclose protected health information under 45 CFR 164.512(i)(1)(i). See the fact sheet and frequently asked questions about the research provisions on this web site for more information about Institutional Review and Privacy Boards.

Q: If research subjects' consent was obtained before the compliance date, but the Institutional Review Board (IRB) subsequently modifies the informed consent document after the compliance date and requires that subjects be reconsented, is authorization now required from these previously enrolled research subjects under the HIPAA Privacy Rule?

A: Yes. If informed consent or reconsent (ie., asked to sign a revised consent or another informed consent) is obtained from research subjects after the compliance date, the covered entity must obtain individual authorization as required at 45 CFR 164.508 for the use or disclosure of protected health information once the consent obtained before the compliance date is no longer valid for the research. The revised informed consent document may be combined with the authorization elements required by 45 CFR 164.508. See the fact sheet and frequently asked questions about the research provisions on this web site for more information about Institutional Review Boards.

Q: Can covered entities continue to disclose adverse event reports that contain protected health information to the Department of Health and Human Services (HHS) Office for Human Research Protections?

A: Yes. The Office for Human Research Protections is a public health authority under the HIPAA Privacy Rule. Therefore, covered entities can continue to disclose protected health information to report adverse events to the Office for Human Research Protections either with patient authorization as provided at 45 CFR 164.508, or without patient authorization for public health activities as permitted at 45 CFR 164.512(b).

Q: Can covered entities continue to disclose protected health information to the HHS Office for Human Research Protections for purposes of determining compliance with the HHS regulations for the protection of human subjects (45 CFR Part 46)?

A: Yes. The Office for Human Research Protections is a health oversight agency under the HIPAA Privacy Rule. Therefore, covered entities can continue to disclose protected health information to the Office for Human Research Protections for such compliance investigations either with patient authorization as provided at 45 CFR 164.508, or without patient authorization for health oversight activities as permitted at 45 CFR 164.512(d).

DISCLOSURES FOR WORKERS' COMPENSATION PURPOSES

[*45 CFR 164.512(l)*]

Background

The HIPAA Privacy Rule does not apply to entities that are either workers' compensation insurers, workers' compensation administrative agencies, or employers, except to the extent they may otherwise be covered entities. However, these entities need access to the health information of individuals who are injured on the job or who have a work-related illness to process or adjudicate claims, or to coordinate care under workers' compensation systems. Generally, this health information is obtained from health care providers who treat these individuals and who may be covered by the Privacy Rule. The Privacy Rule recognizes the legitimate need of insurers and other entities involved in the workers' compensation systems to have access to individuals' health information as authorized by State or other law. Due to the significant variability among such laws, the Privacy Rule permits disclosures of health information for workers' compensation purposes in a number of different ways.

How the Rule Works

Disclosures Without Individual Authorization. The Privacy Rule permits covered entities to disclose protected health information to workers' compensation insurers, State administrators, employers, and other persons or entities involved in workers' compensation systems, without the individual's authorization:

As authorized by and to the extent necessary to comply with laws relating to workers' compensation or similar programs established by law that provide benefits for work-related injuries or illness without regard to fault. This includes programs established by the Black Lung Benefits Act, the Federal Employees' Compensation Act, the Longshore and Harbor Workers' Compensation Act, and the Energy Employees' Occupational Illness Compensation Program Act. See 45 CFR 164.512(*l*).

To the extent the disclosure is required by State or other law. The disclosure must comply with and be limited to what the law requires. See 45 CFR

164.512(a).

For purposes of obtaining payment for any health care provided to the injured or ill worker. See 45 CFR 164.502(a)(1)(ii) and the definition of "payment" at 45 CFR 164.501.

Disclosures With Individual Authorization. In addition, covered entities may disclose protected health information to workers' compensation insurers and others involved in workers' compensation systems where the individual has provided his or her authorization for the release of the information to the entity. The authorization must contain the elements and otherwise meet the requirements specified at 45 CFR 164.508.

Minimum Necessary. Covered entities are required reasonably to limit the amount of protected health information disclosed under 45 CFR 164.512(l) to the minimum necessary to accomplish the workers' compensation purpose. Under this requirement, protected health information may be shared for such purposes to the full extent authorized by State or other law.

In addition, covered entities are required reasonably to limit the amount of protected health information disclosed for payment purposes to the minimum necessary. Covered entities are permitted to disclose the amount and types of protected health information that are necessary to obtain payment for health care provided to an injured or ill worker.

Where a covered entity routinely makes disclosures for workers' compensation purposes under 45 CFR 164.512(*l*) or for payment purposes, the covered entity may develop standard protocols as part of its minimum necessary policies and procedures that address the type and amount of protected health information to be disclosed for such purposes.

Where protected health information is requested by a State workers' compensation or other public official, covered entities are permitted to reasonably rely on the official's representations that the information requested is the minimum necessary for the intended purpose. See 45 CFR 164.514(d)(3)(iii)(A).

Covered entities are not required to make a minimum necessary determination when disclosing protected health information as required by State or other law, or pursuant to the individual's authorization. See 45 CFR 164.502(b).

The Department will actively monitor the effects of the Privacy Rule, and in particular, the minimum necessary standard, on the workers' compensation systems and consider proposing modifications, where appropriate, to ensure that the Rule does not have any unintended negative effects that disturb these systems.

Refer to the fact sheet and frequently asked questions on this web site about the minimum necessary standard, or to 45 CFR 164.502(b) and 164.514(d), for more information.

DISCLOSURES FOR WORKERS' COMPENSATION PURPOSES

Frequently Asked Questions

Q: Won't the HIPAA Privacy Rule's minimum necessary standard impede the ability of workers' compensation insurers, State administrative agencies, and employers to obtain the health information needed to pay injured or ill workers the benefits guaranteed them under the State workers' compensation system?

A: No. The Privacy Rule is not intended to impede the flow of health information to those who need it to process or adjudicate claims, or coordinate care, for injured or ill workers under workers' compensation systems. The minimum necessary standard generally requires covered entities to make reasonable efforts to limit uses and disclosures of, as well as requests for, protected health information to the minimum necessary to accomplish the intended purpose. For disclosures of protected health information made for workers' compensation purposes under 45 CFR 164.512(*l*), the minimum necessary standard permits covered entities to disclose information to the full extent authorized by State or other law. In addition, where protected health information is requested by a State workers' compensation or other public official for such purposes, covered entities are permitted reasonably to rely on the official's representations that the information requested is the minimum necessary for the intended purpose. See 45 CFR 164.514(d)(3)(iii)(A).

For disclosures of protected health information for payment purposes, covered entities may disclose the type and amount of information necessary to receive payment for any health care provided to an injured or ill worker.

The minimum necessary standard does not apply to disclosures that are required by State or other law or made pursuant to the individual's authorization.

Q: Does an individual have a right under the HIPAA Privacy Rule to restrict the protected health information his or her health care provider discloses for workers' compensation purposes?

A: Individuals do not have a right under the Privacy Rule at 45 CFR 164.522(a) to request that a covered entity restrict a disclosure of protected health information about them for workers' compensation purposes when that disclosure is required by law or authorized by, and necessary to comply with, a workers' compensation or similar law. See 45 CFR 164.522(a) and 164.512(a) and (*l*).

Q: Does the HIPAA Privacy Rule permit a health care provider to disclose an injured or ill worker's protected health information without his or her authorization when requested for purposes of adjudicating the individual's workers' compensation claim?

A: Covered entities are permitted to disclose protected health information for such purposes as authorized by, and to the extent necessary to comply with, workers' compensation law. See 45 CFR 164.512(*l*). In addition, the Privacy Rule generally permits covered entities to disclose protected health information in the course of any judicial or administrative proceeding in response to a court order, subpoena, or other lawful process. See 45 CFR 164.512(e).

Q: I am a health care provider and my State law says I have to provide a workers' compensation insurer, upon request, with an injured workers' records that relate to treatment or hospitalization for which compensation is being sought. Am I permitted to disclose the information required by my State law?

A: Yes. The HIPAA Privacy Rule permits a covered entity to disclose protected health information as necessary to comply with State law. No minimum necessary determination is required. See 45 CFR 164.512(a) and 164.502(b).

Q: My State law says I may disclose records, relating to the treatment I provided to an injured worker, to a workers' compensation insurer for purposes of determining the amount of or entitlement to payment under the workers' compensation system. Am I allowed to share this information under the HIPAA Privacy Rule?

A: Yes. A covered entity is permitted to disclose an individual's protected health information as necessary to comply with and to the full extent authorized by workers' compensation law. See 45 CFR 164.512(*l*).

Q: My State law says I may provide information regarding an injured workers' previous condition, which is not directly related to the claim for compensation, to an employer or insurer if I obtain the workers' written release. Am I permitted to make this disclosure under the HIPAA Privacy Rule?

A: A covered entity may disclose protected health information where the individual's written authorization has been obtained, consistent with the Privacy Rule's requirements at 45 CFR 164.508. Thus, a covered entity would be permitted to make the above disclosure if the individual signed such an authorization.

NOTICE OF PRIVACY PRACTICES
FOR PROTECTED HEALTH INFORMATION
[*45 CFR 164.520*]

Background

The HIPAA Privacy Rule gives individuals a fundamental new right to be informed of the privacy practices of their health plans and of most of their health care providers, as well as to be informed of their privacy rights with respect to their personal health information. Health plans and covered health care providers are required to develop and distribute a notice that provides a clear explanation of these rights and practices. The notice is intended to focus individuals on privacy issues and concerns, and to prompt them to have discussions with their health plans and health care providers and exercise their rights.

How the Rule Works

General Rule. The Privacy Rule provides that an individual has a right to adequate notice of how a covered entity may use and disclose protected health information about the individual, as well as his or her rights and the covered entity's obligations with respect to that information. Most covered entities must develop and provide individuals with this notice of their privacy practices.

The Privacy Rule does not require the following covered entities to develop a notice:

Health care clearinghouses, if the only protected health information they create or receive is as a business associate of another covered entity. See 45 CFR 164.500(b)(1).

A correctional institution that is a covered entity (e.g., that has a covered health care provider component).

A group health plan that provides benefits only through one or more contracts of insurance with health insurance issuers or HMOs, and that does not create or receive protected health information other than summary health information or enrollment or disenrollment information.

See 45 CFR 164.520(a).

Content of the Notice. Covered entities are required to provide a notice in *plain language* that describes:

How the covered entity may use and disclose protected health information about an individual.

The individual's rights with respect to the information and how the individual may exercise these rights, including how the individual may complain to the covered entity.

The covered entity's legal duties with respect to the information, including a statement that the covered entity is required by law to maintain the privacy of protected health information.

Whom individuals can contact for further information about the covered entity's privacy policies.

The notice must include an effective date. See 45 CFR 164.520(b) for the specific requirements for developing the content of the notice.

A covered entity is required to promptly revise and distribute its notice whenever it makes material changes to any of its privacy practices. See 45 CFR 164.520(b)(3), 164.520(c)(1)(i)(C) for health plans, and 164.520(c)(2)(iv) for covered health care providers with direct treatment relationships with individuals.

Providing the Notice.

A covered entity must make its notice available to any person who asks for it.

A covered entity must prominently post and make available its notice on any web site it maintains that provides information about its customer services or benefits.

Health Plans must also:

<Provide the notice to individuals then covered by the plan no later than April 14, 2003 (April 14, 2004, for small health plans) and to new enrollees at the time of enrollment.
<Provide a revised notice to individuals then covered by the plan within 60 days of a material revision.
<Notify individuals then covered by the plan of the availability of and how to obtain the notice at least once every three years.

Covered Direct Treatment Providers must also:

<Provide the notice to the individual no later than the date of first service delivery (after the April 14, 2003 compliance date of the Privacy Rule) and, except in an emergency treatment situation, make a good faith effort to obtain the individual's written acknowledgment of receipt of the notice. If an acknowledgment cannot be obtained, the provider must document his or her efforts to obtain the acknowledgment and the reason why it was not obtained.
<When first service delivery to an individual is provided over the Internet, through e-mail, or otherwise electronically, the provider must send an electronic notice automatically and contemporaneously in response to the individual's first request for service. The provider must make a good faith effort to obtain a return receipt or other transmission from the individual in response to receiving the notice.
<In an emergency treatment situation, provide the notice as soon as it is reasonably practicable to do so after the emergency situation has ended. In these situations, providers are not required to make a good faith effort to obtain a written acknowledgment from individuals.
<Make the latest notice (i.e., the one that reflects any changes in privacy policies) available at the provider's office or facility for individuals to request to take with them, and post it in a clear and prominent location at the facility.

A covered entity may e-mail the notice to an individual if the individual agrees to receive an electronic notice.

See 45 CFR 164.520(c) for the specific requirements for providing the notice.

Organizational Options.

Any covered entity, including a hybrid entity or an affiliated covered entity, may choose to develop more than one notice, such as when an entity performs different types of covered functions (i.e., the functions that make it a health plan, a health care provider, or a health care clearinghouse) and there are variations in its privacy practices among these covered functions. Covered entities are encouraged to provide individuals with the most specific notice possible.

Covered entities that participate in an organized health care arrangement may choose to produce a single, joint notice if certain requirements are met. For example, the joint notice must describe the covered entities and the service delivery sites to which it applies. If any one of the participating covered entities provides the joint notice to an individual, the notice distribution requirement with respect to that individual is met for all of the covered entities. See 45 CFR 164.520(d).

NOTICE OF PRIVACY PRACTICES
FOR PROTECTED HEALTH INFORMATION

Frequently Asked Questions

Q: Are hospitals or other health care providers required to provide their notices to patients they treat in an emergency?

A: Hospitals and other covered health care providers with a direct treatment relationship with individuals are not required to provide their notices to patients at the time they are providing emergency treatment. In these situations, the HIPAA Privacy Rule requires only that providers give patients a notice when it is practical to do so after the emergency situation has ended. In addition, where notice is delayed by an emergency treatment situation, the Privacy Rule does not require that providers make a good faith effort to obtain the patient's written acknowledgment of receipt of the notice.

Q: If a health care provider chooses to obtain an individual's consent to use or disclose protected health information about them, does the provider also have to make a good faith effort to obtain the individual's acknowledgment of the notice?

A: Yes. The HIPAA Privacy Rule requires that a covered health care provider with a direct treatment relationship with individuals make a good faith effort to obtain written acknowledgments from those individuals that they have received the provider's notice, regardless of whether the provider also chooses to obtain the individuals' consent. However, those providers that choose to obtain consent from individuals have discretion to design one form that includes both a consent and the acknowledgment of receipt of the notice.

Q: Can covered entities distribute their notices as part of other mailings or distributions?

A: Yes. The HIPAA Privacy Rule provides covered entities with discretion in this area; no special or separate mailings or distributions are required to satisfy the Privacy Rule's notice distribution requirements. Thus, a health plan distributing its notice through the mail, in accordance with 45 CFR 164.520(c)(1), may do so as part of another mailing to the individual (e.g., by including the notice with Summary Plan Descriptions). Similarly, a covered entity that e-mails its notice to an individual, in accordance with 45 CFR 164.520(c)(3), may include additional materials in the e-mail. No separate e-mail is required. However, the Privacy Rule continues to prohibit covered entities from combining the notice in a single document with an authorization form (see 45 CFR 164.508(b)(3)); and direct treatment providers, other than in emergency situations, must provide the notice at or before the date of first service delivery, and must make a good faith effort to obtain the individual's written acknowledgment of receipt of the notice.

Q: Does the HIPAA Privacy Rule require a health care provider to obtain a new acknowledgment of receipt of the notice from patients if the facility changes its privacy policy?

A: No. A covered health care provider with a direct treatment relationship with individuals is required to make a good faith effort to obtain an individual's acknowledgment of receipt of the notice only at the time the provider first gives the notice to the individual--that is, at first service delivery. See 45 CFR 164.520(c)(2).

Q: Does the HIPAA Privacy Rule permit health care providers to obtain an electronic acknowledgment of the notice from individuals?

A: Yes. For notice delivered electrically, an electronic return receipt or other return transmission from the individual is considered a valid written acknowledgment of the notice. A provider who gives his paper notice to a patient during a face-to-face encounter with the individual at first service delivery may also obtain an electronic acknowledgment from the individual, provided that the individual's acknowledgment is in writing. Thus, a receptionist's notation in the provider's computer system of the individual's receipt of the notice would not be considered a valid written acknowledgment of the individual.

Q: Does the HIPAA Privacy Rule require a business associate to create a notice of privacy practices?

A: No. However, a covered entity must ensure through its contract with the business associate that the business associate's uses and disclosures of protected health information and other actions are consistent with the covered entity's privacy policies, as stated in covered entity's notice. Also, a covered entity may use a business associate to distribute its notice to individuals.

Q: Are covered entities permitted to give individuals a "layered" notice?

A: Yes. Covered entities may use a "layered" notice to implement the HIPAA Privacy Rule's requirements, so long as the elements required by 45 CFR 164.520(b) are included in the document that is provided to the individual. For example, a covered entity may satisfy the notice requirements by providing the individual with both a short notice that briefly summarizes the individual's rights, as well as other information; and a longer notice, layered beneath the short notice, that contains all of the elements required by the Privacy Rule. Providing the notice in this fashion is a helpful tool to assure that more individuals will realize that important information is contained in the notice. In addition to ensuring the notice is in plain language (as required by the Privacy Rule), covered entities are encouraged to develop notices that maximize readability and clarity.

Q: Are health plans required to make a good faith effort to obtain from their enrollees a written acknowledgment of receipt of the notice?

A: No. Under the HIPAA Privacy Rule, only covered health care providers that have a direct treatment relationship with individuals are required to make a good faith effort to obtain the individual's acknowledgment of receipt of the notice. See 45 CFR 164.520(c)(2)(ii).

Q: How are health care providers supposed to provide the notice to individuals and obtain their written acknowledgment of the notice when the first treatment encounter is over the phone or in some other manner that is not face-to-face?

A: The HIPAA Privacy Rule is intended to be flexible enough to address the various types of relationships that covered health care providers may have with the individuals they treat, including those treatment situations that are not face-to-face. For example, a health care provider who first treats a patient over the phone satisfies the notice provision requirements of the Privacy Rule by mailing the notice to the individual the same day, if possible. To satisfy the requirement that the provider also make a good faith effort to obtain the individual's acknowledgment of the notice, the provider may include a tear-off sheet or other document with the notice that requests that the acknowledgment be mailed back to the provider. The health care provider is not in violation of the Rule if the individual chooses not to mail back an acknowledgment; and a file copy of the form sent to the patient would be adequate documentation of the provider's good faith effort to obtain the acknowledgment.

Where a health care provider's initial contact with the patient is simply to schedule an appointment or a procedure, the notice provision and acknowledgment requirements may be satisfied at the time the individual arrives at the provider's facility for his or her appointment.

For service provided electronically, the notice must be sent electronically automatically and contemporaneously in response to the individual's first request for service. In this situation, an electronic return receipt or other return transmission from the individual is considered a valid written acknowledgment of the notice.

Q: We participate in an organized health care arrangement (OHCA). How are we to comply with the HIPAA Privacy Rule's requirements for providing notices and obtaining individuals' acknowledgments of the notice?

A: Health care providers and other covered entities that participate in an organized health care arrangement (OHCA) may use a single, joint notice that covers all of the participating covered entities (provided that the conditions at 45 CFR 164.520(d) are met), or may each maintain separate notices. Where a joint notice is provided to an individual by any one of the covered entities to which the joint notice applies, the Privacy Rule's requirements for providing the notice are satisfied for all others covered by the joint notice. If the joint notice is provided to an individual by a direct treatment provider participating in the OHCA, the provider must make a good faith effort to obtain the individual's written acknowledgment of receipt of the joint notice. Where the joint notice is provided to the individual by a participating covered entity other than a direct treatment provider, no acknowledgment need be obtained.

However, where covered entities participating in an OHCA choose to maintain separate notices, each covered entity from which an individual obtains services must provide its notice to the individual in accordance with the applicable requirements of 45 CFR 164.520(c). In addition, each direct treatment provider within the OHCA must make a good faith effort to obtain the individual's acknowledgment of the notice he or she provides.

Q: Does a health plan have to provide a copy of its notice to each dependent receiving coverage under a policy?

A: No. A health plan satisfies the HIPAA Privacy Rule's requirements for providing the notice by distributing its notice only to the named insured of a policy under which coverage is provided both to the named insured and his or her dependents. See 45 CFR 164.520(c)(1)(iii).

Q: For group health plan products, can the health plan send its notice to the administrator of the group product or the plan sponsor for them to distribute to each employee enrolled in the plan?

A: The HIPAA Privacy Rule requires a health plan to distribute its notice to each individual covered by the plan. Health plans may arrange to have another person or entity, for example, a group administrator or a plan sponsor, distribute the notice on their behalf. However, if the other person or entity fails to distribute the notice to the plan's enrollees, the health plan may be in violation of the Privacy Rule.

Q: As a pediatrician, am I required to give my notice of privacy practices to the children I treat?

A: The HIPAA Privacy Rule requires a covered health care provider with a direct treatment relationship with the individual to provide the notice to the individual receiving treatment no later than the date of first service delivery. In cases where the individual has a personal representative, as is generally the case when a parent brings a child in for treatment, the provider satisfies the notice distribution requirements by providing the notice to the personal representative (e.g., the child's parent), and making a good faith effort to obtain the personal representative's acknowledgment of the notice. In the limited cases where the parent is not the personal representative of the unemancipated minor, such as when the minor is authorized under State law to consent to the treatment and does so, the provider must give its notice to the minor and make a good faith effort to obtain the minor's acknowledgment of the notice. See 45 CFR 164.502(g)(3) and 164.520(c)(2).

Q: Are health care providers required by the HIPAA Privacy Rule to post their entire notice at their facility or may they post just a brief description of the notice?

A: Covered health care providers that maintain an office or other physical site where they provide health care directly to individuals are required to post their entire notice at the facility in a clear and prominent location. The Privacy Rule, however, does not prescribe any specific format for the posted notice, just that it include the same information that is distributed directly to the individual. Covered health care providers have discretion to design the posted notice in a manner that works best for their facility, which may be to simply post a copy of the pages of the notice that is provided directly to individuals.

Q: Can a covered entity bypass obtaining an individual's authorization for a use or disclosure not permitted by the HIPAA Privacy Rule simply by informing individuals of the use or disclosure through its notice of privacy practices?

A: No. A covered entity's notice is not a substitute for an individual's authorization. Covered entities are required to obtain the individual's written authorization for any use or disclosure of protected health information not permitted or required by the Privacy Rule. See 45 CFR 164.508. Simply including in the notice a description of such a use or disclosure does not obviate the need for the covered entity to obtain the individual's prior written authorization, when that authorization is required by the Rule. Instead, the notice must reflect the uses and disclosures a covered entity may make without the individual's authorization, as permitted by Privacy Rule, as well as state that any other uses or disclosures only will be made with the individual's written authorization. See 45 CFR 164.520(b).

Q: Is our medical practice required to notify patients through the mail of any changes to our notice?

A: No. The HIPAA Privacy Rule does not require a covered health care provider to mail out its revised notice or otherwise notify patients by mail of changes to the notice. Rather, when a covered health care provider with a direct treatment relationship with individuals makes a change to his notice, he must make the notice available upon request to patients or other persons on or after the effective date of the revision, and, if he maintains a physical service delivery site, post the revised notice in a clear and prominent location in his facility. See 45 CFR 164.520(c)(2)(iv). In addition, the provider must ensure that the current notice, in effect at that time, is provided to patients at first service delivery, and made available on his customer service web site, if he has one. See 45 CFR 164.520(c).

Q: Is a physician required to give her notice to every patient or can she just post the notice in her waiting room and give a copy to those patients who ask for it?

A: The HIPAA Privacy Rule requires a covered health care provider with direct treatment relationships with individuals to give the notice to every individual no later than the date of first service delivery to the individual and to make a good faith effort to obtain the individual's written acknowledgment of receipt of the notice. If the provider maintains an office or other physical site where she provides health care directly to individuals, the provider must also post the notice in the facility in a clear and prominent location where individuals are likely to see it, as well as make the notice available to those who ask for a copy. See 45 CFR 164.520(c) for other notice provision requirements.

Q: It is common practice for hospitals and other health care providers to collect preoperative information over the phone from a new patient prior to the day of surgery in order to determine whether the patient has any special medical concerns or issues that need to be addressed. Does the HIPAA Privacy Rule prohibit this practice if the patient has not yet received or acknowledged the provider's notice?

A: No, the Privacy Rule does not prohibit this practice. Where a health care provider's initial contact with a patient is simply to schedule an appointment or a procedure, or to collect information in anticipation of an appointment or a procedure, the Privacy Rule's requirements for providing the notice and obtaining a patient's acknowledgment of the notice may be satisfied at the time the individual arrives at the provider's facility for his or her appointment or procedure.

Q: Is a pharmacist permitted to have customers acknowledge receipt of the notice by signing or initialing the log book that they already sign when they pick up prescriptions?

A: Yes, provided that the individual is clearly informed on the log book of what they are acknowledging and the acknowledgment is not also used as a waiver or permission for something else that also appears on the log book (such as a waiver to consult with the pharmacist). The HIPAA Privacy Rule provides covered health care providers with discretion to design an acknowledgment process that works best for their businesses.

RESTRICTIONS ON GOVERNMENT ACCESS TO HEALTH INFORMATION

[*45 CFR Part 160, Subpart C; 164.512(f)*]

Background

Under the HIPAA Privacy Rule, government-operated health plans and health care providers must meet substantially the same requirements as private ones for protecting the privacy of individual identifiable health information. For instance, government-run health plans, such as Medicare and Medicaid plans, must take virtually the same steps to protect the claims and health information that they receive from beneficiaries as private insurance plans or health maintenance organizations (HMO). In addition, all Federal agencies must also meet the requirements of the Privacy Act of 1974, which restricts what information about individual citizens – including any personal health information – can be shared with other agencies and with the public.

The only new authority for government involves enforcement of the protections in the Privacy Rule itself. To ensure that covered entities protect patients' privacy as required, the Rule requires that health plans, hospitals, and other covered entities cooperate with efforts by the Department of Health and Human Services (HHS) Office for Civil Rights (OCR) to investigate complaints or otherwise ensure compliance.

RESTRICTIONS ON GOVERNMENT ACCESS TO HEALTH INFORMATION

Frequently Asked Questions

Q: Does the HIPAA Privacy Rule require my doctor to send my medical records to the government?

A: No. The Rule does not require a physician or any other covered entity to send medical information to the government for a government data base or similar operation. This Rule does not require or allow any new government access to medical information, with one exception: the Rule does give the Department of Health and Human Services Office for Civil Rights (OCR) the authority to investigate complaints that Privacy Rule protections or rights have been violated, and otherwise to ensure that covered entities comply with the Rule.

For enforcement purposes, OCR may need to look at how a covered entity handled medical records and other personal health information, as is typical in many enforcement settings. This investigative authority is needed so that the Rule can be enforced, and to ensure the independent review of consumers' concerns over privacy violations. Even so, the Privacy Rule limits disclosures to OCR to information that is "pertinent to ascertaining compliance." OCR will maintain stringent controls to safeguard any individually identifiable health information that it receives. If covered entities could avoid or ignore enforcement requests, consumers would not have a way to ensure an independent review of their concerns about privacy violations under the Rule.

Q: Why would a HIPAA Privacy Rule require covered entities to turn over anybody's personal health information as part of a government enforcement process?

A: An important ingredient in ensuring compliance with the Privacy Rule is the Department of Health and Human Services' (HHS) responsibility to investigate complaints that the Rule has been violated and to follow up on other information regarding noncompliance. At times, this responsibility entails seeing personal health information, such as when an individual indicates to the Department that they believe a covered entity has not properly handled their medical records.

What information would be needed depends on the circumstances and the alleged violations. The Privacy Rule limits HHS Office for Civil Rights' (OCR) access to information that is "pertinent to ascertaining compliance." In some cases, no personal health information may be needed. For instance, OCR would need to review only a business contract to determine whether a health plan included appropriate language to protect privacy when it hired an outside company to help process claims.

Examples of investigations that may require OCR to have access to protected health information include:

Allegations that a covered entity refused to note a request for correction in a patient's medical record, or did not provide complete access to a patient's medical records to that patient.

Allegations that a covered entity used health information for marketing purposes without first obtaining the individuals' authorization when required by the Rule. OCR may need to review information in the marketing department that contains personal health information, to determine whether a violation has occurred.

Q: Will this HIPAA Privacy Rule make it easier for police and law enforcement agencies to get my medical information?

A: No. The Rule does not expand current law enforcement access to individually identifiable health information. In fact, it limits access to a greater degree than currently exists, since the Rule establishes new procedures and safeguards that restrict the circumstances under which a covered entity may give such information to law enforcement officers.

For example, the Rule limits the type of information that covered entities may disclose to law enforcement, absent a warrant or other prior process, when law enforcement is seeking to identify or locate a suspect. It specifically prohibits disclosure of DNA information for this purpose, absent some other legal requirements such as a warrant. Similarly, under most circumstances, the Privacy Rule requires covered entities to obtain permission from persons who have been the victim of domestic violence or abuse before disclosing information about them to law enforcement. In most States, such permission is not required today.

Where State law imposes additional restrictions on disclosure of health information to law enforcement, those State laws continue to apply. This Rule sets a national floor of legal protections; it is not a set of "best practices."

Even in those circumstances when disclosure to law enforcement is permitted by the Rule, the Privacy Rule does not require covered entities to disclose any information. Some other Federal or State law may require a disclosure, and the Privacy Rule does not interfere with the operation of these other laws. However, unless the disclosure is required by some other law, covered entities should use their professional judgment to decide whether to disclose information, reflecting their own policies and ethical principles. In other words, doctors, hospitals, and health plans could continue to follow their own policies to protect privacy in such instances.

Q: Does the HIPAA Privacy Rule create a government database with all individuals' personal health information?

A: No. The Privacy Rule does not create such a government database or require a physician or any other covered entity to send medical information to the Federal government for a government database or similar operation.

Q: How does the HIPAA Privacy Rule affect my rights under the Federal Privacy Act?

A: The Privacy Act of 1974 protects personal information about individuals held by the Federal government. Covered entities that are Federal agencies or Federal contractors that maintain records that are covered by the Privacy Act not only must obey the Privacy Rule's requirements but also must comply with the Privacy Act.

MISCELLANEOUS FREQUENTLY ASKED QUESTIONS ABOUT THE HIPAA PRIVACY RULE

Q:If I believe that my privacy rights have been violated, when can I submit a complaint?

A: By law, health care providers (including doctors and hospitals) who engage in certain electronic transactions, health plans, and health care clearinghouses, (collectively, "covered entities") have until April 14, 2003, to comply with the HIPAA Privacy Rule. (Small health plans have until April 14, 2004, to comply). Activities occurring before April 14, 2003, are not subject to the Office for Civil Rights (OCR) enforcement actions. After that date, a person who believes a covered entity is not complying with a requirement of the Privacy Rule may file with OCR a written complaint, either on paper or electronically. This complaint must be filed within 180 days of when the complainant knew or should have known that the act had occurred. The Secretary may waive this 180-day time limit if good cause is shown. See 45 CFR 160.306 and 164.534. OCR will provide further information on its web site about how to file a complaint (www.hhs.gov/ocr/hipaa/).

In addition, after the compliance dates above, individuals have a right to file a complaint directly with the covered entity. Individuals should refer to the covered entity's notice of privacy practices for more information about how to file a complaint with the covered entity.

Q: If patients request copies of their medical records as permitted by the Privacy Rule, are they required to pay for the copies?

A: The Privacy Rule permits the covered entity to impose reasonable, cost-based fees. The fee may include only the cost of copying (including supplies and labor) and postage, if the patient requests that the copy be mailed. If the patient has agreed to receive a summary or explanation of his or her protected health information, the covered entity may also charge a fee for preparation of the summary or explanation. The fee may not include costs associated with searching for and retrieving the requested information. See 45 CFR 164.524.

Q: Does the HIPAA Privacy Rule protect genetic information?

A: Yes, genetic information is health information protected by the Privacy Rule. Like other health information, to be protected it must meet the definition of protected health information: it must be individually identifiable and maintained by a covered health care provider, health plan, or health care clearinghouse. See 45 C.F.R 160.103 and 164.501.

Q: A provider might have a patient's medical record that contains older portions of a medical record that were created by another/previous provider. Will the HIPAA Privacy Rule permit a provider who is a covered entity to disclose a complete medical record even though portions of the record were created by other providers?

A:Yes, the Privacy Rule permits a provider who is a covered entity to disclose a complete medical record including portions that were created by another provider, assuming that the disclosure is for a purpose permitted by the Privacy Rule, such as treatment.

Q: Can a physician's office FAX patient medical information to another physician's office?

A: The HIPAA Privacy Rule permits physicians to disclose protected health information to another health care provider for treatment purposes. This can be done by fax or by other means. Covered entities must have in place reasonable and appropriate administrative, technical, and physical safeguards to protect the privacy of protected health information that is disclosed using a fax machine. Examples of measures that could be reasonable and appropriate in such a situation include the sender confirming that the fax number to be used is in fact the correct one for the other physician's office, and placing the fax machine in a secure location to prevent unauthorized access to the information. See 45 CFR164.530(c).

Q: Are hospitals able to inform the clergy about parishioners in the hospital?

A: Yes, the HIPAA Privacy Rule allows this communication to occur, as long as the patient has been informed of this use and disclosure, and does not object. The Privacy Rule provides that a hospital or other covered health care provider may maintain in a directory the following information about that individual: the individual's name; location in the facility; health condition expressed in general terms; and religious affiliation. The facility may disclose this directory information to members of the clergy. Thus, for example, a hospital may disclose the names of Methodist patients to a Methodist minister unless a patient has restricted such disclosure. Directory information, except for religious affiliation, may be disclosed only to other persons who ask for the individual by name. When, due to emergency circumstances or incapacity, the patient has not been provided an opportunity to agree or object to being included in the facility's directory, these disclosures may still occur, if such disclosure is consistent with any known prior expressed preference of the individual and the disclosure is in the individual's best interest as determined in the professional judgment of the provider. See 45 CFR 164.510(a).

Q:Are State, county or local health departments required to comply with the HIPAA Privacy Rule?

A: Yes, if a State, county or local health department performs functions that make it a covered entity, or otherwise meets the definition of a covered entity. For example, a state Medicaid program is a covered entity (i.e., a health plan) as defined in the Privacy Rule. Some health departments operate health care clinics and thus are health care providers. If these health care providers transmit health information electronically in connection with a transaction covered in the HIPAA Transactions Rule, they are covered entities. For more information, see the definitions of covered entity, health care provider, health plan and health care clearinghouse in 45 CFR 160.103. See also, the "Covered Entity Decision Tools" posted at **http://www.cms.gov/hipaa/hipaa2/support/tools/decisionsupport/default.asp**. These tools address the question of whether a person, business or agency is a covered health care provider, health care clearinghouse or health plan.

If the health department performs some covered functions (i.e., those activities that make it a provider that conducts certain transactions electronically, a health plan or a health care clearinghouse) and other non-covered functions, it may designate those components (or parts thereof) that perform covered functions as the health care component(s) of the organization and thereby become a type of covered entity known as a "hybrid entity." Most of the requirements of the Privacy Rule apply only to the hybrid entity's health care component(s). If a health department elects to be a hybrid entity, there are restrictions on how its health care component(s) may disclose protected health information to other components of the health department. See 45 CFR 164.504 (a) – (c) for more information about hybrid entities.

Q: Are the following types of insurance covered under HIPAA: long/short term disability; workers compensation; automobile liability that includes coverage for medical payments?

A: No, the listed types of policies are not health plans. The HIPAA Administrative Simplification regulations specifically exclude from the definition of a "health plan" any policy, plan, or program to the extent that it provides, or pays for the cost of, excepted benefits, which are listed in section 2791(c)(1) of the Public Health Service Act, 42 U.S.C. 300gg-91(c)(1). See 45 CFR 160.103. As described in the statute, excepted benefits are one or more (or any combination thereof) of the following policies, plans or programs:

- Coverage only for accident, or disability income insurance, or any combination thereof.
- Coverage issued as a supplement to liability insurance.
- Liability insurance, including general liability insurance and automobile liability insurance.

•Workers' compensation or similar insurance.

•Automobile medical payment insurance.

•Credit-only insurance.

•Coverage for on-site medical clinics

•Other similar insurance coverage, specified in regulations, under which benefits for medical care are secondary or incidental to other insurance benefits.

Q:Is an entity that is acting as a third party administrator to a group health plan a covered entity?

A: No, providing services to or acting on behalf of a health plan does not transform a third party administrator (TPA) into a covered entity. Generally, a TPA of a group health plan would be acting as a business associate of the group health plan. Of course, the TPA may meet the definition of a covered entity based on its other activities (such as by providing group health insurance). See 45 CFR 160.103.

Q:The Social Security Administration (SSA) collects medical records for the Social Security Income (SSI) disability program. Is SSA a covered entity (e.g., a health plan)?

A: The SSA is not a covered entity. The collection of individually identifiable health information is not a factor in determining whether an entity is a covered entity. Covered entities are defined in HIPAA; they are (1) health plans, (2) health care clearinghouses, and (3) health care providers that transmit any health information in electronic form in connection with a transaction covered in the HIPAA Transactions Rule. These terms are defined in detail at 45 CFR 160.103.

Q:Is the Privacy Rule compliance date delayed by the Administrative Simplification Compliance Act (ASCA) that was enacted in December 2001?

A: No, the compliance dates for the Privacy Rule is April 14, 2003, or, for small health plans, April 14, 2004. ASCA does not apply to the HIPAA Privacy Rule. Rather, ASCA delays compliance with the Transaction and Code Set standards adopted by the HIPAA Transactions Rule for covered entities that file a compliance plan. More information about ASCA can be found on the web site for the Centers for Medicare and Medicaid Services at http://cms.hhs.gov/hipaa/.

Q:HIPAA allows "small health plans," defined as health plans having annual receipts of $5 million or less, an additional year (in the case of the Privacy Rule, until April 14, 2004) to come into compliance. How should a health plan determine what receipts to use to decide whether it qualifies as a "small health plan?"

A: Health plans that file certain federal tax returns and report receipts on those returns should use the guidance provided by the Small Business Administration at 13 CFR 121.104 to calculate annual receipts. Health plans that do not report receipts to the IRS - for example, ERISA group health plans that are exempt from filing income tax returns - should use proxy measures to determine their annual receipts. Further information about the relevant provisions of 13 CFR 121.104 and these proxy measures, and additional information related to "small health plans," may be found at http://cms.hhs.gov/hipaa/hipaa2/default.asp.

Q: Does the HIPAA Privacy Rule require that covered entities provide patients with access to oral information?

A: No. The Privacy Rule requires covered entities to provide individuals with access to protected health information about themselves that is contained in their "designated record sets." The term "record" in the term "designated record set" does not include oral information; rather, it connotes information that has been recorded in some manner.

The Rule does not require covered entities to tape or digitally record oral communications, nor retain digitally or tape recorded information after transcription. But if such records are maintained and used to make decisions about the individual, they may meet the definition of "designated record set." For example, a health plan is not required to provide a member access to tapes of a telephone "advice line" interaction if the tape is maintained only for customer service review and not to make decisions about the member.

Q: Does the HIPAA Privacy Rule require that covered entities document all oral communications?

A: No. The Privacy Rule does not require covered entities to document any information, including oral information, that is used or disclosed for treatment, payment or health care operations.

The Rule includes, however, documentation requirements for some information disclosures for other purposes. For example, some disclosures must be documented in order to meet the standard for providing a disclosure history to an individual upon request. Where a documentation requirement exists in the Rule, it applies to all relevant communications, whether in oral or some other form. For example, if a covered physician discloses information about a case of tuberculosis to a public health authority as permitted by the Rule at 45 CFR 164.512, then he or she must maintain a record of that disclosure regardless of whether the disclosure was made orally, by phone, or in writing.

Final Security Rule

[DOCID:fr12au98-28]

[Federal Register: August 12, 1998 (Volume 63, Number 155)]
[Proposed Rules]
[Page 43241-43280]
From the Federal Register Online via GPO Access [wais.access.gpo.gov]

[[Page 43241]]

Part III

Department of Health and Human Services

Office of the Secretary

---

45 CFR Part 142

Security and Electronic Signature Standards; Proposed Rule

[[Page 43242]]

DEPARTMENT OF HEALTH AND HUMAN SERVICES

Office of the Secretary

45 CFR Part 142

[HCFA-0049-P]
RIN 0938-AI57

Security and Electronic Signature Standards

AGENCY: Health Care Financing Administration (HCFA), HHS.

ACTION: Proposed rule.

SUMMARY: This rule proposes standards for the security of individual health information and electronic signature use by health plans, health care clearinghouses, and health care providers. The health plans, health care clearinghouses, and health care providers would use the security standards to develop and maintain the security of all electronic individual health information. The electronic signature standard is applicable only with respect to use with the specific transactions defined in the Health Insurance Portability and Accountability Act of 1996, and when it has been determined that an electronic signature must be used.

The use of these standards would improve the Medicare and Medicaid programs, and other Federal health programs and private health programs, and the effectiveness and efficiency of the health care industry in general. This rule would implement some of the requirements of the Administrative Simplification subtitle of the Health Insurance Portability and Accountability Act of 1996.

DATES: Comments will be considered if we receive them at the appropriate address, as provided below, no later than 5 p.m. on October 13, 1998.

ADDRESSES: Mail written comments (1 original and 3 copies) to the following address: Health Care Financing Administration, Department of Health and Human Services, Attention: HCFA-0049-P, P.O. Box 26585, Baltimore, MD 21207-0519.

If you prefer, you may deliver your written comments (1 original and 3 copies) to one of the following addresses:

Room 309-G, Hubert H. Humphrey Building, 200 Independence Avenue, SW.,
Washington, DC 20201, or
Room C5-09-26, 7500 Security Boulevard, Baltimore, MD 21244-1850.

Comments may also be submitted electronically to the following e-mail address: security@osaspe.dhhs.gov. For e-mail comment procedures, see the beginning of SUPPLEMENTARY INFORMATION. For further information on ordering copies of the Federal Register containing this document and on electronic access, see the beginning of SUPPLEMENTARY information.

FOR FURTHER INFORMATION CONTACT: John Parmigiani, (410) 786-2976.

SUPPLEMENTARY INFORMATION:

E-Mail, Comments, Procedures, Availability of Copies, and Electronic Access

E-mail comments should include the full name, postal address, and affiliation (if applicable) of the sender and must be submitted to the referenced address to be considered. All comments should be incorporated in the e-mail message because we may not be able to access attachments.

Because of staffing and resource limitations, we cannot accept comments by facsimile (FAX) transmission. In commenting, please refer to file code HCFA-0049-P and the specific section or sections of the proposed rule. Both electronic and written comments received by the time and date indicated above will be available for public inspection as they are received, generally beginning approximately 3 weeks after publication of a document, in Room 309-G of the Department's offices at 200 Independence Avenue, SW., Washington, DC, on Monday through Friday of each week from 8:30 a.m. to 5 p.m. (phone: (202) 690-7890). Electronic and legible written comments will also be posted, along with this proposed rule, at the following web site: http://aspe.os.dhhs.gov/admnsimp/.

Copies: To order copies of the Federal Register containing this document, send your request to: New Orders, Superintendent of Documents, P.O. Box 371954, Pittsburgh, PA 15250-7954. Specify the date of the issue requested and enclose a check or money order payable to the Superintendent of Documents, or enclose your Visa or Master Card number and expiration date. Credit card orders can also be placed by calling the order desk at (202) 512-1800 or by faxing to (202) 512-2250. The cost for each copy is $8. As an alternative, you can view and photocopy the Federal Register document at most libraries designated as Federal Depository Libraries and at many other public and academic libraries throughout the country that receive the Federal Register.

This Federal Register document is also available from the Federal Register online database through GPO Access, a service of the U.S. Government Printing Office. Free public access is available on a Wide Area Information Server (WAIS) through the Internet and via asynchronous dial-in. Internet users can access the database by using the World Wide Web, http://www.access.gpo.gov/nara/, by using local WAIS client software, or by telnet to swais.access.gpo.gov, then login as guest (no password required). Dial-in users should use communications software and modem to call (202) 512-1661; type swais, then login as guest (no password required).

I. Background

[Please label written or e-mailed comments about this section with the subject: Background]

In order to administer their programs, the Department of Health and Human Services, other Federal agencies, State Medicaid agencies, private health plans, health care providers, and health care clearinghouses must assure their customers (such as patients, insured, providers, and health care plans) that the confidentiality and privacy of health care information they electronically collect, maintain, use, or transmit is secure. Security of health information is especially important when health information can be directly linked to an individual.

Confidentiality is threatened not only by the risk of improper access to electronically stored information, but also by the risk of interception during electronic transmission of the information.

In addition to the need to ensure electronic health care information is secure and confidential, there is a potential need to associate signature capability with information being electronically stored or transmitted. Today, there are numerous forms of electronic signatures, ranging from biometric devices to digital signature. To satisfy the legal and time-tested characteristics of a written signature, however, an electronic signature must do the following:

<bullet> Identify the signatory individual,

<bullet> Assure the integrity of a document's content, and

<bullet> Provide for nonrepudiation; that is, strong and substantial evidence that will make it difficult for the signer to claim that the electronic representation is not valid. Currently, the only technically mature electronic signature meeting the above criteria is the digital signature. There is no national standard for security or electronic signatures. Of necessity, each health care provider, health care plan, and health care entity

[[Page 43243]]

has defined its own security requirements.

A. Legislation

The Congress included provisions to address the need for security and electronic signature standards and other administrative simplification issues in the Health Insurance Portability and Accountability Act of 1996 (HIPAA), Public Law 104-191, which was enacted on August 21, 1996. Through subtitle F of title II of that law, the Congress added to title XI of the Social Security Act a new part C, entitled ``Administrative Simplification.'' (Public Law 104-191 affects several titles in the United States Code. Hereafter, we refer to the Social Security Act as the Act; we refer to the other laws cited in this document by their names.) The purpose of this part C is to improve the Medicare and Medicaid programs, in particular, and the efficiency and effectiveness of the health care system, in general, by encouraging the development of a health information system through the establishment of standards and requirements to facilitate the electronic maintenance and transmission of certain health information.

Part C of title XI of the Act consists of sections 1171 through 1179. These sections define various terms and impose several requirements on HHS, health plans, health care clearinghouses, and certain health care providers concerning electronic transmission of health information.

The first section, section 1171 of the Act, establishes definitions for purposes of part C of title XI for the following terms: code set, health care clearinghouse, health care provider, health information, health plan, individually identifiable health information, standard, and standard setting organization.

Section 1172 of the Act makes any standard adopted under part C applicable to: (1) Health plans, (2) health care clearinghouses, and (3) health care providers that transmit any health information in electronic form in connection with the transactions referred to in section 1173(a)(1) of the Act. The security standard to be adopted under Part C is not restricted to the transactions referred to in section 1173(a)(1) of the Act, but is applicable to any health information pertaining to an individual that is electronically maintained or transmitted. This section also contains the following requirements concerning standard setting:

<bullet> The Secretary may adopt a standard developed, adopted, or modified by a standard setting organization (that is, an organization accredited by the American National Standards Institute (ANSI)) that has consulted with the National Uniform Billing Committee (NUBC), the National Uniform Claim Committee (NUCC), Workgroup for Electronic Data Interchange (WEDI), and the American Dental Association (ADA).

<bullet> The Secretary may also adopt a standard other than one established by a standard setting organization, if the different standard will reduce costs for health care providers and health plans, the different standard is promulgated through negotiated rulemaking procedures, and the Secretary consults with each of the above-named groups.

<bullet> If no standard has been adopted by any standard setting organization, the Secretary must rely on the recommendations of the National Committee on Vital and Health Statistics (NCVHS) and consult with each of the above-named groups.

In complying with the requirements of part C of title XI, the Secretary must rely on the recommendations of the NCVHS, consult with appropriate State, Federal, and private agencies or organizations, and publish the NCVHS recommendations in the Federal Register.

Paragraph (a) of section 1173 of the Act requires that the Secretary adopt standards for financial and administrative transactions, and data elements for those transactions, to enable health information to be exchanged electronically. Standards are required for the following transactions: health claims, health encounter information, health claims attachments, health plan enrollments and disenrollments, health plan eligibility, health care payment and remittance advice, health plan premium payments, first report of injury, health claim status, and referral certification and authorization. In addition, the Secretary is required to adopt standards for any other financial and administrative transactions that are determined to be appropriate by the Secretary.

Paragraph (b) of section 1173 of the Act requires the Secretary to adopt standards for unique health identifiers for all individuals, employers, health plans, and health care providers and requires further that the adopted standards specify for what purposes unique health identifiers may be used.

Paragraphs (c) through (f) of section 1173 of the Act require the Secretary to establish standards for code sets for each data element for each health care transaction listed above, security standards for health care information systems, standards for electronic signatures (established together with the Secretary of Commerce), and standards for the transmission of data elements needed for the coordination of benefits and sequential processing of claims. Compliance with electronic signature standards will be deemed to satisfy both State and Federal requirements for written signatures with respect to the transactions listed in paragraph (a) of section 1173 of the Act.

In section 1174 of the Act, the Secretary is required to establish standards for all of the above transactions, except claims attachments, by February 21, 1998. The standards for claims attachments must be established by February 21, 1999. Generally, after a standard is established, it cannot be changed during the first year after adoption except for changes that are necessary to permit compliance with the standard. Modifications to any of these standards may be made after the first year, but not more frequently than once every 12 months. The Secretary must also ensure that procedures exist for the routine maintenance, testing, enhancement, and expansion of code sets and that there are crosswalks from prior versions.

Section 1175 of the Act prohibits health plans from refusing to process or delaying the processing of a transaction that is presented in standard format. The Act's requirements are not limited to health plans; however, each person to whom a standard or implementation specification applies is required to comply with the standard within 24 months (or 36 months for small health plans) of its adoption. A health plan or other entity may, of course, comply voluntarily before the effective date. A person may comply by using a health care clearinghouse to transmit or receive the standard transactions. Compliance with modifications to standards or implementation specifications must be accomplished by a date designated by the Secretary. This date may not be earlier than 180 days from the notice of change.

Section 1176 of the Act establishes a civil monetary penalty for violation of the provisions in part C of title XI of the Act, subject to several limitations. Penalties may not be more than $100 per person per violation and not more than $25,000 per person for violations of a single standard for a calendar year. The procedural provisions in section 1128A of the Act, ``Civil Monetary Penalties,'' are applicable.

Section 1177 of the Act establishes penalties for a knowing misuse of unique health identifiers and individually identifiable health information: (1) A fine of not more than $50,000 and/or imprisonment of not

[[Page 43244]]

more than 1 year; (2) if misuse is ``under false pretenses,'' a fine of not more than $100,000 and/or imprisonment of not more than 5 years; and (3) if misuse is with intent to sell, transfer, or use individually identifiable health information for commercial advantage, personal gain, or malicious harm, a fine of not more than $250,000 and/or imprisonment of not more than 10 years. Note that these penalties do not affect any other penalties which may be imposed by other Federal programs, including ERISA.

Under section 1178 of the Act, the provisions of part C of title XI of the Act, as well as any standards established under them, supersede any State law that is contrary to them. However, the Secretary may, for statutorily-specified reasons, waive this provision.

Finally, section 1179 of the Act makes the above provisions

inapplicable to financial institutions or anyone acting on behalf of a financial institution when ``authorizing, processing, clearing, settling, billing, transferring, reconciling, or collecting payments for a financial institution."

(Concerning this last provision, the conference report, in its discussion on section 1178, states:

``The conferees do not intend to exclude the activities of financial institutions or their contractors from compliance with the standards adopted under this part if such activities would be subject to this part. However, conferees intend that this part does not apply to use or disclosure of information when an individual utilizes a payment system to make a payment for, or related to, health plan premiums or health care. For example, the exchange of information between participants in a credit card system in connection with processing a credit card payment for health care would not be covered by this part. Similarly sending a checking account statement to an account holder who uses a credit or debit card to pay for health care services, would not be covered by this part. However, this part does apply if a company clears health care claims, the health care claims activities remain subject to the requirements of this part.") (H.R. Rep. No. 736, 104th Cong., 2nd Sess. 268-269 (1996))

B. Process for Developing National Standards

The Secretary has formulated a five-part strategy for developing and implementing the standards mandated under part C of title XI of the Act:

1. To ensure necessary interagency coordination and required interaction with other Federal departments and the private sector, establish interdepartmental implementation teams to identify and assess potential standards for adoption. The subject matter of the teams includes claims/encounters, identifiers, enrollment/eligibility, systems security and electronic signature, and medical coding classification. Another team addresses cross-cutting issues and coordinates the subject matter teams. The teams consult with external groups such as the NCVHS' Workgroup on Data Standards, WEDI, the ANSI's
Healthcare Informatics Standards Board (HISB), the NUCC, the NUBC, and the ADA. The teams are charged with developing regulations and other necessary documents and making recommendations for the various standards to the HHS Data Council through its Committee on Health Data Standards. (The HHS Data Council is the focal point for consideration of data policy issues. It reports directly to the Secretary and advises the Secretary on data standards and privacy issues.)

2. Develop recommendations for standards to be adopted.

3. Publish proposed rules in the Federal Register describing the standards. Each proposed rule provides the public with a 60-day comment period.

4. Analyze public comments and publish the final rules in the Federal Register.

5. Distribute standards and coordinate preparation and distribution of implementation guides.

This strategy affords many opportunities for involvement of interested and affected parties in standards development and adoption by enabling them to:

<bullet> Participate with standards setting organizations.

<bullet> Provide written input to the NCVHS.

<bullet> Provide written input to the Secretary of HHS.

<bullet> Provide testimony at NCVHS" public meetings.

<bullet> Comment on the proposed rules for each of the proposed standards.

<bullet> Invite HHS staff to meetings with public and private sector organizations or meet directly with senior HHS staff involved in the implementation process.

The implementation teams charged with reviewing standards for designation as required national standards under the statute have defined, with significant input from the health care industry, a set of principles for guiding choices for the standards to be adopted by the Secretary. These principles are based on direct specifications in HIPAA, the purpose of the law, and generally desirable principles. To be designated as an HIPAA standard, each standard should:

1. Improve the efficiency and effectiveness of the health care system by leading to cost reductions for or improvements in benefits from electronic health care transactions.

2. Meet the needs of the health data standards user community, particularly health care providers, health plans, and health care clearinghouses.

3. Be consistent and uniform with the other HIPAA standards--their data element definitions and codes and their privacy and security requirements--and, secondarily, with other private and public sector health data standards.

4. Have low additional development and implementation costs relative to the benefits of using the standard.

5. Be supported by an ANSI-accredited standards developing organization or other private or public organization that will ensure continuity and efficient updating of the standard over time.

6. Have timely development, testing, implementation, and updating procedures to achieve administrative simplification benefits faster.

7. Be technologically independent of the computer platforms and transmission protocols used in electronic health transactions, except when they are explicitly part of the standard.

8. Be precise and unambiguous, but as simple as possible.

9. Keep data collection and paperwork burdens on users as low as is feasible.

10. Incorporate flexibility to adapt more easily to changes in the health care infrastructure (such as new services, organizations, and provider types) and information technology.

A master data dictionary providing for common data definitions across the standards selected for implementation under HIPAA will be developed and maintained. We intend for the data element definitions to be precise, unambiguous, and consistently applied. The transaction-specific reports and general reports from the master data dictionary will be readily available to the public. At a minimum, the information presented will include data element names, definitions, and appropriate references to the transactions where they are used.

This proposed rule would establish the security standard and electronic signature standard for health care information and individually identifiable health care information maintained or transmitted electronically. The remaining standards are grouped, to the extent possible, by subject matter and audience in other regulations. We anticipate publishing

[[Page 43245]]

several separate regulation documents to promulgate the remaining standards required under HIPAA.

II. Provisions of this Proposed Rule

[Please label written comments or e-mailed comments about this section with the subject: Introduction/Applicability]

We propose to add a new part to title 45 of the Code of Federal Regulations for health plans, health care providers, and health care clearinghouses in general. The new part would be part 142 of title 45 and would be titled ``Administrative Requirements." Subpart A would contain the general provisions for this part, including the general definitions and general requirements for health plans. Subpart C would contain provisions specific to securing health information used in any electronic transmission or stored format.

In this proposed rule, we propose a standard for security of health information. This rule would establish that health plans, health care clearinghouses, and health care providers must have the security standard in place to comply with the statutory requirement that health care information and individually identifiable health care information be protected to ensure privacy and confidentiality when health information is electronically stored, maintained, or transmitted. The Congress mandated a separate standard for electronic signature, therefore, this proposed security standard also addresses the selected standard for electronic signature. The proposed security standard does not require the use of an electronic signature, but specifies the standard for an electronic signature that must be followed if such a signature is used. If an entity elects to use an electronic signature, it must comply with the electronic signature standard.

A. Applicability

With the exception of the security provisions, section 262 of HIPAA applies to any health plan, any health care clearinghouse, and any health care provider that transmits any health information in electronic form in connection with transactions referred to in section 1173(a)(1) of the Act. The security provisions of section 262 of HIPAA apply to any health plan, any health care clearinghouse, and any health care provider that electronically maintains or transmits any health information relating to an individual.

Our proposed rules (at 45 CFR 142.102) would apply to the health plans and health care clearinghouses as well, but we would clarify the statutory language in our regulations for health care providers. With the exception of the security regulation, we would have the regulations apply to any health care provider only when electronically transmitting any of the transactions to which section 1173(a)(1) of the Act refers.

Electronic transmissions would include transactions using all media, even when the information is physically moved from one location to another using magnetic tape, disk, or compact disc (cd) media. Transmissions over the Internet (wide-open), Extranet (using Internet technology to link a business with information only accessible to collaborating parties), leased lines, dial-up lines, and private networks are all included. Telephone voice response and ``faxback'' (a request for information made via voice using a fax machine and requested information returned via that same machine as a fax) systems would not be included. We solicit comments concerning any adverse impact the above statement concerning voice response or faxback may have upon the security of the health information in the commenter's care.

With the exception of the security regulation, our regulations would apply to health care clearinghouses when transmitting transactions to, and receiving transactions from, a health care provider or health plan that transmits and receives standard transactions (as defined under ``transaction'') and at all times when transmitting to or receiving electronic transactions from another health care clearinghouse. The security regulation would apply to health care clearing houses electronically maintaining or transmitting any health information pertaining to an individual.

Entities that offer on-line interactive transmission must comply with the standards. The Hypertext Markup Language (HTML) interaction between a server and a browser by which the data elements of a transaction are solicited from a user would not have to use the standards (with the exception of the security standard), although the data content must be equal to that required for the standard. Once the data elements are assembled into a transaction by the server, the transmitted transaction would have to comply with the standards.

With the exception of the security portion, the law would apply to each health care provider when transmitting or receiving any of the specified electronic transactions. The security regulation would apply to each health care provider electronically maintaining or transmitting any health information pertaining to an individual.

The law applies to health plans for all transactions. Section 142.104 would contain the following provisions (from section 1175 of the Act):

If a person desires to conduct a transaction (as defined in Sec. 142.103) with a health plan as a standard transaction, the following apply:

(1) The health plan may not refuse to conduct the transaction as a standard transaction.

(2) The health plan may not delay the transaction or otherwise adversely affect, or attempt to adversely affect, the person or the transaction on the basis that the transaction is a standard transaction.

(3) The information transmitted and received in connection with the transaction must be in the form of standard data elements of health information.

As a further requirement, we would provide that a health plan that conducts transactions through an agent assure that the agent meets all the requirements of part 142 that apply to the health plan.

Section 142.105 would state that a person or other entity may meet the transaction requirements of Sec. 142.104 by either--

(1) Transmitting and receiving standard data elements, or

(2) Submitting nonstandard data elements to a health care clearinghouse for processing into standard data elements and transmission by the health care clearinghouse and receiving standard data elements through the clearinghouse.

Health care clearinghouses would be able to accept nonstandard transactions for the sole purpose of translating them into standard transactions for sending customers and would be able to accept standard transactions and translate them into nonstandard formats for receiving customers. We would state in Sec. 142.105 that the transmission of nonstandard transactions, under contract, between a health plan or a health care provider and a health care clearinghouse would not violate the law.

With the exception of the security standard, transmissions within a corporate entity would not be required to comply with the standards. A hospital that is wholly owned by a managed care company would not have to use the transaction standards to pass encounter information back to the home office, but it would have to use the standard claims transaction to submit a claim to another payer. Another example might be transactions within Federal agencies and their contractors and between State agencies within the same State. For example, Medicare enters into contracts with insurance

companies and common working file sites that process Medicare claims using government furnished software. There is constant communication, on a private network, between HCFA Central Office and the Medicare carriers, intermediaries, and common working file sites. This communication may continue in nonstandard mode. However, these contractors would be required to comply with the transaction standards when exchanging any of the transactions covered by HIPAA with an entity outside these ``corporate'' boundaries.

The security standard is applicable to all health care information electronically maintained or used in an electronic transmission, regardless of format (standard transaction or a proprietary format); no distinction is made between internal corporate entity communication or communication external to the corporate entity.

Although there are situations in which the use of the standards is not required (for example, health care providers may continue to submit paper claims and employers are not required to use any of the standard transactions), we stress that a standard may be used voluntarily in any situation in which it is not required.

This proposed regulation would not mandate the use of electronic signatures with any specific transaction at this time. Instead, the regulation proposes that whenever an electronic signature is required for an electronic transaction by law, regulation, or contract, the signature must meet the standard established in the regulation at Sec. 142.310. Use of this standard would satisfy any Federal or State requirement for a signature, either electronic or on paper.

We note that the ANSI X12N standards for individual transactions which have been proposed for adoption as national standards in a separate proposed rule do not require the use of electronic signatures. Standards for additional transactions that the Secretary may propose for adoption in the future, including one for claims attachments, may contain such requirements. We solicit comments on whether electronic signatures should be required for any specific transactions or under specific circumstances and what effect such requirements would have on electronic health care transactions.

We also note that the NCVHS is required by HIPAA to report to the Secretary recommendations and legislative proposals for uniform data standards for patient medical record information and the electronic exchange of such information, with the implication that HHS should rely on such recommendations to adopt such standards or propose the passage of such legislation by the Congress. We solicit comments on whether the standard proposed below for electronic signatures would be appropriate for consideration as part of such standards.

B. Definitions

[Please label written or e-mailed comments about this section with the subject: Definitions]

Section 1171 of the Act defines several terms and our proposed rules would, for the most part, simply restate the law. The terms that we are defining in this proposed rule follow:

1. Code Set

We would define ``code set'' as section 1171(1) of the Act does: ``code set'' means any set of codes used for encoding data elements, such as tables of terms, medical concepts, medical diagnostic codes, or medical procedure codes.

2. Health Care Clearinghouse

We would define ``health care clearinghouse'' as section 1171(2) of the Act does, but we are adding a further, clarifying sentence. The statute defines a ``health care clearinghouse'' as a public or private entity that processes or facilitates the processing of nonstandard data elements of health information into standard data elements. We would further explain that such an entity is one that currently receives health care transactions from health care providers or other entities, translates the data from a given format into one acceptable to the intended recipient and forwards the processed transaction to appropriate payers and clearinghouses, as necessary, for further action.

There are currently a number of private clearinghouses that perform this function for health care providers. For purposes of this rule, we would consider billing services, repricing companies, community health management information systems or community health information systems, value-added networks, and switches that perform this function to be health care clearinghouses.

3. Health Care Provider

As defined by section 1171(3) of the Act, a ``health care provider'' is a provider of services as defined in section 1861(u) of the Act, a provider of medical or other health services as defined in section 1861(s) of the Act, and any other person who furnishes health care services or supplies. Our regulations would define ``health care provider'' as the statute does and clarify that the definition of a health care provider is limited to those entities that furnish, or bill and are paid for, health care services in the normal course of business.

For a more detailed discussion of the definition of health care provider, we refer the reader to our proposed rule, HCFA-0045-P, Standard Health Care Provider, 63 FR 25320, published May 7, 1998.

4. Health Information

``Health information,'' as defined in section 1171 of the Act, means any information, whether oral or recorded in any form or medium, that--

<bullet> Is created or received by a health care provider, health plan, public health authority, employer, life insurer, school or university, or health care clearinghouse; and

<bullet> Relates to the past, present, or future physical or mental health or condition of an individual; the provision of health care to an individual; or the past, present, or future payment for the provision of health care to an individual.

We propose the same definition for our regulations.

5. Health Plan

We propose that a ``health plan'' be defined essentially as section 1171 of the Act defines it. Section 1171 of the Act cross refers to definitions in section 2791 of the Public Health Service Act (as added by Public Law 104-191, 42 U.S.C. 300gg-91); we would incorporate those definitions as currently stated into our proposed definitions for the convenience of the public. We note that the term ``health plan'' is also defined in other statutes, such as the Employee Retirement Income Security Act of 1974 (ERISA). Our definitions are based on the roles of plans in conducting administrative transactions, and any differences should not be construed to affect other statutes.

For purposes of implementing the provisions of administrative simplification, a ``health plan'' would be an individual or group health plan that provides, or pays the cost of, medical care. This definition includes, but is not limited to, the 13 types of plans listed in the statute. On the other hand, plans such as property and casualty insurance plans and workers compensation plans, which may pay health care costs in the course of administering nonhealth care benefits, are not considered to be health plans in the proposed definition of health plan. Of course, these plans may voluntarily adopt these standards for their own business needs. At some

[[Page 43247]]

future time, the Congress may choose to expressly include some or all of these plans in the list of health plans that must comply with the standards.

Health plans often carry out their business functions through agents, such as plan administrators (including third party administrators), entities that are under ``administrative services only'' (ASO) contracts, claims processors, and fiscal agents. These agents may or may not be health plans in their own right; for example, a health plan acting as another health plan's agent as another line of business. As stated earlier, a health plan that conducts HIPAA transactions through an agent is required to assure that the agent meets all HIPAA requirements that apply to the plan itself.

``Health plan'' includes the following, singly or in combination:

a. ``Group health plan'' (as currently defined by section 2791(a) of the Public Health Service Act). A group health plan is a plan that has 50 or more participants (as the term ``participant'' is currently defined by section 3(7) of ERISA) or is administered by an entity other than the employer that established and maintains the plan. This definition includes both insured and self-insured plans. We define ``participant'' separately below.

Section 2791(a)(1) of the Public Health Service Act defines ``group health plan'' as an employee welfare benefit plan (as defined in current section 3(1) of ERISA) to the extent that the plan provides medical care, including items and services paid for as medical care, to employees or their dependents directly or through insurance, or otherwise.

b. ``Health insurance issuer'' (as currently defined by section 2791(b) of the Public Health Service Act).

Section 2791(b) of the Public Health Service Act currently defines a ``health insurance issuer'' as an insurance company, insurance service, or insurance organization that is licensed to engage in the business of insurance in a State and is subject to State law that regulates insurance.

c. ``Health maintenance organization'' (as currently defined by section 2791(b) of the Public Health Service Act).

Section 2791(b) of the Public Health Service Act currently defines a ``health maintenance organization'' as a Federally qualified health maintenance organization, an organization recognized as such under State law, or a similar organization regulated for solvency under State law in the same manner and to the same extent as such a health maintenance organization. These organizations may include preferred provider organizations, provider sponsored organizations, independent practice associations, competitive medical plans, exclusive provider organizations, and foundations for medical care.

d. Part A or Part B of the Medicare program (title XVIII of the Act).

e. The Medicaid program (title XIX of the Act).

f. A ``Medicare supplemental policy'' as defined under section 1882(g)(1) of the Act.

Section 1882(g)(1) of the Act defines a ``Medicare supplemental policy'' as a health insurance policy that a private entity offers a Medicare beneficiary to provide payment for expenses incurred for services and items that are not reimbursed by Medicare because of deductible, coinsurance, or other limitations under Medicare. The statutory definition of a Medicare supplemental policy excludes a number of plans that are generally considered to be Medicare supplemental plans, such as health plans for employees and former employees and for members and former members of trade associations and unions. A number of these health plans may be included under the definitions of ``group health plan'' or ``health insurance issuer'', as defined in paragraphs a. and b. above.

g. A ``long-term care policy,'' including a nursing home fixed-indemnity policy. A ``long-term care policy'' is considered to be a health plan regardless of how comprehensive it is. We recognize the long-term care insurance segment of the industry is largely unautomated and we welcome comments regarding the impact of HIPAA on the long-term care segment.

h. An employee welfare benefit plan or any other arrangement that is established or maintained for the purpose of offering or providing health benefits to the employees of two or more employers. This includes plans that are referred to as multiple employer welfare arrangements (``MEWAs'').

i. The health care program for active military personnel under title 10 of the United States Code.

j. The veterans health care program under chapter 17 of title 38 of the United States Code.

This health plan primarily furnishes medical care through hospitals and clinics administered by the Department of Veterans Affairs for veterans with a service-connected disability that is compensable. Veterans with nonservice-connected disabilities (and no other health benefit plan) may receive health care under this health plan to the extent resources and facilities are available.

k. The Civilian Health and Medical Program of the Uniformed Services (CHAMPUS), as defined in 10 U.S.C. 1072(4).

CHAMPUS primarily covers services furnished by civilian medical providers to dependents of active duty members of the uniformed services and retirees and their dependents under age 65.

l. The Indian Health Service program under the Indian Health Care Improvement Act (25 U.S.C. 1601 et seq.).

This program furnishes services, generally through its own health care providers, primarily to persons who are eligible to receive services because they are of American Indian or Alaskan Native descent.

m. The Federal Employees Health Benefits Program under 5 U.S.C. chapter 89.

This program consists of health insurance plans offered to active and retired Federal employees and their dependents. Depending on the health plan, the services may be furnished on a fee-for-service basis or through a health maintenance organization.

(Note: Although section 1171(5)(M) of the Act refers to the ``Federal Employees Health Benefit Plan,'' this and any other rules adopting administrative simplification standards will use the correct name, the Federal Employees Health Benefits Program. One health plan does not cover all Federal employees; there are over 350 health plans that provide health benefits coverage to Federal employees, retirees, and their eligible family members. Therefore, we will use the correct name, the Federal Employees Health Benefits Program, to make clear that the administrative simplification standards apply to all health plans that participate in the Program.)

n. Any other individual or group health plan, or combination thereof, that provides or pays for the cost of medical care.

We would include a fourteenth category of health plan in addition to those specifically named in HIPAA, as there are health plans that do not readily fit into the other categories but whose major purpose is providing health benefits. The Secretary would determine which of these plans are health plans for purposes of title II of HIPAA. This category would include the Medicare Plus Choice plans that will become available as a result of section 1855 of the Act as amended by section 4001 of the Balanced Budget Act of 1997 (Public Law 105-33) to the extent that these health plans do not fall under any other category.

[[Page 43248]]

6. Small Health Plan

We would define a ``small health plan'' as a group health plan with fewer than 50 participants.

The HIPAA does not define a ``small health plan'' but instead leaves the definition to be determined by the Secretary. The Conference Report suggests that the appropriate definition of a ``small health plan'' is found in current section 2791(a) of the Public Health Service Act, which is a group health plan with fewer than 50 participants. We would also define small individual health plans as those with fewer than 50 participants.

7. Individually Identifiable Health Information

Section 1171(6) states the term ``individually identifiable health information'' means any information, including demographic information collected from an individual, that--

a. Is created or received by a health care provider, health plan, employer, or health care clearinghouse; and

b. Relates to the past, present or future physical or mental health or condition of an individual, the provision of health care to an individual, or the past, present, or future payment for the provision of health care to an individual, and

(i) Identifies the individual, or

(ii) With respect to which there is a reasonable basis to believe that the information can be used to identify the individual.

8. Standard

Section 1171 of the Act defines ``standard,'' when used with reference to a data element of health information or a transaction referred to in section 1173(a)(1) of the Act, as any such data element or transaction that meets each of the standards and implementation specifications adopted or established by the Secretary with respect to the data element or transaction under sections 1172 through 1174 of the Act.

Under our definition, the security standard would be a set of requirements adopted or established to preserve and maintain the confidentiality and privacy of electronically stored, maintained, or transmitted health information promulgated either by an organization accredited by the ANSI or HHS.

9. Transaction

``Transaction'' would mean the exchange of information between two parties to carry out financial and administrative activities related to health care. A transaction would be (a) any of the transactions listed in section 1173(a)(2) of the Act, and (b) any determined appropriate by the Secretary in accordance with section 1173(a)(1)(B) of the Act. We present them below in the order in which we propose to list them in the regulations text.

A ``transaction'' would mean any of the following:

a. Health claims or equivalent encounter information. This transaction may be used to submit health care claim billing information, encounter information, or both, from health care providers to payers, either directly or via intermediary billers and claims clearinghouses.

b. Health care payment and remittance advice. This transaction may be used by a health plan to make a payment to a financial institution for a health care provider (sending payment only), to send an explanation of benefits remittance advice directly to a health care provider (sending data only), or to make payment and send an explanation of benefits remittance advice to a health care provider via a financial institution (sending both payment and data).

c. Coordination of benefits. This transaction set can be used to transmit health care claims and billing payment information between payers with different payment responsibilities where coordination of benefits is required or between payers and regulatory agencies to monitor the furnishing, billing, and/or payment of health care services within a specific health care/insurance industry segment.

In addition to the nine electronic transactions specified in section 1173(a)(2) of the Act, section 1173(f) directs the Secretary to adopt standards for transferring standard data elements among health plans for coordination of benefits. This particular provision does not state that these should be standards for electronic transfer of standard data elements among health plans. However, we believe that the Congress, when writing this provision, intended for these standards to be an electronic form of transactions for coordination of benefits and sequential processing of claims. The Congress expressed its intent on these matters generally in section 1173(a)(1)(B) of the Act, where the Secretary is directed to adopt ``other financial and administrative transactions * * * consistent with the goals of improving the operation of the health care system and reducing administrative costs.''

d. Health claim status. This transaction may be used by health care providers and recipients of health care products or services (or their authorized agents) to request the status of a health care claim or encounter from a health plan.

e. Enrollment and disenrollment in a health plan. This transaction may be used to establish communication between the sponsor of a health benefit and the payer. It provides enrollment data, such as subscriber and dependents, employer information, and primary care health care provider information. A sponsor is the backer of the coverage, benefit, or product. A sponsor can be an employer, union, government agency, association, or insurance company. The health plan refers to an entity that pays claims, administers the insurance product or benefit, or both.

f. Eligibility for a health plan. This transaction may be used to inquire about the eligibility, coverage, or benefits associated with a benefit plan, employer, plan sponsor, subscriber, or a dependent under the subscriber's policy. It also can be used to communicate information about or changes to eligibility, coverage, or benefits from information sources (such as insurers, sponsors, and payers) to information receivers (such as physicians, hospitals, third party administrators, and government agencies).

g. Health plan premium payments. This transaction may be used by, for example, employers, employees, unions, and associations to make and keep track of payments of health plan premiums to their health insurers. This transaction may also be used by a health care provider, acting as liaison for the beneficiary, to make payment to a health insurer for coinsurance, copayments, and deductibles.

h. Referral certification and authorization. This transaction may be used to transmit health care service referral information between health care providers, health care providers furnishing services, and payers. It can also be used to obtain authorization for certain health care services from a health plan.

i. First report of injury. This transaction may be used to report information pertaining to an injury, illness, or incident to entities interested in the information for statistical, legal, claims, and risk management processing requirements.

j. Health claims attachments. This transaction may be used to transmit health care service information, such as subscriber, patient, demographic, diagnosis, or treatment data for the purpose of a request for review, certification, notification, or reporting the outcome of a health care services review.

k. Other transactions as the Secretary may prescribe by regulation.

[[Page 43249]]

Under section 1173(a)(1)(B) of the Act, the Secretary may adopt standards, and data elements for those standards, and for other financial and administrative transactions deemed appropriate by the Secretary. These transactions would be consistent with the goals of improving the operation of the health care system and reducing administrative costs.

C. Effective Dates--General

[Please label written comments or e-mailed comments about this section with the subject: effective dates]

In general, any given standard would be effective 24 months after the effective date (36 months for small health plans) of the final rule for that standard. Because there are other standards to be established than those in this proposed rule, we specify the date for a given standard under the subpart for that standard.

Health plans would be required by part 142 to comply with our requirements as follows:

1. Each health plan that is not a small plan would have to comply with the requirements of part 142 no later than 24 months after the effective date of the final rule.

2. Each small health plan would have to comply with the requirements of part 142 no later than 36 months after the effective date of the final rule.

Health care providers and health care clearinghouses would be required to begin using the standard by 24 months after the effective date of the final rule.

(The effective date of the final rule will be 60 days after the final rule is published in the Federal Register.)

Provisions of trading partner agreements that stipulate data content, format definitions, or conditions that conflict with the adopted standard would be invalid beginning 36 months from the effective date of the final rule for small health plans, and 24 months from the effective date of the final rule for all other health plans.

If the HHS adopts a modification to an implementation specification or a standard, the implementation date of the modification would be no earlier than the 180th day following the adoption of the modification. HHS would determine the actual date, taking into account the time needed to comply due to the nature and extent of the modification. HHS would be able to extend the time for compliance for small health plans. This provision would be at Sec. 142.106.

Any of the health plans, health care clearinghouses, and health care providers may implement a given standard earlier than the date specified in the subpart created for that standard. We realize that this may create some problems temporarily, as early implementers would have to be able to continue using old standards until the new one must, by law, be in place.

D. Security Standard

[Please label written comments or e-mailed comments about this section with the subject: Security Standard--General]

Section 142.308 would set forth the security standard. There is no recognized single standard that integrates all the components of security (administrative procedures, physical safeguards, technical security services, and technical mechanisms) that must be in place to preserve health information confidentiality and privacy as defined in the law. Therefore, we are designating a new, comprehensive standard, which defines the security requirements to be fulfilled.

In fact, there are numerous security guidelines and standards in existence today, focusing on the different techniques available for implementing the various aspects of security. We thoroughly researched the existing guidelines and standards, and consulted extensively with the organizations that developed them. A list of the organizations with which we consulted can be found in section G. below. As a result of these consultations and our research, we identified several high-level concepts on which the standard is based:

<bullet> The standard must be comprehensive.

<bullet> Consultation with standards development organizations, such as ANSI-accredited organizations, as well as business interest organizations, revealed the need for a standard that addressed all aspects of security in a concerted fashion. The HISB noted in its report to the Secretary that:

``Comprehensive adoption of security standards in health care, not piecemeal implementation, is advocated to provide security to data that is exchanged between health care entities.

By definition, if a system or communications between two systems, were implemented with technology(s) meeting standards in a general system security framework (Identification and Authentication; Authorization and Access Control; Accountability; Integrity and Availability; Security of Communication; and Security Administration.) that system would be essentially secure.

* * * no single standards development organization (SDO) is addressing all aspects of health care information security and confidentiality, and specifically, no single SDO is developing standards that cover every category of the security framework." [Page 189]

<bullet> The standard must be technology-neutral.

Our proposed standard does not reference or advocate specific technology because security technology is changing quickly. We want to give providers/plans/clearinghouses flexibility to choose their own technical solutions. A standard that is dependent on a specific technology or technologies would not be flexible enough to use future advances.

<bullet> The standard must be scalable.

The standard must be able to be implemented by all the affected entities, from the smallest provider to the largest clearinghouse. A single approach would be neither economically feasible nor effective in safeguarding health data. For example, in a small physician practice, a contingency plan for system emergencies might be only a few pages long, and cover issues such as where backup diskettes must be stored, and the location of a backup personal computer (PC). At a large health plan, the contingency plan might consist of multiple volumes and cover issues such as remote hot site operations and secure off-site storage of electronic media. The physician office solution would not protect the large plan's data, and the plan's solution would not be economically feasible (or necessary) for the physician office. Moreover, the statute specifically directed the Secretary to take into account the needs and capabilities of small and rural health care providers, as those terms are defined by the Secretary. The scalability of our approach addresses this direction. We are not proposing specific definitions of ``small" and ``rural" health care providers because the statute provides no exemptions or special benefits for these two groups. However, we solicit comments on the necessity to define these terms.

General Approach

We would define the security standard as a set of requirements with implementation features that providers, plans, and clearinghouses must include in their operations to assure that electronic health information pertaining to an individual remains secure. The implementation features address specific aspects of the requirements. The standard does not reference or advocate specific technology. This would allow the security standard to be stable, yet flexible enough to take advantage of state-of-the-art technology.

[[Page 43250]]

The standard does not address the extent to which a particular entity should implement the specific features. Instead, we would require that each affected entity assess its own security needs and risks and devise, implement, and maintain appropriate security to address its business requirements. How individual security requirements would be satisfied and which technology to use would be business decisions that each organization would have to make.

The recommendations contained in the National Research Council's 1997 report For The Record: Protecting Electronic Health Information support our approach to the development of a security standard. This report presents findings and recommendations related to health data security, and is widely viewed as an authoritative and comprehensive source on the subject. The report concludes that appropriate security practices are highly dependent on individual circumstances, but goes on to suggest that:

``It is therefore not possible to prescribe in detail specific practices for all organizations; rather, each organization must analyze its systems, vulnerabilities, risks, and resources to determine optimal security measures. Nevertheless, the committee believes that a set of practices can be articulated in a sufficiently general way that they can be adopted by all health care organizations in one form or another." (Page 168)

The specific requirements and supporting implementation features detailed in the next section represent this general set of practices. Many health care entities have already implemented some or all of these practices. We believe they represent those practices that are necessary in order to conduct business electronically in the health care industry today and, therefore, are normal business costs.

Inherent in this approach is a balance between the need to secure health data against risk and the economic cost of doing so. Health care entities must consider both aspects in devising their security solutions.

Specific Requirements

The proposed standard requires that each health care entity engaged in electronic maintenance or transmission of health information assess potential risks and vulnerabilities to the individual health data in its possession in electronic form, and develop, implement, and maintain appropriate security measures. Most importantly, these measures must be documented and kept current.

The proposed security standard consists of the requirements that a health care entity must address in order to safeguard the integrity, confidentiality, and availability of its electronic data. It also describes the implementation features that must be present in order to satisfy each requirement. The proposed requirements and implementation features were developed by the implementation team based on knowledge of security procedures and existing standards and guidelines described above. This was an iterative process that involved extensive outreach with a number of health care industry and Department of Commerce security experts. We also drew upon Recommendations 1 and 3 in the National Research Council's 1997 report, For The Record, that were recommended for immediate implementation.

``Recommendation 1: All organizations that handle patient-identifiable health care information--regardless of size--should adopt the set of technical and organizational policies, practices, and procedures described below to protect such information."

The proposed security standard addresses the following policies, practices, and procedures that were listed under Recommendation 1:

<bullet> Organizational Practices

1. Security and confidentiality policies
2. Information security officers
3. Education and training programs, and
4. Sanctions

<bullet> Technical Practices and Procedures

1. Individual authentication of users
2. Access controls
3. Audit trails
4. Physical security and disaster recovery
5. Protection of remote access points
6. Protection of external electronic communications
7. Software discipline, and
8. System assessment

``Recommendation 3: The federal government should work with industry to promote and encourage an informed public debate to determine an appropriate balance between the primary concerns of patients and the information needs of various users of health care information."

This proposed security standard was developed in the spirit of Recommendation 3. The security standard development process has been an open one with invitations to a number of organizations to participate in the security discussions. Although implementation team membership was limited to government employees, nongovernmental organizations; business organizations; individuals knowledgeable in security; and educational institutions have been encouraged to express their views.

As a result of the collaborative security regulation development process, the implementation team has chosen to divide the proposed security requirements, for purposes of presentation only, into the following four categories:

<bullet> Administrative procedures to guard data integrity, confidentiality, and availability--these are documented, formal practices to manage the selection and execution of security measures to protect data and the conduct of personnel in relation to the protection of data.

<bullet> Physical safeguards to guard data integrity, confidentiality, and availability--these relate to the protection of physical computer systems and related buildings and equipment from fire and other natural and environmental hazards, as well as from intrusion. Physical safeguards also cover the use of locks, keys, and administrative measures used to control access to computer systems and facilities.

<bullet> Technical security services to guard data integrity, confidentiality, and availability--these include the processes that are put in place to protect and to control and monitor information access, and

<bullet> Technical security mechanisms--these include the processes that are put in place to prevent unauthorized access to data that is transmitted over a communications network.

It should be noted that the only necessity is that the requirements would be met, not that they be presented in these four categories. Under this proposed rule, a business entity could choose to order the requirements in any manner that suits its business.

We then determined the requirements and implementation features that health plans, providers, and clearinghouses would implement. The implementation features describe the requirements in greater detail. Some requirements do not require this additional level of detail. Within the four categories, the requirements and implementation features are presented in alphabetical order to ensure that no one item is considered to be more important than another. The relative importance of the requirements and implementation features would depend on the characteristics of each organization.

The four categories of the matrix are described in greater detail in Sec. 142.308 and are depicted in tabular form along with the electronic signature standard in

[[Page 43251]]

a combined matrix located at Addendum 1. We have not included the matrix in the proposed regulation text. We invite your comments concerning the appropriateness and usefulness of including the matrix in the final regulation text. We also solicit comments as to the level of detail expressed in requirement implementation features; i.e., do any represent a level of detail that goes beyond what is necessary or appropriate. We have also provided a glossary of terms to facilitate a common understanding of the matrix entries. The glossary can be found at Addendum 2. Finally, we have included currently existing standards and guidelines mapped to the proposed security standard. This mapping is not all inclusive and is located at Addendum 3.

1. Administrative Procedures

[Please label written comments or e-mailed comments about this section with the subject: administrative procedures]

In this proposed rule, the administrative requirements and supporting implementation features are presented at Sec. 142.308(a). We would require each to be documented. We would require the documentation to be made available to those individuals responsible for implementing the procedures and would require it to be reviewed and updated periodically. The following matrix depicts the requirements and supporting implementation features for the Administrative Procedures category. Following the matrix is a discussion of each of the requirements under that category.

Administrative Procedures To Guard Data Integrity, Confidentiality, and Availability

Requirement	Implementation

Certification	
Chain of trust partner agreement	
Contingency plan (all listed implementation features must be implemented).	Applications and data criticality analysis. Data backup plan. Disaster recovery plan. Emergency mode operation plan. Testing and revision.
Formal mechanism for processing records	
Information access control (all listed implementation features must be implemented).	Access authorization. Access establishment. Access modification.
Internal audit	
Personnel security (all listed implementation features must be implemented).	Assure supervision of maintenance personnel by authorized, knowledgeable person. Maintenance of record of access authorizations. Operating, and in some cases, maintenance personnel have proper access authorization. Personnel clearance procedure. Personnel security policy/procedure. System users, including maintenance personnel, trained in security.
Security configuration mgmt. (all listed implementation features must be implemented).	Documentation. Hardware/software installation & maintenance review and testing for security features. Inventory. Security Testing. Virus checking.
Security incident procedures (all listed implementation features must be implemented).	Report procedures. Response procedures.
Security management process (all listed implementation features must be implemented).	Risk analysis. Risk management. Sanction policy. Security policy.
Termination procedures (all listed implementation features must be implemented).	Combination locks changed. Removal from access lists. Removal of user account(s). Turn in keys, token or cards that allow access.
Training (all listed implementation features must be implemented).	Awareness training for all personnel (including mgmt) Periodic security reminders. User education concerning virus protection. User education in importance of monitoring log in success/failure, and how to report discrepancies. User education in password management

----

a. Certification. Each organization would be required to evaluate its computer system(s) or network design(s) to certify that the appropriate security has been implemented. This evaluation could be performed internally or by an external accrediting agency.

We are, at this time, soliciting input on appropriate mechanisms to permit independent assessment of compliance. We would be particularly interested in input from those engaging in health care electronic data interchange (EDI), as well as independent certification and auditing organizations addressing issues of documentary evidence of steps taken for compliance; need for, or desirability of, independent verification, validation, and testing of system changes; and certifications required for off-the-shelf products used to meet the requirements of this regulation.

[[Page 43252]]

We also solicit comments on the extent to which obtaining external certification would create an undue burden on small or rural providers.

b. Chain of Trust Partner Agreement. If data are processed through a third party, the parties would be required to enter into a chain of trust partner agreement. This is a contract in which the parties agree to electronically exchange data and to protect the transmitted data. The sender and receiver are required and depend upon each other to maintain the integrity and confidentiality of the transmitted information. Multiple two-party contracts may be involved in moving information from the originating party to the ultimate receiving party. For example, a provider may contract with a clearinghouse to transmit claims to the clearinghouse; the clearinghouse, in turn, may contract with another clearinghouse or with a payer for the further transmittal of those claims. These agreements are important so that the same level of security will be maintained at all links in the chain when information moves from one organization to another.

c. Contingency Plan. We would require a contingency plan to be in effect for responding to system emergencies. The organization would be required to perform periodic backups of data, have available critical facilities for continuing operations in the event of an emergency, and have disaster recovery procedures in place. To satisfy the requirement, the plan would include the following:

<bullet> Applications and data criticality analysis,
<bullet> A data backup plan,
<bullet> A disaster recovery plan,
<bullet> An emergency mode operation plan, and
<bullet> Testing and revision procedures.

d. Formal Mechanism for Processing Records There would be a formal mechanism for processing records, that is, documented policies and procedures for the routine and nonroutine receipt, manipulation, storage, dissemination, transmission, and/or disposal of health information. This is important to limit the inadvertent loss or disclosure of secure information because of process issues.

e. Information Access Control. An entity would be required to establish and maintain formal, documented policies and procedures for granting different levels of access to health care information. To satisfy this requirement, the following features would be provided:

<bullet> Access authorization policies and procedures.
<bullet> Access establishment policies and procedures.
<bullet> Access modification policies and procedures.

Access control is also discussed later in this document in the personnel security requirement and under the physical safeguards, technical security services, and technical security mechanisms categories.

f. Internal Audit. There would be a requirement for an ongoing internal audit process, which is the in-house review of the records of system activity (for example, logins, file accesses, security incidents) maintained by an entity. This is important to enable the organization to identify potential security violations.

g. Personnel Security. There would be a requirement that all personnel with access to health information must be authorized to do so after receiving appropriate clearances. This is important to prevent unnecessary or inadvertent access to secure information. The personnel security requirement would require entities to meet the following conditions:

<bullet> Assure supervision of personnel performing technical systems maintenance activities by authorized, knowledgeable persons.
<bullet> Maintain access authorization records.
<bullet> Insure that operating, and in some cases, maintenance personnel have proper access.
<bullet> Employ personnel clearance procedures
<bullet> Employ personnel security policy/procedures.
<bullet> Ensure that system users, including technical maintenance personnel are trained in system security.

h. Security Configuration Management. The organization would be required to implement measures, practices, and procedures for the security of information systems. These would be coordinated and integrated with other system configuration management practices in order to create and manage system integrity. This integration process is important to ensure that routine changes to system hardware and/or software do not contribute to or create security weaknesses. This requirement would include the following:

<bullet> Documentation.
<bullet> Hardware/software installation and maintenance review and

testing for security features.
<bullet> Inventory procedures.
<bullet> Security testing.
<bullet> Virus checking.

i. Security Incident Procedures. There would be a requirement to implement accurate and current security incident procedures. These are formal, documented instructions for reporting security breaches, so that security violations are reported and handled promptly. These instructions would include the following:
<bullet> Report procedures.
<bullet> Response procedures.

j. Security Management Process. A process for security management would be required. This involves creating, administering, and overseeing policies to ensure the prevention, detection, containment, and correction of security breaches. We would require the organization to have a formal security management process in place to address the full range of security issues. Security management includes the following mandatory implementation features:
<bullet> Risk analysis.
<bullet> Risk management.
<bullet> A sanction policy.
<bullet> A security policy.

k. Termination Procedures. There would be a requirement to implement termination procedures, which are formal, documented instructions, including appropriate security measures, for the ending of an employee's employment or an internal/external user's access. These procedures are important to prevent the possibility of unauthorized access to secure data by those who are no longer authorized to access the data. Termination procedures would include the following mandatory implementation features:
<bullet> Changing combination locks.
<bullet> Removal from access lists.
<bullet> Removal of user account(s).
<bullet> Turn in of keys, tokens, or cards that allow access.

l. Training. This proposed rule would require security training for all staff regarding the vulnerabilities of the health information in an entity's possession and procedures which must be followed to ensure the protection of that information. This is important because employees need to understand their security responsibilities and make security a part of their day-to-day activities. The implementation features that would be required to be incorporated follow:
<bullet> Awareness training for all personnel, including management, (this is also included as a requirement under physical safeguards).
<bullet> Periodic security reminders.
<bullet> User education concerning virus protection.
<bullet> User education in importance of monitoring login success/failure, and how to report discrepancies.
<bullet> User education in password management.

[[Page 43253]]

2. Physical Safeguards To Guard Data Integrity, Confidentiality, and Availability
[Please label written comments or e-mailed comments about this section with the subject: Physical Safeguards]

The requirements and implementation features for physical safeguards are presented at Sec. 142.308(b) of this proposed rule. We would require each of these safeguards to be documented. We would require this documentation to be made available to those individuals responsible for implementing the safeguards and to be reviewed and updated periodically. The following matrix depicts the requirements and implementation features for the Physical Safeguards category. Following the matrix is a discussion of each of the requirements under that category.

Physical Safeguards To Guard Data Integrity, Confidentiality, and Availability

Requirement	Implementation
Assigned security responsibility	
Media controls (all listed implementation features must be implemented).	Access control. Accountability (tracking mechanism). Data backup. Data storage. Disposal.
Physical access controls (limited access) (all listed implementation features must be implemented).	Disaster recovery. Emergency mode operation. Equipment control (into and out of site). Facility security plan. Procedures for verifying access authorizations prior to physical access. Maintenance records. Need-to-know procedures for personnel access. Sign-in for visitors and escort, if appropriate. Testing and revision.
Policy/guideline on work station use	
Secure work station location	
Security awareness training.	

a. Assigned Security Responsibility. We would require the security responsibility to be assigned to a specific individual or organization, and the assignment be documented. These responsibilities would include the management and supervision of (1) the use of security measures to protect data, and (2) the conduct of personnel in relation to the protection of data. This assignment is important to provide an organizational focus and importance to security and to pinpoint responsibility.

b. Media Controls. Media controls would be required in the form of formal, documented policies and procedures that govern the receipt and removal of hardware/software (for example, diskettes, tapes) into and out of a facility. They are important to ensure total control of media containing health information. These controls would include the following mandatory implementation features:
<bullet> Controlled access to media.
<bullet> Accountability (tracking mechanism).
<bullet> Data backup.
<bullet> Data storage.
<bullet> Disposal.

c. Physical Access Controls. Physical access controls (limited access) would be required. These would be formal, documented policies and procedures for limiting physical access to an entity while ensuring that properly authorized access is allowed. These controls would be extremely important to the security of health information by preventing unauthorized physical access to information and ensuring that authorized personnel have proper access. These controls would include the following mandatory implementation features:
<bullet> Disaster recovery.
<bullet> Emergency mode operation.
<bullet> Equipment control (into and out of site).
<bullet> A facility security plan.
<bullet> Procedures for verifying access authorizations prior to physical access.
<bullet> Maintenance records.
<bullet> Need-to-know procedures for personnel access.
<bullet> Sign-in for visitors and escort, if appropriate.
<bullet> Testing and revision.

d. Policy/Guideline on Workstation Use. Each organization would be required to have a policy/guideline on workstation use. These documented instructions/procedures would delineate the proper functions to be performed and the manner in which those functions are to be performed (for example, logging off before leaving a terminal unattended). This would be important so that employees will understand the manner in which workstations must be used to maximize the security of health information.

e. Secure Workstation Location. Each organization would be required to put in place physical safeguards to eliminate or minimize the possibility of unauthorized access to information. This would be important especially in public buildings, provider locations, and in areas where there is heavy pedestrian traffic.

f. Security Awareness Training. Security awareness training would be required for all employees, agents, and contractors. This would be important because employees would need to understand their security responsibilities based on their job responsibilities in the organization and make security a part of their daily activities.

3. Technical Security Services To Guard Data Integrity, Confidentiality, and Availability

[Please label written comments or e-mailed comments about this section with the subject: Technical Security Services]

The proposed requirements and implementation features for technical security services are presented at Sec. 142.308(c). We would require each of these services to be implemented and documented. The documentation would be made available to those individuals responsible for implementing the services and would be reviewed and updated periodically. The following matrix depicts the requirements and implementation features for the Technical Security Services category. Following the matrix is a discussion of

[[Page 43254]]

each of the requirements under that category.

Technical Security Services To Guard Data Integrity, Confidentiality, and Availability

Requirement	Implementation
Access control (The following implementation feature must be implemented: Procedure for emergency access. In addition, at least one of the following three implementation features must be implemented: Context-based access, Role-based access, User-based access. The use of Encryption is optional).	Context-based access. Encryption. Procedure for emergency access. Role-based access. User-based access.
Audit controls	
Authorization control (At least one of the listed implementation features must be implemented).	Role-based access. User-based access.
Data Authentication	
Entity authentication (The following implementation features must be implemented: Automatic logoff, Unique user identification. In addition, at least one of the other listed implementation features must be implemented).	Automatic logoff. Biometric. Password. PIN. Telephone callback. Token. Unique user identification.

a. Access Control. There would be a requirement for access control which would restrict access to resources and allow access only by privileged entities. It would be important to limit access to health information to those employees who have a business need to access it. Types of access control include, among others, mandatory access control, discretionary access control, time-of-day, classification, and subject-object separation. The following implementation feature would be used:

<bullet> Procedure for emergency access.

In addition, at least one of the following three implementation features would be used:

<bullet> Context-based access.

<bullet> Role-based access.

<bullet> User-based access.

The use of the encryption implementation feature would be optional.

b. Audit Controls. Each organization would be required to put in place audit control mechanisms to record and examine system activity. They would be important so that the organization can identify suspect data access activities, assess its security program, and respond to potential weaknesses.

c. Authorization Control. There would be a requirement to put in place a mechanism for obtaining consent for the use and disclosure of health information. These controls would be necessary to ensure that health information is used only by properly authorized individuals. Either of the following implementation features may be used:

<bullet> Role-based access.

<bullet> User-based access (see access control, above.).

d. Data Authentication. Each organization would be required to be able to provide corroboration that data in its possession has not been altered or destroyed in an unauthorized manner. Examples of how data corroboration may be assured include the use of a check sum, double keying, a message authentication code, or digital signature.

e. Entity Authentication. Each organization would be required to implement entity authentication, which is the corroboration that an entity is who it claims to be. Authentication would be important to prevent the improper identification of an entity who is accessing secure data. The following implementation features would be used:

<bullet> Automatic log off.

<bullet> Unique user identification.

In addition, at least one of the following implementation features would be used:

<bullet> A biometric identification system.

<bullet> A password system.

<bullet> A personal identification number (PIN).

<bullet> Telephone callback.

<bullet> A token system which uses a physical device for user identification.

4. Technical Security Mechanisms To Guard Against Unauthorized Access to Data That Is Transmitted Over a Communications Network

[Please label written comments or e-mailed comments about this section with the subject: Technical Security Mechanisms]

In this proposed rule, the requirements and implementation features for technical security mechanisms are presented at Sec. 142.308(d). Each of these mechanisms would need to be documented. The documentation would be made available to those individuals responsible for implementing the mechanisms and would be reviewed and updated periodically. The following matrix depicts the requirement and implementation features for the Technical Security Mechanisms category. Following the matrix is a discussion of the requirement under that category.

[[Page 43255]]

Technical Security Mechanisms To Guard Against Unauthorized Access to Data That Is Transmitted Over a Communications Network

Requirement	Implementation
Communications/network controls (If communications or networking is employed, the following implementation features must be implemented: Integrity controls, Message authentication. In addition, one of the following implementation features must be implemented: Access controls, Encryption. In addition, if using a network, the following four implementation features must be implemented: Alarm, Audit trail, Entity authentication, Event reporting).	Access controls. Alarm. Audit trail. Encryption. Entity authentication. Event reporting. Integrity controls. Message authentication.

Each organization that uses communications or networks would be required to protect communications containing health information that are transmitted electronically over open networks so that they cannot be easily intercepted and interpreted by parties other than the intended recipient, and to protect their information systems from intruders trying to access systems through external communication points. When using open networks, some form of encryption should be employed. The utilization of less open systems/networks such as those provided by a value-added network (VAN) or private-wire arrangement provides sufficient access controls to allow encryption to be an optional feature. These controls would be important because of the potential for compromise of information over open systems such as the Internet or dial-in lines.

The following implementation features would be in place:

<bullet> Integrity controls.

<bullet> Message authentication.

One of the following implementation features would be in place:

<bullet> Access controls.

<bullet> Encryption.

In addition, if using a network for communications, the following implementation features would be in place:

<bullet> Alarm.

<bullet> Audit trail.

<bullet> Entity authentication.

<bullet> Event reporting.

Small or Rural Provider Example. The size and organizational structure of the entities that would be required to implement this standard vary tremendously. Therefore, it would be impossible to provide examples that would cover every possible implementation of security in the health care industry. Nevertheless, we have included an example describing the manner in which a small or rural provider might choose to implement the requirements of the standard. (For purposes of this example, we would describe a small or rural provider as a one to four physician office, with two to five additional employees. The office uses a PC-based practice management system, which is used to communicate intermittently with a clearinghouse for submission of electronic claims. The number of providers is of less importance for this example than the relatively simple technology in use and the fact that there is insufficient volume or revenue to justify employment of a computer system administrator.) We want to emphasize that there are numerous ways in which an entity could implement these requirements and features. This example does not necessarily represent the best way or the only way in which an entity could choose to implement security.

We anticipate that the small or rural provider office, as described above, would normally evaluate and self-certify that the appropriate security is in place for its computer system and office procedures. This evaluation could be done by a knowledgeable person on the staff, or more likely, by a consultant or by the vendor of the practice management system as a service to its customers. First, the office might assess actual and potential risks to its information assets. Then, to establish appropriate security, the office would develop policies and procedures to mitigate and manage those risks. These would include an overall framework outlining information security activities and responsibilities, and repercussions for failure to meet those responsibilities.

Next, this office might develop contingency plans to reduce or negate the damage resulting from processing anomalies; for example, establish a routine process for maintaining back up floppy disks at a second location, obtain a PC maintenance contract, and arrange for use of a backup PC should the need arise. This office would need to periodically review its plan to determine whether it still met the office's needs.

The office would need to create and document a personnel security policy and procedures to be followed. A key individual on the office staff should be charged with the responsibility for assuring the Personnel Security requirement is met. This responsibility would include seeing that the access authorization levels granted are documented and kept current (for example, records are kept of everyone who is permitted to use the PC and what files they may access), and training all personnel in security. Again, we emphasize that these requirements are scalable. The requirement for Personnel Clearance Procedures could be met in a small office with standard personal and professional reference checks, while a large organization may employ more formal, rigorous background investigations.

This same individual could also be charged with the responsibility for Security Configuration Management and Termination Procedures. For our small provider, the Security Configuration Management requirement would be relatively easy to satisfy; the necessary features could be part of a purchased hardware/software package (for example, a new PC might be equipped with virus checking software), or included as part of the support supplied with the purchase of equipment and software. Termination procedures would incorporate specific security actions to be taken as a result of an employee's termination, such as obtaining all keys and changing combinations or passwords. A ``position description'' document describing this person's duties could specify the level of detail necessary.

The small or rural provider office would also need to ensure that they have activated the internal auditing capability of the software used to manage health data files so that it tracks who has accessed the data. (We expect that the capability of keeping audit trails will become standard in all health care software in the near future, spurred on by the health information privacy debates in the Congress and elsewhere.)

A small or rural provider may document compliance with many of the

[[Page 43256]]

foregoing administrative security requirements by including them in an ``office procedures'' type of document that should be required reading by new employees and always available for reference. Requirements that would lend themselves to inclusion in an ``office procedures'' document include: contingency plans, formal records processing procedures, information access controls (rules for granting access, actual establishment of access, and procedures for modifying such access), security incident procedures (for example, who is to be notified if it appears that medical information has been accessed by an unauthorized party), and training. Periodic security reminders could include visual aids, such as posters and screen savers, and oral reminders in recurring meetings.

Physical Access controls would be relatively straightforward for this small or rural office, using locked rooms and/or closets to secure equipment and media from unauthorized access. The ``office procedures/ policies'' manual should include directions for authorizing access and keeping records of authorized accesses. Media Controls and Workstation Use policy instructions would be developed by the office and would include additional instructions on such items as where to store backed-up data, how to dispose of data no longer needed, or logging off when leaving terminals unattended.

Safeguards for the security of workstation location(s) would depend upon the physical surroundings in the small or rural office. Our small or rural provider may meet the requirements by locating equipment in areas that are generally populated by office staff and have some degree of physical separation from the public. Security Awareness Training would be part of the new employee orientation process and would be a periodic recurring discussion item in staff meetings.

The Technical Security Services requirements for Access Control, Entity Authentication, and Authorization Control may be achieved simply by implementing a user-based data access model (assigning a user-name and password combination to each authorized employee). Other access models could be employed if desired, but would prove unwieldy for the small office. For example, the role-based access process groups users with similar data access needs, and context-based access is based upon the context of a transaction--not on the attributes of the initiator. By assigning full access rights to a minimum of two key individuals in the office, implementation of the Emergency Access feature could be satisfied. Audit control mechanisms, by necessity, would be provided by software featuring that capability. By establishing and using a message authentication code, Data Authentication would be achieved. Use of the password system mentioned above could also satisfy the Unique User Identification requirement.

As our example provider contracts with a third party to handle claims processing, the claims processing contract would be the vehicle to provide for a chain of trust (requiring the contractor to implement the same security requirements and take responsibility for protecting the data it receives).

If this provider chooses to use the Internet to transmit or receive health information, some form of encryption must be used. For example, the provider could procure and use commercial software to provide protection against unauthorized access to the data transmitted or received. (This decision must take into account what encryption system the message recipient uses.) On the other hand, health information when transmitted via other means such as VANs, private wires, or even dial-up connections may not require such absolute protection as is provided by encryption. This small or rural provider would likely not be part of a network configuration, therefore, only integrity controls and message authentication would be required and could be provided by currently available software products, most likely provided as part of their contract with their health care clearinghouse.

Small providers may need guidance regarding the content of the documents required by this rule (for example, specifics of a chain of trust partner agreement). We would expect models of the documentation discussed in this example to be developed by industry associations and vendors. If this model documentation is not developed, DHHS would work with the industry to develop them.

E. Electronic Signature Standard

[Please label written comments or e-mailed comments about this section with the subject: Electronic Signature Standard]

HIPAA directs the Secretary of the Department of Health and Human Services to coordinate with the Secretary of the Department of Commerce in adopting standards for the electronic transmission and authentication of signatures with respect to the transactions referred to in the law. This rule was developed in coordination with the Department of Commerce's National Institute of Standards and Technology. We propose to adopt a cryptographically based digital signature as the standard.

Whenever a HIPAA specified transaction requires the use of an electronic signature, the standard must be used. It should be noted that an electronic signature is not required for any of the currently proposed standard transactions.

In the electronic environment, the same legal weight associated with an original signature on a paper document may be needed for electronic data. Use of an electronic signature refers to the act of attaching a signature by electronic means. The electronic signature process involves authentication of the signer's identity, a signature process according to system design and software instructions, binding of the signature to the document and non-alterability after the signature has been affixed to the document. The generation of electronic signatures requires the successful identification and authentication of the signer at the time of the signature.

The proposed standard for electronic signature is presented at Sec. 142.310 and would be digital.

The following matrix depicts the requirement and implementation features for electronic signatures. Following the matrix is a discussion of the electronic signature requirement.

[[Page 43257]]

Electronic Signature

Requirement	Implementation
Digital signature (If digital signature is employed, the following three implementation features must be implemented: Message integrity, Nonrepudiation, User authentication. Other implementation features are optional).	Ability to add attributes.
	Continuity of signature capability.
	Countersignatures.
	Independent verifiability.
	Interoperability.
	Message integrity.
	Multiple Signatures.
	Nonrepudiation.
	Transportability.
	User authentication.

Various technologies may fulfill one or more of the requirements specified in the matrix. Authentication systems (passwords, biometrics, physical feature authentication, behavioral actions and token-based authentication) can be combined with cryptographic techniques to form an electronic signature. However, a complete electronic signature system may require more than one of the technologies mentioned above. If electronic signatures would be used, certain implementation features must be included, specifically:

<bullet> Message integrity.
<bullet> Nonrepudiation.
<bullet> User authentication.

Currently there are no technically mature techniques that provide the security service of nonrepudiation in an open network environment, in the absence of trusted third parties, other than digital signature-based techniques. Therefore, if electronic signatures are employed, we would require that digital signature technology be used. A digital signature is formed by applying a mathematical function to the electronic document. This process yields a unique bit string, referred to as a message digest. The digest (only) is encrypted using the originator's private key and the resulting bit stream is appended to the electronic document. The recipient of the transmitted document decrypts the message digest with the originator's public key, applies the same message hash function to the document, then compares the resulting digest with the transmitted version. If they are identical, then the recipient is assured that the message is unaltered and the identity of the signer is proven. Since only the signatory authority can hold the Private Key used to digitally sign the document, the critical feature of nonrepudiation is enforced. Other electronic signature implementation features that may be used follow:

<bullet> Ability to add attributes.
<bullet> Continuity of signature capability.
<bullet> Countersignatures capability.
<bullet> Independent verifiability.
<bullet> Interoperability.
<bullet> Multiple signatures.
<bullet> Transportability.

This standard is described in greater detail in Sec. 142.310 of the regulation text and is depicted in tabular form along with the security standard in a combined matrix located at Addendum 1. We have not included the matrix in the proposed regulation text. We invite your comments concerning the appropriateness and usefulness of including the matrix in the final regulation text. We have also provided a glossary of terms to facilitate a common understanding of the matrix entries. The glossary can be found at Addendum 2. Finally, we have included currently existing standards and guidelines mapped to the proposed electronic signature standard. This mapping is not all inclusive and is located at Addendum 3.

F. Selection Criteria

Each individual implementation team weighted the criteria described in section I.B. above, Process for Developing National Standards, in terms of the standard it was addressing. As we assessed security and electronic signatures, it became apparent that while the security standard set forth in Sec. 142.308 and the electronic signature standard set forth in Sec. 142.310 satisfy all the criteria described above, they most strongly address criteria 1, 3, 7, 9, and 10. These criteria are described below in the specific context of these standards.

1. Improve the efficiency and effectiveness of the health care system.

The security and electronic signature standards would be integrated with the electronic transmission of health care information to improve the overall effectiveness of the health care system. This integration would assure that electronic health care information would not be accessible to any unauthorized person or organization, but would be both accurate and available to those who are authorized to receive it.

3. Be consistent and uniform with the other HIPAA standards and, secondly, with other private and public sector health data standards.

The security and electronic signature standards were developed after a comprehensive review of existing standards and guidelines, with significant input by a wide range of industry experts. As indicated in Addendum 3, the standards map well to existing standards and guidelines.

7. Be technologically independent of computer platforms and transmission protocols.

We have defined the security and electronic signature standards in terms of requirements that would allow businesses in the health care industry to select the technology that best meets their business requirements while still allowing them to comply with the standards.

9. Keep data collection and paperwork burdens on users as low as is feasible.

The security and electronic signature standards would allow individual health care industry businesses to ascertain the level of security information that would be needed. The confidentiality level associated with individual data elements concerning health care information would determine the appropriate security application to be used. The security standard would define the requirements to be met to achieve the privacy and confidentiality goal, but each business entity, driven by its business requirements, would decide what techniques and controls would provide appropriate and adequate electronic data protection. This would allow data collection and the paperwork burden to be as low as is feasible.

10. Incorporate flexibility to adapt more easily to changes in the health care infrastructure and information technology.

A technologically neutral security standard would be more adaptable to changes in infrastructure and information technology.

[[Page 43258]]

G. Consultations

In the development of the security and electronic signature standards, we consulted with many organizations, including those the legislation requires (section 1172(c)(3)(B) of the Act):

1. The NCVHS held two days of public hearings on security issues in August 1997, and made a recommendation to the Secretary of HHS, as required by the legislation. The NCVHS recommendation to the Secretary of HHS, as required by the legislation, was for a technologically neutral standard. It identified certain criteria to be established for a health information system to be secure. The proposed security standard complies with the NCVHS security recommendation.

2. The ANSI Accredited Standards Committee (ASC) X12 subcommittees on communication and control, insurance and government were contacted. Their current standards development effort is focused on messaging rather than on security requirements.

3. American Society for Testing and Materials (ASTM), Committee E31 on Computerized Systems participated in the security discussions.

4. Association for Electronic Health Care Transactions (AFEHCT), the clearinghouse organization, provided information on its health care transaction process requirements and emphasized that the security standard must be adaptable to different business needs.

5. Computer-based Patient Record Institute (CPRI) was consulted because the Work Group on Confidentiality, Privacy and Security is working on the establishment of guidelines, confidentiality agreements, security requirements, and frameworks. CPRI works closely with accredited standards development organizations.

6. Health Level Seven (HL-7) has been contacted through its participation at the HISB meetings.

7. NUCC and the NUBC were apprised of the different implementation teams' efforts. NUBC has not addressed security issues at any of the public meetings. NUCC identified a number of issues at its November 18-19 meeting and provided written comments to us.

H. Rules for Security Standards and Electronic Signature Standard

1. Health Plans

a. In Sec. 142.306(a), we would require health plans to accept and apply the security standard to all health care information pertaining to an individual that is electronically maintained or electronically transmitted. Federal agencies and States may place additional requirements on their health plans. In addition, trading partners may mutually agree to implement additional security measures.

b. In Sec. 142.310(a), entities would not be required to use an electronic signature. However, if a plan elects to use an electronic signature in one of the transactions named in the law, it would be required to apply the electronic signature standard described in Sec. 142.310(b) to that transaction. In the future, we anticipate that the standards for other transactions may include requirements for signatures. In particular, the proposed standard for claims attachments, which will be issued in a separate regulations package later, may include signature requirements on some or all of the attachments. If the proposed attachments standard includes such signature requirements, we will address the issue of how to reconcile such requirements with existing State and Federal requirements for written signatures as part of the proposed rule.

2. Health Care Clearinghouses

a. We would require in Sec. 142.306(b) that each health care clearinghouse comply with the security standard to ensure all health care information and activities are protected from unauthorized access. If the clearinghouse is part of a larger organization, then security must be imposed to prevent unauthorized access by the larger organization. The security standards apply to all health information pertaining to an individual that is electronically maintained or electronically transmitted.

b. In Sec. 142.310(a), entities would not be required to use an electronic signature. However, if a plan elects to use an electronic signature in one of the transactions named in the law, it would be required to apply the electronic signature standard described in Sec. 142.310(b) to that transaction. In the future, we anticipate that the standards for other transactions may include requirements for signatures. In particular, the proposed standard for claims attachments, which will be issued in a separate regulations package later, may include signature requirements on some or all of the attachments. If the proposed attachments standard includes such signature requirements, we will address the issue of how to reconcile such requirements with existing State and Federal requirements for written signatures as part of the proposed rule.

3. Health Care Providers

a. In Sec. 142.306(a), we would require each health care provider to apply the security standard to all health information pertaining to an individual that is electronically maintained or electronically transmitted.

b. In Sec. 142.310(a), entities would not be required to use an electronic signature. However, if a plan elects to use an electronic signature in one of the transactions named in the law, it would be required to apply the electronic signature standard described in Sec. 142.310(b) to that transaction. In the future, we anticipate that the standards for other transactions may include requirements for signatures. In particular, the proposed standard for claims attachments, which will be issued in a separate regulations package later, may include signature requirements on some or all of the attachments. If the proposed attachments standard includes such signature requirements, we will address the issue of how to reconcile such requirements with existing State and Federal requirements for written signatures as part of the proposed rule.

I. Effective Dates

Health plans would be required to comply with the security and electronic signature standards as follows:

1. Each health plan that is not a small health plan would have to comply with the requirements of Secs. 142.306, 142.308, and 142.310 no later than 24 months after publication of the final rule.

2. Each small health plan would have to comply with the requirements of Secs. 142.306, 142.308, and 142.310 no later than 36 months after the date of publication of the final rule.

3. If the effective date for the electronic transaction standards is later than the effective date for the security standard, implementation of the security standard would not be delayed until the standard transactions are in use. The security standard would still be effective with respect to electronically stored or maintained data. Security of health information would not be solely tied to the standard transactions but would apply to all individual health information electronically stored, maintained, or transmitted.

4. Under this proposed rule, in some cases, a health plan could choose to convert from paper to standard EDI transactions prior to the effective date of the security standard. We would recommend that the security standard be implemented at that time in order to safeguard the data in those transactions. We invite comments on this issue.

[[Page 43259]]

Failure to comply with standards may result in monetary penalties. The Secretary is required by statute to impose penalties of not more than $100 per violation on any person who fails to comply with a standard, except that the total amount imposed on any one person in each calendar year may not exceed $25,000 for violations of one requirement.

We are not proposing any enforcement procedures at this time, but we plan to do so in a future Federal Register document once the industry has some experience with using the standards. These procedures will be in place by the time the standards are implemented by industry. We envision the monitoring and enforcement process as a partnership between the Federal government and the private sector. Some private accreditation bodies have already exhibited interest in certifying compliance with the security requirements as part of their accreditation reviews. Small providers may be able to self-certify through industry-developed checklists. HHS would likely retain the final responsibility for determining violations and imposing the penalties specified by the statute. We welcome comments on this approach.

III. Implementation

If an entity elects to use an electronic signature in a transaction, or if an electronic signature is required by a transaction standard adopted by the Secretary, the entity must apply the electronic signature standard described in Sec. 142.310(b).

How the security standard would be implemented is dependent upon industry trading partner agreements for electronic transmissions. The health care industry would be able to adapt the security matrix to meet its business needs. We propose that the requirements of the security standard be implemented over time. However, we would require implementation to be complete by the applicable effective date. We would encourage, but not require that entities comply with the security standard as soon as practicable, preferably before implementing the transactions standards.

The security standard would supersede contrary provisions of State law including State law requiring medical or health plan records to be maintained or transmitted in other electronic formats. There are certain exceptions when the standards would not supersede contrary provisions of State law; section 1178 identifies those conditions and directs the Secretary to determine whether a particular State provision falls within one or more of the exceptions.

The electronic signature standard (digital signature) would be deemed to satisfy Federal and State statutory requirements for written signatures with respect to the named transactions referred to in the legislation.

Several accreditation organizations such as the Electronic Healthcare Network Accreditation Commission (EHNAC), the Joint Commission on Accreditation of Healthcare Organizations (JCAHO), and the National Committee for Quality Assurance (NCQA), indicate that one of their accreditation requirements will be compliance with the HIPAA security and electronic signature (if applicable) standards.

IV. New and Revised Standards

To encourage innovation and promote development, we plan to establish a process to allow an organization to request a revision or replacement to any adopted standard or standards. An organization could request a revision or replacement to an adopted standard by requesting a waiver from the Secretary of Health and Human Services to test a revised or new standard. The organization would be required, at a minimum, to demonstrate that the revised or new standard offers a clear improvement over the adopted standard. If the organization presents sufficient documentation that supports testing of a revised or new standard, we want to be able to grant the organization a temporary waiver to test while remaining in compliance with the law. We do not intend to establish a process that would allow an organization to avoid using any adopted standard.

We would welcome comments on the following: (1) How we should establish this process, (2) the length of time a proposed standard should be tested before we decide whether to adopt it, (3) whether we should solicit public comments before implementing a change in a standard, and (4) other issues and recommendations we should consider. Comments should be submitted to the addresses presented in the ADDRESSES section of this document.

The following is one possible process:

<bullet> Any organization that wishes to revise or replace an adopted standard would submit its waiver request to an HHS evaluation committee (to be established or defined). The organization would do the following for each standard it wishes to revise or replace:

+ Provide a detailed explanation, no more than 10 pages, of how the revision or replacement would be a clear improvement over the current standard.

+ Provide specifications and technical capabilities on the revised or new standard, including any additional system requirements.

+ Provide an explanation, no more than five pages, of how the organization intends to test the standard.

<bullet> The committee's evaluation would, at a minimum, be based on the following:

+ A cost-benefit analysis.

+ An assessment of whether the proposed revision or replacement demonstrates a clear improvement to an existing standard.

+ The extent and length of time of the waiver.

<bullet> The evaluation committee would inform the organization requesting the waiver within 30 working days of the committee's decision on the waiver request. If the committee decides to grant a waiver, the notification may include the following:

+ Committee comments such as the following:

--The length of time for which the waiver applies if it differs from the waiver request.

--The sites the committee believes are appropriate for testing if they differ from the waiver request.

--Any pertinent information regarding the conditions of an approved waiver.

<bullet> Any organization that receives a waiver would be required to submit a report containing the results of the study, no later than 3 months after the study is completed.

<bullet> The committee would evaluate the report and determine whether the benefits of the proposed revision or new standard significantly outweigh the disadvantages of implementing it and make a recommendation to the Secretary.

V. Response to Comments

Because of the large number of items of correspondence we normally receive on Federal Register documents published for comment, we are not able to acknowledge or respond to them individually. We will consider all comments we receive by the date and time specified in the DATES section of this preamble, and, if we proceed with a subsequent document, we will respond to the major comments in the preamble of that document.

VI. Impact Analysis

As the effect of any one standard is affected by the implementation of other standards, it can be misleading to discuss the impact of one standard by itself. Therefore, we did an impact

[[Page 43260]]

analysis on the total effect of all the standards in the proposed rule concerning the national provider identifier (HCFA-0045-P), which was published on May 7, 1998 (63 FR 25320).

We intend to publish in each proposed rule an impact analysis that is specific to the standard or standards proposed in that rule, but the impact analysis will assess only the relative cost impact of implementing a given standard. Thus, the following discussion contains the impact analysis for the security standard and the electronic signature standard proposed in this rule. As stated in the general impact analysis in HCFA-0045-P, we do not intend to associate costs and savings to specific standards.

Although we cannot determine the specific economic impact of the standards being proposed in this rule (and individually each standard may not have a significant impact), the overall impact analysis makes clear that, collectively, all the standards will have a significant impact of over $100 million on the economy. Also, while each standard may not have a significant impact on a substantial number of small entities, the combined effects of all the proposed standards may have a significant effect on a substantial number of small entities. Therefore, the following impact analysis should be read in conjunction with the overall impact analysis.

The following describes the specific impacts that relate to the security and electronic signature standards. Security protection for health care information is not a ``stand-alone'' type requirement. Appropriate security protections will be a business enabler, encouraging the growth and use of electronic data interchange. The synergistic effect of the employment of the recommended security practices, procedures and technologies will enhance all aspects of HIPAA's Administrative Simplification requirements. In addition, it is important to recognize that security is not a product, but is an on-going, dynamic process.

In accordance with the provisions of Executive Order 12866, this proposed rule was reviewed by the Office of Management and Budget.

A. Security Standard

HIPAA requires that all health plans, health care providers, and health care clearinghouses that maintain or transmit health information electronically establish and maintain reasonable and appropriate administrative, technical, and physical safeguards to ensure integrity, confidentiality, and availability of the information. The safeguards also protect the information against any reasonably anticipated threats or hazards to the security or integrity of the information and protect it against unauthorized use or disclosure. Recommendation 1 from the National Research Council's (NRC) report For the Record: Protecting

Electronic Health Information (``All organizations that handle patient-identifiable health care information-- regardless of size--should adopt the set of technical and organization policies, practices, and procedures described * * * to protect such information.") would apply to all health care providers regardless of size, health care clearinghouses, and health plans. We agree with the NRC's belief that implementation of the practices and technologies delineated in Recommendation 1 would be possible today, and at a reasonable cost.

Health care providers that conduct electronic transactions with health plans would have to comply with the recommendation(s) for security protection. There is, however, no requirement to maintain health records electronically or transmit health care information by electronic means. There may also be health care providers that currently submit health care information on paper but archive records electronically. These entities will need to ensure that their existing electronic systems conform to security requirements for maintaining health information. Once they have done so, however, they may also take advantage of all the other benefits of electronic recordkeeping and transmittal. Therefore, no individual small entity is expected to experience direct costs that exceed benefits as a result of this rule. Furthermore, because almost all of the NRC recommendations reflect contemporary security measures and controls, most organizations that currently have security measures should have to make few, if any, modifications to their systems to meet the requirements proposed in the security standard.

The singular exception to the above lies in the area of providing security for the electronic transmission of health care information over insecure, public media. Here, the choice of a method to use is driven by economic factors. If an organization wishes to use an insecure transmission media such as the Internet, and take advantage of the low costs involved, off-setting costs may need to be incurred to provide for an acceptable form of encryption so that health information will be protected from intercept and possible misuse.

One alternative course of action to encrypting the information would be to use the services of a VAN. VANs do not manipulate data, but rather transmit data in its native form over telecommunication lines. We anticipate that VANs would be positively affected by administrative simplification, because use of the proposed transactions standards would eliminate the need for data to be reformatted. This would allow providers to purchase the services of a VAN directly, rather than as a service bundled with the functions of other clearinghouses. Another course of action might be to use private lines which would provide an appropriate level of protection for data in transmission.

B. Electronic Signature Standard

HIPAA does not require the use of electronic signatures. This particular capability, however, would be necessary for a completely paperless environment. Certain features of the digital signature type of electronic signature make this particular system the most desirable. Only digital signatures, using current technology, provide the combination of authenticity, message integrity, and nonrepudiation which is viewed as a desirable complement to the security standards required by the law.

The use of digital signatures requires a certain infrastructure (Public Key Infrastructure) that may necessitate the expenditure of initial and recurring costs for users. We do not know what these costs are presently, due to the lack of maturity of digital signature technology, and minimal use in the marketplace today. It is noted that public key certificate management systems and services do exist today, and it is presumed more quantifiable information will be forthcoming, as to potential costs and savings that can be associated with the use of digital signature systems. Other forms of electronic signature were considered, such as biometric and digitized signatures. While they provide a useful capability in certain circumstances, we believe that digital signature technology is most appropriate for this particular application.

C. Guiding Principles for Standard Selection

The implementation teams charged with designating standards under the statute have defined, with significant input from the health care industry, a set of common criteria for evaluating potential standards. These criteria are based on direct specifications in the HIPAA, the purpose of the law, and principles that support the regulatory

[[Page 43261]]

philosophy set forth in EO 12866 of September 30, 1993. In order to be designated as a standard, EO 12866 requires that a proposed standard:

<bullet> Improve the efficiency and effectiveness of the health care system by leading to cost reductions for or improvements in benefits from electronic HIPAA health care transactions. This principle supports the regulatory goals of cost-effectiveness and avoidance of burden.

<bullet> Meet the needs of the health data standards user community, particularly health care providers, health plans, and health care clearinghouses. This principle supports the regulatory goal of cost-effectiveness.

<bullet> Be consistent and uniform with the other HIPAA standards (that is, their data element definitions and codes and their privacy and security requirements) and, secondarily, with other private and public sector health data standards. This principle supports the regulatory goals of consistency and avoidance of incompatibility, and it establishes a performance objective for the standard.

<bullet> Have low additional development and implementation costs relative to the benefits of using the standard. This principle supports the regulatory goals of cost-effectiveness and avoidance of burden.

<bullet> Be supported by an ANSI-accredited standards developing organization or other private or public organization that would ensure continuity and efficient updating of the standard over time. This principle supports the regulatory goal of predictability.

<bullet> Have timely development, testing, implementation, and updating procedures to achieve administrative simplification benefits faster. This principle establishes a performance objective for the standard.

<bullet> Be technologically independent of the computer platforms and transmission protocols used in HIPAA health transactions, except when they are explicitly part of the standard. This principle establishes a performance objective for the standard and supports the regulatory goal of flexibility.

<bullet> Be precise and unambiguous but as simple as possible. This principle supports the regulatory goals of predictability and simplicity.

<bullet> Keep data collection and paperwork burdens on users as low as is feasible. This principle supports the regulatory goals of cost-effectiveness and avoidance of duplication and burden.

<bullet> Incorporate flexibility to adapt more easily to changes in the health care infrastructure (such as new services, organizations, and provider types) and information technology. This principle supports the regulatory goals of flexibility and encouragement of innovation.

We assessed a wide variety of security standards, guidelines and electronic signature standards against the principles listed above, with the overall goal of achieving the maximum benefit for the least cost. We found that there exists no single standard for security or electronic signature that encompasses all the requirements that have been deemed necessary. However, in this particular area, technology is rapidly developing enhancements and better means for accomplishing the stated goals.

D. Affected Entities

1. Health Care Providers

Health care providers that conduct business using electronic transactions with other health care participants (such as other health care providers, health plans, and employers) or maintain electronic health information are encouraged, but are not required to simultaneously implement the proposed security standard. However, if the effective date for the electronic transaction standards is later than the effective date for the security standard, the implementation of the security standard will not be delayed until the standard transactions are in use.

Health care providers that transmit, receive, or maintain health information would incur implementation costs for establishing or updating their security systems. Any negative impact on these health care providers caused by implementing the proposed security standard would generally be related to the initial implementation period for the specific requirements of the security standard. Health care providers that are indirectly involved in electronic transactions (for example, those who submit a paper claim that the health plan transmits electronically to a secondary payer) and do not maintain electronic health information would not be affected.

2. Health Plans

Health plans that engage in electronic health care transactions would have to modify their systems to use the security standard and the electronic signature standard, if used. Health plans that maintain electronic health information would also have to modify their systems to use the security standard. This conversion would have a one-time cost impact on Federal, State and private plans alike.

We recognize that this conversion process has the potential to cause business disruption of some health plans. However, health plans would be able to schedule their implementation of the security standard and other standards in a way that best fits their needs, as long as they meet the deadlines specified in the law.

Implementation of the security standard and the electronic signature standard, if used by the entities, would enhance payment safeguard activities and protect the integrity of the Medicare trust fund by reducing fraud and abuse that occurs when health care information is used by those who are not authorized to receive it. In addition these standards would assist the plans, providers, and clearinghouses to more effectively maintain the security of all health information in their databases.

3. Clearinghouses

Health care clearinghouses would face impacts similar to those experienced by health care providers and health plans. Systems vendors, that provide computer software applications to health care providers and other billers of health care services, would likely be positively affected. These vendors would have to develop software solutions that would allow health care providers and other billers of health care transactions to protect the information in their databases from unwanted access to their systems.

4. Unfunded Mandates

This proposed rule has been reviewed in accordance with the Unfunded Mandates Reform Act of 1995 (UMRA) (U.S.C. 1501 et seq.) and Executive Order 12875. As discussed in the combined impact analysis referenced above (see Federal Register, Volume 63, No. 88), DHHS estimates that implementation of the standards will require the expenditure of more than $100 million by the private sector. Therefore, the rule establishes a Federal private sector mandate and is a significant regulatory action within the meaning of section 202 of UMRA (2 U.S.C. 1532). DHHS has included this statement to address the anticipated effects of the proposed rules pursuant to section 202.

These standards also apply to State and local governments in their roles as health plans or health care providers. Thus, the proposed rules impose unfunded mandates on these entities. While we do not have sufficient information to provide estimates of these impacts, several State Medicaid agencies have estimated that it would cost $1 million per State to implement

[[Page 43262]]

all of the HIPAA standards. However, the Congressional Budget Office analysis stated that ``States are already in the forefront in administering the Medicaid program electronically; the only costs--which should not be significant--would involve bringing the software and computer systems for the Medicaid programs into compliance with the new standards."

The anticipated benefits and costs of this proposed standard, and other issues raised in section 202 of the UMRA, are addressed in the analysis below, and in the combined impact analysis. In addition, under section 205 of the UMRA (2 U.S.C. 1535), having considered a reasonable number of alternatives as outlined in the preamble to this rule and in the following analysis, the Department has concluded that the rule is the most cost-effective alternative for implementation of DHHS" statutory objective of administrative simplification.

5. Regulatory Flexibility Act

The Regulatory Flexibility Act (RFA) of 1980, Public Law 96-354, requires us to prepare a regulatory flexibility analysis if the Secretary certifies that a proposed regulation would have a significant economic impact on a substantial number of small entities. The security and electronic signature standards will affect small entities, such as providers. A more detailed analysis of the impact on small entities is part of the impact analysis we published on May 7, 1998 (63 FR 25320) for all the HIPAA standards. A detailed illustration of the potential impact of the security standard on a small health care provider can be found in the preamble in section D.

E. Factors in Establishing the Security Standard

1. Selection of Security Systems and Procedures

Because there is no national security standard in widespread use throughout the industry, adopting any of the candidate standards would require most health care providers, health plans and health care clearinghouses to conform to the new standard. Implementation of the security standard would require all health plans, health care providers, and health care clearinghouses to establish or revise their security precautions because the proposed standard is not currently in use. The selection of the security standard does not impose a greater burden on the industry than the nonselected options, and presents significant advantages in terms of universality, uniqueness and flexibility.

Only those plans, providers, and clearinghouses that decide to use the digital signature would be affected by the electronic signature standard. Some large health plans, health care providers, and health care clearinghouses that currently exchange health information among trading partners may have security systems and procedures in place to protect the information from unauthorized access. These entities may not incur significant costs to meet the proposed security standard and if they opt not to use the digital signature they would not incur costs to meet the electronic signature requirements. Also, some entities that currently use electronic signatures as an added security measure may also be using digital signature technology. At most, large entities that may have sophisticated security systems in place may only need to revise or update their systems to meet the proposed security standard and electronic signature standard.

2. Complexity of Conversion

The complexity of the conversion would be significantly affected by the volume of claims health plans process electronically and the desire to transmit the claims themselves or to use the services of a VAN or a clearinghouse. If they chose to transmit themselves, they would need to convert to the proposed transaction standards. Specific technology limitations of existing systems could affect the complexity of the conversion. For example, some entities may only have a minimum level of security and procedures in place and therefore may require a full upgrade, while others may already have a very sophisticated system and procedures and require very little enhancement.

3. Cost of Conversion

We expect that most providers, health plans, and clearinghouses that transmit or store data electronically have already implemented some security measures and will primarily need to assess existing security, identify areas of risk, and implement additional measures. We cannot estimate the per-entity cost of implementation because there is no information available regarding the extent to which providers', plans', and clearinghouses' current security practices are deficient. Moreover, some security solutions are almost cost-free to implement (e.g., reminding employees not to post passwords on their monitors) while others are not.

Affected entities will have many choices regarding how they will implement security. Some may choose to assess security using in-house staff, while others will utilize consultants. Practice management software vendors may also provide security consultation services to their customers. Entities may also choose to implement security measures that require hardware or software purchases at the time they do routine equipment upgrades.

The security requirements we are proposing were developed with considerable input from the health care industry, including providers, health plans, clearinghouses, vendors, and standards organizations. Industry members strongly advocated this flexible approach, which permits each affected entity to develop cost-effective security measures. We believe that this approach will yield the lowest implementation cost to industry while assuring that health information is safeguarded. We solicit input regarding implementation costs.

We are unable to estimate, of the nation's 4 million-plus health plans and 1.2 million-plus providers, the number of entities that would require security systems and procedures because they conduct electronic transactions or maintain electronic health information. Nor are we able to estimate the number of entities that neither conduct electronic transactions nor maintain electronic health information but may choose to do so at some future time. (These would be entities that send and receive paper transactions and maintain paper records and thus would not be affected because they would have no need to implement security standards.) However, we are aware of the possibility that those small entities that currently process claims electronically or maintain electronic health information may not be able to continue to do so due to the cost of establishing security systems to meet the requirements of the proposed security standard. Those entities that are not able to bill and exchange health information electronically may use clearinghouses. We believe that the proposed security standard represents the minimum necessary for adequate protection of health information in an electronic format. As discussed earlier in this preamble, the security requirements are both scalable and technically flexible; and while the law requires each health plan that is not a small plan to comply with the security and electronic signature requirements no later than 24 months after the effective date of the final rule, small plans will be allowed an additional 12 months to comply.

Since we are unable to estimate the number of entities, we are also unable to estimate the cost to the entities that will process electronic transactions.

[[Page 43263]]

However, we believe that the cost of establishing security systems and procedures is a portion of the costs associated with converting to the transaction standards that are required under HIPAA.

This discussion on conversion costs relates only to health plans, health care providers, and health care clearinghouses that are required to follow the security standard to maintain, transmit or receive electronic health information. Other entities would not be required to follow the security standard and procedures until they choose to maintain, transmit, or receive electronic health information. The cost of establishing security systems and procedures for entities that do not transmit, receive or maintain health information electronically is not included in our estimates.

VII. Collection of Information Requirements

Under the Paperwork Reduction Act of 1995, we are required to provide 60-day notice in the Federal Register and solicit public comment before a collection of information requirement is submitted to the Office of Management and Budget (OMB) for review and approval. In order to fairly evaluate whether an information collection should be approved by OMB, section 3506(c)(2)(A) of the Paperwork Reduction Act of 1995 requires that we solicit comment on the following issues:

<bullet> The need for the information collection and its usefulness in carrying out the proper functions of our agency.

<bullet> The accuracy of our estimate of the information collection burden.

<bullet> The quality, utility, and clarity of the information to be collected.

<bullet> Recommendations to minimize the information collection burden on the affected public, including automated collection techniques.

As discussed below, we are soliciting comment on the recordkeeping requirements, as referenced in Sec. 142.308 of this document. In addition, we are soliciting comment on the applicability of the PRA as it may relate to the requirement to use the standard adopted in Sec. 142.310 of this regulation.

Section 142.308 Security Standard

In summary, each entity designated in Sec. 142.302 must maintain documentation demonstrating the development, implementation, and maintenance of appropriate security measures that include, at a minimum, the requirements and implementation features set forth in this section. In addition, entities must maintain necessary documentation to demonstrate that these measures have been periodically reviewed, validated, updated, and kept current.

While we solicit comment on these recordkeeping requirements we explicitly solicit comment on the burden associated with maintaining documentation related to the implementation the requirements set forth in Sec. 142.308. Since the level of documentation necessary to demonstrate compliance with these requirements is dependent upon individual business needs and the fact that we do not prescribe the form, format, or degree of documentation necessary to demonstrate compliance, we are currently unable to accurately estimate the degree of recordkeeping burden that will be experienced by the varying entities. Therefore, commentors should provide an estimate of: (1) the initial recordkeeping burden associated with meeting these requirements and (2) the recordkeeping burden associated with maintaining documentation to demonstrate that the measures have been periodically reviewed, validated, updated, and kept current.

Below is a discussion of the applicability of the PRA as it may relate to the adoption of the standard referenced in Sec. 142.310 of this regulation.

Section 142.310 Electronic Signature Standard

In summary, any entity electing to use an electronic signature in a transaction as defined in Sec. 142.103, or if an electronic signature is required by a transaction standard adopted by the Secretary, the entity must apply the electronic signature standard described in paragraph (b) of this section to that transaction.

Discussion

The emerging and increasing use of health care EDI standards and transactions raises the issue of the applicability of the PRA. The question arises whether a regulation that adopts an EDI standard used to exchange certain information constitutes an information collection subject to the PRA.

In particular, we are still considering whether the use of any EDI transaction standard, such as the electronic signature described in this regulation, should be viewed or regarded as a standardized electronic collection of information. If it is a standardized electronic information collection, then the requirement by the Federal government on the industry to accept and transmit the information may be subject to OMB review and approval under the PRA.

We invite public comment on the issues discussed above. If the requirements, as set forth in Sec. 142.310 are determined to be subject to the PRA, we will submit these requirements to OMB for PRA approval. If you comment on these information collection and recordkeeping requirements, please e-mail comments to JBurke1@hcfa.gov (Attn: HCFA-0049) or mail copies directly to the following:

Health Care Financing Administration, Office of Information Services, Security and Standards Group, Division of HCFA Enterprise Standards, Room N2-14-26, 7500 Security Boulevard, Baltimore, MD 21244-1850. Attn: John Burke HCFA-0049, HCFA Reports Clearance Officer

And

Office of Information and Regulatory Affairs, Office of Management and Budget, Room 10235, New Executive Office Building, Washington, DC 20503, Attn: Allison Herron Eydt, HCFA Desk Officer

List of Subjects in 45 CFR Part 142

Administrative practice and procedure, Health facilities, Health insurance, Hospitals, Medicaid, Medicare, Report and recordkeeping requirement.

45 CFR subtitle A, subchapter B, would be amended by adding part 42 to read as follows:

Note to Reader: This proposed rule is one of several proposed rules that are being published to implement the administrative simplification provisions of the Health Insurance Portability and Accountability Act of 1996. We propose to establish a new 45 CFR Part 142. Proposed Subpart A--General Provisions is exactly the same in each rule unless we have added new sections or definitions to incorporate additional general information. The subparts that follow relate to the specific provisions announced separately in each proposed rule. When we publish the first final rule, each subsequent final rule will revise or add to the text that is set out in the first final rule.

PART 142--ADMINISTRATIVE REQUIREMENTS

Subpart A--General Provisions

Sec.

142.101 Statutory basis and purpose.

142.102 Applicability.

142.103 Definitions.
142.104 General requirements for health plans.
142.105 Compliance using a health care clearinghouse.
142.106 Effective dates of a modification to a standard or implementation specification.

[[Page 43264]]

Subpart B--Reserved

Subpart C--Security and Electronic Signature Standards

Sec.
142.302 Applicability and scope.
142.304 Definitions.
142.306 Rules for the security standard.
142.308 Security standard.
142.310 Electronic signature standard.
142.312 Effective date of the initial implementation of the security and electronic standards.

Authority: Sections 1173 and 1175 of the Social Security Act (42 U.S.C. 1320d-2 and 1320d-4).

Subpart A--General Provisions

Sec. 142.101 Statutory basis and purpose.

Sections 1171 through 1179 of the Social Security Act, 42 U.S.C. 1320d, as added by section 262 of the Health Insurance Portability and Accountability Act of 1996, require HHS to adopt national standards for the electronic exchange of health information in the health care system. The purpose of the sections of this part is to promote administrative simplification.

Sec. 142.102 Applicability.

(a) The standards adopted or designated under this part apply, in whole or in part, to the following:
(1) A health plan.
(2) A health care clearinghouse when doing the following:
(i) Transmitting a standard transaction (as defined in Sec. 142.103) to a health care provider or health plan.
(ii) Receiving a standard transaction from a health care provider or health plan.
(iii) Transmitting and receiving the standard transactions when interacting with another health care clearinghouse.
(3) A health care provider when transmitting an electronic transaction as defined in Sec. 142.103.
(b) Means of compliance are stated in greater detail in Sec. 142.105.

Sec. 142.103 Definitions.

For purposes of this part, the following definitions apply:
Code set means any set of codes used for encoding data elements, such as tables of terms, medical concepts, medical diagnostic codes, or medical procedure codes.
Health care clearinghouse means a public or private entity that processes or facilitates the processing of nonstandard data elements of health information into standard data elements. The entity receives health care transactions from health care providers or other entities, translates the data from a given format into one acceptable to the intended payer or payers, and forwards the processed transaction to appropriate payers and clearinghouses. Billing services, repricing companies, community health management information systems, community health information systems, and ``value-added" networks and switches are considered to be health care clearinghouses for purposes of this part.
Health care provider means a provider of services as defined in section 1861(u) of the Social Security Act, 42 U.S.C. 1395x, a provider of medical or other health services as defined in section 1861(s) of the Social Security Act, and any other person who furnishes or bills and is paid for health care services or supplies in the normal course of business.
Health information means any information, whether oral or recorded in any form or medium, that--
(1) Is created or received by a health care provider, health plan, public health authority, employer, life insurer, school or university, or health care clearinghouse; and
(2) Relates to the past, present, or future physical or mental health or condition of an individual, the provision of health care to an individual, or the past, present, or future payment for the provision of health care to an individual.
Health plan means an individual or group plan that provides, or pays the cost of, medical care. Health plan includes the following, singly or in combination:
(1) Group health plan. A group health plan is an employee welfare benefit plan (as currently defined in section 3(1) of the Employee Retirement Income and Security Act of 1974, 29 U.S.C. 1002(1)), including insured and self-insured plans, to the extent that the plan provides medical care, including items and services paid for as medical care, to employees or their dependents directly or through insurance, or otherwise, and--
(i) Has 50 or more participants; or
(ii) Is administered by an entity other than the employer that established and maintains the plan.
(2) Health insurance issuer. A health insurance issuer is an insurance company, insurance service, or insurance organization that is licensed to engage in the business of insurance in a State and is subject to State law that regulates insurance.
(3) Health maintenance organization. A health maintenance organization is a Federally qualified health maintenance organization, an organization recognized as a health maintenance organization under State law, or a similar organization regulated for solvency under State law in the same manner and to the same extent as such a health maintenance organization.
(4) Part A or Part B of the Medicare program under title XVIII of the Social Security Act.
(5) The Medicaid program under title XIX of the Social Security Act.
(6) A Medicare supplemental policy (as defined in section 1882(g)(1) of the Social Security Act, 42 U.S.C. 1395ss).
(7) A long-term care policy, including a nursing home fixed-indemnity policy.
(8) An employee welfare benefit plan or any other arrangement that is established or maintained for the purpose of offering or providing health benefits to the employees of two or more employers.
(9) The health care program for active military personnel under title 10 of the United States Code.
(10) The veterans health care program under 38 U.S.C. chapter 17.
(11) The Civilian Health and Medical Program of the Uniformed Services (CHAMPUS), as defined in 10 U.S.C. 1072(4).
(12) The Indian Health Service program under the Indian Health Care Improvement Act (25 U.S.C. 1601 et seq.).
(13) The Federal Employees Health Benefits Program under 5 U.S.C. chapter 89.
(14) Any other individual or group health plan, or combination thereof, that provides or pays for the cost of medical care.
Medical care means the diagnosis, cure, mitigation, treatment, or prevention of disease, or amounts paid for the purpose of affecting any body structure or function of the body; amounts paid for transportation primarily for and essential to these items; and amounts paid for insurance covering the items and the transportation specified in this definition.
Participant means any employee or former employee of an employer, or any member or former member of an employee organization, who is or may become eligible to receive a benefit of any type from an employee benefit plan that covers employees of that employer or members of such an organization, or whose beneficiaries may be eligible to receive any of these benefits. ``Employee" includes an individual who is treated as an employee under section 401(c)(1) of the Internal Revenue Code of 1986 (26 U.S.C. 401(c)(1)).
Small health plan means a group health plan or individual health plan with fewer than 50 participants.

[[Page 43265]]

Standard means a set of rules for a set of codes, data elements, transactions, or identifiers promulgated either by an organization accredited by the American National Standards Institute or HHS for the electronic transmission of health information.

Transaction means the exchange of information between two parties to carry out financial and administrative activities related to health care. It includes the following:

(1) Health claims or equivalent encounter information.
(2) Health care payment and remittance advice.
(3) Coordination of benefits.
(4) Health claims status.
(5) Enrollment and disenrollment in a health plan.
(6) Eligibility for a health plan.
(7) Health plan premium payments.
(8) Referral certification and authorization.
(9) First report of injury.
(10) Health claims attachments.
(11) Other transactions as the Secretary may prescribe by regulation.

Sec. 142.104 General requirements for health plans.

If a person conducts a transaction (as defined in Sec. 142.103) with a health plan as a standard transaction, the following apply:

(a) The health plan may not refuse to conduct the transaction as a standard transaction.

(b) The health plan may not delay the transaction or otherwise adversely affect, or attempt to adversely affect, the person or the transaction on the ground that the transaction is a standard transaction.

(c) The health information transmitted and received in connection with the transaction must be in the form of standard data elements of health information.

(d) A health plan that conducts transactions through an agent must assure that the agent meets all the requirements of this part that apply to the health plan.

Sec. 142.105 Compliance using a health care clearinghouse.

(a) Any person or other entity subject to the requirements of this part may meet the requirements to accept and transmit standard transactions by either--

(1) Transmitting and receiving standard data elements; or

(2) Submitting nonstandard data elements to a health care clearinghouse for processing into standard data elements and transmission by the health care clearinghouse and receiving standard data elements through the health care clearinghouse.

(b) The transmission, under contract, of nonstandard data elements between a health plan or a health care provider and its agent health care clearinghouse is not a violation of the requirements of this part.

Sec. 142.106 Effective dates of a modification to a standard or implementation specification.

HHS may modify a standard or implementation specification after the first year in which HHS requires the standard or implementation specification to be used, but not more frequently than once every 12 months. If HHS adopts a modification to a standard or implementation specification, the implementation date of the modified standard or implementation specification may be no earlier than 180 days following the adoption of the modification. HHS determines the actual date, taking into account the time needed to comply due to the nature and extent of the modification. HHS may extend the time for compliance for small health plans.

Subpart B--[Reserved]

Subpart C--Security and Electronic Signature Standards

Sec. 142.302 Applicability and scope.

The standards adopted or designated under this subpart apply, in whole or in part, to the following:

(a) A health plan.

(b) A health care clearinghouse or health care provider that takes one of the following actions:

(1) Processes any electronic transmission between any combination of health care entities listed in this section.

(2) Electronically maintains any health information used in an electronic transmission that has been sent or received between any combination of health care entities listed in this section.

Sec. 142.304 Definitions.

For purposes of this subpart, the following definitions apply:

Access refers to the ability or the means necessary to read, write, modify, or communicate data/information or otherwise make use of any system resource.

Access control refers to a method of restricting access to resources, allowing only privileged entities access. Types of access control include, among others, mandatory access control, discretionary access control, time-of-day, and classification.

Authentication refers to the corroboration that an entity is the one claimed.

Contingency plan refers to a plan for responding to a system emergency. The plan includes performing backups, preparing critical facilities that can be used to facilitate continuity of operations in the event of an emergency, and recovering from a disaster.

Encryption (or encipherment) refers to transforming confidential plaintext into ciphertext to protect it. An encryption algorithm combines plaintext with other values called keys, or ciphers, so the data becomes unintelligible. Once encrypted, data can be stored or transmitted over unsecured lines. Decrypting data reverses the encryption algorithm process and makes the plaintext available for further processing.

Password refers to confidential authentication information composed of a string of characters.

Role-based access control (RBAC) is an alternative to traditional access control models (e.g., discretionary or non-discretionary access control policies) that permits the specification and enforcement of enterprise-specific security policies in a way that maps more naturally to an organization's structure and business activities. With RBAC, rather than attempting to map an organization's security policy to a relatively low-level set of technical controls (typically, access control lists), each user is assigned to one or more predefined roles, each of which has been assigned the various privileges needed to perform that role.

Token refers to a physical item necessary for user identification when used in the context of authentication. For example, an electronic device that can be inserted in a door or a computer system to obtain access.

User-based access refers to a security mechanism used to grant users of a system access based upon the identity of the user.

Sec. 142.306 Rules for the security standard.

(a) An entity must apply the security standard described in Sec. 142.308 to all health information pertaining to an individual that is electronically maintained or electronically transmitted.

(b) If a health care clearinghouse is part of a larger organization, it must assure that all health information pertaining to an individual is protected from unauthorized access by the larger organization.

[[Page 43266]]

Sec. 142.308 Security standard.

Each entity designated in Sec. 142.302 must assess potential risks and vulnerabilities to the individual health data in its possession and develop, implement, and maintain appropriate security measures. These measures must be documented and kept current, and must include, at a minimum, the following requirements and implementation features:

(a) Administrative procedures to guard data integrity, confidentiality, and availability (documented, formal practices to manage the selection and execution of security measures to protect data, and to manage the conduct of personnel in relation to the protection of data). These procedures include the following requirements:

(1) Certification. (The technical evaluation performed as part of, and in support of, the accreditation process that establishes the extent to which a particular computer system or network design and

implementation meet a pre-specified set of security requirements. This evaluation may be performed internally or by an external accrediting agency.)

(2) A chain of trust partner agreement (a contract entered into by two business partners in which the partners agree to electronically exchange data and protect the integrity and confidentiality of the data exchanged).

(3) A contingency plan, a routinely updated plan for responding to a system emergency, that includes performing backups, preparing critical facilities that can be used to facilitate continuity of operations in the event of an emergency, and recovering from a disaster. The plan must include all of the following implementation features:

(i) An applications and data criticality analysis (an entity's formal assessment of the sensitivity, vulnerabilities, and security of its programs and information it receives, manipulates, stores, and/or transmits).

(ii) Data backup plan (a documented and routinely updated plan to create and maintain, for a specific period of time, retrievable exact copies of information).

(iii) A disaster recovery plan (the part of an overall contingency plan that contains a process enabling an enterprise to restore any loss of data in the event of fire, vandalism, natural disaster, or system failure).

(iv) Emergency mode operation plan (the part of an overall contingency plan that contains a process enabling an enterprise to continue to operate in the event of fire, vandalism, natural disaster, or system failure).

(v) Testing and revision procedures (the documented process of periodic testing of written contingency plans to discover weaknesses and the subsequent process of revising the documentation, if necessary).

(4) Formal mechanism for processing records (documented policies and procedures for the routine, and nonroutine, receipt, manipulation, storage, dissemination, transmission, and/or disposal of health information).

(5) Information access control (formal, documented policies and procedures for granting different levels of access to health care information) that includes all of the following implementation features:

(i) Access authorization (information-use policies and procedures that establish the rules for granting access, (for example, to a terminal, transaction, program, process, or some other user.)

(ii) Access establishment (security policies and rules that determine an entity's initial right of access to a terminal, transaction, program, process or some other user).

(iii) Access modification (security policies and rules that determine the types of, and reasons for, modification to an entity's established right of access, to a terminal, transaction, program, process, or some other user.)

(6) Internal audit (in-house review of the records of system activity (such as logins, file accesses, and security incidents) maintained by an organization).

(7) Personnel security (all personnel who have access to any sensitive information have the required authorities as well as all appropriate clearances) that includes all of the following implementation features:

(i) Assuring supervision of maintenance personnel by an authorized, knowledgeable person. These procedures are documented formal procedures and instructions for the oversight of maintenance personnel when the personnel are near health information pertaining to an individual.

(ii) Maintaining a record of access authorizations (ongoing documentation and review of the levels of access granted to a user, program, or procedure accessing health information).

(iii) Assuring that operating and maintenance personnel have proper access authorization (formal documented policies and procedures for determining the access level to be granted to individuals working on, or near, health information).

(iv) Establishing personnel clearance procedures (a protective measure applied to determine that an individual's access to sensitive unclassified automated information is admissible).

(v) Establishing and maintaining personnel security policies and procedures (formal, documentation of procedures to ensure that all personnel who have access to sensitive information have the required authority as well as appropriate clearances).

(vi) Assuring that system users, including maintenance personnel, receive security awareness training.

(8) Security configuration management (measures, practices, and procedures for the security of information systems that must be coordinated and integrated with each other and other measures, practices, and procedures of the organization established in order to create a coherent system of security) that includes all of the following implementation features:

(i) Documentation (written security plans, rules, procedures, and instructions concerning all components of an entity's security).

(ii) Hardware and software installation and maintenance review and testing for security features (formal, documented procedures for connecting and loading new equipment and programs, periodic review of the maintenance occurring on that equipment and programs, and periodic security testing of the security attributes of that hardware/software).

(iii) Inventory (the formal, documented identification of hardware and software assets).

(iv) Security testing (process used to determine that the security features of a system are implemented as designed and that they are adequate for a proposed applications environment; this process includes hands-on functional testing, penetration testing, and verification).

(v) Virus checking. (The act of running a computer program that identifies and disables:

(A) Another ``virus'' computer program, typically hidden, that attaches itself to other programs and has the ability to replicate.

(B) A code fragment (not an independent program) that reproduces by attaching to another program.

(C) A code embedded within a program that causes a copy of itself to be inserted in one or more other programs.)

(9) Security incident procedures (formal documented instructions for reporting security breaches) that include all of the following implementation features:

(i) Report procedures (documented formal mechanism employed to document security incidents).

[[Page 43267]]

(ii) Response procedures (documented formal rules or instructions for actions to be taken as a result of the receipt of a security incident report).

(10) Security management process (creation, administration, and oversight of policies to ensure the prevention, detection, containment, and correction of security breaches involving risk analysis and risk management). It includes the establishment of accountability, management controls (policies and education), electronic controls, physical security, and penalties for the abuse and misuse of its assets (both physical and electronic) that includes all of the following implementation features:

(i) Risk analysis, a process whereby cost-effective security/ control measures may be selected by balancing the costs of various security/control measures against the losses that would be expected if these measures were not in place.

(ii) Risk management (process of assessing risk, taking steps to reduce risk to an acceptable level, and maintaining that level of risk).

(iii) Sanction policies and procedures (statements regarding disciplinary actions that are communicated to all employees, agents, and contractors; for example, verbal warning, notice of disciplinary action placed in personnel files, removal of system privileges, termination of employment, and contract penalties). They must include employee, agent, and contractor notice of civil or criminal penalties for misuse or misappropriation of health information and must make employees, agents, and contractors aware that violations may result in notification to law enforcement officials and regulatory, accreditation, and licensure organizations.

(iv) Security policy (statement(s) of information values, protection responsibilities, and organization commitment for a system). This is the framework within which an entity establishes needed levels of information security to achieve the desired confidentiality goals.

(11) Termination procedures (formal documented instructions, which include appropriate security measures, for the ending of an employee's employment or an internal/external user's access) that include procedures for all of the following implementation features:

(i) Changing locks (a documented procedure for changing combinations of locking mechanisms, both on a recurring basis and when personnel knowledgeable of combinations no longer have a need to know or require access to the protected facility or system).

(ii) Removal from access lists (physical eradication of an entity's access privileges).

(iii) Removal of user account(s) (termination or deletion of an individual's access privileges to the information, services, and resources for which they currently have clearance, authorization, and need-to-know when such clearance, authorization and need-to-know no longer exists).

(iv) Turning in of keys, tokens, or cards that allow access (formal, documented procedure to ensure all physical items that allow a terminated employee to access a property, building, or equipment are retrieved from that employee, preferably before termination).

(12) Training (education concerning the vulnerabilities of the health information in an entity's possession and ways to ensure the protection of that information) that includes all of the following implementation features:

(i) Awareness training for all personnel, including management personnel (in security awareness, including, but not limited to, password maintenance, incident reporting, and viruses and other forms of malicious software).

(ii) Periodic security reminders (employees, agents, and contractors are made aware of security concerns on an ongoing basis).

(iii) User education concerning virus protection (training relative to user awareness of the potential harm that can be caused by a virus, how to prevent the introduction of a virus to a computer system, and what to do if a virus is detected).

(iv) User education in importance of monitoring log-in success or failure and how to report discrepancies (training in the user's responsibility to ensure the security of health care information).

(v) User education in password management (type of user training in the rules to be followed in creating and changing passwords and the need to keep them confidential).

(b) Physical safeguards to guard data integrity, confidentiality, and availability. Protection of physical computer systems and related buildings and equipment from fire and other natural and environmental hazards, as well as from intrusion. It covers the use of locks, keys, and administrative measures used to control access to computer systems and facilities. Physical safeguards must include all of the following requirements and implementation features:

(1) Assigned security responsibility (practices established by management to manage and supervise the execution and use of security measures to protect data and to manage and supervise the conduct of personnel in relation to the protection of data).

(2) Media controls (formal, documented policies and procedures that govern the receipt and removal of hardware/software (such as diskettes and tapes) into and out of a facility) that include all of the following implementation features:

(i) Access control.

(ii) Accountability (the property that ensures that the actions of an entity can be traced uniquely to that entity).

(iii) Data backup (a retrievable, exact copy of information).

(iv) Data storage (the retention of health care information pertaining to an individual in an electronic format).

(v) Disposal (final disposition of electronic data, and/or the hardware on which electronic data is stored).

(3) Physical access controls (limited access) (formal, documented policies and procedures to be followed to limit physical access to an entity while ensuring that properly authorized access is allowed) that include all of the following implementation features:

(i) Disaster recovery (the process enabling an entity to restore any loss of data in the event of fire, vandalism, natural disaster, or system failure).

(ii) An emergency mode operation (access controls in place that enable an entity to continue to operate in the event of fire, vandalism, natural disaster, or system failure).

(iii) Equipment control (into and out of site) (documented security procedures for bringing hardware and software into and out of a facility and for maintaining a record of that equipment. This includes, but is not limited to, the marking, handling, and disposal of hardware and storage media.)

(iv) A facility security plan (a plan to safeguard the premises and building (exterior and interior) from unauthorized physical access and to safeguard the equipment therein from unauthorized physical access, tampering, and theft).

(v) Procedures for verifying access authorizations before granting physical access (formal, documented policies and instructions for validating the access privileges of an entity before granting those privileges).

(vi) Maintenance records (documentation of repairs and modifications to the physical components of a facility, such as

[[Page 43268]]

hardware, software, walls, doors, and locks).

(vii) Need-to-know procedures for personnel access (a security principle stating that a user should have access only to the data he or she needs to perform a particular function).

(viii) Procedures to sign in visitors and provide escorts, if appropriate (formal documented procedure governing the reception and hosting of visitors).

(ix) Testing and revision (the restriction of program testing and revision to formally authorized personnel).

(4) Policy and guidelines on work station use (documented instructions/procedures delineating the proper functions to be performed, the manner in which those functions are to be performed, and the physical attributes of the surroundings of a specific computer terminal site or type of site, dependent upon the sensitivity of the information accessed from that site).

(5) A secure work station location (physical safeguards to eliminate or minimize the possibility of unauthorized access to information; for example, locating a terminal used to access sensitive information in a locked room and restricting access to that room to authorized personnel, not placing a terminal used to access patient information in any area of a doctor's office where the screen contents can be viewed from the reception area).

(6) Security awareness training (information security awareness training programs in which all employees, agents, and contractors must participate, including, based on job responsibilities, customized education programs that focus on issues regarding use of health information and responsibilities regarding confidentiality and security).

(c) Technical security services to guard data integrity, confidentiality, and availability (the processes that are put in place to protect information and to control individual access to information). These services include the following requirements and implementation features:

(1) The technical security services must include all of the following requirements and the specified implementation features:

(i) Access control that includes:

(A) A procedure for emergency access (documented instructions for obtaining necessary information during a crisis), and

(B) At least one of the following implementation features:

(1) Context-based access (an access control procedure based on the context of a transaction (as opposed to being based on attributes of the initiator or target)).

(2) Role-based access.

(3) User-based access.

(C) The optional use of encryption.

(ii) Audit controls (mechanisms employed to record and examine system activity).

(iii) Authorization control (the mechanism for obtaining consent for the use and disclosure of health information) that includes at least one of the following implementation features:

(A) Role-based access.

(B) User-based access.

(iv) Data authentication. (The corroboration that data has not been altered or destroyed in an unauthorized manner. Examples of how data corroboration may be assured include the use of a check sum, double keying, a message authentication code, or digital signature.)

(v) Entity authentication (the corroboration that an entity is the one claimed) that includes:

(A) Automatic logoff (a security procedure that causes an electronic session to terminate after a predetermined time of inactivity, such as 15 minutes), and

(B) Unique user identifier (a combination name/number assigned and maintained in security procedures for identifying and tracking individual user identity).

(C) At least one of the following implementation features:

(1) Biometric identification (an identification system that

identifies a human from a measurement of a physical feature or repeatable action of the individual (for example, hand geometry, retinal scan, iris scan, fingerprint patterns, facial characteristics, DNA sequence characteristics, voice prints, and hand written signature)).

(2) Password.

(3) Personal identification number (PIN) (a number or code assigned to an individual and used to provide verification of identity).

(4) A telephone callback procedure (method of authenticating the identity of the receiver and sender of information through a series of ``questions" and ``answers" sent back and forth establishing the identity of each). For example, when the communicating systems exchange a series of identification codes as part of the initiation of a session to exchange information, or when a host computer disconnects the initial session before the authentication is complete, and the host calls the user back to establish a session at a predetermined telephone number.

(5) Token.

(2) [Reserved]

(d) Technical security mechanisms (processes that are put in place to guard against unauthorized access to data that is transmitted over a communications network).

(1) If an entity uses communications or network controls, its security standards for technical security mechanisms must include the following:

(i) The following implementation features:

(A) Integrity controls (a security mechanism employed to ensure the validity of the information being electronically transmitted or stored).

(B) Message authentication (ensuring, typically with a message authentication code, that a message received (usually via a network) matches the message sent).

(ii) One of the following implementation features:

(A) Access controls (protection of sensitive communications transmissions over open or private networks so that they cannot be easily intercepted and interpreted by parties other than the intended recipient).

(B) Encryption.

(2) If an entity uses network controls (to protect sensitive communication that is transmitted electronically over open networks so that it cannot be easily intercepted and interpreted by parties other than the intended recipient), its technical security mechanisms must include all of the following implementation features:

(i) Alarm. (In communication systems, any device that can sense an abnormal condition within the system and provide, either locally or remotely, a signal indicating the presence of the abnormality. The signal may be in any desired form ranging from a simple contact closure (or opening) to a time-phased automatic shutdown and restart cycle.)

(ii) Audit trail (the data collected and potentially used to facilitate a security audit).

(iii) Entity authentication (a communications or network mechanism to irrefutably identify authorized users, programs, and processes and to deny access to unauthorized users, programs, and processes).

(iv) Event reporting (a network message indicating operational irregularities in physical elements of a network or a response to the occurrence of a significant task, typically the completion of a request for information).

Sec. 142.310 Electronic signature standard.

(a) General rule. If an entity elects to use an electronic signature in a

[[Page 43269]]

transaction as defined in Sec. 142.103, or if an electronic signature is required by a transaction standard adopted by the Secretary, the entity must apply the electronic signature standard described in paragraph (b) of this section to that transaction.

(b) Standard.

(1) An electronic signature is the attribute affixed to an electronic document to bind it to a particular entity. An electronic signature secures the user authentication (proof of claimed identity) at the time the signature is generated; creates the logical manifestation of signature (including the possibility for multiple parties to sign a document and have the order of application recognized and proven); supplies additional information such as time stamp and signature purpose specific to that user; and ensures the integrity of the signed document to enable transportability of data, interoperability, independent verifiability, and continuity of signature capability. Verifying a signature on a document verifies the integrity of the document and associated attributes and verifies the identity of the signer.

(2) The standard for electronic signature is a digital signature. A ``digital signature" is an electronic signature based upon cryptographic methods of originator authentication, computed by using a set of rules and a set of parameters so that the identity of the signer and the integrity of the data can be verified.

(c) Required implementation features. If an entity uses electronic signatures, the signature method must assure all of the following features:

(1) Message integrity (the assurance of unaltered transmission and receipt of a message from the sender to the intended recipient).

(2) Nonrepudiation (strong and substantial evidence of the identity of the signer of a message, and of message integrity, sufficient to prevent a party from successfully denying the origin, submission, or delivery of the message and the integrity of its contents).

(3) User authentication (the provision of assurance of the claimed identity of an entity).

(d) Optional implementation features. If an entity uses electronic signatures, the entity may also use, among others, any of the following implementation features:

(1) Ability to add attributes (one possible capability of a digital signature technology; for example, the ability to add a time stamp as part of a digital signature).

(2) Continuity of signature capability (the concept that the public verification of a signature must not compromise the ability of the signer to apply additional secure signatures at a later date).

(3) Countersignatures. (The capability to prove the order of application of signatures. This is analogous to the normal business practice of countersignatures, where a party signs a document that has already been signed by another party.)

(4) Independent verifiability (the capability to verify the signature without the cooperation of the signer).

(5) Interoperability (the applications used on either side of a communication, between trading partners and/or between internal components of an entity, are able to read and correctly interpret the information communicated from one to the other).

(6) Multiple signatures. (With this feature, multiple parties are able to sign a document. Conceptually, multiple signatures are simply appended to the document.)

(7) Transportability of data (the ability of a signed document to be transported over an insecure network to another system, while maintaining the integrity of the document, including content, signatures, signature attributes, and (if present) document attributes).

Sec. 142.312 Effective date of the initial implementation of the security and electronic signature standards.

(a) General rules.

(1) Except for a small health plan (defined at Sec. 142.103), each entity designated in Sec. 142.302 must comply with the requirements of this subpart by [24 months after the effective date of the final rule in the Federal Register].

(2) A delay in an effective date for using a standard transaction described in this part does not delay the effective dates described in paragraphs (a)(1) and (b) of this section.

(3) The requirements of the security standard may be implemented over time. Implementation must be completed by the applicable effective date.

(b) Small health plans. A small health plan must comply with the requirements of this subpart by [36 months after the effective date of the final rule in the Federal Register].

Authority: Sections 1173 and 1175 of the Social Security Act (42 U.S.C. 1320d-2 and 1320d-4).

Dated: July 15, 1998.
Donna E. Shalala,

Secretary.

Note: The following appendix will not appear in the Code of Federal Regulations.

Addendum 1

HIPAA Security Matrix

Please Note: (1) While we have attempted to categorize security requirements for ease of understanding and reading clarity, there are overlapping areas on the matrix in which the same requirements are restated in a slightly different context. (2) To ensure that no Requirement or Implementation feature is considered more important than another, this matrix has been presented, within each subject area, in alphabetical order.

Administrative Procedures To Guard Data Integrity, Confidentiality, and Availability

Requirement	Implementation
Certification	
Chain of trust partner agreement	
Contingency plan (all listed implementation features must be implemented).	Applications and data criticality analysis. Data backup plan. Disaster recovery plan. Emergency mode operation plan. Testing and revision.
Formal mechanism for processing records.	
Information access control (all listed implementation features must be implemented).	Access authorization. Access establishment. Access modification.
Internal audit	

[[Page 43270]]

Requirement	Implementation
Personnel security (all listed implementation features must be implemented).	Assure supervision of maintenance personnel by authorized, knowledgeable person. Maintainance of record of access authorizations. Operating, and in some cases, maintenance personnel have proper access authorization. Personnel clearance procedure. Personnel security policy/ procedure. System users, including maintenance personnel, trained in security.
Security configuration mgmt. (all listed implementation features must be implemented).	Documentation. Hardware/software installation & maintenance review and testing for security features. Inventory. Security Testing. Virus checking.
Security incident procedures (all listed implementation features must be implemented).	Report procedures. Response procedures.
Security management process (all listed implementation features must be implemented).	Risk analysis. Risk management. Sanction policy. Security policy.
Termination procedures (all listed implementation features must be implemented).	Combination locks changed. Removal from access lists. Removal of user account(s). Turn in keys, token or cards that allow access.
Training (all listed implementation features must be implemented).	Awareness training for all personnel (including mgmt). Periodic security reminders. User education concerning virus protection. User education in importance of monitoring log in success/ failure, and how to report discrepancies. User education in password management.

Physical Safeguards To Guard Data Integrity, Confidentiality, and Availability

Requirement	Implementation
Assigned security responsibility	
Media controls (all listed implementation features must be implemented).	Access control. Accountability (tracking mechanism). Data backup. Data storage. Disposal.
Physical access controls (limited access) (all listed implementation features must be implemented).	Disaster recovery. Emergency mode operation. Equipment control (into and out of site). Facility security plan. Procedures for verifying access authorizations prior to physical access. Maintenance records. Need-to-know procedures for personnel access. Sign-in for visitors and escort, if appropriate. Testing and revision.
Policy/guideline on work station use	
Secure work station location	
Security awareness training	

Technical Security Services To Guard Data Integrity, Confidentiality, and Availability

Requirement	Implementation
Access control (The following implementation feature must be implemented: Procedure for emergency access. In addition, at least one of the following three implementation features must be implemented: Context-based access, Roll-based access, User-based access. The use of Encryption is optional).	Context-based access. Encryption. Procedure for emergency access. Role-based access. User-based access.
Audit controls	
Authorization Control (At least one of the listed implementation features must be implemented).	Role-based access. User-based access
Data Authentication	

[[Page 43271]]

Requirement	Implementation
Entity Authentication (The following implementation features must be implemented: Automatic logoff, Unique user identification. In addition, at least one of the other listed implementation features must be implemented).	Automatic logoff. Biometric. Password. PIN. Telephone callback. Token. Unique user identification.

Technical Security Mechanisms To Guard Against Unauthorized Access to

Data That Is Transmitted Over a Communications Network

Requirement	Implementation
Communications/network controls (The following implementation features must be implemented: Integrity controls, Message authentication. If communications or networking is employed, one of the following implementation features must be implemented: Access controls, Encryption. In addition, if using a network, the following four implementation features must be implemented: Alarm, Audit trail, Entity authentication, Event reporting).	Access controls. Alarm. Audit trail. Encryption. Entity authentication. Event reporting. Integrity controls. Message authentication.

Electronic Signature

Requirement	Implementation
Digital signature (If digital signature is employed, the following three implementation features must be implemented: Message integrity, Non-repudiation, User authentication. Other implementation features are optional).	Ability to add attributes. Continuity of signature capability. Counter signatures. Independent verifiability. Interoperability. Message integrity. Multiple Signatures. Non-repudiation. Transportability. User authentication.

Addendum 2--HIPAA Security and Electronic Signature Standards Glossary of Terms

Please Note:

(1) While we have attempted to categorize security requirements for ease of understanding and reading clarity, there are overlapping areas on the matrix in which the same requirements are restated in a slightly different context.

(2) While not appearing on the matrix, a number of terms listed below do appear in the glossary descriptions and have been supplied for additional clarity:

(3) The definitions provided in this document have been obtained from multiple sources.

Ability to add attributes:

One possible capability of a digital signature technology, for example, the ability to add a time stamp as part of a digital signature.

Part of digital signature on the matrix.

Access:

The ability or the means necessary to read, write, modify, or communicate data/information or otherwise make use of any system resource.

Access authorization:

Information-use policies/procedures that establish the rules for granting and/or restricting access to a user, terminal, transaction, program, or process.

Part of information access control on the matrix.

Access control:

A method of restricting access to resources, allowing only privileged entities access. (PGP, Inc.)

Types of access control include, among others, mandatory access control, discretionary access control, time-of-day, classification, and subject-object separation.

Part of Media Controls on the matrix.

Part of technical security services to control and monitor access to information on the matrix.

Access controls:

The protection of sensitive communications transmissions over open or private networks so that it cannot be easily intercepted and interpreted by parties other than the intended recipient.

Part of mechanisms to prevent unauthorized access to data that is transmitted over a communications network on the matrix.

Access establishment:

The security policies, and the rules established therein, that determine an entity's initial right of access to a terminal, transaction, program, or process.

Part of information access control on the matrix.

Access Level:

A level associated with an individual who may be accessing information (for example, a clearance level) or with the information which may be accessed (for example, a classification level). (NRC, 1991, as cited in HISB, DRAFT GLOSSARY OF TERMS RELATED TO INFORMATION SECURITY IN HEALTH CARE INFORMATION SYSTEMS draft
Glossary of Terms Related to Information Security in Health Care Information Systems)

Access modification:

The security policies, and the rules established therein, that determine types of, and reasons for, modification to an entity's established right of access to a terminal, transaction, program, or process.

Part of information access control on the matrix.

Accountability:

The property that ensures that the actions of an entity can be traced uniquely to that entity. (ASTM E1762--95)

[[Page 43272]]

Part of media controls on the matrix.

Administrative procedures to guard data integrity, confidentiality and availability:

Documented, formal practices to manage (1) the selection and execution of security measures to protect data, and (2) the conduct of personnel in relation to the protection of data.

A section of the matrix.

Alarm, event reporting, and audit trail:

(1) Alarm: In communication systems, any device that can sense an abnormal condition within the system and provide, either locally or remotely, a signal indicating the presence of the abnormality.
(188) NOTE: The signal may be in any desired form ranging from a simple contact closure (or opening) to a time-phased automatic shutdown and restart cycle. (Glossary of INFOSEC and INFOSEC Related Terms--Idaho State University)

(2) Event reporting: Network message indicating operational irregularities in physical elements of a network or a response to the occurrence of a significant task, typically the completion of a request for information. (Glossary of INFOSEC and INFOSEC Related Terms--Idaho State University)

(3) Audit trail: Data collected and potentially used to facilitate a security audit. (ISO 7498-2, as cited in HISB, DRAFT GLOSSARY OF TERMS RELATED TO INFORMATION SECURITY IN HEALTH CARE
INFORMATION SYSTEMS draft Glossary of Terms Related to Information Security in Health Care Information Systems)

Part of mechanisms to prevent unauthorized access to data that is transmitted over a communications network on the matrix.

Applications and data criticality analysis:

An entity's formal assessment of the sensitivity, vulnerabilities, and security of its programs and information it receives, manipulates, stores, and/or transmits.

Part of contingency plan on the matrix.

Assigned security responsibility:

Practices put in place by management to manage and supervise (1) the execution and use of security measures to protect data, and (2) the conduct of personnel in relation to the protection of data.

Part of Physical safeguards to guard data integrity, confidentiality, and availability on the matrix.

Assure supervision of maintenance personnel by authorized, knowledgeable person:

Documented formal procedures/instruction for the oversight of maintenance personnel when such personnel are in the vicinity of health information pertaining to an individual.

Part of personnel security on the matrix.

Asymmetric encryption:

Encryption and decryption performed using two different keys, one of which is referred to as the public key and one of which is referred to as the private key.

Also known as public-key encryption. (Stallings)

Asymmetric key:

One half of a key pair used in an asymmetric (``public-key") encryption system. Asymmetric encryption systems have two important properties: (1) the key used for encryption is different from the one used for decryption (2) neither key can feasibly be derived from the other. (CORBA Security Services, 1997)

Audit controls:

The mechanisms employed to record and examine system activity.

Part of technical security services to control and monitor access to information on the matrix.

Authorization control:

The mechanism for obtaining consent for the use and disclosure of health information.

Part of technical security services to control and monitor access to information on the matrix.

Automatic logoff:

After a pre-determined time of inactivity (for example, 15 minutes), an electronic session is terminated.

Part of entity authentication on the matrix.

Availability:

The property of being accessible and useable upon demand by an authorized entity. (ISO 7498-2, as cited in the HISB draft Glossary of Terms Related to Information Security In Health care Information Systems)

Awareness training for all personnel (including management):

All personnel in an organization should undergo security awareness training, including, but not limited to, password maintenance, incident reporting, and an education concerning viruses and other forms of malicious software.

Part of Training on the matrix.

Biometric:.

A biometric identification system identifies a human from a measurement of a physical feature or repeatable action of the individual (for example, hand geometry, retinal scan, iris scan, fingerprint patterns, facial characteristics, DNA sequence characteristics, voice prints, and hand written signature). (ASTM E1762--95, as cited in the HISB draft Glossary of Terms Related to Information Security In Health care Information Systems)

Part of entity authentication on the matrix.

Certification:

The technical evaluation performed as part of, and in support of, the accreditation process that establishes the extent to which a particular computer system or network design and implementation meet a pre-specified set of security requirements. This evaluation may be performed internally or by an external accrediting agency.

Part of administrative procedures to guard data integrity, confidentiality, and availability.

Chain of Trust Partner Agreement:

Contract entered into by two business partners in which it is agreed to exchange data and that the first party will transmit information to the second party, where the data transmitted is agreed to be protected between the partners. The sender and receiver depend upon each other to maintain the integrity and confidentiality of the transmitted information. Multiple such two-party contracts may be involved in moving information from the originator to the ultimate recipient, for example, a provider may contract with a clearing house to transmit claims to the clearing house; the clearing house, in turn, may contract with another clearing house or with a payer for the further transmittal of those same claims.

Part of administrative procedures to guard data integrity, confidentiality and availability on the matrix..

Classification:

Protection of data from unauthorized access by the designation of multiple levels of access authorization clearances to be required for access, dependent upon the sensitivity of the information.

A type of access control on the matrix.

Clearing House:

* * * a public or private entity that processes or facilitates the processing of nonstandard data elements of health information into standard data elements. (HIPAA, Subtitle F, Section 262(a) Section 1171(2))

Combination locks changed:

Documented procedure for changing combinations of locking mechanisms, both on a recurring basis and when personnel knowledgeable of combinations no longer have a need to know or a requirement for access to the protected facility/system.

Part of termination procedures on the matrix.

Confidentiality:

The property that information is not made available or disclosed to unauthorized individuals, entities or processes. (ISO 7498-2, as cited in the HISB draft Glossary of Terms Related to Information Security In Health care Information Systems) .

Context-based access:

An access control based on the context of a transaction (as opposed to being based on attributes of the initiator or target). The ``external" factors might include time of day, location of the user, strength of user authentication, etc.

Part of access control on the matrix.

Contingency Plan:

A plan for responding to a system emergency. The plan includes performing backups, preparing critical facilities that can be used to facilitate continuity of operations in the event of an emergency, and recovering from a disaster. (O'Reilly, 1992, as cited in the HISB draft Glossary of Terms Related to Information Security In Health care Information Systems) Contingency plans should be updated routinely.

Part of Administrative procedures to guard data integrity, confidentiality and availability on the matrix.

Continuity of signature capability:

The public verification of a signature shall not compromise the ability of the signer to apply additional secure signatures at a later date. (ASTM E 1762--95)

[[Page 43273]]

Part of digital signature on the matrix.

Counter signatures:

It shall be possible to prove the order of application of signatures. This is analogous to the normal business practice of countersignatures, where some party signs a document which has already been signed by another party. (ASTM E 1762 -95)

Part of digital signature on the matrix.

Data:

A sequence of symbols to which meaning may be assigned. (NRC, 1991, as cited in the HISB draft Glossary of Terms Related to Information Security In Health care Information Systems)

Data authentication:

The corroboration that data has not been altered or destroyed in an unauthorized manner. Examples of how data corroboration may be assured include the use of a check sum, double keying, a message authentication code, or digital signature.

Part of technical security services to control and monitor access to information on the matrix

Data backup:

A retrievable, exact copy of information.

Part of media controls on the matrix.

Data backup plan:

A documented and routinely updated plan to create and maintain, for a specific period of time, retrievable exact copies of information.

Part of contingency plans on the matrix.

Data Integrity:

The property that dat has [sic] not been altered or destroyed in an unauthorized manner. (ASTM E1762-95).

Data storage:

The retention of health care information pertaining to an individual in an electronic format.

Part of media controls on the matrix.

Digital signature:

An electronic signature based upon cryptographic methods of originator authentication, computed by using a set of rules and a set of parameters such that the identity of the signer and the integrity of the data can be verified. (FDA Electronic Record; Electronic Signatures; Final Rule)

Part of electronic signature on the matrix.

Disaster recovery:

The process whereby an enterprise would restore any loss of data

in the event of fire, vandalism, natural disaster, or system failure. (CPRI, 1996c, as cited in HISB, DRAFT GLOSSARY OF TERMS RELATED TO INFORMATION SECURITY IN HEALTH CARE INFORMATION SYSTEMS
draft Glossary of Terms Related to Information Security in Health Care Information Systems)
Part of physical access controls (limited access) on the matrix.
Disaster recovery plan:
Part of an overall contingency plan. The plan for a process whereby an enterprise would restore any loss of data in the event of fire, vandalism, natural disaster, or system failure. (CPRI, 1996c, as cited in HISB, DRAFT GLOSSARY OF TERMS RELATED TO INFORMATION
SECURITY IN HEALTH CARE INFORMATION SYSTEMS draft Glossary of Terms
Related to Information Security in Health Care Information Systems)
Part of contingency plan on the matrix.
Discretionary access control:
Discretionary Access Control (DAC) is used to control access by restricting a subject's access to an object. It is generally used to limit a user's access to a file. In this type of access control it is the owner of the file who controls other users' accesses to the file.
A type of access control on the matrix.
Disposal:
The final disposition of electronic data, and/or the hardware on which electronic data is stored.
Part of media controls on the matrix.
Documentation:
Written security plans, rules, procedures, and instructions concerning all components of an entity's security.
Part of security configuration mgmt on the matrix.
Electronic data interchange (EDI):
Intercompany, computer-to-computer transmission of business information in a standard format. For EDI purists, ``computer-to-computer'' means direct transmission from the originating application program to the receiving, or processing, application program, and an EDI transmission consists only of business data, not any accompanying verbiage or free-form messages. Purists might also contend that a standard format is one that is approved by a national or international standards organization, as opposed to formats developed by industry groups or companies. (EDI Security, Control, and Audit)
Electronic signature:
The attribute that is affixed to an electronic document to bind it to a particular entity. An electronic signature process secures the user authentication (proof of claimed identity, such as by biometrics (fingerprints, retinal scans, hand written signature verification, etc.), tokens or passwords) at the time the signature is generated; creates the logical manifestation of signature (including the possibility for multiple parties to sign a document and have the order of application recognized and proven) and supplies additional information such as time stamp and signature purpose specific to that user; and ensures the integrity of the signed document to enable transportability, interoperability, independent verifiability, and continuity of signature capability. Verifying a signature on a document verifies the integrity of the document and associated attributes and verifies the identity of the signer. There are several technologies available for user authentication, including passwords, cryptography, and biometrics. (ASTM 1762-95, as cited in the HISB draft Glossary of Terms Related to Information Security In Health care Information Systems)
Emergency mode operation:
Access controls in place that enable an enterprise to continue to operate in the event of fire, vandalism, natural disaster, or system failure.
Part of physical access controls (limited access) on the matrix.
Emergency mode operation plan:
Part of an overall contingency plan. The plan for a process whereby an enterprise would be able to continue to operate in the event of fire, vandalism, natural disaster, or system failure.
Part of contingency plan on the matrix.
Encryption:
Transforming confidential plaintext into ciphertext to protect it. Also called encipherment. An encryption algorithm combines plaintext with other values called keys, or ciphers, so the data becomes unintelligible. Once encrypted, data can be stored or transmitted over unsecured lines. (EDI Security, Control, and Audit)
Decrypting data reverses the encryption algorithm process and makes the plaintext available for further processing.
Part of access control on the matrix.
Entity authentication:
1. The corroboration that an entity is the one claimed. (ISO 7498-2, as cited in the HISB draft Glossary of Terms Related to Information Security In Health care Information Systems)
Part of technical security services to control and monitor access to information on the matrix.
2. A communications/network mechanism to irrefutably identify authorized users, programs, and processes, and to deny access to unauthorized users, programs and processes.
Part of mechanisms to prevent unauthorized access to data that is transmitted over a communications network on the matrix.
Equipment control (into and out of site):
Documented security procedures for bringing hardware and software into and out of a facility and for maintaining a record of that equipment. This includes, but is not limited to, the marking, handling, and disposal of hardware and storage media.
Part of physical access controls (limited access) on the matrix.
Facility security plan:
A plan to safeguard the premises and building(s) (exterior and interior) from unauthorized physical access, and to safeguard the equipment therein from unauthorized physical access, tampering, and theft.
Part of physical access controls (limited access) on the matrix.
Formal mechanism for processing records:
Documented policies and procedures for the routine, and non-routine, receipt, manipulation, storage, dissemination, transmission, and/or disposal of health information.

[[Page 43274]]

Part of administrative procedures to guard data integrity, confidentiality, and availability on the matrix.
Hardware/software installation & maintenance review and testing for security features:
Formal, documented procedures for (1) connecting and loading new equipment and programs, (2) periodic review of the maintenance occurring on that equipment and programs, and (3) periodic security testing of the security attributes of that hardware/software.
Part of security configuration mgmt on the matrix.
Independent verifiability:
The capability to verify the signature without the cooperation of the signer. Technically, it is accomplished using the public key of the signatory, and it is a property of all digital signatures performed with asymmetric key encryption
Part of digital signature on the matrix.
Information:
Data to which meaning is assigned, according to context and assumed conventions. (National Security Council, 1991, as cited in the HISB draft Glossary of Terms Related to Information Security In Health care Information Systems)
Information access control:
Formal, documented policies and procedures for granting different levels of access to health care information.
Part of administrative procedures to ensure integrity and confidentiality on the matrix.
Integrity controls:
Security mechanism employed to ensure the validity of the information being electronically transmitted or stored.
Part of mechanisms to prevent unauthorized access to data that is transmitted over a communications network on the matrix.
Internal audit:
The in-house review of the records of system activity (for example, logins, file accesses, security incidents) maintained by an organization.
Part of administrative procedures to guard data integrity, confidentiality, and availability on the matrix.
Interoperability:
The applications used on either side of a communication, between trading partners and/or between internal components of an entity,

being able to read and correctly interpret the information communicated from one to the other.
Part of digital signature on the matrix.
Inventory:
Formal, documented identification of hardware and software assets.
Part of security configuration mgmt on the matrix.
Key:
An input that controls the transformation of data by an encryption algorithm (NRC, 1991, as cited in the HISB draft Glossary of Terms Related to Information Security In Health care Information Systems)
Maintenance of record of access authorizations:
Ongoing documentation and review of the levels of access granted to a user, program, or procedure accessing health information.
Part of personnel security on the matrix.
Maintenance records:
Documentation of repairs and modifications to the physical components of a facility, for example, hardware, software, walls, doors, locks.
Part of physical access controls (limited access) on the matrix.
Mandatory Access Control (MAC):
A means of restricting access to objects that is based on fixed security attributes assigned to users and to files and other objects. The controls are mandatory in the sense that they cannot be modified by users or their programs. (Stallings, 1995) (as cited in the HISB draft Glossary of Terms Related to Information Security In Health care Information Systems)
A type of access control on the matrix.
Media controls:
Formal, documented policies and procedures that govern the receipt and removal of hardware/software (for example, diskettes, tapes) into and out of a facility.
Part of physical safeguards to guard data integrity, confidentiality, and availability on the matrix.
Message:
A digital representation of information. (ABA Digital Signatures Guidelines)
Message authentication:
Ensuring, typically with a message authentication code, that a message received (usually via a network) matches the message sent. (O'Reilly, 1992, as cited in the HISB draft Glossary of Terms Related to Information Security In Health care Information Systems)
Part of mechanisms to prevent unauthorized access to data that is transmitted over a communications network on the matrix
Message authentication code:
Data associated with an authenticated message that allows a receiver to verify the integrity of the message. (Glossary of INFOSEC and INFOSEC Related Terms--Idaho State University)
Message integrity:
The assurance of unaltered transmission and receipt of a message from the sender to the intended recipient. (ABA Digital Signature Guidelines)
Part of digital signature on the matrix.
Multiple signatures:
It shall be possible for multiple parties to sign a document. Multiple signatures are conceptually, simply appended to the document. (ASTM E 1762-95)
Part of digital signature on the matrix.
Need-to-know procedures for personnel access:
A security principle stating that a user should have access only to the data he or she needs to perform a particular function. (O'Reilly, 1992, as cited in the HISB draft Glossary of Terms Related to Information Security In Health care Information Systems)
Part of physical access controls (limited access) on the matrix.
Nonrepudiation:
Strong and substantial evidence of the identity of the signer of a message and of message integrity, sufficient to prevent a party from successfully denying the origin, submission or delivery of the message and the integrity of its contents. (ABA Digital Signature Guidelines)
Part of digital signature on the matrix.
Operating, and in some cases, maintenance personnel have proper access authorizations:
Formal, documented policies and procedures to be followed in determining the access level to be granted to individuals working on, or in the vicinity of, health information.
Part of personnel security on the matrix.
Password:
Confidential authentication information composed of a string of characters. (ISO 7498--2, as cited in the HISB draft Glossary of Terms Related to Information Security In Health care Information Systems)
Part of entity authentication on the matrix.
Periodic security reminders:
Employees, agents and contractors should be made aware of security concerns on an ongoing basis.
Part of training on the matrix.
Personnel clearance procedure:
A protective measure applied to determine that an individual's access to sensitive unclassified automated information is admissible. The need for and extent of a screening process is normally based on an assessment of risk, cost, benefit, and feasibility as well as other protective measures in place. Effective screening processes are applied in such a way as to allow a range of implementation, from minimal procedures to more stringent procedures commensurate with the sensitivity of the data to be accessed and the magnitude of harm or loss that could be caused by the individual (DOE 1360.2A, as cited in Glossary of INFOSEC and INFOSEC Related Terms--Idaho State University)
Part of personnel security on the matrix.
Personnel security:
The procedures established to ensure that all personnel who have access to sensitive information have the required authority as well as appropriate clearances. (NCSC Glossary of Computer Security Terms, October 21, 1988)
Part of administrative procedures to guard data integrity, confidentiality and availability on the matrix.
Personnel security policy/procedure:
Formal, documentation of policies and procedures established to ensure that all personnel who have access to sensitive information have the required authority as well as appropriate clearances. (Glossary of INFOSEC and INFOSEC Related Terms--Idaho State University)
Part of personnel security on the matrix.
Physical access controls (limited access):
Those formal, documented policies and procedures to be followed to limit

[[Page 43275]]

physical access to an entity while ensuring that properly authorized access is allowed.
Part of Physical safeguards to guard data integrity, confidentiality, and availability on the matrix.
Physical safeguards:
Protection of physical computer systems and related buildings and equipment from fire and other natural and environmental hazards, as well as from intrusion. Also covers the use of locks, keys, and administrative measures used to control access to computer systems and facilities. (O'Reilly, 1992, as cited in HISB, draft Glossary of Terms Related to Information Security in Health Care Information Systems)
A section of the matrix covering physical security requirements.
PIN (Personal Identification Number):
A number or code assigned to an individual and used to provide verification of identity.
Part of entity authentication on the matrix.
Policy/guideline on work station use:
Documented instructions/procedures delineating the proper functions to be performed, the manner in which those functions are to be performed, and the physical attributes of the surroundings, of a specific computer terminal site or type of site, dependant upon the sensitivity of the information accessed from that site.
Part of Physical safeguards to guard data integrity, confidentiality, and availability on the matrix.
Procedure for emergency access:
Documented instructions for obtaining necessary information during a crisis.
Part of access control on the matrix.

Procedures for verifying access authorizations prior to physical access:

Formal, documented policies and instructions for validating the access privileges of an entity prior to granting those privileges.

Part of physical access controls (limited access) on the matrix.

Provider:

A supplier of services as defined in section 1861(u) of the HIPAA.

A supplier of medical or other services as defined in section 1861(s) of the HIPAA.

Public key:

One of the two keys used in an asymmetric encryption system. The public key is made public, to be used in conjunction with a corresponding private key. [Stallings, 1995]

Removal from access lists:

The physical eradication of an entity's access privileges.

Part of termination procedures on the matrix.

Removal of user account(s):

The termination or deletion of an individual's access privileges to the information, services, and resources for which they currently have clearance, authorization, and need-to-know when such clearance, authorization and need-to-know no longer exists.

Part of termination procedures on the matrix.

Report procedures:

The documented formal mechanism employed to document security incidents.

Part of security incident procedures on the matrix.

Response procedures:

The documented formal rules/instructions for actions to be taken as a result of the receipt of a security incident report.

Part of security incident procedures on the matrix.

Risk analysis:

Risk analysis, a process whereby cost-effective security/control measures may be selected by balancing the costs of various security/ control measures against the losses that would be expected if these measures were not in place.

Part of the security management process on the matrix.

Risk management:

Risk is the possibility of something adverse happening. Risk management is the process of assessing risk, taking steps to reduce risk to an acceptable level and maintaining that level of risk. (NIST Pub. 800-14)

Part of the security management process on the matrix.

Role-based access control:

Role-based access control (RBAC) is an alternative to traditional access control models (e.g., discretionary or non-discretionary access control policies) that permits the specification and enforcement of enterprise-specific security policies in a way that maps more naturally to an organization's structure and business activities. With RBAC, rather than attempting to map an organization's security policy to a relatively low-level set of technical controls (typically, access control lists), each user is assigned to one or more predefined roles, each of which has been assigned the various privileges needed to perform that role.

Part of access control on the matrix.

Part of authorization control on the matrix.

Sanction policy:

Organizations must have policies and procedures regarding disciplinary actions which are communicated to all employees, agents and contractors, for example, verbal warning, notice of disciplinary action placed in personnel files, removal of system privileges, termination of employment and contract penalties (ASTM E 1869)

In addition to enterprise sanctions, employees, agents, and contractors must be advised of civil or criminal penalties for misuse or misappropriation of health information. Employees, agents and contractors, must be made aware that violations may result in notification to law enforcement officials and regulatory, accreditation and licensure organizations. (ASTM)

Part of the security management process on the matrix.

Secure work station location:

Physical safeguards to eliminate or minimize the possibility of unauthorized access to information, for example, locating a terminal used to access sensitive information in a locked room and restricting access to that room to authorized personnel, not placing a terminal used to access patient information in any area of a doctor's office where the screen contents can be viewed from the reception area.

Part of physical safeguards to guard data integrity, confidentiality, and availability on the matrix.

Security:

Security encompasses all of the safeguards in an information system, including hardware, software, personnel policies, information practice policies, disaster preparedness, and the oversight of all these areas. The purpose of security is to protect both the system and the information it contains from unauthorized access from without and from misuse from within.

Through various security measures, a health information system can shield confidential information from unauthorized access, disclosure and misuse, thus protecting privacy of the individuals who are the subjects of the stored data. (Privacy and Health Information Systems: A Guide to Protecting Patient Confidentiality)

Security awareness training:

All employees, agents, and contractors must participate in information security awareness training programs. Based on job responsibilities, individuals may be required to attend customized education programs that focus on issues regarding use of health information and responsibilities regarding confidentiality and security. (ASTM)

Part of Physical safeguards to guard data integrity, confidentiality, and availability on the matrix.

Security configuration management:

Measures, practices and procedures for the security of information systems should be coordinated and integrated with each other and other measures, practices and procedures of the organization so as to create a coherent system of security. (OECD Guidelines, as cited in NIST Pub 800-14)

Part of administrative procedures to guard data integrity, confidentiality, and availability on the matrix.

Security incident procedures:

Formal, documented instructions for reporting security breaches.

Part of administrative procedures to guard data integrity, confidentiality and availability on the matrix.

Security management process:

A security management process encompasses the creation, administration and oversight of policies to ensure the prevention, detection, containment, and correction of security breaches. It involves risk analysis and risk management, including the establishment of accountability, management controls (policies and education), electronic controls, physical security, and penalties for the abuse and misuse of its assets, both physical and electronic.

[[Page 43276]]

Part of administrative procedures to guard data integrity, confidentiality and availability on the matrix.

Security policy:

The framework within which an organization establishes needed levels of information security to achieve the desired confidentiality goals. A policy is a statement of information values, protection responsibilities, and organization commitment for a system. (OTA, 1993) The American Health Information Management Association recommends that security policies apply to all employees, medical staff members, volunteers, students, faculty, independent contractors, and agents. (AHIMA, 1996c) (as cited in HISB, DRAFT GLOSSARY OF TERMS RELATED TO INFORMATION SECURITY IN
HEALTH CARE INFORMATION SYSTEMS draft Glossary of Terms Related to
Information Security in Health Care Information Systems)

Part of the security management process on the matrix

Security testing:

A process used to determine that the security features of a system are implemented as designed and that they are adequate for a proposed applications environment. This process includes hands-on functional testing, penetration testing, and verification. (Glossary of INFOSEC and INFOSEC Related Terms--Idaho State University)

Part of security configuration mgmt on the matrix.

Sign-in for visitors and escort, if appropriate:

Formal, documented procedure governing the reception and hosting

of visitors.
Part of physical access controls (limited access) on the matrix.
Subject/object separation:
Access to a subject does not guarantee access to the objects associated with that subject.
Subject is defined as an active entity, generally in the form of a person, process, or device that causes information to flow among objects or changes the system state. Technically, a process/domain pair. (Glossary of INFOSEC and INFOSEC Related Terms--Idaho State University)
Object is defined as a passive entity that contains or receives information. Access to an object potentially implies access to the information it contains. Examples of objects are: records blocks, pages, segments, files, directories, directory trees, and programs, as well as bits, bytes, words, fields, processors, video displays, keyboards, clocks, printers, network nodes, etc. (Glossary of INFOSEC and INFOSEC Related Terms--Idaho State University)
A type of access control.
System users, including maintenance personnel, trained in security:
See Awareness training (including management).
Part of personnel security on the matrix.
Technical security mechanisms:
The processes that are put in place to guard against unauthorized access to data that is transmitted over a communications network,
A section of the matrix.
Technical security services:
The processes that are put in place (1) to protect information and (2) to control and monitor individual access to information.
A section of the matrix.
Telephone callback:
A method of authenticating the identity of the receiver and sender of information through a series of ``questions'' and ``answers'' sent back and forth establishing the identity of each. For example, when the communicating systems exchange a series of identification codes as part of the initiation of a session to exchange information, or when a host computer disconnects the initial session before the authentication is complete, and the host calls the user back to establish a session at a predetermined telephone number.
Part of Entity authentication on the matrix.
Termination procedures:
Formal, documented instructions, which include appropriate security measures, for the ending of an employee's employment, or an internal/external user's access.
Part of administrative procedures to guard data integrity, confidentiality and availability on the matrix.
Testing and revision:
(1) Testing and revision of contingency plans refers to the documented process of periodic testing to discover weaknesses in such plans and the subsequent process of revising the documentation if necessary.
Part of contingency plan on the matrix.
(2) Testing and revision of programs should be restricted to formally authorized personnel.
Part of physical access controls (limited access) on the matrix.
Time-of-day:
Access to data is restricted to certain time frames, e.g., Monday through Friday, 8:00 a.m. to 6:00 p.m.
A type of access control on the matrix.
Time-stamp:
To create a notation that indicates, at least, the correct date and time of an action, and the identity of the person that created the notation.
Token:
A physical item that's used to provide identity. Typically an electronic device that can be inserted in a door or a computer system to obtain access. (O'Reilly, 1992) (as cited in HISB, DRAFT GLOSSARY OF TERMS RELATED TO INFORMATION SECURITY IN HEALTH CARE
INFORMATION SYSTEMS draft Glossary of Terms Related to Information Security in Health Care Information Systems)
Part of entity authentication on the matrix
Training:
Education concerning the vulnerabilities of the health information in an entity's possession and ways to ensure the protection of that information.
Part of administrative procedures to guard data integrity, confidentiality and availability on the matrix.
Transportability:
A signed document can be transported (over an insecure network) to another system, while maintaining the integrity of the document.
Part of digital signature on the matrix.
Turn in keys, token or cards that allow access:
Formal, documented procedure to ensure all physical items that allow a terminated employee to access a property, building, or equipment are retrieved from that employee, preferably prior to termination.
Part of termination procedures on the matrix.
Unique user identification:
The combination name/number assigned and maintained in security procedures for identifying and tracking individual user identity. (ASTM)
Part of Entity authentication on the matrix.
User authentication:
The provision of assurance of the claimed identity of an entity. (ASTM E1762-5)
Part of digital signature on the matrix.
User-based access:
A security mechanism used to grant users of a system access based upon the identity of the user.
Part of access control on the matrix.
Part of authorization control on the matrix.
User education in importance of monitoring log in success/failure, and how to report discrepancies:
Training in the user's responsibility to ensure the security of health care information.
Part of training on the matrix.
User education concerning virus protection:
Training relative to user awareness of the potential harm that can be caused by a virus, how to prevent the introduction of a virus to a computer system, and what to do if a virus is detected.
Part of training on the matrix.
User education in password management:
A type of user training in the rules to be followed in creating and changing passwords and the need to keep them confidential.
Part of training on the matrix.
Virus checking:
A computer program that identifies and disables:
(1) another ``virus'' computer program, typically hidden, that attaches itself to other programs and has the ability to replicate. (Unchecked virus programs result in undesired side effects generally unanticipated by the user.)
(2) A type of programmed threat. A code fragment (not an independent program) that reproduces by attaching to another program. It may damage data directly, or it may degrade system performance by taking over system resources which are then not available to authorized users. (O'Reilly, 1992, as cited in HISB, DRAFT GLOSSARY OF TERMS RELATED TO INFORMATION SECURITY IN HEALTH
CARE INFORMATION SYSTEMS draft Glossary of Terms Related to Information

Security in Health Care Information Systems)
(3) Code embedded within a program that causes a copy of itself to be inserted in one or more other programs. In addition to propagation, the virus usually performs some unwanted function. (Stallings, 1995, as cited in HISB, DRAFT GLOSSARY OF TERMS RELATED
TO INFORMATION SECURITY IN HEALTH CARE INFORMATION SYSTEMS draft
Glossary of Terms Related to Information Security in Health Care Information Systems)
Part of security configuration mgmt on the matrix.

Acronyms

ABA American Bar Association

ADA American Dental Association
ANSI American National Standards Institute
AHIMA American Health Information Management Association
ASTM American Society for Testing and Materials
CDT Center for Democracy & Technology
CEN Central European Nations
CORBA Common Object Request Broker
CPRI Computer-based Patient Record Institute
DAC Discretionary Access Control
DEA Data Encryption Algorithm
EDI Electronic Data Interchange
EHNAC Electronic Healthcare Network Accreditation Commission
FDA Food and Drug Administration
HISB Health Care Informatics Standards Board
ISO International Organization for Standardization
MAC Mandatory Access Control
NCSC National Computer Security Center
NCQA National Council for Quality Assurance
NCVHS National Committee on Vital and Health Statistics
NUBC National Uniform Billing Committee
NUCC National Uniform Claim Committee
PGP Pretty Good Privacy
PIN Personal Identification Number
NIST National Institutes of Standards and Technology
SDO Standards Development Organization
WEDI Workgroup for Electronic Data Interchange

Bibliography

ABA, Digital Signature Guidelines.
ANSI, ASC X12.58, Security Structures, June, 1997.
ASTM, E1762-95, Standard Guide for Electronic Authentication of Health Care Information. ASTM Committee E-31 on Computerized Systems, Subcommittee E31.20 on Authentication. West Conshohocken, PA, October 10, 1995.
ASTM, A Security Framework for Healthcare Information. ASTM Committee E-31 on Computerized Systems, Subcommittee E31.20 on Authentication. West Conshohocken, PA, February 11, 1997.
EDI Security, Control, and Audit, Marcells, Albert J. & Chan, Sally. Artech House, 685 Canton Street, Norwood, MA 01602, 1993.
FDA, Electronic Record; Electronic Signatures; Final Rule.
For the Record--Protecting Electronic Health Information, Computer Science and Telecommunications Board, NRC, National Academy Press, 2102 Constitution Avenue, NW, Box 285, Washington, DC, 20055, 1997.
Glossary of INFOSEC and INFOSEC Related Terms, Version 6. Schou, Corey D., Center for Decision Support, Idaho State University. August, 1996
HISB, DRAFT GLOSSARY OF TERMS RELATED TO INFORMATION SECURITY IN
HEALTH CARE INFORMATION SYSTEMS Glossary of Terms Related to Information Security in Health Care Information Systems draft, 1997
NCSC, Glossary of Computer Security Terms, October 21, 1988.
NIST Pub 800-14, ``Generally Accepted Principles and Practices for Securing Information Technology Systems", Swanson, Marianne, & Guttman, Barbara, September, 1996. PGP, Inc., Cryptology Reference Chart, August, 1997
Privacy and Health Information Systems: A Guide to Protecting Patient Confidentiality, Goldman, Janlori & Mulligan, Deirdre, CDT, 1996.

Addendum 3

HIPAA SECURITY MATRIX--mapping

Please Note: While we have attempted to categorize security requirements for ease of understanding and reading clarity, there are overlapping areas on the matrix in which the same requirements are restated in a slightly different context.

Administrative Procedures To Guard Data Integrity, Confidentiality, and Availability

```
---------------------------------------------------------------------
    Requirement          Implementation      Mapped standards
---------------------------------------------------------------------
Certification.............. ................... 47.
Chain of trust partner      ................... 12, 47.
 agreement.
Contingency plan (all listed  Applications and    17, 47, 53.
 implementation features      data criticality   12, 17, 47.
 must be implemented).        analysis.          12, 17, 47, 53.
                       Data backup plan.... 47, 53.
                       Disaster recovery   12, 17, 47.
                        plan.
                       Emergency mode
                        operation plan.
                       Testing and revision
Formal mechanism for        ................... 12, 17.
 processing records.
Information access control  Access authorization 12, 17, 47, 53.
 (all listed implementation  Access establishment 17, 47, 53.
 features must be        Access modification. 12, 17, 47, 53.
 implemented).
Internal audit.............. ................... 12, 17, 43, 44, 47.
 Personnel security (all   Assure supervision   17, 47.
  listed implementation     of maintenance
   features must be       personnel by
    implemented)          authorized,
                        knowledgeable
                        person.
                       Maintainance of     12, 17, 47.
                        record of access
                        authorizations.
                       Operating, and in   17, 47.
                        some cases,
                        maintenance
                        personnel have
                        proper access
                        authorization.
                       Personnel clearance  17, 47.
                        procedure.
                       Personnel security   17, 47, 53.
                        policy/procedure.
                       System users,       12, 17, 47, 53.
                        including
                        maintenance
                        personnel, trained
                        in security.
Security configuration mgmt. Documentation....... 12, 17, 47, 53.
 (all listed implementation
 features must be
 implemented).
                       Hardware/software   12, 17, 47.
                        installation &
                        maintenance review
                        and testing for
                        security features.
                       Inventory........... 12, 17.
                       Security testing.... 12, 17, 47.
                       Virus checking...... 12, 17, 47, 53.
Security incident procedures Report procedures... 12, 17, 47.
 (all listed implementation  Response procedures. 17, 47.
 features must be
 implemented).

[[Page 43278]]

Security management process  Risk analysis....... 12, 17, 47, 53.
 (all listed implementation  Risk management..... 17, 47.
 features must be         Sanction policy..... 12, 17, 47, 53.
 implemented).            Security policy..... 17, 47, 53.
Termination procedures (all  Combination locks   12, 17.
 listed implementation       changed.          12, 17, 47, 53.
 features must be         Removal from access 12, 17, 47.
 implemented).            lists.            12, 17, 47.
                       Removal of user
                        account(s).
                       Turn in keys, token
                        or cards that allow
                        access.
```

Training (all listed Awareness training 12, 17, 18, 47, 53.
implementation features for all personnel
must be implemented). (including mgmt).
Periodic security 12, 18.
reminders.
User education ....
concerning virus
protection.
User education in 12, 17, 18.
importance of
monitoring log in
success/failure,
and how to report
discrepancies.
User education in 12, 18, 47
password management.

Physical Safeguards To Guard Data Integrity, Confidentiality, and Availability

----
Requirement Implementation Mapped standards

Assigned security .... 47.
responsibility.
Media controls (all listed Access control...... 17, 47, 53.
implementation features Accountability 17, 18, 47.
must be implemented). (tracking 12, 17, 47, 53.
mechanism). 12, 17, 47.
Data backup......... 17, 47, 53.
Data storage........
Disposal............
Physical access controls Disaster recovery... 17.
(limited access) (all Emergency mode 17.
listed implementation operation. 17, 47.
features must be Equipment control 12, 17, 47.
implemented). (into and out of
site).
Facility security
plan.
Procedures for 17, 18, 47.
verifying access
authorizations
prior to physical
access.
Maintenance records. 17
Need-to-know 12, 17, 47, 53
procedures for
personnel access.
Sign-in for visitors 17
and escort, if
appropriate.
Testing and revision 17, 47
Policy/guideline on work .... 18.
station use.
Secure work station location .... 17, 53.
Security awareness training. .... 12, 17, 47.

Technical Security Services To Guard Data Integrity, Confidentiality, and Availability

----
Requirement Implementation Mapped standards

Access control (The Context-based 5, 12, 14, 16, 17,
following implementation access,. 40, 47.
feature must be Encryption.......... 1, 6, 12, 14, 17,
implemented: Procedure for 21, 22, 23, 24, 26,
emergency access, In Procedure for 36, 28, 29, 30, 31,
addition, at least one of emergency access. 47, 49, 53, 54, 55.
the following three Roll-based access,.. 14, 17, 53.
implementation features User-based access... 14, 16, 17, 40, 41,
must be implemented: 47, 53.
Context-based access, Roll- 11, 12, 14, 16, 17,
based access, User-based 40, 41, 47, 53.
access. The use of
Encryption is optional).
Audit controls............. .... 12, 14, 18, 47, 53.
Authorization control (At Role-based access... 5, 14, 16, 17, 47,
least one of the listed User-based access... 53.
implementation features 14, 16, 47, 53.
must be implemented).
Data authentication......... .... 11, 53.
Entity Authentication (The Automatic logoff.... 14, 16, 17, 18, 40,
following implementation Biometric........... 53
features must be Password............ 14, 16, 18, 40, 47,
implemented: Automatic PIN................. 53.
logoff, Unique user Telephone callback.. 14, 16, 17, 18, 19,
identification. In Token............... 40, 47, 53.
addition, at least one of Unique user 14, 16, 18, 19, 40,
the other listed identification. 47.
implementation features 14, 17, 18, 47, 53.
must be implemented). 14, 17, 47, 50, 53.
14, 47, 53.

[[Page 43279]]

Technical Security Mechanisms To Guard Data Integrity, Confidentiality, and Availability

----
Requirement Implementation Mapped standards

Communications/network Access controls..... 14, 17, 22, 23, 39,
controls (If communications Alarm, event 47, 48, 53.
or networking is employed, reporting, and 14, 17, 18, 35, 36,
the following audit trail. 37, 38, 44.
implementation features Audit trail
must be implemented: Encryption.......... 1, 6, 12, 14, 17,
Integrity controls, Message 21, 22, 23, 24, 26,
authentication. In Entity 27, 28, 29, 30, 31,
addition, one of the authentication. 47, 49, 52, 53.
following implementation 12, 14, 17, 18, 20,
features must be Event reporting 22, 23, 31, 32, 33,
implemented: Access Integrity controls.. 34, 51, 53.
controls, Encryption. In Message
addition, if using a authentication. 14, 15, 17, 18, 22,
network, the following four 23, 45, 46.
implementation features 14, 15, 17, 18, 22,
must be implemented: Alarm, 23, 25, 45, 46, 52.
Audit trail, Entity
authentication, Event
reporting).

Electronic Signature

Requirement Implementation Mapped standards

Digital signature (If Ability to add 3, 4, 10, 11, 13, 20
digital signature is attributes. 3, 4, 11, 13, 14, 18
employed, the following Continuity of 3, 4, 10, 11, 13,
three implementation signature 14, 18
features must be capability. 3, 4, 11, 13, 20
implemented: Message Counter signatures.. 3, 4, 7, 8, 9, 13,
integrity, Non-repudiation, Independent 14, 48
User authentication. Other verifiability. 3, 4, 10, 11, 13,
implementation features are Interoperability.... 14, 18
optional). Message integrity... 3, 4, 10, 11, 13, 20
Multiple signatures. 2, 3, 4, 10, 11, 13,
Non-repudiation..... 14, 42
Transportability.... 3, 4, 11, 13, 14, 18
User authentication. 3, 4, 10, 11, 13, 20

Mapped Standards

1. ANSI X3.92--Data Encryption Standard
2. ANSI X9.30--Part 1: Public Key Cryptography Using Irreversible Algorithms: Digital Signature Algorithm

3. ANSI X9.30--Part 2: Public Key Cryptography Using Irreversible Algorithms: Secure Hash Algorithm (SHA-1)
4. ANSI X9.31--Reversible Digital Signature Algorithms
5. ANSI X9.45--Enhanced Management Controls Using Digital Signatures and Attribute Certificates
6. ANSI X9.52--Triple DES Modes of Operation
7. ANSI X9.55--Extensions to Public Key Certificates and CRLs
8. ANSI X9.57--Certificate Management
9. ANSI X9.62--Elliptic Curve Digital Signature Algorithm (draft)
10. ANSI X12.58--Security Structures (version 2)
11. ASTM E 1762--Standard Guide for Authentication of Healthcare Information
12. ASTM E 1869--Draft Standard for Confidentiality, Privacy, Access and Data Security Principles
13. ASTM PS 100-97--Standard Specification for Authentication of Healthcare Information Using Digital Signatures
14. ASTM PS 101-97--Security Framework for Healthcare Information
15. ASTM PS 102-97--Standard Guide for Internet and Intranet Security
16. ASTM PS 103-97 Authentication & Authorization Guideline
17. CEN--European Pre-Standard
18. FDA--Electronic Records--Electronic Signatures--Final Rule
19. FIPS PUB 112--Password Usage
20. FIPS PUB 196--Entity Authentication Using Public Key Cryptography
21. FIPS PUB 46-2--Data Encryption Standard
22. IEEE 802.10: Interoperable LAN/MAN Security (SILS), 1992-1996 (multiple parts)
23. IEEE 802.10c--LAN/WAN Security--Key Management
24. IETF ID--Combined SSL/PCT Transport Layer Security Protocol
25. IETF ID--FTP Authentication Using DSA
26. IETF ID--Secure HyperText TP Protocol (S-HTTP)
27. IETF ID--SMIME Cert Handling
28. IETF ID--SMIME Message Specification
29. IETF RFC 1422--Privacy Enhanced Mail: Part 1: Message Encryption and Authentication Procedures
30. IETF RFC 1424--Privacy Enhanced Mail: Part 2: Certificate-Based Key Management
31. IETF RFC 1423--Privacy Enhanced Mail: Part 3: Algorithms, Modes, and Identifiers
32. ISO/IEC 9798-1: Information Technology--Security Techniques--Entity Authentication Mechanisms--Part 1: General Model
33. ISO/IEC 9798-2: Information Technology--Security Techniques--Entity Authentication Mechanisms--Part 2: Entity Authentication Using Asymmetric Techniques
34. ISO/IEC 9798-2: Information Technology--Security Techniques--Entity Authentication Mechanisms--Part 2: Entity Authentication Using Symmetric Techniques
35. ISO/IEC 10164-4--Information Technology--Open Systems Connection--System Management: Alarm Reporting Function
36. ISO/IEC 10164-5--Information Technology--Open Systems Connection--System Management: Event Report Management Function
37. ISO/IEC 10164-7--Information Technology--Open Systems Connection--System Management: Security Alarm Reporting Function
38. ISO/IEC 10164-8--Information Technology--Open Systems Connection--System Management: Security Audit Trail Function
39. ISO/IEC 10164-9--Information Technology--Open Systems Connection--System Management: Objects and Attributes for Access Control
40. ISO/IEC 10181-2--Information Technology--Security Frameworks in Open Systems--Authentication Framework
41. ISO/IEC 10181-3--Information Technology--Security Frameworks in Open Systems--Access Control Framework
42. ISO/IEC 10181-4--Information Technology--Security Frameworks in Open Systems--Non-repudiation Framework
43. ISO/IEC 10181-5--Information Technology--Security Frameworks in Open Systems--Confidentiality Framework
44. ISO/IEC 10181-7--Information Technology--Security Frameworks in Open Systems--Security Audit Framework
45. ISO/IEC 10736--Information Technology--Telecommunications and Information Exchange Between Systems--Transport Layer Security Protocol (TLSP)

[[Page 43280]]

46. ISO/IEC 11577--Information Technology--Telecommunications and Information Exchange Between Systems--Network Layer Security Protocol (NLSP)
47. NIST--Generally Accepted Principles and Practices for Secure Information Technology Systems
48. NIST MISPC--Minimum Interoperability Specification for PKI Components Version 1
49. PKCS #7--Cryptographic Message Syntax Standard Version 1.5 or later
50. PKCS #11--Cryptoki B A Cryptographic Token Interface
51. RFC 1510--Kerberos Authentication Service
52. RFC 2104--HMAC:Keyed-Hashing for Message Authentication
53. For the Record--Protecting Electronic Health Information
54. ANSI X9.42--Management of Symmetric Keys Using Diffie-Hellman
55. ANSI X9.44--Key Transport Using RSA

[FR Doc. 98-21601 Filed 8-7-98; 1:23 pm]
BILLING CODE 4120-01-P